THROUGH WOOD AND DALE

Through Wood and Dale

DIARIES, 1975–1978

James Lees-Milne

JOHN MURRAY
Albemarle Street, London

First published in 1998
by John Murray (Publishers) Ltd,
50 Albemarle Street, London W1X 4BD

A catalogue record for this book is available from the British Library

ISBN 0-7195-5599 X

Typeset in 11.5/13pt Bembo by Servis Filmsetting Ltd, Manchester
Printed and bound in Great Britain by The University Press, Cambridge

Contents

Preface

When this selection from Jim's diaries opens in 1975, he and Alvilde were about to move from 19 Lansdown Crescent, Bath, to Essex House in Badminton – amidst some anxiety. Jim worried that the new house was small, dark and depressing. It was not. It was a pretty Queen Anne house at the gates of Badminton House, limewashed the colour of pale blood oranges. Although it had only three downstairs rooms, a kitchen, a sitting-room and a book room, it was quickly decorated by Alvilde in elegant Anglo-French style and they entertained there almost every weekend – all meals being eaten in the kitchen, the light shining memorably through the carved albaster cow and calf on the window sill.

The flat at Lansdown Crescent was kept as a place to work and, during the week, Jim's routine was to drive to there and write most mornings in what had been William Beckford's library. In these diaries he writes a short life of Beckford and a novel (*Round the Clock*), publishes a second volume of diaries (*Prophesying Peace*) and embarks on a biography of his friend Harold Nicolson. It was characteristic of him that whenever he had finished one book he worried until he had decided upon another. In this his diary played a part too, providing a solace, a way of observing and thinking when other projects were lacking.

These diaries are not a record of his work, as the early volumes were, but a portrait of his way of life and, most distinctively, his personality. They show both a shy individual and a social, gregarious man who can write with feeling after a meal, 'I would have preferred less talk about literature and art, and more fun and jokes.' They are full of perceptive and occasionally barbed observations of people, places, animals and birds – for he noticed everything – until one becomes familiar with his likes and dislikes, his foibles and the byways of his character as one does with an old and valued friend.

For those who were his friends, the entries that recall him most vividly and affectionately are the beautifully turned portraits of moments or incidents: Alvilde cutting his hair as he munches his toast at breakfast or his pleasure at the spotted flycatcher nesting in the coronet beneath a window. Amidst the entries in these diaries it is strange to find myself revived as a young man – I appear irregularly at meals and family gatherings – but also moving, at this distance, to recall the great kindness and tolerance he showed a great-nephew.

NICK ROBINSON, 1988

Five miles meandering with a mazy motion
Through wood and dale the sacred river ran,
Then reached the caverns measureless to man,
And sank in tumult to a lifeless ocean:

Samuel Taylor Coleridge, *Kubla Khan*

1975

Curious that lately I have been reading about my visits in 1942 or 3 to St Catherine's Court on behalf of the National Trust. This afternoon on my return from London Jeremy Fry* rang me up from that house, where he was lunching with the new owner, Strutt, who then spoke to me. Told me he was the grandson of the Geoffrey Strutt† I knew. Said he was a bloody man. I replied that he was nice enough to me. Young Strutt has heavy death duties to pay and wonders if the Trust can help him by asking the Treasury to take the place in part payment of death duties. I said I would go and talk to him on Friday.

Tuesday, 7th January

I have received a letter from Martin Gilbert,‡ who is engaged on vol. 5 of Winston Churchill's Life. Among Sir Winston's archives he has come upon my name as a guest at Chartwell for four nights in January 1928. Can I give him any recollections of the visit? I have replied that I remember it fairly well. I was terrified of W.C., who would come in to dinner late, eat his soup aggressively, growl in expostulation at Randolph's cheek, then melt so as to be gallant with the girls and tolerant of the boys: that one night we remained at the dinner table till midnight while W.C. gave us a demonstration of how the Battle of Jutland was fought, with decanters and wine glasses in place of ships, while puffing cigar smoke to represent gun smoke. He was like an enthusiastic schoolboy on that occasion. The rest of the visit he was in waders in the lake or building a wall, or pacing backwards and forwards in his upstairs room dictating a book to his secretaries. Thump, thump on floorboards overhead.

John Jolliffe§ telephoned. Would I write a book for a small pub-

---

* Inventor and entrepreneur (b. 1924).
† Major Geoffrey Strutt of St Catherine's Court, Somerset; see *Ancestral Voices*.
‡ Fellow of Merton College, Oxford since 1962; Official Biographer of Sir Winston Churchill since 1968 (b. 1936).
§ Author, editor, reviewer (b. 1935).

lishing firm he is now interested in, called the Compton Press, about Beckford, 40,000 words to be delivered by May? The book must coincide with a Beckford exhibition due to be held in the autumn. I hate being taken unawares on the telephone and said No, I had not the time, for I have to do my contribution to the Mitchell Beazley book, plus an article on Stratfield Saye for *Apollo*. Then I thought, to hell, if someone else can do this book, which cannot be good no matter by whom within so short a time, why not I? Besides, I am interested in Beckford. So the next morning I rang him up to that effect. He said he had not in the meanwhile approached any other author.

A young Bath solicitor called Wiltshire asked A. and me to dinner on Saturday to meet a friend and client of his, Bernard Luce,[*] American, of the Luce family (*Time & Tide*). Luce a nice, quiet little man. His absorbing interest is English country houses. He is setting up a foundation financed by himself and other rich men to buy and save English buildings of merit. Rather an agonizing dinner. Next morning, Sunday, Luce and Wiltshire came here to see the library.

Today I went to London for a meeting of Paul Methuen's[†] trustees with Philip Hay[‡] and another man at Sotheby's, to discuss why they had not recommended that the whole Corsham collection should be exempted from death duties as one famous collection. Medley[§] pointed out that none of the books and none of the silver have been exempted, yet Sotheby's have valued many books, like a first edition of Hobbes's *Leviathan*, at several thousand pounds. The silver comprises some of the best Paul Storr pieces in England. Sotheby's were bewildered, and agreed to review their entire valuation, which in the meantime we shall pretend never to have seen, if the Treasury question us. I thought to myself that all of us in the room, with the single exception of Paul's solicitor, were of one mind, and indeed a unanimous understanding was at once come to, an unexpressed determination that so fine a place as Corsham must be kept intact as far as

---

[*] Bernard Luce, son of Henry Robinson Luce, founder-publisher of *Time* (1923), *Life* (1936) and other American magazines.

[†] Paul Methuen, RA, 4th Baron Methuen (1886–1974); during P.M.'s lifetime J.L.-M. was a Trustee of the Methuen Estate.

[‡] Sir (Alan) Philip Hay (1918–86); Secretary to HRH The Princess Marina of Kent 1948–68; Director of Sotheby's 1969–86.

[§] Christopher Medley, Yorkshire squire and Trustee of the Methuen Estate.

possible. 'We' were Christopher Medley, George Howard* who is immensely sharp and clever, Daniel Awdry† the youngish MP, and self; Hay told us he was a brother-in-law of Hugh Hertford.‡ The meeting was satisfactory, for we achieved our objective by this heart-to-heart talk. Medley and I went to Paddington together. He told me John Methuen§ was quite impossible and, he agreed, a little mad. He said that a month ago he was had up for being badly drunk in his Land Rover, in which he was driving a number of boy scouts. The case is coming up shortly and must go against him. Paul would be furious. I told him and Wood, the solicitor, that Paul would be horrified if Corsham were given to Bath Academy and not the N. Trust, which the executors are now considering.

Wednesday, 8th January

A good day – not climatically, for it is pitch dark. Kathleen, the daily, came back from nursing both her in-laws who have had strokes in Newhaven – she is a saintly woman. Breakfast at eight and cleaned Feeble the canary's cage, A. being away till Thursday and going to Switzerland tomorrow. I have come to love this little yellow bird who sings lustily while I type, and is touching and in need of protection, and is brave and never minds what you do with him. He sang in the car all the way back from the Droghedas' after Xmas. All morning I wrote the last spread of my contribution to the *Great Architecture of the World* – such rot – and typed out the whole six pages, and posted them to the publishers, Mitchell Beazley. Walked to Lansdown Grove Hotel where I snacked at one. Dewey the nice furniture repairer came at 2.15 with a new handrail which he inserted in the staircase. Walked down to the reference library in Queen Square and read four *Country Life* articles on Stratfield Saye of 1948, making notes. Cooked myself dinner, or rather heated what A. had prepared, and walked down to 1 Royal Crescent for an Architectural Committee meeting at 7.30.

* George Howard (1920–84), of Castle Howard, Yorkshire; a Governor of the BBC from 1972; Chairman, 1980–3; cr. Baron Howard of Henderskelfe (Life Peer) 1983.
† MP for Chippenham Division of Wiltshire; solicitor (b. 1924).
‡ Hugh Seymour, 8th Marquess of Hertford (1930–97), of Ragley Park, Warwickshire.
§ Paul Methuen's nephew, who succeeded his father, as 6th Baron, in 1975.

Friday, 10th January

A charming man, Michael Russell of the Compton Russell Press, telephoned me. It seems that they do want me to write the Beckford book. In fact I am much cheered because they are postponing the exhibition until March 1976, which means I shall have more time, seeing that the book is intended to coincide with the exhibition; secondly, only 25,000 words instead of 40,000 will be required. I am rather thrilled, yet apprehensive. I have not yet written a biography which has been accepted, and much will depend upon how I acquit myself.

Yesterday I went to Stratfield Saye to glean for my article for *Apollo*. The new duke is a new broom. Many alterations, several of which Gerry* would not have approved. Has certainly improved the outside, planted avenues and greatly tidied up the lawns between the river and house; also has cleaned and dredged the river, which is now a feature from the windows. Has made a swimming pool in the Orangery, which is acceptable if people must have these ridiculous heated pools, but I did not like the ignoble blue plastic roof in place of paned glass. Fitted carpets in several rooms, and a certain amount of pastel paint on walls and doors.

A nice secretary, Mrs Wilson, conducted me round and took me to a snack luncheon at the Wellington Arms. She never knew Gerry. It is odd seeing houses in which formerly one had been received as a friend of the host under different auspices. The present duke has little idea who I am – an old friend of his father. I did not bother to enlighten him. Why should he wish to know?

Sunday, 12th January

I find myself unwittingly supposing myself superior to, or rather having an advantage over, someone who may be older than myself. It is quite irrational, and regrettable. For instance, when someone's name that interests me crops up, I at once wish to know how old he or she is. I am pleased if that person should be older, which is seldom enough the case nowadays. In some way I feel I have the lead over those who

---

* Gerald Wellesley, 7th Duke of Wellington (1885–1972); long-standing friend of J.L.-M.; 8th Duke – 'the new duke' – (b. 1915) succeeded his father, 1972.

are dead, particularly those who were my contemporaries. In other words, I suppose, it is a realization that the old are never wanted by the young. So one deceives oneself into believing one is younger than one is because one is still alive, however decayed.

Tuesday, 14th January

To Jack Rathbone,[*] who was lunching with me today, I mentioned Derek Hill's[†] sensitivity about his paintings. Whenever he came to Alderley the first thing he did was to look for them, and if he could not find them, ask where they were and why they were not hung in conspicuous places. Jack told me the following story, told him by Derek himself. During the war Derek, who was a conscientious objector, worked on a farm. He made friends with the Italian prisoners. After the war he happened to be in the neighbourhood of one of the prisoners near Naples, and called. The boy was away from home, but Derek found a huge family, very impoverished. After explaining who he was, he told them that he had painted the boy's portrait and given it him as a signal favour. He asked to see it. Much embarrassment ensued, which surprised Derek, until he noticed that one of the brothers was wearing an old pair of trousers, which had been patched with pieces of canvas from the portrait.

Friday, 17th January

At luncheon time A. pointed out to me a large blue car parked on the far side of our road, with one man sitting at the wheel. She said he had been there since 8.30 this morning. After luncheon she and I drove off in our own car for a walk. She dropped me back at the door at four and the blue car and driver were still there. So I telephoned the police, who asked for the car's number. Within three minutes my doorbell rang, and the man from the blue car stood on the doorstep. He showed me his pass and announced himself as Inspector So-and-So. Very polite, said he was keeping a watch on something at this end of the Crescent. I excused myself. He said I was quite right to be

---

[*] John Francis Warre Rathbone (1909–95); Secretary of the N.T. 1949–68; President, London Centre of the N.T., from 1968.
[†] Landscape and portrait painter (b. 1916).

suspicious, and went back to his watch. I told Miss Long, our upstairs neighbour. She said he was undoubtedly keeping a watch through the mirror of his car, which was cunningly parked facing the other way, on 4 Lansdown Place West, where a group of drug pushers lodged. They had been ordered by the Court to leave by tomorrow morning at latest.

Wednesday, 22nd January

Last night had a vivid dream - all my dreams are too vivid - that Rick Stewart-Jones* (who died in 1957) came up to me and in the presence of his wife hugged me to his heart, saying, 'Let there never be a misunderstanding between us again. We love one another.' I felt the warmth of his body, and was surprised by the spontaneous gesture, for Rick was never demonstrative. This may have had something to do with Jeremy Fry, who a few evenings ago got locked out and rang me at midnight to let him in. This I did and went up to his flat and talked for a quarter of an hour. I was in my pyjamas with a rug round my shoulders. When I left he threw his arms round me and hugged me, with thanks. That was all. Perhaps it was not enough for my subconscious. In which sad case my subconscious will never again have enough.

Friday, 24th January

Last night at dinner here Rick Stewart-Jones's name cropped up, and Robert Henshaw† said he had never met a man who left on him a deeper impression of goodness. R. was somebody very special, very precious and when Robert heard about his death he felt a light had gone out. Now I, who knew R. so well, and greatly loved him at one time, never felt this spiritual aura around him. His extreme goodness, yes.

Two days ago A. dropped me on the main Bath–Stroud road at the old gates to Boxwell Court. I walked from there to Newark. Down the Boxwell drive was amazed to see masses of primroses already out. Last year's roses are still in flower. There can seldom have been such a mild winter, nor one so wet. Water and mud along the old London

---

* Richard Stewart-Jones (1914–57); conservationist.
† Resident of Bath; musician and conservationist.

road to Ozleworth such that I had to leave the path and climb into the woods to avoid getting stuck. I met John Huntley* neatly breaking twigs and making a bonfire near the house. Stopped, and we talked about the Transfer Tax. He did not seem unduly depressed. I told him we were not very happy in Bath and hoped to return to the country. He said, 'All day and every day of the year I do what you see me doing now, pottering here at Boxwell. I often think it is of no use to anybody and an absurd way of life.' 'No, no, no,' I exclaimed. 'You are leading the true life, the only life that matters. The real life.' I spoke with so much vehemence and conviction that I think he was startled. I meant it. His family have lived at Boxwell for 400 years without a break. He is a typical squire, and a through-and-through countryman, who is in touch with the earth, knows its every fibre.

A. and I went round Miss Taylor's house† with a builder by ourselves the following day [23 January] in pouring rain. We found the house terribly damp. Most of the walls of most of the rooms saturated, and no windows fitting properly. We wonder how we can face this, unless the estate really means to correct it. I am very uncertain about this Badminton venture.

Saturday, 25th January

I read in *The Times* the verbatim debate in the Commons on the Transfer Tax, which was passed by a Labour majority, a foregone conclusion. This is an historic week, for it means the end of the country estate. It is the end of the English parkscape scene; the end of a long, tired tradition. We shall be a full Communist state within ten years.

Monday, 3rd February

I remembered to say 'Hares' and 'Rabbits' at 11.58 and 12.02, out loud and with precision, so that Providence (or whosoever is the recipient of these magic formulae) could make no mistake for once. This of course was the night the month changed. Instead of bringing me luck,

---

* The Huntleys of Boxwell Court, Leighterton, have been Gloucestershire landowners since the Dissolution of the Monasteries, the Huntley of the time having been steward to the Abbot of Gloucester.
† Essex House, Badminton.

it has brought me one of the worst colds of my life, just on the eve of
our departure for Egypt. For the past three days I have not gone out
of doors, and have nursed myself to the extent of taking penicillin at
Dr Jones's orders. I have read a great deal lately, Julian Fane's* new *Tug
of War*, which because it moves him to another sphere, is better. The
book is far from boring and the descriptive Welsh passages are evocative, but he analyses his love affairs too much; goes over and over them
again. That is a bit too self-exposing. Also there is one passage, the
critical incident of the whole story, which I find shocking. In a flash
of lightning he sees the girl he is in love with with her face in the
crotch of another man, in the garden.

On Saturday Peter Hood† brought and nailed up my bullion fringes
for the yellow curtains in the library. Since we came here I have longed
for them. And now they are at last set up I am pleased as Punch, and
I sit and admire them, and decide that now my library is finished. All
I need is a hanging Colza-oil lantern for the hook in the ceiling
rosette, and I shall, when we go to Badminton, take away the pair of
Marlowes, of Naples, which are wasted, skyed over the bookcases, and
substitute the two Puleston and Bailey quarter-length portraits, which
are more suitable.

Egyptian tour   *Thursday, 6th February*

Cairo: The ninth century Mosque of Ibn Tulun. Congregational mosque to
be distinguished from other types. Outside courtyard (Zyada). A fellah
sweeping the dust on the floor with a huge palm branch. The kites
flying overhead. The silence in the heart of the great, bustling city.
Pointed arches, slightly shouldered. The dusty brickwork. Peculiar
crenellation of the long encompassing wall resembles manikins with
linked arms. The brick courses in English bond.

The Mosque of Sultan Hassan. Fourteenth-century. A teaching mosque.
Divided into four halls. The immense verticality of the street façade,
four huge pointed arches of the 'sahn'. The plan a Greek cross, and a
step up from the 'sahn'. Pavements of marble inlay. The students' quarters in the extreme four corners that infill the Greek cross. The heavy
architraves slotted.

---

* Hon. Julian Fane (b. 1927); yr son of Diana, Countess of Westmorland.
† Interior designer; worked with John Fowler of Colefax & Fowler.

Muhammed Ali Mosque. c. 1830. Alabaster. Santa Sofia influence. Ottoman not Egyptian. No wonder the modern Egyptians wanted to rid themselves of this usurping Turkish family of rulers. The rings of glass lanterns, all with glass dome shades; hung very low, just above head height, at the same level. Why can't western Christian churches imitate this example? The central dome, and four semi-domes.

al-Nasir Mosque. Fourteenth-century. Congregational.

The University. Tenth-century. Keel arch.

Friday, 7th February

Saqqâra. Bundles of reeds. Columns slant upwards rather than entasis. Sandstone. Vertical emphasis of façade. Proto-Doric engaged columns to tomb of Caliphs. Fluted columns. Imitation timber soffit, all in stone, a kind of Mannerist touch.

Giza. Solid blocks of granite of Valley Temple. Floor of alabaster. More awesome than Saqqâra.

Saturday, 8th February

Cairo Museum. Astonishingly badly maintained. Sparrows in the galleries. None of the exhibits protected from the light. Tutankhamun's gloves rotting before one's eyes. Heaps of powder beneath wooden caskets. Within decades the treasures of millennia are disintegrating. These bloody Egyptians are hopeless people. Akhnaton's epicene figure that of a woman, with broad thighs, breasts and no genitalia. An extraordinary *fin-de-siècle* almost Aubrey Beardsley face, long, pointed chin, sensuous lips, amused, cynical expression. Saw a framed photograph of the treasure of Tutankhamun as it was discovered by Carter and Carnarvon. The objects heaped one on top of another, higgledy-piggledy, untidily, just like the stables at Erddig with motor-bicycles, old mowing machines, carriages, etc. It was not the robbers, for they never reached this tomb. It was because the King died pre-maturely aged nineteen and had not had time to prepare and arrange these things. Not only T's gloves but his under-garments under full glare of light from skylights. His walking-sticks flaking. Wonderful as these gold and jewelled treasures are, I could not help comparing the workmanship unfavourably with French eighteenth-century workmanship, which was far more delicate. There's no questioning that the last reached the world heights in respect of artefact quality.

The Pyramids of Cheops and Chephren are far steeper than I imagined. Were these buildings still isolated in the desert as heretofore, I would have been more impressed than I was. In themselves they are more remarkable than illustrations suggest. But today they are practically surrounded by ignoble blocks of unfinished flats and houses, fences, car parks, '*son et lumière*' paraphernalia, an auditorium of cheap seats, and trash of every sort. Rising from the sand, they must have been the most impressive buildings of man. The damned archaeologists have ruined the Sphinx by digging a trench round her and restoring the base in an insensitive manner. Robin Fedden,* our guide throughout, once climbed Chephren's pyramid to the top by means of mountaineering tackle. He said the experience more alarming than a mountain face. Greater sense of isolation and detachment from the earth. Under the projecting cap, where the original polished surface remains, falcons have their eyries, jackals their lairs, and serpents abound. It was difficult to credit this.

Sunday, 9th February

Luxor. The clarity of the light here reminds me of mistral weather in the south of France. A magnified brightness; exaggerated cleanness of the air. Luxor Temple not axial. All of the New Kingdom. Once an avenue of sphinxes to Karnak, and at the Karnak end remains of these truncated objects at regular intervals, some now merely rounded stones. Outer court added by Amenhotep III. Deformed entasis at bottom of the columns of entrance. Temple begun by Tuthmosis III. Dedicated to God Amon and wife Mut. Statues and carving always done in situ. Amenhotep III's columns more orthodox, namely Doric, with lotus capitals. In my total ignorance and lack of investigation never realized before this expedition how Greek architecture totally derived from the Egyptian. Papyrus contours sharp, lotus contours rounded. The stone vaulting slabs over Alexander the Great's apartments remain, heavy monoliths, the cornice still painted in strips. Ante-hall papyrus columns. Here they have extended the charming

---

* Writer and Secretary (1951–74) of Historic Buildings Committee of the N.T. (1909–77).

old, low-storeyed Winter Palace Hotel by a tall, projecting block which towers over the adjacent temple and dissolves the ethos.

Monday, 10th February

The drive from Luxor gave the first close, intimate view of Egyptian landscape of the cultivated land. Beautiful it is too. An oasis, fertile, mud hovels of no age, hundreds of years old or of yesterday, traditional, no glass to windows, no doors; and sheep, chicken, goats and humans sharing the indoors.

Dendera. The local god Hathor, cow, of love and joy. I grew to detest her. Hall of columns (twenty-four), capital heads of Horus. Roof complete, a blue painted ground. A cobweb ribbon was floating from Horus's lips. At first I thought it must have been intentional, something left over from Egyptian times. The great long, stretching hands of goddess Mut are predatory, rapacious.

Abydos. The capital of Upper Egypt. God Osiris buried here, or the main part of him. A Mecca. Temple of Site 1 (Sethos, 1304–1290 BC) dedicated to seven deities. The vaulting intact. This greatly impresses me, the monstrous thickness of the stone in monoliths. The painted stone blocks.

Tuesday, 11th February

The Tombs of the Nobles. Tomb of Nas. Not torches but mirrors or reflectors were used for the decoration of these tombs. Today a fellah crouches at the entrance with a board plastered with silver paper, another at the first turning, and a third flashes the light on to whatever graffito the guide is explaining. The density of the light seems not to be dissipated by each reflection, and has a peculiar bright natural quality down there. In these nobles' tombs everyday scenes of life, wine-pressing, threshing, bird-netting, in strong colours. Even bee-keeping. One deep tomb ceiling constructed to undulate and then painted over with drooping vines and vine leaves, the collage most convincing.

Temple of Amenhotep II. You enter a transverse hall first. Everything done by Egyptians for glorification of the gods. Was no slavery. No foreign captives, no Jews (our guides emphasized) permitted the privilege of working at these temples. Honour and eternal life the motives. Tomb of Ramones, Aknaton's minister, realistic reliefs.

The Ramesseum. One of thirteen found. Funerary temples always on the west side of the Nile. The necropolis on side on which the sun goes down. One understands their beliefs of the nether world, the uncharted desert, the finitude of their narrow strip of world, desert on either side whence and whither the sun rises and descends daily. Effigy of Ramesses I fallen broken on the ground is Shelley's Ozymandias: 'I met a traveller from an antique land . . . who said . . .'

Wednesday, 12th February

Karnak. Proceeded by avenue of rams. Temple of God Amon. Pair of vast pylons. Hypostyle hall vastest of all; and are the columns ranged regularly? Couldn't decide. Karnak means 'ruin' in Arabic. God Amon wears two feathers like rolling-pins on his head. Papyrus represents Lower Egypt. Lotus Upper Egypt. In a house-boat in Cairo we were shown the newly discovered process of making papyrus sheets from the plant. Electrom, a mixture of gold, brown. Was painted on the apex of obelisks.

Temple of Hatshepsut. First instance of landscape layout in the world. Three terraces under a hemi-cycle of rock mountain, steep, stark, must be baking hot in summer under this precipice and no vegetation now whatever. Defaced by Tutmosis III. God Anubis, the jackal, represented like a glorious whippet, the god of necropolises and mummies. Not desert then but green avenue to the Nile. Senenmut her architect. Frieze in low relief of warriors painted red, and the holy barque much in evidence. Goddess Hathor, cow with sun between horns, of music, and delight. Temple of Anubis, coloured vultures with outspread wings, three-dimensional. Columns fluted or canted.

Thursay, 13th February

At last we board the *Osiris* and spend four nights on this delicious boat on the Nile. Not enough.

Valley of the Kings. Long, twisting, lunar landscape of grey stones. Tomb of Ramesses III. Goddess Nut of sky and night, protective, wide open arms. Sarcophagus room richly painted; railway-carriage arch in yellow and black. Long, long, stepped passages under horizontal vaults and landings.

Tutankhamun's Tomb. Unfinished because the King died so young. Baboons symbolize hours. Decoration of King's tomb chamber best of all. Large, life-size painted figures of King and gods. Seti I's tomb v. deep.

Very shocking that the roadway along the Valley of Kings has electric light standards with curved heads, thus totally nullifying the romance.

Friday, 14th February

Esna city. A caravan halt. Graeco-Roman temple of Ram (Clun), 185–54 BC. Had been completely buried by sand and now twenty feet below level of modern houses. Composite capitals of lotus. Defaced by Copts, especially gods' faces. Stone screens between columns. Traces of colour on screen frieze. Here hieroglyphics meaningless. Hypostyle caps v. beautiful, Composite include grapes. Temple swarming with swallows. Intact vault, painted.

Edfu. Apollinopolis Magna. Dedicated to God Horus whose wife Hator lived at Dendera where he visited her annually. Thirty-five metres high. Vertical openings on front of propylon for flags. Begun 237 BC. First court twelve columns on either side. Copts defaced again. Horus as falcon crowned before hall. I become sick of Horus. Back wall of hypostyle hall was front of original temple. Sanctuary tabernacle of polished granite and slab in front of it for holy barque. Cut out of one block of black granite from Aswan. Ambulatory with v. high wall surrounds this temple.

Saturday, 15th February

Niolisus. Pharaonic. Crocodile, dedicatee. Well for purifications. Pylon (Roman) entirely destroyed. A calendar of feasts incised on one wall. Surgical instruments displayed.

Philae. Was on an island, now at bottom of the lake. The 1902 dam covered half of the temple during flooding season. Now barricaded and water constantly pumped out while army of workmen dismantle in order to remove the whole structure to higher land. The best preserved Ptolemaic temple, observed from rampart above. Not allowed to descend. A Roman pavilion to Hadrian does not look so much Roman as Egyptian. Asymmetrical colonnades to the pylon.

Aswan. Straw-coloured sand of the dunes and porphyry rocks the east side of the river. Egyptian granite quarries here. This place likewise spoilt by huge beastly hotel we stayed in, facing Elephantine Island on which an enormous coloured photograph of General Sadat on advertisement hoarding.

In the evening Robin [Fedden], [his wife] Renée and an eighteen-year-old girl and I took the felucca from the hotel to the Aga Khan's mausoleum. From distance an impressive building, but on close inspection the corner turrets too small, the blocks of masonry too small. On the tomb, which is marble and vast, one tiny silver vase with a single rose which is grown in the Begum's garden below and every day changed. We walked past it. Saw a desert hare squatting on the edge of the sand. Walked to the convent deserted by the Copts in twelfth century. Robin thrilled by seeing a flock of trumpeter finches. Dull little birds. Proceeded across golden sand and stones, quartz and sparkling. Going heavy. Climbed a hill to a little mausoleum (Muslim) overlooking the city and river. Thence descended precipice of sand, like skiing. Rather frightening. My shoes so full of and heavy with sand that they half came off. Robin said just as well I managed to keep them on, for vipers. Within four minutes their bite kills. Along the path by Nile our boy in a pink jellaba met us. Only a narrow strip of mangy grass between bank and desert. Watched hawks. Watched dung beetles, which on sensing our approach, feigned death. Noticed their tracks across sand just like those of a minefield tractor; phenomenon of sand falling while simultaneously a wave of sand moved uphill. In evening light the Nile dark purple. Back on the felucca gliding home across the river, listening to the barking of frogs.

Sunday, 16th February

Flew to Abu Simbel in a Polish plane, very rickety. The flies here terrible. Very remarkable feat in removing these temples, rocks and all. But rather a disillusion to go behind into the wings, so to speak, and see how the rock hill is really some stones fixed to the outside of an enormous hangar. Nevertheless much impressed, although debased bas reliefs. Formerly the Nile water lapped the feet of the colossi.

Wadi Natrun. Half a dozen of us hired a mini-bus and motored a hundred miles into the desert. Only had time to visit two monasteries. *Deir Suriani* with tenth-century stucco work beside the iconostasis. The church screen of ivory inlaid in ebony and cedar, doors folding, alabaster window openings. Within sanctuary stone carved panels, very early. In the west end of this, the summer church - for it was very chilly - a pile of wheat for the holy bread with an iron cross stuck in the top of the pile. Went into St Bishoi's cell carved from the rock, with a chimney-like shaft for minimum of light and air. Here he knelt at night in prayer with a wire attached to his hair from a stay. When he nodded with sleep the wire pulled his scalp. A marble-rimmed hole in the west end of the church for washing the feet of the monks. Even here one has to remove one's shoes before entry. The monks – there are thirty – very poor and very dirty. Ostrich eggs hanging, as in Jerusalem. The monk explained that they symbolize care of the faithful by the Church, the ostrich caring more for its offspring than any other bird. The winter church now in use is smaller and warmer. Given holy bread to eat. Nice, crackly, wheaten, and light brown. At St Macarius we rang the portal bell. Taken into a guests' room like a waiting room in an aerodrome. After an interval a monk brought us tea in a tin pot. It was dark as treacle. Then the Father Rector, impressive with a beard, conducted us round, ceaselessly explaining, not one word of which we understood. This a rich monastery. Consequence, the monks are rebuilding it with their own hands in the most monstrous way, totally ruining the buildings. Use of concrete and abominable pointing.

Tommy Gillespie, nice old Canadian in our group. I said to him, 'One sometimes makes mistakes in pressing people one meets on group tours to call on one at home.' 'Oh,' he said, 'I never do after my horrid experience.' Years ago he called on some people he had met on a boat. They lived in a manor house in Devon. He drove up to the door and rang the bell. Door was opened by a parlour maid, stark naked except for a parlourmaid's cap with strings. She led him into the great hall. There he was greeted by his host and hostess, both stark naked. Tea on a silver tray was brought in by the stark naked maid. The hostess was nervous of the crumbs, the host of spilling hot tea on his stomach. After tea they said to Tommy, 'Shall we play croquet now?' He too was now obliged to strip. 'So', he explained solemnly, 'I never follow up new friendships.'

Renée Fedden said the last time she left Egypt was at four in the morning. At the gate of the flight at the airport they searched her hand-bag and discovered £40 of Egyptian money. They told her she was forbidden to take it abroad. She said, 'I cannot possibly change it now. The bank is shut and even the restaurant is shut. Here, take it!' And she thrust it at the officer. He refused, saying he was unable to accept it. Renée, in despair of missing her plane and by then in a rage, tore the notes up and threw them on the ground, saying, 'Damn your beastly money, which is worthless to me anyway.' Whereupon she was promptly arrested for infringing the law.

The Egyptian country women carry on their heads empty water pots, sideways up, called 'goollahs', exactly the same as those used by the ancient Egyptians.

One evening I came into the Hilton, Cairo, where we were staying, to find a wedding reception in progress. A band of dervishes, naked to the waist, wearing sashes and pantaloons were playing pipes. Bride and bridegroom carried lit candles in their hands, she clad in white raiment. Behind came bagpipers, followed by a long procession of unsmiling guests in western dress.

The most sinister experience in Egypt was the visit to the Serapeum or tomb of the sacred bulls, at Memphis. We descended down, down, down into the bowels of the earth. There was no light but what our feeble torches gave. The dust was stifling. Suffered throughout from tomb throat. Indeed I had a bad cold the whole fortnight, it having begun before we left England. The most beautiful and unforgettable experience was watching the sunsets from the boat on the Nile. Every night the same thing happened. The orange sun went down rapidly, with a practically audible plonk into the desert. At this moment it became cold. One felt shivery and reached for the pullover. For twenty minutes nothing much happened. A dull, toneless, dead twilight. One decided there was to be no sunset that evening. Then the sunset swept across the sky. A wondrous, orange and purple clarity, the sky becoming feathery with refractions. Edward Lear has captured these skies. Each sunset was a Lear water-colour.

Wednesday, 26th February

J.K.-B.,* just returned from America, says that John Pope-Hennessy†
is the most revered of Englishmen in the museum world there. He is
far more highly thought of than K. Clark.‡ His name is one to conjure
with. He is regarded as the foremost scholar of painting in the world.
John supports this opinion without question.

A remarkable and satisfactory thing about Egypt is the number of
birds and the great variety. They have so far survived because the
Egyptians have no guns, I suppose, being still too poor, thank goodness. Everywhere we saw hoopoes, black and white kingfishers,
herons, egrets, falcons, and swallows flying in and out of the tombs. I
have since my return read Amelia Edwards's *Thousand Miles up the
Nile*, written in 1875. Conditions have not changed much since that
date in the country, away from horrid Cairo. The fellahin still work
primitive wheels, with jugs tied on them, which they propel by means
of rotating oxen, and so raise water from the Nile in driblets which
flow slowly down little channels scooped in the mud flats of the river
bank.

Tuesday, 11th March

Met Anne Scott-James§ in the London Library. I told her how good
A. thought her Sissinghurst book was. She said if it pleased A. then
she felt all right, for A. was the severest and best qualified critic to
judge it.

Sat yesterday afternoon in a small, stuffy room in Mitchell Beazley
the publishers' office off Shaftesbury Avenue, going through photographs and colour plates with female secretary for my section in the
Architecture of the World book. We sat together so intimate and close that
I defy any man in such situation, even of my age, to have been
unmoved by the proximity. It was when we were bending over a small

---

* John Kenworthy-Browne (b. 1931); on staff of N.T. and Christie's; expert on neo-clas-
sical sculpture.
† Sir John Pope-Hennessy (1913–94); Director of the V. & A., 1967–73; Director of
British Museum, 1974–6; art historian.
‡ Baron Clark of Saltwood (Life Peer, 1969); but best remembered as Sir Kenneth Clark,
art historian (1903–85).
§ Journalist and gardener; m. 1967 Sir Osbert Lancaster (1908–86), cartoonist, painter,
theatrical designer, writer. The book was *Sissinghurst: The Making of a Garden*.

plate, each with a magnifying glass in hand, that her hair just brushed my cheek, sending sparks of electricity or a surge of sap within me. I can honestly say it was no more libidinous than cerebral. I mean it was, let me be honest, physical, because I had physical reactions, without feeling libidinous. What I mean is that I did not feel impelled to do more than put an arm round her and embrace. Needless to say, I didn't even dare do that.

Friday, 21st March

Poor old Tom Goff* is dead. The first I knew was from seeing an appreciation in *The Times* by his friend David McKenna. A. telephoned John Gwynne who told her Tom had taken an overdose. He was guarded and would not explain what had happened, beyond hinting that Tom was very worried by some man who was claiming the right to his Pont Street flat. There had been a terrible row, with David M. present. All seemed to end well when the others left. Tom there and then killed himself. He had inherited from his father a mental instability. He was a difficult though a fundamentally good man. He made great trouble for me years ago in accusing me to the Chairman of having persuaded his father to give The Courts, Holt [near Lacock in Wiltshire], to the N.T. when I knew him to be out of his mind. This was very unfair because all the negotiations with the father took place in the presence of Lady Cécilie Goff, who appeared to approve them. Tom was meanwhile in Canada. This was during the war. The Chairman, who I think was at the time David Crawford, agreed to a most sensible compromise, such as only the N.T. would come to, namely that for his lifetime Tom should retain the FitzClarence portraits which his father had made over to the Trust with the house. I was led to believe at the time that the father had obtained the son's consent in writing. How was I to know otherwise? Tom was an intimate friend of Ted Lister,† and belonged to that now extinct generation of *bien*, high-to-middle-brow bachelors, endowed with money, privilege and nice houses and possessions; queers with an Edwardian sense of the proprieties, snobbish, yet full of confidence,

---

* Thomas Goff, maker of harpsichords; son of Major T.C.E. Goff, a descendant of William IV and Mrs Jordan; see *Ancestral Voices*.
† E.G. Lister (1873–1956), of Westwood Manor, Wiltshire, which he saved and reinstated, and left to the N.T.

men with whom it was in my youth an education to be with. Tom was a particularly brilliant raconteur, but unable to pronounce his *r*s.

Last night at 1.15 when I was just asleep the telephone rang loudly beside my bed. It was Mrs Schuster from next door, number 20, to say that her manservant had just been rung up in his flat at the top of the house. 'A common voice' addressed him by name (he is not in the telephone book) thus: 'There is a bomb in yer place, two o'clock. There is a bomb in yer place, two o'clock,' and rang off. The police were round in a few minutes; having investigated and found nothing, they kept guard for the rest of the night. Mrs Schuster said she was sure it was a hoax but I had better look out, for anarchists had a habit of chucking bombs through basement windows. Since I sleep in the basement, albeit on the garden side, I closed my shutters, and drew the curtains, and hoped for the best.

Sunday, 23rd March

We put Feeble the canary on the window-sill of the library during the daytime because he likes being in the sun and watching the people go by in the road – so we choose to think. Anyway he gives me pleasure in singing, which does not disturb me at work; on the contrary, he is company. Twice lately I have seen a black cat on the ledge outside clawing at the shut window trying to get at the bird. Now, I have grown to love Feeble, and I hate cats. This morning I seized a walking stick, crept out of the front door, and managed to catch the cat a smart blow with the stick. Taken aback, it jumped down the area onto the paving below, and ran off. A. said I should not have done this; one must never hurt animals however much one may dislike them. Besides, if anyone had seen me do this to a neighbour's cat it would have caused bad blood. Ever since this incident I have pondered. The dreadful truth is that the old hunting instinct in me derives pleasure in – not being positively cruel, but in catching the quarry.

This morning at the eight o'clock Holy Communion service in the Abbey [in Bath] a man beside me blew his nose with the utmost violence, making a truly disgusting noise. I thought how frightful this was, and scarcely less disgusting than if he had relieved himself of some other superfluous bodily waste. How absurd polite conventions are. They are based on what's possible and what's not. The anus and penis can be concealed. Therefore what the nose and mouth do has come to be accepted as perfectly respectable.

The Tony Powells[*] to luncheon. A. says she never feels entirely at ease with them. I do because one can talk, they both being highly companionable. In our talking of grubby girls of today and asking why young men found them attractive, Tony said he did. He had always been attracted by girls who looked as though they had slept under a hedge for a week. I respect him, and love her for her warmth.

I have received an appeal for money towards Cyril Connolly's[†] fund. Apparently he has left debts amounting to £27,000 and no assets whatever, a widow and two children without a *sou*. A. says this is an appeal which we need not answer for latterly Cyril was very off-hand with us, did not answer letters when invited to stay or acknowledge occasional fagging I did for him over his Pavilions book,[‡] etc. But I am not sure.

Wednesday, 2nd April

We went to Scotney [Castle, Kent] for Easter, the coldest I ever remember. It snowed nearly every day and there was a bitter wind. On the Saturday A. and I visited Penshurst; paid and went the round. The house well shown, well arranged, notices in good taste. As I was leaving the gatehouse Lord De L'Isle passed me, turned and said I must come in for tea, Peggy[§] would be so pleased to see me. I said A. was with me, and was looking at the garden. I retrieved her and we both had tea with him, and Peggy, in their new tea room, just opened. They showed us round their part of the house, where they live quite apart from the public sector. She told A. she did not much care for Penshurst, which was for her a duty. She infinitely preferred Wales. I got the impression that neither cared very much for the other. Relations formal and strained. He seemed a very sad man, now superannuated, and apparently much embittered because she prevented his being made Lord-Lieutenant through constantly taking him away from Kent. He told A.

---

[*] Anthony Powell (b. 1905), author; m. 1934 Lady Violet Pakenham, dau. of 5th Earl of Longford.
[†] Author, journalist and literary reviewer (1903–74).
[‡] This was *Les Pavillons* (1962), '(with Jerome Zerbe)'.
[§] Margaret, wife of 1st Viscount De L'Isle, VC, and formerly of 3rd Baron Glenusk (who d. 1948); she was a family connection through J.L.-M's great-grandfather, Sir Joseph Bailey.

he had 'known Jim for years'. Yet I do not think I know him at all well. We had a few words in his library about the state of the country. He is appalled by what is happening. Thinks we shall go Marxist within a matter of years. Says he would far sooner be dead, and agrees that we at our time of life have nothing to lose in fighting it to the death. Exhorts me to write and enrol myself in General What's-his-name's register.* Says at least he would be glad to have my name on his list. Bill De L'Isle thinks Heath† was the cause of our ills, through sheer weakness, feebleness. The conversation arose from my asking him about his Shelley ancestry, and his telling me he had inherited two separate Shelley baronetcies. I deplored the fact that no more baronets were created. He said Heath had been determined to stop hereditary honours, that he was the most class-conscious of men. I liked De L'Isle very much. Peggy surprised and embarrassed me by saying she was giving me a print in a maplewood frame of my gt-grandfather.

Staying at Scotney were a lady from Devon, a friendly dumpling, uninteresting, and John Cornforth‡ and Lanning [Roper].§ Lanning is a dull man, though unexceptionable as to character, slightly tragedy queen, and name-dropping. John Cornforth has a single-track but a good mind. Is acknowledged successor to Christopher Hussey at *Country Life*.

In the Scotney library I found two large folio volumes on the land-owners of Great Britain in 1873. Dukes and the smallest squireens were included. Abram Crompton owned 58 acres at Crompton; Henry Travis Milne owned 260 acres at Crompton. They were my gt-gt-uncles, I think. My gt-grandfather, Joseph Lees, to my surprise owned 746 acres at Lees. Now, my maternal gt-grandfather Joseph Bailey owned 600 acres in Radnorshire, 4,800 in Herefordshire and 22,000 in Brecon.

Wednesday, 16th April

Eardley said to me last week, 'I hate going into churches. Churches remind me of death.'

---

* David Stirling, DSO, OBE (b. 1915); founder of SAS.
† Rt Hon. Edward Heath (b. 1916; KG 1992); Conservative Prime Minister 1970–4.
‡ Architectural historian and writer, notably for *Country Life*.
§ Landscape gardener and writer (1912–83); American-born, but spent most of his working life in England; garden correspondent of the *Sunday Times*, 1951–75.

Yesterday afternoon at Badminton A. was planting things in the garden of Taylor's [Essex House]. I started walking back towards Bath. I watched a brimstone butterfly accompany me, like a cat, back and forth along the hedge by the park. I wanted it to settle so that I might see the markings on the outside of its wings. But it would settle with folded wings. I easily picked it up, by very slowly and gently moving my hand to within nine inches of it, and rapidly pouncing with finger and thumb. Between my fingers it remained absolutely still. It did not move a leg or antenna. I feared I had killed it from fright. So I threw it into the air, and away it flew quite undeterred.

I have grave doubts about this Badminton house. It is dark and depressing inside. And I fear that it will be difficult, far worse than here in Lansdown Crescent, to preserve anonymity. I don't want to have to bid good morning and enquire after every inhabitant's health whenever I walk, not necessarily through the garden gate, but through the front door into the front garden. Today the village was pandemonium with horse boxes and police cars and caravans containing those thousands of people organizing the beastly horse trials. If we do live in Badminton we shall have to leave the village for at least a week every April.

Dined with Christopher Chancellor;[*] or rather, ate from a tray on a stool in his library, from a most uncomfortable, low armchair, toast and marmalade, and a banana; and, I concede, drank some excellent white grapy wine which he had brought back from Lucca. Until 11.30 I had to listen to him complaining about his tribulations arising from the Preservation Trust, and to him reading articles and letters to the Bath papers about the Pres. Trust. He read me a very long and very strong letter he has just sent to the new City Planning Officer, and asked me what I thought of it. I told him I thought it would sever all decent relations between the Trust and the Corporation for all time. He was clearly disturbed, but not convinced.

Thursday, 17th April

This morning received, quite unsolicited, a charming letter from John Saumarez Smith[†] of Heywood Hill's shop about my diaries, which he

---

[*] Sir Christopher Chancellor (1904–89); General Manager of Reuters Ltd, 1944–59; Chairman of Bowaters, 1962–9; Chairman of Bath Preservation Trust, 1969–76.
[†] Bibliophile and Managing Director of G. Heywood Hill, booksellers (b. 1943).

has read in proof. Says his shop will sell hundreds of copies. Gratifying indeed, but oh dear, the triviality of the stuff. He did say I would make enemies, and arouse contradictions, but interest.

Friday, 18th April

Having missed buying from Heywood Hill's shop the copy of Maddox's *Views of Lansdown Tower*, 1844, which I longed for, I found another copy at Weinreb's shop. When I sent them a cheque and letter, saying I would call for it the next time I came to London, I received a reply that Mr Weinreb hoped I would forewarn him. So I telephoned the shop to say I would call that morning. I was put through to Mr Weinreb, who promptly invited me to luncheon. I was very surprised and flattered, and thanked him warmly but declined because I had another engagement. Nevertheless, when I called for the book I was made to visit him in his room, where he gave me coffee. He said he merely wished to make my acquaintance. I was much pleased.

The day before yesterday I motored to Fonthill, and beginning with the 'Inigo Jones' gateway went all the way round the estate in the car, stopping at certain points. Called on John Goodall who lives in Lawn Cottage, where there is a ruinous circular dovecote with the Beckford crest over the doorway. Goodall has a glass mug with 'P.G.' engraved thereon. It was given by Beckford to the dwarf.* I walked from the road to Bitham Lake and looked up the steep slope, wondering where exactly the Abbey had stood. This I discovered on reaching the great western avenue. At the entrance I left the car, and walked. Was embarrassed at being overtaken by a motorist who stopped and politely asked me what I was doing. I explained, hoped I was not trespassing, etc. He was the owner of the Abbey grounds, a man called Rimington. He allowed me to walk round the site of the Abbey and I marvelled that it covered so small an area. To the south is a steep declivity to the American garden, now overgrown, the terrace, and Bitham Lake below. Still a marvellous situation, and unspoilt part of country. It was a rewarding visit.

I am so steeped in Beckford that I identify myself with him – a horrid character, it cannot be denied.

Yesterday was motored by Tony Mitchell† to Hagley to talk to

---

* William Beckford of Fonthill Abbey had in his service a dwarf, Piero (Pierre de Grailly).
† Anthony Mitchell, local N.T. representative.

Charles Cobham* about the house. He is a jolly man, full of stories and fun, very astute, and talks well. The salt of the earth, a splendid man, who reminded me of Bill De L'Isle. He too is a KG. He showed us a drawing of a pretty Lyttelton girl who was to have married A.J. Balfour. She died at twenty-three and was buried wearing her engagement ring. Balfour never really recovered from this loss. Charles Cobham once asked Baldwin his opinion of A.J.B. Baldwin replied that Balfour regarded the ways of men with the interest of a choirboy at a funeral. Cobham showing us the portrait of his gt-grandfather in the dining room, said he killed himself. There is still a strong streak of melancholia in the Lyttelton family. His youngest son suffers, and from time to time has to go to a home. He has eight children. The gt-grandfather, when driving to Worcester and discerning a 'proletarian bottom', used to flick it with his whip. When the workmen in one factory past which he drove saw the Lord coming, they used to assemble by the wayside and pelt his carriage with dead cats, stones, old bottles and rotten eggs. When Lord Lyttelton died and was buried in Worcester Cathedral, a concourse followed the bier, including all the workmen of the factory, who declared that never had there been a greater gentleman or one more beloved.

Tony Mitchell told me that when he lunched with John Cadbury† and his wife the other day, he heard John say to the wife, 'Wilt thou have sugar in thy coffee?' I knew he was a practising Quaker, but I never knew he was as old-fashioned as that. It is delightful.

Cobham has lately had the exterior walls at Hagley cleaned of the dirt of Birmingham smog. Done by sand blasting, which means ⅛th of the ashlar being scraped or blown off, a questionable proceeding. Has had the balustrade of the perron remade in a composition which is bright scarlet, and very hideous. I fear his taste is deplorable, and choice of new carpets and furnishings altogether awful. Yet some fine furniture still there. I noticed the absence from the Gallery of the frail Chippendale wall lights, and remarked rather tactlessly on it. C. said he had to sell them to help pay death duties.

---

* 10th Viscount Cobham, KG (1909–77), of Hagley Hall, Stourbridge, Worcestershire.
† National Trust supporter (1889–1982); m. 1925 Joyce Matthews.

Saturday, 26th April

On Thursday we went to dear old Raymond's* eightieth birthday party given by Desmond† and Patrick Trevor-Roper‡ in Pat's house in Regent's Park. It was extremely hot; I was quite unable to drink, merely one sip of champagne. Both Desmond and Raymond told me separately that they had read my *Ancestral Voices* in proof, which annoys me rather. So too of course had the boy from Chatto's, Sebastian Walker,§ who was staying at Crichel. R. said, 'I do not mind your calling me a rattle-snake, but I do mind your quoting me for comparing Helen Dashwood to a holly. Can you please substitute a fictitious name?' Consequence is I have had to get on to Norah Smallwood,¶ involving much last-minute confabulation and fuss, and alteration to print.

Monday, 28th April

I almost had a breakthrough with Nick,** my gt-nephew, when he and I went to Stourhead last Sunday, by ourselves. I mean that although I have long loved him dearly and longed to become intimate with him, a shyness on both sides has hindered this. The other day, he driving me there and back, we managed to talk more naturally than hitherto. He is an exceedingly clever boy which should make our companionship easy; yet, with someone of two generations' difference it is hard to click in a hurry. When he talks feelingly about the philosophy behind Ezra Pound's poetry I feel totally at sea, and ignorant. When I talk about Bernini, of whom he, the budding art historian, has never heard, he feels at sea. The result is that I get on to bantering terms with him, and this does not always work. Clearly the more we do see of one another, the easier we shall become. He is an enormous youth, over my height, stronger built, and handsome as can be

---

* Raymond Mortimer (1895–1980); literary reviewer; of Long Crichel House, Dorset.

† Desmond Shawe-Taylor (1907–95); literary and music critic for *New Statesman* and the *Sunday Times*; also of Long Crichel.

‡ Ophthalmic surgeon and lecturer (b. 1916); brother of historian Hugh Trevor-Roper (cr. 1979 Baron Dacre of Glanton); also of Long Crichel.

§ Director of Chatto & Windus, 1977–79; founder (1978) and Chairman of Walker Books Ltd, children's book publishers (1942–91).

¶ Publisher; Chairman of Chatto & Windus (1909–84).

** Nicholas Robinson, eldest son of J.L.-M's sister Audrey's daughter Prudence.

with his sleek dark hair, fine brows and what's called a well-cut profile. If only he would not chain-smoke, and dress like a tramp!

Drawing a bow at a venture I telephoned last night to a stranger named Goodridge in the Bath telephone book. A young man answered with a cheery and common voice. Yes, he was descended from H.E. Goodridge, the architect of Lansdown Tower: that he knew, but nothing beside. Advised me to telephone his father, whose name was the other I had spotted in the book. Spoke to the father. He too very friendly, not the least minding my enquiries. Again, common voice, almost working-class I should guess; charming, called me 'Sir'. Said he knew nothing about H.E. Goodridge papers, and added, 'I have never cared to probe too closely.' By which I assume he did not mean there were skeletons in the family cupboards, but merely that he had never had the curiosity to ask questions. By process of elimination and synthesis I deduced that he was the great-grandson of H.E. His mother is alive in a 'home'. He visits her once a week, and will ask her and ring me back. Stupidly I forgot to enquire whether there was a portrait of Goodridge in the family. The short obituary of Goodridge in an old *Bath Chronicle* states that he was of an old Wessex family which migrated to Bath in the eighteenth century. Certainly H.E. Goodridge who was on close terms with Beckford and bought things from his sale in 1844 was a cultivated and skilled architect. How is it that descendants can be so ignorant?

Tuesday, 29th April

Spring comes to Barzaba,* with a nip in the air today. He walks from Bathampton along the canal to Freshford and back. The trees and hedgerows, such as are left, are vivid green. So is the scum on the canal water, which on the end of his dipped walking stick presents the prettiest little floral fronds with hardly any stalks at all, wisps merely. But he notices very little, apart from the moorhens which scuttle across the water as though leaving behind them a nest with eggs, in their fright. Never a nest to be seen. Why do they bob with their tails in such an ungainly, silly fashion? Neither does Barzaba come to any conclusion how he is to begin his book, which worries him very much. He fears he may not be able either to begin, or continue, cer-

---

* William Beckford personified himself as Barzaba in letters to his friend of many decades, Gregorio Franchi.

tainly not end. Instead he is fascinated by a group of young people by an old broken-down lock where there is a motor-boat which plies on Saturdays for gain - through the thick duckweed. One of the group is bending almost double, while kneeling over a piece of machinery. In the way of the young today his shirt does not fit into his trousers, and leaves a space of six inches of skin visible. The skin is faintly bronzed, smooth as a nectarine and with the down of a nectarine, glistening in the sunlight. It is a cold afternoon, with a north-west wind. Another facing him is naked to the waist. How on such a day he can be so is extraordinary. In consequence his nipples are protuberant and hard, as though they are gooseflesh. Barzaba nods a 'Good afternoon', is looked upon as he retreats as an old, good man, and immediately forgotten. But he does not forget. At the end of an hour and a half he is back at Bathampton Bridge, and motors home. The expedition has done nothing to stimulate his mind, only his curiosity, which profits him nothing.

Wednesday, 30th April

I used to think a man ceased to live when he ceased to be in love. Now I know that he ceases to live when he ceases to love his fellows – how trite and pious *and* untrue when meant in the aggregate. Only a handful of persons is worth loving. What is incontrovertible is that a man ceases to live when he can no longer look forward. Looking forward is the spice of life – to the article coming out next week, the book next year, the coin cabinet which belonged to Beckford (and which he ought not to have spent money on buying) being delivered. The moment when I have nothing to look forward to, then I shall be dead. Oh, the sadness of old age, and me!

On the radio I listened to an opera by Mercadente, whom I had never heard of, a contemporary of Donizetti, or rather an older generation to and eclipsed in popularity by. It was full of melody, passion, swing, and bangings and buglings and drummings. I enjoyed it immensely, and was thrilled.

Did I record that Mattei Radev* offered to stay and gild the rosettes of my library ceiling? He said he might bring his best gilder, who was a blackamoor boy from Jamaica, by name – Beckford! I don't think Mattei had ever heard of William Beckford when he told me this.

---

* Picture-frame-gilder; Bulgarian immigrant.

Clearly this boy's forbears were among B's large number of slaves on his vast estates. It would be fun to have Mr Beckford working on the ceiling of Mr Beckford's own library.

Saturday, 3rd May

I have bought for fifty pence a rubber stamp, and having arranged the letters I put on the backs of envelopes 'Down with the Marxists'. The stamp looks just like those tiresome advertisement scrawls with which the Post Office disfigures post cards sent to one, so that one cannot read the text.

I must be very dense. Over and over again I read in books sentences which I entirely fail to understand, *viz.*, in Michael Holroyd's *Augustus John* the sentence '(Love affairs) discovered aspects of himself he had never imagined before; they taught him to get away from the dull old stamping grounds, to become another person. This was their fatal charm. For when the new continent had been thoroughly explored, the new self mapped and assimilated into the central empire of the self, there was no more mystery: and interest died.' Having read this sentence three times (at midnight, it is true), I gave up, and passed on. Michael Holroyd is a very clever man indeed. I am amazed at his industry and his power of analysis. This 'analysis' is what I utterly fail to reach; and the failure explains why I cannot write biography. Holroyd's book (Vol. 1) is however far too long. Horrible man, John, and those loathsome filthy gypsies.

Curious how one does not mind, on the contrary almost relishes, one's own smells. I am constantly smelling myself; hot vapours arise from me to my nostrils. I only hope others do not notice them. I wonder if they do, and do not like to say so? Yet I believe A. would. We have a pact to tell each other. I would hesitate to tell her. As yet I have *never* had cause. I fear that the older one becomes, the more and worse one smells. Most of my contemporaries smell, and I back away lest I catch a whiff.

Dick and Elaine[*] lunched yesterday on their way from Worcester to Sussex. Have not seen them since Christmas 1973. Not greatly changed. Rather on the defensive about Simon and ready to criticize Lois.[†]

---

[*] Richard Crompton Lees-Milne (1910–84) and his wife (née Brigstocke), J.L.-M's brother and sister-in-law.
[†] Richard and Elaine L.-M's son and his first wife.

When the old express disapproval of the young I always recall their own past foibles, which usually were no less unsavoury than those which they deplore. I fear Dick and I look much alike now. I say fear, for although I love him, I do not like his lanky build. It saddens me that I cannot make any contact whatever with him beyond the family. And that is not a very improving subject.

Friday, 9th May

A young man called Laurence Lee having written to me some days ago arrived punctually by appointment at four with an enormous Gladstone bag filled with all the books I have ever written. These he made me sign one by one. He had two copies of several. I gave him a cup of tea and we packed him off. He had no car and had walked up Lansdown hill carrying this heavy bag, and walked back again to the station. I believe he was not a dealer, but a collector. He told me he had 2,000 books, and was a land agent by profession.

I rushed off to Corsham to inspect an elm tree which yesterday fell on the main road, decapitating a bus driver and injuring several passengers. The inside of the bole and branches was black. John Methuen assured me this was no indication of decay. I would have thought it was.

Brian Fothergill dined. He arrived in Bath two days ago to look at Beckford houses and the Tower, which I took him to see, for his forthcoming book.* Has very good manners which appealed to A. Looks ill and saturnine; is astringent, and bookish; but sympathetic and easy to talk to.

It was such a surprise to be approached by Graham Monsell† at the theatre the other evening in London, with outstretched hand. He held my hand and said how delighted he was to see me and would so much like us to meet to talk over old times. Old times, my foot! I was terrified of Graham as a boy. At children's tennis tournaments he used to bash his racquet in rage over my head so that I looked like a clown peering through a broken drum, and once at Wickhamford he let out my father's pet parrot so that it flew away, and drove his car out of the motor-house into a ditch. At Oxford he was considered extremely

---

* *Beckford of Fonthill* (1979).
† Henry Bolton Graham Eyres Monsell (1905–93), 2nd Viscount Monsell.

dashing, the 'fastest' man in the university, wore a black polo sweater, and allegedly took drugs. Was excessively supercilious, rich and disdainful. I was terrified of him. Now he is rather bent, blind, sallow, dusty and shy and diffident. How the late worms change places with the early birds.

Thursday, 15th May

Further Beckford thoughts. Beckford's life was ruined at the age of twenty-four by the vicious persecution of Lord Loughborough, later 1st Earl of Rosslyn, who claimed to be deeply shocked by Beckford's criminal relations with his nephew (in-law), young William Courtenay. I recall at Oxford this Lord Rosslyn's g-gt-gt-gt-nephew, Hamish Erskine,[*] sleeping with Desmond Parsons,[†] who was Beckford's gt-gt-gt-gt-grandson. Now, was Lord Rosslyn squirming in his grave with rage during the late Twenties when his collateral descendant was thus indulging in carnal relations with the descendant of his bitter enemy?

Dining at Sally W[estminster]'s[‡] on Monday Clare Crossley[§] was describing the *Great Splash* film which she had seen, in which two boys are photographed having an affair. She said, 'I had never before seen two men sleeping together. Have you? Or perhaps you have?' I said nothing, but was overcome with embarrassment and blushed scarlet. George Dix[¶] who was sitting opposite me observed this, and said afterwards he had never seen me at a loss for words before. I should have replied to Clare that I had not, which in a sense is true, in that one did not presumably 'see' oneself or anyone else in such conditions.

Thursday, 22nd May

Last week A. went to France to stay with Clarissa[**] and the grandchildren. I stayed here and began upon my Beckford book, not

---

[*] Hon. James (but always known as Hamish) St Clair-Erskine, MC (1909–73).
[†] Hon. Desmond Parsons (1910–37), brother of 6th Earl of Rosse.
[‡] Sally Perry (1911–91), widow of Gerald Grosvenor, 4th Duke of Westminster.
[§] Clare (b. 1907), m. 1927 Anthony Crossley (1909–84).
[¶] Friend of J.L.-M. since 1945, at which time he was a US naval officer.
[**] A.L.-M's daughter by her first marriage (1933) to Anthony, 3rd Viscount Chaplin (1906–82); she m. 1958 Michael Luke.

without difficulty. By dint of working uninterruptedly I managed to rough out a schedule and to write a prologue of some fifteen pages. The appalling and daunting slog is to abbreviate. I have enough notes for a book of 200,000 words, not 40,000, which is my limit.

Mrs Thatcher's* eyebrows are similar to Mr Macmillan's.† They slope downwards in a leonine fashion which denotes wisdom. I think this woman has spirit and convictions. If only she has powers of leadership.

I myself interrupted my work by going to London on Tuesday for the night. Freda Berkeley‡ told me that Charlotte Bonham Carter§ was expecting us to dinner. A. had already chucked, and I felt I must go because the poor thing has just escaped death from a dreadful motor accident, and goes on to Freda about the Beckford books she intends giving me, and which she fears owing to her incapacity she cannot bring to London. To indicate that I am not greedily expecting this magnificent present, and to show my general good will and affection for this dear old person, I must go.

Lunched alone in the cafeteria of the V. & A. Filthy. Dirty trays and nasty snacks, the sort one gets on the train. Negro waitresses grumbling loudly about the nastiness of a white lady who quite rightly showed some delicacy about a dirty dish of food. She *was* a 'lady'. This was the real reason. The hatred of the proletariat for the upper classes is manifested on all occasions now.

Sunday, 25th May

I went to Holy Communion in the Abbey at eight. By myself, A. too late, which is unusual for her. Wrote several letters in the morning – I only write on Sundays now, limiting them to about six a week at most because of the increased postage. Also corrected the proofs of my contribution to the *Great Architecture* book. The Gibbses¶ and Jack Rathbone came to lunch. The Gibbses are a sterling couple, and

---

* Rt Hon. Margaret Thatcher, who in 1975 became Leader of the Conservative Party (then in Opposition); Prime Minister 1979–90; cr. 1992 Baroness Thatcher of Kesteven.
† Rt Hon. Harold Macmillan (1894–1986); Conservative Prime Minister 1957–63; cr. Earl of Stockton, 1984.
‡ Freda Bernstein (b. 1923); m. 1946 the composer Lennox Berkeley (1903–90; Kt 1974).
§ Charlotte Ogilvy (1893–1989); m. 1926 Sir Edgar Bonham Carter (1870–1956), jurist and colonial administrator; she was a well-known and idiosyncratic social figure.
¶ Christopher and Peggy; friends of long standing.

Peggy by no means devoid of humour or intelligence. I used in my odious salad days to underestimate them. They are worth one hundred of me joined together, being pure gold. After they left, A. and I drove to Brockham End, and walked across the golf course and down the valley to the west. Stormy skies and distant prospects of angry hills. Very lovely, but already the earth is one appreciable week older since I walked there alone the previous Sunday. Now the green deeper, the promise gone. Besides, no cuckoo today. I heard it last week. On return read the newspapers. At eight concert in the Theatre Royal. Alfred Brendel at the piano, playing three Beethoven sonatas – with more gusto than reverence.

He is a cold, ungracious man, but his playing interested me. His grimaces and contortions were embarrassing. I felt like a voyeur watching a man making love. He crouched over the piano, he recoiled. He stretched, and at times flung back his right arm as though it were a rapier withdrawn from a corpse. His facial muscles worked wildly. He gazed into space, he shut his eyes and saw nothing. He caressed the keys. He struck them viciously. He pouted. He grinned. He gritted his teeth and ground them. He was mouthing, masticating, almost masturbating. No, there was no need, because he had the object of his love there under him. It was the piano. We encored him again and again. He returned, made the most perfunctory bows, would not give us an encore. He had a job to do, and he did it superbly. It cost him the utmost physical energy. And I suppose what we were witnessing was a spiritual agony, such as mystics undergo.

Back at ten to hear a talk by K. Clark on Michelangelo as painter, suavely, smoothly spoken by the professional broadcaster who introduces little laughs as though they are impromptus and the whole talk is improvised, whereas the announcer said it was a translation (by K.) of a lecture delivered in Italian to the Florentine Academy last year. K. is one of our great men because he understands the meaning as well as the trappings of art. Always a sentence to ponder.

Monday, 2nd June

Genuinely sad to read in *The Times* this morning of the death of Olive Lloyd-Baker.* A. says I must not get kicks out of deaths of those I

---

* Miss Olive Lloyd-Baker, of Hardwicke Court, Gloucestershire; landowner and neighbour.

know in the obituary column. It is true that old people do, and I
suppose I do too at times. This time I am genuinely sorry, for I liked
this spirited, tough, old-fashioned, dutiful spinster who was a grand
landlord with a great sense of responsibility for her estates and tenants
at Hardwicke and in London. Just as well I wrote the article on
Hardwicke: in no stretch of the word a great house, but the seat of a
good old county family, and I daresay it is now doomed to be vacated.
Olive made a remark which I shall always remember and which John
Betjeman relished: 'An ounce of heredity is worth a pound of merit.'

Wednesday, 4th June

Watched on TV the debate in the Oxford Union on the European
Community. Most interesting. The two antis were Peter Shore[*] and
Barbara Castle;[†] the two pros Jeremy Thorpe[‡] and Heath. Shore was
emotional and boring. Thorpe demolished him with much wit and
foolery, an amusing, brilliant speaker. Then that Mrs Castle, who
made snide remarks about the Union officials in black ties – the
traditional dress – referring to them offensively as sprigs of the
Establishment. And what is she today, pray, if not the Establishment?
Bloody woman. The entire gist of her speech was anti, anti-us. But
Heath spoke like a true statesman in the best tradition. I call it a truly
great speech, in which he called upon us to honour our word and our
great history, and pull ourselves together. Oh yes, it was a great speech,
even if the delivery was not magnificent and the words lacking the
oratorical zeal Churchill would have shown. Heath was in deadly
earnest, unemotional and controlled. He delivered no back-hand
blows, and indulged in no snide jibes. He showed himself to be a big
man. So.

Thursday, 5th June

I am already more than half-way through my Beckford booklet, by
which I mean it is more than half down, though still helter-skelter,
muddled and mixed. It has not flown; there has been little flow,

---

[*] Rt Hon. Peter Shore, Labour MP; Secretary of State for Trade, 1974–6.
[†] Rt Hon. Barbara Castle (née Betts); Labour MP; Secretary of State for Social Services,
1974–6; cr. Baroness Castle of Ibstone, 1990.
[‡] Rt Hon. Jeremy Thorpe, MP; Leader of the Liberal Party.

indeed, mostly grind. I think it is nearly all repetitious staff, without a new thought or idea, but that was inevitable from the start. I rather fear what those bright young people in Compton Russell Press will think. Father D'Arcy,[*] much to my surprise - I even thought he might be dead - has written me a fan letter about *Another Self*. Also received one from Helen Dashwood,[†] just come round to it. This disconcerts me because in my forthcoming *Ancestral Voices* I am rather nasty about her.

Thursday, 12th June

I had a nightmare that I was between two platforms in a tube station, having the greatest difficulty not to stand on a live line. The lines were infinite and criss-crossed. People were shouting advice to me about where I could safely put my feet, but there was scarcely any ground between the lines and I did not know which were live and which were not.

Often during the day I am visited by, or I manufacture, dreams of hate. These are very dreadful. I argue against somebody (it used to be my father in the old days), and work myself into terrible rages while I think of arguments to floor my opponent.

On Sunday last A. and I spent the day at Fonthill. A meeting in the morning at the cottage (called Beckford's Cottage) of nice young Julian Berry,[‡] who gave us delicious cold luncheon cooked by his girl-friend, pretty and charming, name undiscovered and embarrassment in consequence what to call her, how to refer to her. The other attendants Humphrey Stone, son of Reynolds,[§] beaky, yet with latent charm, and wife so big with child I expected her to drop it on the carpet, Clive Wainwright,[¶] expert on Victorian furniture, and [Christopher] Thacker, a Garden History Society pundit, not dull but very difficult to elicit anything from. The two last bearded. It was a

---

[*] Father M. D'Arcy, SJ (1888–1976); known to J.L.-M. since his conversion to Catholicism.

[†] Widow of Sir John Dashwood, 10th Bt (1896–1966), of West Wycombe Park, Buckinghamshire.

[‡] Publisher; Chairman of Compton Russell Press.

[§] Reynolds Stone (1909–70); designer, graphic engraver and printer; m. 1938 Janet Woods.

[¶] Now (1998) a senior curator at the V. & A. and expert on the work of Augustus Pugin.

boiling, heat-wave day. Wainwright dressed in thickest tweeds, with waistcoat and watch-chain and fob, a Victorian paterfamilias, pontifical, and vastly hot. We walked from Bittern Wood* to the Abbey remains, which we entered. Filled with junk and some interesting early Victorian chairs and benches which we queried whether they were Beckford's, little framed Italian water-colour scenes mouldering. Too strange for words, this neglect. The place belongs to Neil Rimington who inherited it from the Shaw-Stewarts, and cares not a fig what happens to these things. Then went to tea with the Margadales† in the new house [Fonthill House, Tisbury] they have built on the site of the recently demolished Detmar Blow house. Uninspired, conventional, derivative, and devoid of taste or fancy. Lord M. deaf and stuffy and philistine; she, Peggy Smith, a sweet woman. She took us to see the Palladian boathouse and is worried about its deteriorating condition. Says her husband hates it and wishes it to disintegrate, which it is rapidly doing, because he does not want the public to discover and visit it lest they disturb the pheasants!

The hot, hirsute experts, all so knowing about Beckford, are enough to put one off him for ever. How *he* would have hated them.

On Tuesday in London Colin McMordie‡ dined with me. I did not enjoy it much. It was so hot in Brooks's and the club was so full that I took him out, thinking we might eat in a less stuffy atmosphere. I made a mistake. We had a perfectly filthy and expensive meal at Rowleys in Jermyn Street, £9 without tip. Then returned to Brooks's. At midnight I told him I must go to bed. So we walked to Knightsbridge where we parted. He is a very nice, intelligent, handsome youth, dressed in blue striped suit and blue shirt and tie, most dandy. But he is rather precious. Told me he was twenty-five. Rolls his large eyes and looks one intensely in the face. Talks in a brittle manner about artists I have never heard of. Says he has read all my books and much likes *Heretics*. In spite of all this I was rather bored by him and sensed myself to be a failure in his eyes. What is lacking in him? He was endearing about himself. Laughed at himself. Said he knew he was too romantic, given to purple passages in his writing;

---

* The lake and woods at Fonthill have been variously and often simultaneously known as Bitham, Bittern, even Bottom, since before Beckford's time.

† John Granville Morrison, 1st Baron Margadale; Lord-Lieutenant of Wiltshire, 1969–81; m. 1928 Hon. Margaret Lucie Smith, dau. of 2nd Viscount Hambleden; she d. 1980.

‡ Oxford post-graduate, friend of J.L.-M. since 1973; architectural historian.

admitted preciosity, but said he had a soft inner core. Told me the present generation of undergraduates quite different from his. They are conventional in ideas and dress, and are intolerant of the foibles of others. Sound hell to me. Now, what I would have preferred was less talk about literature and art, and more fun and jokes. Intenseness in the young I find an impediment to intimacy and freedom of speech.

I lunched with Archie [Aberdeen]* in the House [of Lords]. Years since I was there. How conventional it is. It is like being inside Fonthill Abbey, which surely influenced Barry. The 1830s were really a suitable decade for that particular place to be burnt down and built again from the ground up, save only St Stephen's Hall which is an inestimable medieval treasure. I admired the encaustic tiled floors, the brass Gothic chandeliers, enormous, and the stained-glass windows. Must admit the portraits of the recent sovereigns are pretty poor, and some of the wall paintings of historic events nauseating.

Each peer in alphabetical order, his title and rank on a large card, has a hat peg for (no longer hat) coat, umbrella and briefcase. I wonder what confusion is caused when a peerage becomes extinct or a new creation is made. From A to Z the whole lot has to be shuffled up or down. Archie was waiting for me beside the equestrian statue of Richard Coeur de Lion. He said he was descended from him, but I said I thought he liked the boys and had no offspring. Archie was astonished, didn't know about Blondel, and was disappointed by my disclosure.

Sunday, 15th June

Went alone – I have hardly missed a Sunday since we came here – to Holy Communion in the Abbey, very devout and all attention. Nevertheless during the Confession (which I always recite with fervour) I found my mind wandering from 'our manifold sins and wickedness' to the £100 cheque I received from *Apollo* last week and passed on to X, and thought, had I not done so, I would have bought for myself . . . and checked myself. I see Father D'Arcy is 87 today. Wrote a letter of condolence to Sheila Birkenhead,† but

---

* Archibald Gordon, 5th Marquess of Aberdeen (1913–84); writer and broadcaster.
† Hon. Sheila Berry, dau. of 1st Viscount Camrose; writer; m. 1935 Frederick Smith, 2nd Earl of Birkenhead (1907–75).

no letter about Jack Spencer* for I do not know anyone who loved him.

Saturday, 21st June

Denys† said at dinner tonight that the English proletariat did not work less hard than Continentals but were far stupider. They could not see that by demanding more wages than the country could afford they were overstretching the goose that provided the golden egg. The French had more common sense, and so had the Germans.

Saturday, 28th June

It is satisfactory that some past emotions are as strong now as formerly. John Cornforth and I motored to Moccas [Court, Herefordshire] on Wednesday, for I am to write an article on the house for *Country Life*. Although one or two horrors have arisen since my first visit twenty or twenty-five years ago, notably a sort of factory by the village cross, and a handful of mean houses too close to the front drive gate, yet once inside the purlieus I still find myself in another world. I have never known a place in the UK seemingly so remote, in a setting so tranquil, so inductive of ecstatic dreams and ancient history. In Moccas I am invaded with the very same sensations, a suspension from all mundane associations, reducing me to a sort of coma and enveloping me as though in a cloud of wonder and exultation, which I have encountered only in certain Spanish churches where time stands still – or did so twenty years ago. (I can never return to them in case the magic has flown.) Now, time does stand still at Moccas. Possibly the slowly, imperceptibly moving river below the house contributes to the suspension. There is nothing like a river sluggish since time immemorial to induce a sense of eternity.

Yesterday I went to Olive Lloyd-Baker's memorial service in Gloucester Cathedral. I sat at the back of the nave, and again thought this the most beautiful of all our cathedrals. Excellent address about Olive by the old Dean, Siriol Evans. I congratulated him in the porch afterwards. Never remarkable for humility, he said, 'Yes, I recaptured her, I think.'

Then to Evesham where I had a session with Noel Saunders over

---

* 7th Earl Spencer (1892–1975).
† Denys Sutton (b. 1917); Editor of *Apollo*, 1967–87; art historian and dilettante.

my new will. The old one which lists my belongings in detail has to
be scrapped. The briefest document has to be prepared, and I am to
leave a letter of wishes which I must rely on my executors to carry
out. Asked Noel to be one, A. the other. He agreed. Then to
Wickhamford, where I sat in the church and thought. What I thought
was – this is one of the loveliest little churches in England, and the
memorial plaque which I got Reynolds (Stone) to do for my parents
over the manor pew is about the most *digne* modern memorial I have
seen anywhere. What a success it is, of black slate incised with an
intoxication of whirligig lettering!

Sunday, 29th June

At Holy Communion this morning thought over John [Cornforth]'s
telling me he would be in Durham looking for Nollekens busts in
country houses next week; and wished I too was on the track of
undiscovered tangible treasure instead of researching for literary data
in musty old documents. Thought, too, one should not look as
though one is endeavouring to be devout, like the Pharisee. Yet it is
difficult not to look it when one is it, sunk deep in prayer or the
endeavour at communication, that most lip-curling spectacle to non-
believers I feel sure. I still can't think why more do not go to HC
which is the setting of the seal of unity with the good and beautiful,
shared by most religions and not only the Christian churches; which
should be every man's fragile but determined pact with the Supreme
Being, however shaky his faith, whatever his creed of God may be.
An involved sentence, this.

Last night we went to Charlecote on a £3 ticket each. A delightful evening arranged by Alice Lucy,* namely readings, poetry and
singing on the very best amateur lines. Alice read in a slightly precious
manner, but on the whole well, extracts from the diary of a continental tour made in 1841 and '42 by Mary Elizabeth Lucy and spouse,
in the manner of Queen Victoria's Journal, followed by arias sung by
Jane Fawcett, excellent contralto, and daughter, a soprano of great
merit. Really wonderful, powerful, controlled voices. Ted Fawcett
read poetry from Byron and other romantics.

---

* Hon. Alice Buchan, dau. of 1st Baron Tweedsmuir (the author John Buchan); m. 1933
Brian Cameron-Ramsay-Fairfax-Lucy, later 5th Bt (1898–1974), of Charlecote Park,
Warwickshire.

Tuesday, 1st July

I have 'got down' my Beckford book, which is not too bad; but owing to brevity it is slight stuff. I mean that I have written it all now, having of course to correct, add, delete, and re-write before retyping and sending to the publishers.

A. went off this afternoon to the garden party at Montacute at which the Queen Mother is to be received, to mark the 80th birthday of the N.T. She can't understand why I don't want to go. My reasons may not be wholly untinged with pique, in that dear Mr Fowler* has done the whole place up at great cost from top to toe, whereas Eardley† and I spent hours of our life struggling to make a silk purse out of a sow's ear at that house which I love. Moreover, in its simple way I believe it to have been more sympathetic. We had the minimum of funds allowed us, and I consider we made a good job within our limitations. Now Montacute is a bit too dolled-up. Although splendid architecture, the house was throughout the Phelips centuries undemonstrative and sparsely furnished. I shall go quietly there on my own one day.

Sunday, 6th July

Found such a good word by chance in the dictionary – opsimath. I am an opsimath, one who develops slowly.

The Times apparently wish to reproduce extracts of my diaries in their Saturday Review page on 13th Sept. Will pay me £200 for the privilege. This means the agents take off £20 plus VAT for serving me, then the Income Tax will take another £80, so I shall with luck clear £80 – no, that is too optimistic, more like £60.

Yesterday I went to Salisbury to see a nice old Lady Lighton‡ hoping to acquire information about Goodridge. I got nothing, and she got something from me. Surprising how ignorant people are about their ancestors. Then at six went to see poor Cecil [Beaton].§ He was sitting in an upright chair to the left of the fireplace in his drawing-room.

---

* John Fowler (1905–77); interior decorator of historic country houses and partner in decorating firm of Colefax & Fowler.

† Eardley Knollys (1902–91); painter, and N.T. representative in south-west counties.

‡ Rachel Gwendoline, yr dau. of Rear Admiral W.W.S. Goodridge, CIE; m. 1926 as his 1st wife Sir Christopher Lighton, 8th Bt; m. diss. 1953.

§ Sir Cecil Beaton (1904–80); artist, stage designer, photographer and society figure.

Immaculately dressed in white ducks, white linen coat and blue scarf
through a ring round his neck. Looked white, and his eyes very dark.
Did not rise when I came in. Was cheerful but is extremely sad. He
walks in great awkwardness with a stick, his feet sticking out sideways
like a disjointed doll's. Has absolutely no feeling in his right hand
which he nurses and rubs. Is longing for life to return to it but I doubt
if it will. He says it is hell being unable to work, the one thing he
wants to do. 'Shall I ever be better?' he asked. His memory too is poor.
Cannot remember anyone's name, not even his secretary's. Says
strange things, like 'How is that person who lives near you with a
name like Mouse?' When one cannot guess he waves his left hand as
though to erase the query and says 'Never mind. Don't let's bother.' I
stayed an hour and a quarter, I hope not too long, and as always in
these circumstances talked too much. Hope I did not tire him. He
gave me a gloxinia to take to A. who had sent him a pot of her marmalade. Dreadful to see that man, the sharpest I have ever known with
an eye like a lynx's, dulled by a stroke. There were flashes of the old
malice, and he laughed, throwing back his head, over gossip.

Thursday, 10th July

Interesting but disturbing example of the Leftist anarchical rot which
has crept in, even in the small world of amenities. The Bath
Preservation Trust last week was riven. Three trustees have revolted
against the way in which a new article has been inserted into the Rules
and Regulations of the Trust. They take exception to a small, futile
and frivolous point concerning associate membership. One of them,
David Brain, has complained of his Chairman's conduct to the Civic
Trust which has written to the Chairman a letter intimating that the
Civic Trust may withhold whatever privileges we as a small town body
derive from its custody. Another has written a letter to the local press.
All these three trustees are Leftists whose jargon is repeatedly that 'we
must be democratic', just like the extreme Leftists among the Unions.
Their intention is to disrupt the Trust and bring it to an end. They
may well succeed.

Yesterday in London I was waiting for a bus at Tottenham Court
Road, in my place in a queue. Behind me a woman under thirty was
pushing her way forward. I deliberately elbowed her back to the rear
where she belonged and was myself the last person allowed on the bus.
I had to stand inside. The conductress politely asked the woman to get

off the platform where she had placed herself, saying 'There is no more room for standing.' The woman, who was foreign, almost coffee-coloured, shouted abusively, 'The English always say No to one.' Irked by this remark, and also by the woman's presence preventing the bus from moving on, it being exceedingly hot, I said to her tartly: 'Perhaps they only say No to you.' She spat in my face. I wiped my face and spat in hers. She spat back. Quick as lightning I slapped her face as hard as I dared. Enraged, I said, 'Get off this bus immediately, you odious woman,' and she did. Awkward silence. In that typically British way no one said a word. At the next stop I got off, having I suppose behaved badly.

Tuesday, 22nd July

We motored to Send for the weekend. The environment is disfigured by dead elms, dried-up grass and vegetation, for there has been less rain in Surrey than here, and roses with black spot and dying and mouldering plants. Loelia* calls it Pest Corner, with some reason. We motored to London Monday morning after breakfast to fetch two heavy parcels at Warwick Avenue and out again to Odiham, and back here. Result is that today we are completely worn out.

Sunday afternoon we visited Lady Heald's† garden, open to the public. A charming old house of red brick, all sorts of dates, chiefly seventeenth-century I should guess, with Artisan Mannerist gables and door pilasters in moulded brick, very 'rude' so to speak. A fine high buttressed wall supposedly built by Sarah Duchess of Marlborough, and garden terraces underneath Bunyan's Hill of Difficulty. A sylvan retreat near beastly Guildford. Lady Heald told A. she had been on a deputation, she representing the Garden Opening people, to the Government over this protest against Wealth Tax. She said she was still seething with rage over the behaviour of Hugh Jenkins the Minister.‡ He said he did not love the aristocracy and would do nothing to relieve them of tax. All large houses and gardens

* Hon. Loelia Ponsonby (1902–93), dau. of 1st Baron Sysonby, Treasurer to HM King George V; wife of Sir Martin Lindsay of Dowhill, Bt (m. 1969) and formerly (1930–47) of 2nd Duke of Westminster.
† Daphne Constance, CBE, 2nd wife of Sir Lawrence Frederick Heald, PC, QC (1897–1981), of Chilworth Manor, Guildford, Surrey.
‡ Labour MP; Minister for the Arts, 1974–6; cr. Baron Jenkins of Putney (Life Peer), 1981 (b. 1908).

should belong to the people, and the small ones could look after themselves. Lady Heald said in that case if places like hers disappeared the charities would suffer. Reply to this was that there must be no charities; the State was going to take them over. She remarked upon Michael Rosse's[*] recent visit to him and his excellent evidence given. Jenkins said that Lord Rosse was nice enough as an individual but he detested all he stood for. Lady Heald said we would get nothing out of this particular man, who was ghastly.

Then visited Royal Holloway College, which I have always wished to see. Gigantic and extraordinary. *Tour de force.* The guide who showed us round took us into the picture gallery. In the middle of the gallery a large picture of two polar bears on an ice-floe. He said the authorities had discovered that at examinations held in the gallery every student who had been seated in front of this picture failed. Now during examinations they cover the picture with a Union Jack. He told us that the present Principal of the College was the first man to be appointed. Hitherto women only. Moreover, the guide said to me, 'The statues (*sic*) lay down that they have to be virgins.' Surprised, I said, 'Do you mean spinsters?' 'No,' he said, 'virgins.' I did not have the chance of asking him if candidates were obliged to undergo a medical examination.

Monday, 28th July

The horrors of the night persist. I seldom get through a night without a disagreeable dream. Dreams are the result of nightly Mogadon I am sure. In fact I resemble the opium takers of old, Coleridge, Shelley, de Quincey, so very many of whom became addicts, and consequently subject to hair-raising nightmares, illusions (Shelley's attack in Wales), miseries. At times I find that sleep exhausts me more than being wide awake. It would be ghastly to dread falling asleep. I hope never to reach that stage.

Monday, 4th August

Today I finished the Beckford book and have given it to A. to read. She is always my first reader and invariably has commonsense crit-

---

[*] Michael Parsons, 6th Earl of Rosse (1906–79), of Birr Castle, Co. Offaly, Ireland; m. 1935 Anne Armstrong-Jones (née Messel).

icisms. She knows at a glance when my work is boring. She spots grammatical absurdities, involved statements and indiscretions. I don't think it is too bad, although it contains no original contribution of any kind. It is a little over the limit of 40,000 words set: about 49,500 I would guess.

On Saturday Charlotte Bonham Carter came for luncheon and the day. A boiling, grilling day. She motored herself from her Hampshire house to Reading, then took the train here. Brought with her two books her grandfather had bought at the Hamilton Palace sale in 1882–3 which had belonged to Beckford;* one is Byron's *Vision of Judgment*. Most kind, and I am deeply touched. Her grandfather was William Wickham (bookplate – Manners maketh Man). We had Diana Westmorland[†] lunching too, just about the same age – what? 82 or thereabouts? Charlotte in spite of her deplorable accident is by far the brisker. Walked up and down in spite of our steep little staircase without holding the banister rail, insisted on visiting number 1 Royal Crescent[‡] in the afternoon. Her mind is very active and sharp. She is well informed indeed on most subjects and her memory retentive and clear. She never hesitates in her speech. Yet she seldom listens and keeps exclaiming, 'My dear, how lovely, how too wonderful!' – which, Freda Berkeley told me, she said to a friend who announced that his wife had died a fortnight ago, and then added '– and terrible.'

Wednesday, 6th August

Had to go to London yesterday to take the chair at the N.T. Architectural Panel meeting. Heat in London asphyxiating. Throughout the meeting I sweated like a pig. Such nice people, *viz.*, staff and members. How I like them, and all so helpful. Martin Drury[§] taking the place of Bobby Gore[¶] away in Venice. Ian

---

* William Beckford's younger daughter married the Marquess of Douglas who became 10th Duke of Hamilton.
† Hon. Diana Lister, dau. of 4th and last Baron Ribblesdale; m. 1923, as her 3rd husband, the 14th Earl of Westmorland (d. 1948); she d. 1983.
‡ Number 1 Royal Crescent, Bath, by John Wood the Younger, had been decorated and furnished by the Bath Preservation Trust as a fine example of a house of its period, and was opened to the public.
§ N.T. Historic Buildings representative; now (1998) Director-General of the Trust.
¶ F. St John Gore; N.T. Adviser on Pictures, 1956–86.

McCallum,* Sherban Cantacuzino† (a Romanian prince I think, for
he wears a huge signet ring with a crown), Mark Girouard,‡ John
Cornforth.

Went to Heywood Hill's shop to buy something for A. John
Saumarez Smith showed me a pile of books stacked in a corner. Said,
'Do you know whose book that is?' It was mine, to be out on 18th
September. I had not seen a copy before this. Pleased with the look
of it but much disturbed by the price – £6. Was shown Harold Acton's
Nancy Mitford, with photographs, at only £5.25. Hideous jacket of a
coloured photograph of N. at her pretty writing-table I knew so well,
looking like the Duchess of Windsor with high scooped hair. John
says he has already taken 75 orders for my book, and that Ali Forbes§
is reviewing it for the *TLS*. I somehow can't face up to looking
through it.

Got back at six. A. gave me the most beautiful little thin ring of
rubies set in gold, which is the nicest present I have ever had. Clarissa
and Michael Luke called at Eardley [Knollys]'s at 9.30 bringing with
them a heavy parcel, present for A. and me. A. and I opened it on A's
bed. A romantic oil view of Rome from Tivoli by a French artist, G.F.
Ronmy, done about 1830–40 I should guess, most accomplished in a
tight Caspar D. Friedrich style. Also I brought with me a bag of more
books collected from Charlotte's house, containing five of Beckford's,
two with holograph notes of his in the flyleaves. Three lovely presents
– no, a fourth, from Audrey, of a telephone note-pad with pencil,
magnetized. Indeed four treats.

Thursday, 7th August

The Bath Preservation Trust rows are simply loathsome. I long to be
quit of the whole thing, and can't until Christopher Chancellor

---

* Curator of the American Museum, Claverton, near Bath (1919–87).
† FRIBA; in 1975, Executive Editor of the *Architectural Review*. There were several
Cantacuzino emperors of Byzantium in the second half of the fourteenth century; the
family subsequently migrated to Romania, where an earlier Sherban (1640–88) was
Hospodar of Wallachia and a great benefactor of his country; in the seventeenth and
eighteenth centuries Cantacuzinos were Princes of Moldavia and Wallachia, known as
the Old Kingdom (of Romania); but the Romanian Royal Family of the mid-nineteenth
to the twentieth century were Hohenzollerns.
‡ Writer and architectural historian; Slade Professor of Fine Art, Oxford, 1975–6.
§ Alastair Forbes, journalist and book reviewer (b. 1918).

retires. This evening a meeting of the trustees was called. Graham and
Brain thought fit to attend. The Chairman, Greening, simply said in
a dignified way, 'We do not usually meet in August. This meeting was
called specially to discuss the Extraordinary General Meeting on the
19th. Several trustees have told me they are reluctant to discuss the
subject in the presence of Mr G. and Mr B. Perhaps they would like
to retire?' A pause. 'No. Hands up those who do not wish to continue
the meeting.' All but two of us held up our hands. 'Then the meeting
is adjourned.' We all rose and a little self-consciously gathered together
in one corner. The two dissident trustees murmured, 'How childish!'
and left.

Thursday, 14th August

This afternoon we had a downpour, the first proper rain for weeks and
weeks. Never do I remember a finer summer. I was sitting in the car
in Victoria Park, waiting for the shower to end before getting out. I
watched two pigeons on the path. I thought both had been run over
and were sick. They kept toppling over from one leg to the other,
spreading out their wings as though incapable of flying. I thought,
how dreadful, I suppose I must kill them. When I got out of the car
they flew away happily. They were merely having their first bath,
turning over their wings to receive the rain. A. says this is usual prac-
tice among birds.

   A. and I have exchanged rings for our birthdays. The one I have
given her, which she chose, consists of diamond hearts mounted in
emeralds.

Friday, 15th August

After a Bath Preservation meeting this evening – I attended another
from twelve to two today – Christopher Chancellor came to dinner
with us. During dinner both A. and I had a revelation: this tough,
ruthless, efficient, high-powered business tycoon was a broken man.
He sat slumped over his plate, his head on his chest. When he repeated
for the third time that evening a long story word for word, we understood that he was senile. It was a sad experience.

Monday, 18th August

Today I tore up and threw in the dustbin the original manuscript-typescript of my diaries for 1942 and 1943. I had a few misgivings, but decided that what was omitted from the published version was worthless, and worse than that, shaming. Thoroughly illiterate too. I hope in the autumn to go through the ensuing years and edit them, possibly for publication. It will depend on the reception *Ancestral Voices* gets.

Not a word from the Compton Russell Press to whom I delivered the manuscript of Beckford last Tuesday. But Bevis Hillier* who lunched on Sunday said Julian Berry pronounced it good. Which is something. Bevis Hillier very bright and on the spot. Short, dark, stubbled, *Bohème*. Square-cut features. A. thought it odd that he came to luncheon with us, for the first time seen, without a tie. An old-fashioned thought. He wants me to write an article on Beckford's marginalia for the April issue of *The Connoisseur*. He is poor old Gwynne Ramsay's successor, and was surprisingly charitable about him.

Austria   *Friday, 22nd August*

George Dix motored us to Altötting in Germany from Salzburg. Saw the marvellous gold, enamel and jewelled object in the Schatzkammer, made in the fourteenth century for a Duke of Burgundy. Quite a small object with Our Lady and Child within an arbour of Gothic design encrusted with flowers. Donor and his groom with horse below. Workmanship in minutest detail, and very moving as only Gothic jewel-work can be. He also took us to two Rococo churches, Marienberg, approached by pilgrimage steps, and Raitenhaslach. The last as good as any I have seen. Each time one turns an eye upon a detail in these Rococo churches here one notices something overlooked the previous time. From the arch separating nave from sanctuary a pair of blue and silver curtains. What structural liberties the Rococo artists took, too. This was once a Cistercian church of five aisles. All the aisles removed and the building gloriously transformed by the Rococoists. The Portuguese under Salazar would have removed the Rococo features and reimposed the Gothic aisles.

---

* FRSA; journalist and writer on fine arts and antiques, and biographer of Betjeman; in 1975 he was Editor of *The Connoisseur*, and Antiques Correspondent of *The Times*.

On our return a hail storm ensued. All cars on the motorway were obliged to draw up along the side lane and wait. The noise of the hail stones as large as marbles on the tin roof of the car was deafening. When this happens to people with bare heads they are often knocked out.

George Dix says some funny things. His snobbishness or rather interest in the aristocracy is deliciously uninhibited. He is not a good sleeper. This morning he told us gleefully that he had found a wonderful way of getting to sleep. Instead of counting sheep he counted English dukes. There are twenty-six, he informed us, and he got to twenty before snoring.

The Kollegienkirche in Salzburg is caviare to the general, but to architectural appreciators it is something quite extraordinarily wonderful: the oval theme of the chapels, the open oval eye above each, with balustrade and view above that of the oval domelet. Below on the pavement, the oval marble slab. The stucco walls are painted the palest pink, grey and blue. The chandeliers of small crystal drops. Indeed, the Germans and Austrians light their churches better than any. Often naked bulbs are concealed under a metal shade entirely covered with a large tassel. This church is very high and narrow.

Saturday, 23rd August

George insisted on our going to lunch at Schloss Blühnbach high up in the mountains. I was very reluctant to go because it was to be a party of 150 guests. But it was an unforgettable experience. The house belonged to the Archduke Franz-Ferdinand who added a storey and made other alterations to an older building. After his assassination it was bought by Krupps, the grandfather of the present owner, who is called von Bolen Halberg Krupps when the 'Krupps' is not dropped altogether. He is one of the richest men in Europe. Big Bertha's grandson to boot. His wife a Countess Augsburg. He an astonishing figure, extremely sinister. House inside has walls plastered with horns of elks and chamois. Chandeliers of horns, friezes of horns, curtain boxes of horns. Primitive portraits of shooting dogs and owners.

Tony Pawson* staying there, whom we met on the aeroplane from

---

* Journalist and sportsman (b. 1921).

Zürich to Salzburg, and through him we were invited. Our host slightly round-shouldered, wearing a tight brown jersey with sleeves and tight brown trousers, a long gold chain round the neck. He had cropped hair, Eton crop, which accentuated his resemblance to Avis Gurney* of the Twenties. One of the most sinister figures I have ever seen. Does absolutely nothing, ever. The house full of servants in *lederhosen*. All the doorhandles covered with little chamois-leather fingerstalls, most curious. George explained that in the cold weather one gets electric shocks in the bare hand from brass handles. Unfortunately a rainy day, low clouds, so that the impressive view of mountain peaks from this eyrie invisible.

Sunday, 24th August

This morning A. remained in bed with a bad throat and swollen glands. I went for a walk through Anif park, past the Leeds-like castle standing in a lake, down a sycamore avenue to the Salzer river. Turned sharp right and walked along the path to the first bridge over the motorway. The swollen green river dashing on my left side. Picked a wild nettle-like flower with purple and yellow stamens. Also came across stones, embedded in the path so that I could not uproot them, stones streaked with what must be lapis.

Monday, 25th August

George Dix says that he never notices animals or birds. He complains that the latter keep him awake in the mornings. He finds 'the barking of cuckoos most disturbing', he said. We both expressed bewilderment.

Tuesday, 26th August

In the air bus from the plane at Zürich a youngish woman offered me her seat. I strongly deprecated the gesture with profuse thanks. This is an indication of my age.

The Swiss may have no souls. But they do have a sense of profound

---

* Hon. Mrs Gurney, sister of John Morgan of Tredegar; in *Midway on the Waves* J.L.-M. said 'she is just as ugly to look upon [now] as she was when a girl'.

material well-being. This we find attractive. In Geneva we had a royal suite in the Richmond Hotel, for one night. Never do I remember staying in such luxury. One enormous bed and an enormous sitting room next to the enormous bedroom, through which we had to walk to the bathroom.

Salzburg is totally unspoilt. Only the outskirts have been added to within recent years, like all outskirts, as George and I studied from the terrace in front of Maria Plein church, newly redecorated in palest pink and lapis blue. The ironwork shop signs hanging over the narrow street in which is Mozart's birthplace, are fanciful. The country so green and lush, and window boxes dribbling with geraniums and begonias. Every house outside the towns is a chalet, whether sixteenth century or 1975. The traditional manner of building in Austria certainly is a relief to nerves jaded by concrete whimsy in all other parts of the world.

We attended two operas in the new Festspielhaus, *Don Carlos* and *Figaro*. The first a magnificent performance, the largest stage and orchestra I have ever seen. Scenery and clothes very good but no better than Visconti's at Covent Garden. In fact I thought the old performance with Boris Christoff was better. Von Karajan allows no air conditioning and only one interval in each performance. Consequently the heat and discomfort of the seating a great trial to me. When one begins to wonder if one can survive before being able to get up and go out, one is in no condition to appreciate an opera. Such a pity, and the seats cost the earth.

Friday, 29th August

Darling Mama's birthday. She would be 91 today. How I love her and how I suffer remorse for not having demonstrated my love in fuller measure, for she drove me mad towards the end. Went to London for the day to see Dr Norman, for in Austria I developed a recurrence of bladder trouble – cystitis. The funny old man always reassures me when I work myself into a state. But when I have sharp pain in peeing, and then pee in fits and starts – I overheard myself describing it to him as in 'stits and farts' – I get anxious. He gave me pills which he assures me will stop it within days. God, I hope so.

How I love the autumn. From the train I watched a Turneresque sun sweep the fields, and though I could not smell the world I knew there was a soft tang in the air of dew and wood smoke. I love the autumn in England beyond all the other seasons rolled into one. Am reading Harold [Acton]'s memoir of Nancy which he has sent us. It is an enjoyable read, well done within the limitations imposed on him: affectionate and nostalgic. Interesting to see how Nance's letters develop from schoolgirl *naïveté* to a clever, well informed, extremely sharp adult prose. She was a very well-read woman indeed, but uneducated.

Standing in the corridor waiting to get out at Bath station was amused to read on the lavatory door: 'Tools and appliances are kept in the guard's compartment for use in emergency.' What emergency? If the carriage were to be telescoped, upside-down in a ravine in the middle of the night . . . ? What then? And where is the guard's compartment?

Monday, 1st September

Last night we went to the Robinsons for a dinner of twenty-five to celebrate Audrey's seventieth birthday.* I can't pretend I enjoyed it in particular, but I was delighted in general. Amazing how my dear little sister has come through, so to speak. She has taken a turn upwards since that awful Tony's death, and reached a serenity, and I believe contentment. There she was, the centre of a large family's affection, the marvellous Robinson boys. Henry adorable now (easier than Nick) and a jolly boy who has just left Oxford with a 2nd. Splendid I think. Nick back from France where he has spent the vacation working as a waiter in Bordeaux, followed home by his girl-friend, a beautiful, tongue-tied, *racée*, bad-tempered from all accounts, spoilt, Franco-Vietnamese without one word of English. Audrey made to open all her presents in front of a ring of admirers. She seemed very happy. I made a tiny speech towards the end of dinner and we drank health. Such a din that with my incipient deafness I heard not a word anyone said. Both Henry and Nick have invited themselves to meals here this week, which delights us. Goodness, they are nice boys!

I asked Nick if he had found many customers were bloody, as they so often are to waiters. He said seldom, but the French employers

---

* J.L.-M's sister Audrey (1905–90) m., 1st, Matthew Arthur, later 3rd Baron Glenarthur; 2nd, Anthony Stevens; her daughter Prudence Arthur m. 1953 Major Edwin Winwood Robinson, of Moor Wood, Gloucestershire; their sons were Henry, Nicholas and Richard.

were. They constantly tried to cheat the waiters of the wages agreed upon. One employer withheld part of his wage on the outrageous pretence that he had taken tips to which he was not entitled. Nick made such a scene that the man gave way, which he would not have done had Nick been guilty. Lois [Lees-Milne], who works for the manager of a Birmingham firm, complained that the workers jeer her because she is the boss's secretary, and threaten to expose her to her union authorities if she works overtime. What utter hell workers are today, in England at least!

As a memoir, Harold Acton's book on Nancy is well done, a difficult task for him with the sisters breathing down his neck; his references to Gaston Palewski* are discreet. Most of Nance's letters that Harold quotes from were written to Alvilde, whose name features on every other page. Interesting to see how N. adapted herself, as all corre-spondents do, to the person she addressed. Also, towards the end, when she was suffering such tortures of pain and was under drugs, her letters improve, lose their schoolgirl frivolity, and without losing their sharp wit, become wise and learned. My word, she was a clever woman.

Friday, 5th September

Ian McCallum has lent me the journals of Roger Hinks.† They are in typescript, for no publisher will take them. They are astonishing. They scarcely deal with friends unless friends illustrate an argument, or contribute to a discussion. They are about his thoughts, his reading of philosophy and art. An intellectual man, not likeable, prim, prissy, censorious, sitting as I remember stiffly, upright like a ramrod, very ugly indeed, with a supercilious look on his pursed lips, as though he despised the world and all its inhabitants. But these journals are unusual. They are very German, might be Goethe's thoughts. They make heavy reading, though I find them irresistible, if at times boring. Is this because I am not clever enough to understand what he is getting at, perchance? The milk of human kindness is absent, yet much moral sensibility and responsibility remain. Idiot publishers including Jock Murray have turned them down. They require drastic editing, and breaking into shorter paragraphs.

---

* Colonel Gaston Palewski (1901–84); Chef du Cabinet to General de Gaulle, and French Ambassador to Rome; close friend of Nancy Mitford.
† Art historian and British Council representative overseas; prolific diarist (1903–63).

Saturday, 6th September

Yesterday morning I spent drafting a letter to the *Architects' Journal* on this perennial Bath Preservation Trust issue. I am so sick of it I can hardly bear it. Then was obliged to take it to the office where [Christopher] Chancellor and Pamela Lock went through it, making further suggestions for me to type out again. A rush luncheon and off to Badminton to adjudicate between the builder and plumber as to who is responsible for the hole in a new radiator pipe which last week leaked and brought down the newly decorated ceiling of my room there. Then rushed to Bristol BBC to be interviewed about *Ancestral Voices*. A very uncosy experience. Since I could not and they would not meet me in London or here, I was obliged to speak to a young man in London down the line. I had earphones and spoke into a megaphone like a rubber galosh, which went wrong and then broke down. I thought the interrogator slightly hostile. He kept asking: didn't I think it extraordinary, a young man at the time paying visits to country houses during the worst war in history? I explained that I had been invalided out of the Army and worked in an office as well, but foolishly did not say that my journeys were not all to country houses but also to existing Trust properties, which someone had to manage. One always thinks too late, and too slow. This is for Radio 4, programme called 'P.M.', presumably at the date of issue of said book. On Sunday I have Theo Richmond* of the *Guardian* coming from London to do a profile of me. Another woman telephoned asking to interview me for West of England Radio. We couldn't hit on a date before my departure on Monday, so she is giving a review on radio instead.

The year of Roger Hinks's journal which I read last night was his 34th. He was the same age as me when *I* was writing *A. Voices*. His brightness compares with my dimness at the same age.

Sunday, 7th September

The free-lance journalist Theo Richmond came from London to interview me for a profile for the *Guardian*. He was charming, and sympathetic. He arrived at three, just as the Christopher Chancellors and Diana Westmorland were leaving after luncheon. His first words

---

* Journalist, documentary film maker and author (*Konin: A Quest*, 1995).

were: 'I am afraid I am the wrong Theo,' in reference to *Another Self* which he professed to admire. Then he said, 'I have interviewed many people, but have never been so alarmed as I am by the prospect of interviewing you.' I expressed astonishment. He said, 'You notice every blemish, and that terrifies me.' It was a good beginning. We talked for an hour or more, he having put a dictaphone on the table between us, which alarmed *me*, although he did promise that he would not take from it every word of inanity I uttered. It was to remind him, he said. He took copious notes. I don't think I was very good, and after he left I thought of many better retorts than the ones I gave. He ended by photographing me from every angle, about twenty times I guess. I notice this is how people photograph today, random snaps. Told me he was a Jew from the East End.

Scandinavian tour   *Tuesday, 9th September*

Eardley and I flew to Copenhagen. The Danes are utterly shameless with their porn shops. Old and young, middle-aged husbands and wives go to them, leaf through magazines of the most indecent photo-graphs in colour, and attend non-stop blue films of indescribable revoltingness. In some shops there are rows of cubicles like telephone kiosks or confessionals, into which they put two kroner, whereupon through an aperture they watch a minute or two minutes' reel of pornography. You see the backs of Danes of both sexes and all ages glued to these apertures – mostly little old ladies with ashen grey buns and string bags. We spent hours in the new Glyptotek. In the National Museum there is a Bernini bust of Urban VII's mother, a Batoni of Peter Beckford in Rome in 1766 and a Pieter de Hooch of *The Concert Players*.

Thursday, 11th September

Trained to Roskilde. The Cathedral like all Scandinavian churches is too clinically clean, and quite without spirit. Some fine Baroque royal tombs nevertheless. Then the Viking ships – rather boring. Then Ledreborg Slott gardens. We walked down a long lime avenue from the bus stop. Limes formerly pollarded so that today they fork upwards a great height. The house with dependencies on the flat side, over-looks a deep dell towards wooded slopes. In a central clearing a statue of Adam and Eve, the apple at their feet with toothmarks in it, a thing

I have not seen before in sculpture. A tranquil, drizzly day, the autumnal trees a variety of greens and pale mauves. A most beautiful garden.

Saturday, 13th September

Helsinki has not much to offer. Famous art deco station, pretty hideous. Our great discovery was the Empire Square, built by the Russian Czars, with cathedral of St Nicholas dominating it. A very remarkable, clean-cut, austere neo-Greek building by C.L. Engel. The University Library, part of this group, one of the best things we saw in our fortnight's tour of Scandinavian capitals. I made notes of these quarters for a possible article. Stockholm where we spent only two nights is of course the best of the four by a long chalk. We went to the Haga Slott pavilion, my third visit. Beautiful little building, not well kept, and too bare of contents. Was much moved by the monumental effigy on a pier of the Storkyrkan Church. It was of Nicodemus Tessin holding an open sheaf of papers; one leg raised on steps, head bent down reverentially. At the Haga pavilion the pillow of the Crown Prince's bed was dated Ano. 1751, and had a coronet embroidered thereon.

Eardley told me how he introduced Graham Sutherland[*] to portraiture. He accompanied the Sutherlands on a visit years ago to Willie Maugham's[†] villa on Cap Ferrat. On the way they lunched and Cathie drew caricatures on the paper cover of a restaurant table. Eardley was struck by them. After the visit he suggested that Cathie draw some caricatures of Willie. This she did most successfully. Whereupon Eardley suggested that Graham do a portrait of Willie with the help of Cathie's sketches. Graham asked Willie if he would like him to do his portrait, and W. consented.

Thursday, 25th September

We stayed five nights on the outskirts of Oslo with Eardley's niece Anne and her husband, Peter Hudson, who is a Major-General and attached to NATO. Sweet, good couple, living in a rented house among a hundred other 'Sunningdale' residences, each with swim-

---

[*] Graham Sutherland, OM (1903–80), m. 1927 Kathleen (Cathie) Barry.
[†] W. Somerset Maugham (1874–1965).

ming pool (illuminated at nights, electricity being so cheap), no fences between, Hollywood-like. Dinner parties of NATO Commander-in-Chief and generals and admirals, all quite out of our world, and a slight strain. Oslo a most dreary city, and the most expensive of the four. E. and I had a snack luncheon of an open sandwich and one cup of coffee each. Total bill over £2.

Wednesday, 8th October

The National Trust meetings are the most enjoyable of any I have attended over a longish life of committee experience. Relations between staff and committee members are as good as could possibly be. Respect from staff, confidence from chairmen and members, at times affection. Lunching at Brooks's after the Properties Cttee today met Gerry Coke* in the lavatory who greeted me effusively. Said he seldom came to the club, and seldom saw old friends. So we sat together at the round table in the window of the coffee room, and were joined by two other old friends, Sam Lloyd† and Ran Antrim.‡ I told Ran that Terence Morrison-Scott§ was the best chairman I had sat under (or nearly), and hoped he might succeed Michael Rosse on the Properties. Rather shame-facedly Ran said that Peter Chance¶ had already been chosen. He is a stuffed dummy with none of Terence's bewitching charm, and exactly the same age as T., who was considered too close to Michael's age. I said T. and P. were my exact contemporaries at Eton, and Michael was a year and a half older.

Friday, 31st October

I have been very negligent of my diary lately. The chief reason is our move to Essex House, Badminton. Every evening when I get back there from Bath I hang pictures with A. or arrange something. A year

---

* Gerald Edward Coke, CBE (1907–90); Eton College contemporary of J.L.-M.

† Sampson Llewellyn Lloyd (b. 1907); lived with his wife Margaret (Peggy) Parker at Bagpath Court, Gloucestershire.

‡ Randal McDonell (1911–77), 13th Earl of Antrim; Chairman of N.T., 1965–77.

§ Sir Terence Morrison-Scott (1908–91); eminent zoologist; member of N.T. Properties Committee 1963–83; Chairman of Nature Conservancy Panel, 1970–81; Chairman of Architectural Panel, 1973–82.

¶ Ivan Oswald Chance (1910–84); Chairman of Christie's International, 1973–6; Chairman of the Properties Committee, N.T. 1976–80.

ago precisely we were doing this very thing in Bath and I thought and hoped it was for the last time.

I have resumed Roger Hinks's diaries; am just about half-way through. Difficult to read. The type is faint and foolscap pages are too big for ease on the eye and understanding. My goodness, how introspective he was, and what store he set by his diaries. They were sacred to him. Every day he refers to them, and every six months states that he is about to begin his 'Book', what he calls the autobiography of his imagination. He did have imagination, great powers of analysis, great understanding of the arts, but no heart. He admits that he was never in love. That is what makes these diaries unacceptable to publishers. Yet they ought to be published, they must be. I talked to Norah Smallwood last week and she suggested Angus Davidson* as a possible editor. A good suggestion, and I shall speak to Ian McCallum this evening when we dine with him. Strange indeed that my diaries which are trivia, tosh compared with his, have been published. I feel embarrassed when people come up to me holding the book in their hands and asking for my autograph. Although I have received some flattering letters, all are from friends. What gives me pleasure is well-informed letters from strangers, with kindly comments of course.

Motoring back from London last Saturday I stopped on the motorway at a service station, still pondering over Roger's diaries and upon a passage written in Stockholm during the War. He referred to the civilizing effect the English way of life would have on the Germans, always eager to heed the English example, when the War should be over. I went to the WC and while relieving, in came a horde of football fans on their way back to Wales, I suppose. Such yahoos I never saw or heard, yelling, behaving like savages. Not one of them was born when Roger was writing his words. And so, I thought, this is where the English civilizing influence has got to, this is where it has brought our own people, the present generation, to. Can the greatest optimist deny that our civilization has regressed since the early 1940s when we still believed we were contriving a better world than what preceded the War?

I was returning from a Service of Thanksgiving for the life of Diona Murray (Stewart-Jones)† whose death in July I had not noticed,

---

* Literary contemporary of J.L.-M.; author of *Edward Lear*.
† Mrs Patrick Murray; sister of Richard Stewart-Jones. During the war years J.L.-M. frequently stayed with the Stewart-Jones family in Chelsea.

indeed knew nothing of until I received a card of invitation from Beanie, the last survivor of that large family of siblings. Service was in Chelsea Old Church. I sat close to and read afterwards the fine tablet to Rick's memory. The party in Crosby Hall afterwards was like something in the last volume of Proust's novels. Old furrowed, rugged ladies came up and said, 'I am Hester', or 'Janet', and after a palsied look of un-recognition, something dawned and a embrace ensued. I was curious to meet Rick's boy, Barnaby. I had cherished a vision of a young man looking just like his father, which he used to aged four when I last saw him. Instead he looked like his mother, who withheld her presence today. He wore a yellow beard and was covered with yellow hair. Didn't seem interested in his father, barely remembered him. Was polite, and left no impression on me at all. Emma, the mother, will, I was told, have nothing to do with the Stewart-Jones family. Edward [Stewart-Jones]'s widow Hester a nice, sensible, wise woman, I thought. She claimed that all the gushing things which friends habitually say about Rick could be confirmed *and* contradicted. He had every counter-virtue to virtue. He could be cruel, malevolent and everything that's horrid. I daresay she came up against him. My opinion of Rick is that he was something of a saint, but maddening. He was late for every engagement, which denotes utter selfishness. There was much of the prude in his disposition. But he had humour, and understanding. And he was virtuous. Curious how today I do not think of him with particular tenderness, regret or love, although I loved him greatly for a time. I know now what I knew at the time but refused to admit to myself, that he was *not* my 'sort'. He thought me a reactionary, and a person lacking public spirit and philanthropic ideology. For he was a Roundhead, and I am a Cavalier.

Monday, 10th November

I was upset to receive a letter a week ago from Sir Humphry Tollemache beginning 'Dear Sir'. My heart sank because of the form of address, and the ominous name. Ham House, I thought, and my flippant story of the visit there in 1943. *The Times* would select it. This Sir Humphry is a brother of the man I mistook for the alcoholic family butler. I should have checked that there was no such close relation living. Somehow I imagined the line was extinct. Anyway, he took grave exception to what I wrote. So I sent him a grovelling apology and this morning, thank God, he has written me a very decent letter beginning, 'You could not have written a nicer letter to me and in the circumstances I am grateful for it.' Although I brought this entirely on myself, nevertheless all this past week I have felt upset.[*] On Saturday at the National Trust annual meeting in Bristol Midi,[†] with whom I had a fleeting word, told me that Helen Dashwood was furious. I have heard this from several quarters. Midi went on, 'People ask why on earth Jim published these diaries.' I said to Midi, 'Have you read them?' She confessed that she hadn't, although I sent her a copy weeks ago.

I am feeling very low, as if life were ebbing out of me. Singularly depressed for no apparent reason. I ought to be so happy but, as I tried to explain to A. last night, despondency is based on no reason. It just assails one. She thinks I am taking it out on her, which I certainly don't intend. I merely want to be left alone. I don't want to see people, I don't want to be harassed, asked questions, asked for explanations. When in these moods I am, I know, intolerable to live with and I appear ungrateful, inconsiderate, introspective and impossible. I concede all these things. I am sorry. But I want to be ignored, left. And this I never am, or can be. In my youth these moods were worse than they are now. Then I was working and so had to continue consorting with people. Now I no longer work for a living, but am married, and still cannot be left to myself.

It is flattering when the young wish to see one and confide their troubles. That sweet girl Diana Keith Neal[‡] told me all her tribulations the other evening when she cooked me eggs, about her lover who is a rich playboy living abroad for tax reasons, won't stick at any work, is quickly bored, and desperately attractive. Drop him, I tried to tell her, as kindly as I could. Drop him at once!

---

[*] Recounted in *Ancestral Voices*. Major-General Sir Humphry Tollemache, 6th Bt, was a younger son of Sir Lyonel Tollemache, 4th Bt (1854–1952), and succeeded his brother in 1969; the line is by no means extinct.

[†] Hon. Mary O'Neill, Mrs Derick Gascoigne; Alderley neighbour, mother of writer and broadcaster Bamber Gascoigne.

[‡] Daughter of W. Keith Neal, collector of antique guns.

Monday, 17th November

Heywood and Anne* lunched on their way home from staying with the Lees Mayalls,† who complain that they are constantly being confused with us. Heywood is nowadays a funny, little old man with a round, red face and plump little body, just as quiet, quizzical, clever and humorous as heretofore. Anne gets more distinguished every day. They are a beloved pair, and perfectly suited and devoted. Heywood still amused by everything Anne says and does. 'Now do look out, Anne. Be careful with that coffee cup. You know how you drop things.'

Wednesday, 19th November

Harold Acton‡ lunched with me at Brooks's. I was enchanted with him. We indulged in blissful comparison of the complaints made by individuals of our recent books. He has been assailed by Rosamond and, on R's behalf, her brother John,§ for including a passage in a letter from Nance to, I think, Alvilde: 'Rosamond has been trying to get the Wid [Mrs Hammersley] to intercede with the Almighty on behalf of her little girl', or words to that effect, wounding doubtless to poor Ros who has never got over the death of her daughter Sally, and words which would have been in worse taste if Harold's instead of Nancy's own. Then Palewski has been on to him because Ali Forbes disclosed his name in a review of Harold's book in the *TLS*. David Higham¶ is most indignant with Forbes who, he complains, writes about himself and not the books he is reviewing. I said he was a friend of mine. He can't still be a friend of yours, he replied, after what he wrote about you in the last paragraph of his review of *A. Voices*. David Horner** told Harold that he thought of suing me for calling him epicene, but refrained because he did not wish to give the book further publicity.

---

* George Heywood Hill, bookseller (d. 1986); m. 1938 Lady Anne Gathorne-Hardy.
† Sir Alexander Lees Mayall, KCVO (1915–93); diplomat; m. (2nd) 1947 Hon. Mary Ormsby Gore, dau. of 4th Baron Harlech.
‡ Sir Harold Acton (1904–95; Kt 1974); writer and aesthete; resident in Florence.
§ Rosamond Lehmann (1901–90), novelist; John Lehmann, FRSL (1907–87), poet, editor and publisher.
¶ J.L.-M.'s literary agent.
** Companion of Sir Osbert Sitwell.

I said to Harold that D.H. ought to be flattered, because to be called epicene implied that he had qualities of both sexes.

I closely watched Harold's expressive face across the table. The eyelids are small and semi-circular which contributes to the oriental aspect; the nostrils are tiny and tucked back as though they have been operated upon. Harold's mischievous, extremely courteous, almost dancing voice and gait make him unique among men. We had a good heart-to-heart. He told me that his German companion now lives in Florence. I said I hoped he was nice to Harold. Yes, said H., but he is very expensive, fast cars, elaborate cameras, travel, entertainment without end. 'It is a little sad,' he said, 'having to pay even for affection, on top of everything else. But what can we expect at our age, my dear?'

To *Ballo in Maschera* with John Pope-Hennessy in the Royal Box. Visually a little disappointing, but musically without flaw. There is not a dull phrase in this opera. If only the King this evening had looked a little more classical, instead of looking like Soame Jenyns[*] (who incidentally has written me a long, amusing letter, beginning by reference to the description I gave of his Jewish features in those accursed diaries).

Friday, 21st November

Was deeply distressed to read this morning a brief notice in *The Times* of dear Monica [Baldwin]'s[†] death. It was so sudden, and the announcement so brief and inexplicit that at once I feared something terribly wrong. And so it proved. This evening I telephoned Bloggs[‡] who had just returned from Long Melford where she had moved a few weeks ago. She told me in her last letter of September she was going to a nice Catholic refuge. Only yesterday I said to myself it was high time I wrote to her again. Bloggs in his slow way began, 'I only returned one hour ago, and have since been reading with Elspeth Monica's letter of farewell, which arrived in my absence.'

---

[*] Of Bottisham Hall, Cambridgeshire (b. 1904); ceramic expert; descendant of Dr Johnson's friend Soame Jenyns.

[†] One-time nun, and author of *I Leap over the Wall*; cousin of the politician Stanley Baldwin; she and J.L.-M. corresponded for many years.

[‡] A.W. Baldwin, 3rd Earl Baldwin of Bewdley (1904–76); biographer; m. 1936 Elspeth Tomes.

Then I knew the worst. Evidently she was treated very badly, or supposed she was. She wrote to her friend Joan Arbuthnot, whom she had left behind at the Curry Mallet house, that she was ill-treated, half starved and spied upon. That she dared not telephone for fear of being overheard and abused afterwards. Can this have been true? Bloggs said it was a good thing she had taken her life, half a bottle of sleeping pills and half a bottle of whisky: 'Poor Monica, she never understood about these things.' She grew increasingly miserable, as I can testify from her letters to me, and could not reconcile herself to the changes within the Church and the condition of world affairs. Yet for her, who remained staunchly Catholic and devout, albeit latterly refusing to attend Mass, and who (she assured me) went through her Offices daily, and prayed, to have acted so far contrary to express Catholic doctrine by taking her own life is very tragic indeed. Bloggs maintains she did the right thing (though whether in the right way, I question). He said, 'Extreme old age is an extremely melancholy business. We all have to face it in time. I have given a few broad hints to the Almighty. Whether He will heed them is another matter.' I feel sure Monica's life was ruined by the Catholic Church, those thirty lost years of doubt and self-questioning in an enclosed order, to return to a changed and alien world, to which she failed to adapt herself, then to be let down in the end by the Church taking from her all those anchors to which she still clung after her decision to abandon the convent. In ending her life she must have lost her faith, and died without hope, fearing, wretched, despairing. This makes me very sad indeed. A. keeps saying, 'I wish you had seen her. I told you you ought to have seen her.' Still I am not sure. But I am sure that I should have written to her recently instead of letting our correspondence subside. I should have done that. Perhaps her other pen friends did the same, so that she was reduced to total loneliness.

Monday, 24th November

Am at present engaged in writing long captions for the illustrations to *Beckford*, which I believe is, in spite of its brevity, a rather good little book. I have already begun editing the next series of diaries, *Prophesying Peace*; and am most anxious to dispose of them so that I may tear up and destroy the original manuscript, as I have done of *A. Voices*. My embarrassment over those to-be-excised passages is extreme. I am terrified of dying before I have finished. When this work is over, then 'The Squires' I suppose.

Woke up this morning with a funny ache in the left jaw, where I have few teeth left.

Such a to-do when I called at the Nat. Portrait Gallery last week, wishing to look up portraits of some obscure musicians who featured in Beckford's life. The attendant downstairs said I must make an appointment to see the Librarian. I said I had never done such a thing before, and always used to walk into the library. He refused, then asked me what I wanted from the library. I was not going to explain to this uneducated person what my needs were, and insisted on seeing someone more responsible. After I had waited half an hour a lady in brown descended in a lofty manner. I remonstrated with her, with the result that I was received in the library by a charming, painstaking lady, Miss Evans; was given every facility, and got most of what I wanted. Miss Evans all over me. But why should members of the public with serious needs be treated in this aggressive, putting-off fashion? Damn it all, the NPG is there to serve the public, not to give cushy jobs of filing to dry-as-dust officials.

Tuesday, 25th November

I used to be surprised and shocked because old people accepted the calamities and deaths of their old friends with seeming equanimity. Now I realize that had they not done so, they would have gone mad. I have reached the age when I am beset with deaths and calamities. Monica has gone; Miss Long has had a serious fall and is in hospital; John Fowler has had a fit; dear old Florence* is dying in a London hospital, and I am waiting to know whether to go to London tomorrow to see her. Jack Rathbone is telephoning this evening to tell me whether or not she will recognize me, if I do go. Eve Gregory,† Audrey's greatest friend, died yesterday in Scotland with Audrey in attendance.

---

* Miss Florence Paterson; N.T. co-worker; during the war years she had shuttled about with J.L.-M. between London and the N.T's billet at West Wycombe Park in Buckinghamshire.
† Eve Hill, wife of Vice-Admiral Sir David Gregory; he also d. 1975.

Wednesday, 26th November

To London specially to see poor Florence in the Royal Free Hospital. To my surprise she was sitting in an armchair beside her bed. Looking however the ghost of her former self. When she saw me she opened wide her arms and I bent low to embrace her. Totally changed from the well-filled, plump and bright old Florence whom I last saw when we lunched with Jack Rathbone, in the early summer. Her wide smile was the same. Spoke in a tiny voice, so quietly that I could hardly hear, yet laughed at old jokes. Said she could not understand what had happened to her, she was suddenly stricken with illness and misery. Was just able to converse. Mostly consisted in expressions of gratitude to everyone for their kindness. I said, 'But, Florence darling, of course people are kind to you because all your life you have been good to others', which is the truth. After an hour I left for fear of tiring her if I stayed longer. Still the same sweet smiling eyes. I knew I should never see her again. And already Jack has telephoned that she has relapsed and does not know him.

Saturday, 29th November

Sylvia Chancellor,* to whom I was remarking upon the bad taste of our kind neighbour Mrs Schuster's house, and the austerity of the rooms, said: 'The trouble is there is too little of it. With bad taste such as hers the rooms ought to be crammed.'

By some extraordinary miracle the silver pencil Vita† gave me in 1947 has reappeared. Sitting in the car I noticed it on the floor in front of the passenger's seat. It must have dropped through a hole in the dashboard ledge where it disappeared a month ago. I knew this must have happened, but the garage who sold me this beastly little car swore such a thing was impossible. Another garage even took the dashboard to pieces – or said they had – and denied that the pencil was there. Anyway I am overjoyed. I adore this pencil, and I wouldn't like to say how many times it has disappeared and reappeared. This last time I really believed I had lost it for good.

The Badminton agent told A. that with the latest rise of £6 in the agricultural worker's wage, the estate will be liable to an extra £20,000 a year.

---

* Sylvia Paget, wife of Sir Christopher Chancellor (m. 1926).
† Hon. Vita Sackville-West; writer and gardener (d. 1962).

Monday, 1st December

In the critics' choice of books for 1975 in *The Times* last Thursday, someone spoke of my book in disparaging terms, i.e., faint praise modified by 'Oh, but such ghastly people', or words to that effect. And in the *Sunday Times* yesterday Robert Harling[*] gave it as his choice, referring to my hermaphroditic malice towards friends, acquaintances and myself, etc. I am greatly distressed that people evidently think the book full of rancour. I don't see myself as bitchy but as an *ingénu*, I mean I see myself as such when I wrote these diaries over thirty years ago.

Yesterday we lunched with Tony and Violet Powell at the Chantry. Violet has read it twice, she says, and Tony confirmed this. She evidently liked it immensely, and talked about little else. Enjoyable interlude in an extremely foggy day. Curry cooked by Tony. I always enjoy seeing them. Both so stimulating. I understand how young Hugh Montgomery-Massingberd[†] felt. He longed to talk to Tony about his novels which he admires intensely; and Tony would only discuss genealogy. He is hipped on the subject, and his shelves are filled with every sort of reference book, *The Complete Peerage* among them. I of course share this interest to some extent. Some people find him sinister. He is not the least so; but he is inscrutable behind his very affable manner. It is his form of defence. And why not, for he is our most renowned novelist living. He has an *enormous* behind, much in evidence, and badly fitting teeth. He has reviewed for next Thursday's *Telegraph* Cyril [Connolly]'s letters to Noel Blakiston, called *A Romantic Friendship*. Says they are fascinating for Cyril even as a boy wrote like an angel. 'I am quite certain they tucked up together,' Tony said – quite wrongly.

Tuesday, 2nd December

Florence died yesterday about an hour after Jack went to see her. Just faded away. Strange that someone who could talk so rationally to me four days before should be extinct. She said she had glanced at my book which someone had lent her; had read the passage about Forsyth,[‡] and

---

[*] Novelist; Editor of *House & Garden*.
[†] Genealogist, writer, and Obituaries Editor of the *Daily Telegraph*, 1986–94.
[‡] W.A. Forsyth, an architect consulted by the N.T. during the war years; of 'Uriah Heep-like humility'.

twinkled. I said it was rather irreverent, wasn't it? Yes, she said, and 'Monica Dance thought you had not been nice enough about the SPAB',* which surprised me, for I thought I had been. So I told Florence I would immediately send her the copy which I was going to give her for Xmas. I sent it, and don't suppose she even opened the parcel. I am sure Florence Paterson never thought, said or did an unkind thing all her life long. For this reason alone I enshrine her amongst the elect I have come across.

Monday, 8th December

On 4th I motored to Oxford for the day. Drove to Colin McMordie's lodgings in Marlborough Road. He lunched with me in a French bistro off the High Street, and in the afternoon until dark conducted me round the colleges. The purpose was to show me the new buildings, new quads which have been built since the war, and recently. I would say that three-quarters are a success. All have been built with care for their environment. The St John's quad and St Edmund Hall quads about the best, being sensitive, original, and yet conformist. Far and away the worst, and by the best-known architect, is St Catherine's College. It is an absolute beast, hideous, shoddy, cheap and unpractical. Unpractical in that the undergraduates' rooms, being bed-sitters, have walls entirely of glass, so that the blinds have to be completely drawn when the inmates want either to work or to change their clothes unseen. With curtains drawn back the rooms reveal underclothes hanging on a rail behind the glass walls. The same raw brick surface is found inside as well as outside the entire building. Flimsy metal struts project from the outside walls; the 'campanile' is contemptible and the whole air is one of meagreness and futility.

Colin rather pathetic at the end. The brave façade did not crumble, but it wilted. He confessed that he was anxious about his future; he has no job in view at the end of a three-years' course in Art as a graduate. He is submitting his final thesis on which I imagine much depends, and fears he, so gifted, is unemployable at the age of twenty-six. He is an extremely handsome fellow and when alone with me drops his tiresome affectation.

Badminton is a village isolated from the present. All the cottages

---

* Mrs Monica Dance was the Secretary of the Society for the Protection of Ancient Buildings, 1943–78.

are inhabited by people working on the estate. They are all friendly, contented, and respectful of one another. All the men say, 'Good morning, Good night, sir', as of old.

Thursday, 11th December

This morning at 9.30 I went for an interview with a Mrs Goodman of East Anglia Radio on, of course, the book, in her flat in Hanover Steps behind Tyburn. I was not good. Too early in the morning. At this hour my mind works sluggishly. When we had a preliminary talk I was all right, but the moment I was confronted with that microphone, held in front of my mouth, I halted. I find myself hesitating, fumbling for words, pausing, conscious of the intervals and fearing lest I dry up, deterred too by the beseeching smile of expectancy and reproach on the face of the too-close interlocutor. When she plays back what I have said, I am appalled. As well as being die-away, my voice is horribly affected. When speaking I am totally unaware of that mincing, slightly middle-class, pedagogic, Twentyish intonation. I always suppose, when I consider the matter at all, that my voice is normal, straightforward, educated certainly, but not like that of an aesthete don from Leeds University. Confronted with the microphone I also become banal. When asked finally what advice I would give to country house owners faced with today's penal taxation and the impending Wealth Tax, all I can find to say is, 'Give your house to the National Trust or turn it into flats.' What I should have said was, 'Burn your treasures the moment you see the tax collector approaching, sooner than let an ungrateful nation of Leftists confiscate them.'

Returned in time for the Bath Preservation Trust annual meeting in the Guildhall. I must get out of this Trust. The new chairman Lord Raglan* was introduced and made a speech about nothing – pious platitudes and phrases like, 'We must not let Bath city die of inanition. Business must thrive,' etc. But I could not concentrate on his words – only on the back view of his totally bald pate and strings of too-long, lank hair over his collar. Instead I was fascinated by the exceeding beauty of the chandeliers, finer than those in the Assembly Rooms. Illuminated by a few candle bulbs, they glittered like diamond tiaras made for some oriental giant goddesses. Amazed I was by the brilliant

---

* FitzRoy Somerset, 5th Baron Raglan (b. 1927); Chairman of Bath Preservation Trust 1975–7; founder of the Bath Society, 1977.

mauve and orange facets mingling with the overall silver. How is this spectrum of colour explained? – for the mauve and orange were in individual segments of the drops. They were not in lengths, like the silver. The loops and swags truly magnificent. I thought I had seldom seen anything more splendidly satisfying.

Saturday, 13th December

Last night in bed I finished Christopher Sykes's[*] *Evelyn Waugh*. What a repulsive fellow! I doubt whether his writings are good enough to justify his abominable character. Yet in a ghastly way I see myself as a pale reflection of the man Evelyn. The same bad temper, grousiness, melancholy, pessimism, disillusion with the Catholic Church, to the extent that I have apostasized, whereas he had the strength and loyalty not to succumb. Everyone I meet criticizes Christopher's book, or damns it with faint praise. Of course it is far too long. But it is a competent affair. Harold [Acton] said it was repetitive, David Somerset[†] who lent me his copy said how stilted and ponderous the prose. It is rather old-fashioned and a bit pedantic. On the other hand, I don't think a biography of this length can be written in sparkling or spanking prose. Its very length and factualness prohibit artistry. Lytton Strachey's *Queen Victoria* is art, because it is a short work, much contrived; and, in being so sparkling and spanking, is largely untrue. I like to imagine, castle in the air, that my *Beckford* is like this.

Poor Diana [Westmorland] telephoned in tears to tell that her old peke had died. I dared not be too commiserative on the telephone lest she break down. So I wrote a letter of condolence and walked across the fields to deliver it at Lyegrove. A hard frost, and as I walked through our village, along the disused drive, across the belt of beeches known as The Verge, over a ploughed field, across a grass field, the golden sun waxed bigger and bigger, then dived. On the way home a waxing moon stood stock-still in a sky of powder blue, one bright star twinkling beside it. The rooks flew overhead. Otherwise not a sound but my footfalls on the crackling ice puddles and the rimy tufts of grass. Then a dying horn and the hounds coming home to Badminton after a day of what must have been hard going.

---

[*] Traveller, journalist, writer (1907–86).
[†] Cousin and heir of 10th Duke of Beaufort; m. 1950 Lady Caroline Thynne, dau. of 6th Marquess of Bath (she d. 1995); living at The Cottage, Badminton, Gloucestershire.

Sunday, 14th December

During my walk yesterday I decided to write a novel, to be called 'A Seven Day Week', then 'A Day in the House'. Alderley was to be the setting, and seven inmates, including a whippet, were to record their thoughts about each other and themselves in an absolutely uninhibited manner. I got extremely worked up and excited, because walking always inspires ideas, and was determined to jot them down on paper the moment I returned. When I got home A. bustled me to change and go off to the beastly carols in the church and supper with the boring X——s in the next village afterwards. All my ideas have evaporated.

I am reading the *Romantic Friendship*, comprising Cyril Connolly's letters to Noel Blakiston while they were at Eton and Oxford and Cambridge. Cyril was at that time a thorough romantic, no cynic, no gross materialist. His intellect, already formidable, amazes me. His learning was immense, and his ability to quote from Milton and the Greek and Latin classics astonishing. His ideas hardly adolescent at all, on the contrary adult. It is an extraordinary picture of the thoughts and interests of Eton scholars in the Twenties, no less remarkable than the correspondence of, say, Robert Bridges and Digby Dolben in the 1860s, which always impressed me.

Tuesday, 16th December

Now David Crawford* is dead. His obituary in today's *Times* must indicate even to the most prejudiced Leftist that men such as he are unique not just to England but to the world. Such sense of duty, such dedication to the arts and civilized being, such utter selflessness. This race of patricians must disappear through taxation, if through nothing else. Mrs Lanchberry, the telephonist at the N.T., told me only last week that David C. had called at the office. She went and talked to him in his car. 'A darling man,' this uneducated woman called him. 'And do you know, Mr L.-M., he said to me he regretted that when he was chairman he never got to know individual members of the staff better, or asked their views on how the Trust was managed. Wasn't

---

* David Lindsay, KT, GBE, 28th Earl of Crawford and 11th of Balcarres, Premier Earl of Scotland and Head of the House of Lindsay (1900–75); *inter alia*, Chairman of N.T. 1945–65.

that nice of him?' I had the greatest veneration for him. He was an extremely proud man, something of a Puritan, censorious and very fastidious. Yet his charm was irresistible, and – as charm usually is – a dangerous quality. You could not discern what he was really thinking. Whenever I saw him I fancied that he liked my company and agreed with all I said. The moment he left me, I realized that he was assessing me at what I am worth. Ran Antrim, to whom I was talking about David C., said, 'He was certainly a saint.' I don't think he was this, not at all. Then I asked Ran how he thought Michael Rosse was. I was alarmed by Michael's sunken eyes. 'He is finished,' Ran said succinctly. We talked of dying. He was alarmed by the prospect. I said I feared the process, lest it was like a nightmare. No, he didn't think so, because a few years ago he very nearly died of heart failure, and was dragged back to life just in time. He said the sensation was a gentle sinking into nothingness. When Ran smiles, his rugged, creased face becomes smooth for a moment and alight. He is a far more sensitive man than one might think from his cynical manner.

On returning to Badminton this evening I found Tim Mitchell, the agent, having a drink with A. His conversation is fixed on the Beauforts. He venerates them, is fascinated by them, adores them, and has a loyalty of the sort which I imagine Cavaliers bestowed upon Charles I. When he came he found it very difficult to carry out any reforms of the estate. When he made a new suggestion, everyone on the estate said, 'I don't think his Grace would like that.' For that reason incumbents don't stay long at the church here. Unlike the agents, they don't feel the same loyalty: why should they, for they are not strictly speaking the Duke's servants. And mercifully the Duke will not tolerate Series 2 or 3 of the liturgy. The incumbents feel they lack scope for their beastly improvements. Mitchell thinks this vicar has settled, because he lacks ambition to rise in the clerical hierarchy. When the Queen was here in the spring the vicar and wife, just arrived, were bidden to dinner at 8.30. No one warned them that they should have arrived at 8.15. They were punctual at 8.30, just when the Queen was coming down the stairs. The butler rushed to the front door and beckoned to the vicar to run for it. He slipped, poor man, and fell on the wet paving stone, covering his evening suit with mud. Imagine the horror of his situation! The Queen was all affability; the Duchess in presenting him said, 'See the state he's in, Ma'am. He is drunk of course.' This little joke did not reassure the new vicar. Mitchell said that only dukes may be buried beside Great Badminton church; even duchesses have to be interred in Little Badminton graveyard. The present couple won't have a wood fire in the one dark sitting room they use, but an electric fire. And of course the radiators are not on this winter. The butler spends from May till the following April polishing the silver to be used for the Horse Trials house party and the assembled royals.

Thursday, 18th December

Went to see dear old Patrick [Kinross]* in the King Edward VII hospital. He told me unconcernedly that the growth they cut out of his colon a fortnight ago was malignant. He doesn't seem perturbed, and talks about his new book on Aubrey Herbert, which he is longing to begin. Is totally forward-looking. Discussed Cyril's youthful letters to Noel. Patrick has forty of Cyril's letters, which he thinks even more brilliant than these published ones.

---

* 3rd Baron Kinross (1904–76); author, journalist and broadcaster.

1976

Friday, 2nd January

We lunched with the Beauforts[*] in the large dining room, helping ourselves. The butler, having announced us, disappeared and was not seen again. I sat next to her. She said, 'Your wife says I may call you Jim. My name is Mary,' as though I did not know it, but it was kindly put. A. sat next to him and in spite of her misgivings got on well, chatting about Westonbirt and the Menzieses.[†] He said to me after that the reason why he had not called on us was that he was so fond of Aileen Taylor he could not bring himself to enter our house. I liked him for this. He said he worried about her death, hoping she had not been in pain or distress, for she was found dead by Peggy[‡] one morning in her kitchen. We were shown the Worcester porcelain she left the Duke. It is in a showcase at the top of the stairs. Just as well it is, for there it will remain longer than the Somerset family, in all probability.

She has a funny little-girl manner of speaking, and is often sharp and to the point. She took us into the bedroom the Queen has, and which Queen Mary used during her long stay.[§] It faces south and is darkened by the great cedar. Q. Mary urged the Duchess to have it cut down, her objection being the insects which she claimed harboured there and came through the window. The Duchess said, 'It will come down over my dead body, Ma'am.' The reply was, 'Very well, it must remain, my dear.' Odd little incidental remarks she drops, like, 'Yes, I have been to Vienna. I stayed at Schönbrunn, with the old Emperor. He was very nice to children.' And, 'You know my grandmother the Duchess of Teck was rather fat.'

John Betjeman[¶] telephoned from Cornwall to congratulate on *A.*

---

[*] Henry Somerset, 10th Duke of Beaufort (1990–84), of Badminton House, Gloucestershire; m. 1923 Lady Mary Cambridge, dau. of 1st Marquess of Cambridge, elder brother of Queen Mary (of Teck).
[†] Angus Menzies (1910–73) was A.L.-M's first cousin.
[‡] Daily to Miss Taylor and then the L.-Ms at Essex House.
[§] During the Second World War.
[¶] Sir John Betjeman (1906–84; Kt 1969); poet, broadcaster, and writer on architecture; succeeded Cecil Day-Lewis as Poet Laureate, 1972.

Voices. He has just read it. Says it is good, and so funny. I asked if he thought it was in poor taste. 'No, no, no,' he said. Nevertheless the more I think about it, the more I fear it is. I wish I could forget it.

Monday, 12th January

A. and I dined with John Betj. and Elizabeth* in her house. He holding my book in his hand as I entered and throughout the evening reading extracts. And when he read them, they did seem funny. I accompanied him to his house three doors away to collect a bottle of Australian wine he wanted us to sample. Jolly good it was too. His house is astonishingly spick and span, far more so than E's. I opened a volume of Alfred Douglas's poems, with a dedication to J., addressed as 'Moth', from A.D., dated 1923. I said, How did you know him so early? He said he wrote him a fan letter from Marlborough. They at once became friends, of a totally innocent sort. But Mr Betjeman, father, discovering several letters from Bosie, sent for John, then aged about fifteen, to tell him he would not allow the correspondence to continue. He said to John, 'Do you know what a bugger is?' 'No,' said John, knowing perfectly well. 'Well, a bugger is a man who gets hold of another, and by a process of mutual admiration, so works upon him that he puts his piss-pipe up the arse of the other. And can anything be more disgusting than that?' 'No, father.' As we were leaving I told John that Bamber Gascoigne's tele series on Christianity was going to be very anti-Christianity. Midi, whom I saw at six, told me so. John said it is no matter how many millions watch a film that is anti, they are not influenced by it. It is pro films that influence people. Then he said something that shook me a little, namely that he didn't mind about religion going, it was the churches going that mattered to him. I said, 'Yes, but John, you and I know that it is the Eucharist that matters to us above everything else.' And he said, 'Yes, it is.'

Wednesday, 14th January

Went to Dr Allison about my stiff neck, which he said I ricked three months ago, and it would right itself. Damned long time it has taken so far. At the same time he removed a wart from above my right eye by cauterizing, and a local anaesthetic. Said that last night John and

---

* Lady Elizabeth Cavendish, dau. of 10th Duke of Devonshire.

Elizabeth dined with him and his wife. I said how much it worried me the way J. walked. Allison said John was older than he should be for his years. The shuffling was not caused by some physical inability to walk properly, but by some mechanism in the brain, something which governs the involuntary muscles, that it was not put on, and could not be prevented. This I find very strange.

Every single night I have nightmares. They are either anxiety or guilt dreams, and very occasionally, still, sexual. Mostly guilt. Very often too I am struggling to free myself from some bondage, trying to catch a train, say, and unable to budge, or, as the other night, trying to get out of a building in which I was trespassing.

Allison said John B. brought my book with him and read out extracts all through dinner. I said, 'How very boring for you.' I do hope he is not doing this to everyone. It sounds almost senile to me. Dear John, his senility, if it is such, exceeds my maturity by a hundred thousand miles.

Monday, 19th January

This morning there arrived by post from Switzerland a Xerox sent by Ali Forbes of a letter written to him by Stephen Spender,[*] abusing me. In it Stephen says he has always loathed the sight of me, and disliked my very appearance, which is that of a sinister undertaker who with his spade thrusts moribund, not yet dead corpses into the grave. That he sees my soul as a brown fungus upon a coffin, etc. That he has never spoken more than a dozen sentences to me in his life. Now this is pretty mischievous of Ali Forbes, I consider. I am affected by Spender's letter. No, not gravely, because I do not like him and know that what he writes is pretentious tripe, yet affected by the knowledge that there is someone alive who can write such disagreeable things about me. I have replied to Ali, saying what a pity Nancy [Mitford] is not alive; that she would have hooted with laughter; that I have forwarded the letter to the Poet Laureate, and will ask Heywood Hill's shop to frame and exhibit it; that it always interests me that Communists use such extravagant language, and I presume Spender still to be a Communist, although I doubt whether he admits to being a Party member, since all socialite Communists prefer not to disclose this fact. I hope the mischievous Ali may send a Xerox of my letter back to Spender.

---

[*] Poet and man of letters (1909–95; Kt 1983).

Saturday, 24th January

Dined tonight at the House [Badminton House]. Rather surprised to be asked so soon after lunching there. We took Eardley [Knollys], who was staying. This time a butler and footman, or their equivalents out of livery, were waiting. That poor, tiresome old Mrs Durant* staying again, and Lady Londesborough, looking dreadfully ill, ashen grey and taciturn: A. said, like Lady Macbeth. Duke dressed in the Hunt livery, E. and I in dinner jackets. She can be very funny. She said she received a letter from the Bishop of Malmesbury, signed Frankie Malmesbury, and a † after his name. She wrote back, asking if the cross signified a kiss. She is always ready to tell stories about Aunt Queen Mary when she was staying here during the war. One day the Queen sat next to another bishop during luncheon. She gave the bishop a large piece of hard, coarse dog biscuit, telling him to give it to the labrador which was nuzzling the other side of him. The bishop, who was slightly deaf and very old, with new false teeth, proceeded to gnaw it himself, with evident pain. Queen Mary relished the spectacle.

The Duke has a limited charm, and his manners are almost the best I have encountered. He told that when he was a boy the family was obliged to leave Badminton every summer for two or three months, for Troy House, Monmouthshire, because the water supply dried up. The house was not on the main, and the wells became exhausted. He told us that the game of Badminton was invented by his great-aunts to amuse themselves on wet days in the great hall. The objective was not to defeat your opponent, but to keep up a rally as long as possible. The old scores give outstanding rallies of 250-odd. I imagine that Victorian lawn tennis, which was pat-ball, had the same objective.

Friday, 30th January

Much to my surprise I notice the death of Gyles Isham.† I suppose it was heart. He belonged to the last generation, I should say, of cultivated squires in the eighteenth-century tradition. He *was* cultivated, and *the* historian of Northamptonshire. No one knew more about that

---

* '. . . an ancient cousin of the Somersets, and a great-great-granddaughter of Nelson' (*Ancient as the Hills*).
† Sir Gyles Isham (1903–76), 12th Bt, of Lamport Hall, Northamptonshire; landowner, actor and connoisseur.

county, in which his family had been established for centuries. His life was dedicated to local interests, archives and good works; for years he was chairman of the grand Northampton loony bin, in which so many of my friends and acquaintances languished, and languish – Diane Abdy,* Leigh Ashton (still).† I had not seen Gyles lately, alas! He was a charming, informative, companionable man, and to stay with him was a joy, there was always so much to discuss. Lamport was his overriding love. I don't suppose anything superseded it, not even Trevor his agent whom he worshipped in the discreetest, Edwardian fashion, or the stage in his early years. For he acted with Greta Garbo in the Twenties in the *La Dame aux Camélias* film [*Camille*], and others. It was a wonder how so beautiful a young man (which he evidently was) could have turned into the sconey dumpling, all jowl and smile, whom I knew. He resembled his great friend Wyndham Ketton-Cremer‡ in his interests, writings, and ownership of an inherited historic house. Such a type of squire must be almost extinct. Myles Hildyard§ is another and he, dear old thing, still survives, thank God.

Monday, 2nd February

Read in Saturday's *Times* a long obituary of Frank Ashton-Gwatkin,¶ Violet Trefusis's** adorer and most loyal swain. He was 87 and had had a most distinguished diplomatic career. He was another cultivated old man. This morning I received from him a letter of congratulations on my book – which I never for one instant would have supposed he might like – full of praise, accompanied by a brochure of the Elegies of Maximianus, a Latin poet of the fifth/sixth century AD [*recte* sixth] translated by him, and inscribed. The letter was posted on 28th January, so he must have died the following day. Rather pathetically,

---

* Lady Diana Bridgeman, dau. of 5th Earl of Bradford; 2nd wife of Sir Robert Abdy (1896–1976), 5th Bt; she d. 1967.
† Sir Leigh Ashton (Kt, 1948); Director and Secretary, V. & A., 1945–55.
‡ Squire of Felbrigg Hall, near Cromer, Norwich; man of letters and Norfolk historian (1906–69).
§ Squire of Flintham Hall, Nottinghamshire; local historian (b. 1914).
¶ CB, CMG (b. 1889); retired 1947 as Assistant Under-Secretary at the Foreign Office; wrote novels about Japan under the *nom de plume* of John Paris, having been attached to the suite of the Crown Prince of Japan on his visit to England in 1921.
** Violet Trefusis (1894–1972), dau. of Colonel The Hon. George Keppel and his wife Alice; novelist; lover of Vita Sackville-West.

he said he was a broken man, and inveighed against the horrors of old age.

Sunday, 15th February

We motored to Broadway, to tea with Toty and Dorothy De Navarro.[*]
A. is to write for the N.T. periodical an article on Lawrie Johnston.[†]
We hoped Toty would cough up more information than he was able
to do. No one seems to know the date of L.J's birth, whether he was
trained as an architect, or anything about his background. Toty, who
is nearly eighty, told several amusing stories about Elgar and Barrie at
the Court Farm, all of which I have already forgotten. He said his
parents moved to Broadway in 1896, enticed there by Alfred Parsons
and Millais; that William Morris and his family used to stay in
Broadway Tower during the summer, picnicking, like gypsies. Morris
was the virtual discoverer.

Toty told me that when an undergraduate in Cambridge in 1914
he went to tea with Montague Butler, President of Trinity. Butler told
him that his father was sent to Germany as a young man with letters
of introduction to Goethe and Schiller.

Gerald Brenan's[‡] book *A Life of One's Own* is extremely well
written, although the story he recounts of his early life is not a
remarkable one. He learnt to discard God, of course. Was illuminat-
ing when describing the few occasions when ecstasy overtook him, at
unforeseen unexpected moments, such as in the trenches during the
first war. He calls them revelations of wishing to become part of the
universe, to understand. K. Clark describes very lucidly and beautifully too in his autobiography the moment when as a boy his instant
revelation of art took place, likewise an ecstasy.

---

[*] José Maria De Navarro (1896–1979), only surviving son of the actress Mary Anderson
(1859–1940) who retired from the stage in the 1880s to marry Antonio De Navarro
(1860–1932), a wealthy Spanish-American, and settle at Court Farm, Broadway,
Worcestershire, which became a meeting-place for such luminaries as Elgar, Toscanini,
Henry James, James Barrie, etc; Toty De Navarro, archaeologist and Fellow of Trinity
College, Cambridge, m. 1940 (Agnes) Dorothy MacKenzie Hoare (1901–87), Fellow of
Newnham College, Cambridge.
[†] Major Lawrence Johnston, creator of Hidcote Manor Garden, Hidcote Bartrim,
Gloucestershire.
[‡] Writer (1894–1987).

Tuesday, 17th February

I have received this week two letters which in different ways have much moved me. One from K. Clark congratulating me on *Another Self*, which he has only just read – aloud, to Jane. Found it hilarious, the stories hardly credible, approves the art of recounting incidents without following up the sequels, and so forth. V. gratifying and flattering to receive such a letter from this man, who is almost God. The other letter, yesterday, came from Mrs Spender,[*] beginning politely, saying how sorry that they were the cause of my not accepting Ann Fleming's[†] invitation to luncheon last Sunday. Then screeds followed about the injury I had done Stephen, 'he will have to live with it', etc., 'he is a public figure, a creative writer', insinuating that I am neither of these things – too true. Now I understand, having received a copy of Spender's letter to Ali Forbes, how one feels when wounded. I have replied perfectly politely, saying I am indeed sorry to have caused pain, but making light of the matter; disclaiming any intentional injury, but feigning amusement over his rudeness about me. Oh dear, the silliness of it all.

Sunday, 22nd February

Candida Lycett Green[‡] is a strange girl. Very beautiful, with regular features which can't be inherited from either parent. From the mouths of babes and sucklings an older person can imbibe wisdom. When she arrived I went into the road to greet her and in that tiresome way we all have today, I embraced her. To show how much she disrelished it she gave me a furious, resounding kiss on the mouth, enough to freeze me to eternity. It was like a whip-lash. Now I agree with her sentiment and in future shall be more sparing of my oscular favours towards the young.

Wednesday, 3rd March

I motored John Kenworthy-Browne to see three churches with monuments by Nollekens, beginning with Cirencester, the 1st and

---

[*] Natasha Litvin; m. Stephen Spender 1941, as his 2nd wife.
[†] Ann Charteris, dau. of Hon. Guy Charteris, m. (3rd) Ian Fleming (1907–64), novelist.
[‡] Mrs Rupert Lycett Green, dau. of Sir John Betjeman and Hon. Penelope Chetwode; writer on the smaller houses and cottages.

2nd Earls Bathurst; then to a charming, isolated little church called Hankerton; and lastly, North Wraxall. The Methuen chapel has a ceiling of tinctured armorial shields, which must have been done at the same date and by the same craftsmen as the little dining room in Corsham Court. Surprisingly Paul Methuen never told me about it. In the centre of the chapel a splendid, smooth polished marble sarcophagus to Methuens, presumably by Nollekens. Great scrolls at the four corners. A satisfactory thing.

Thursday, 4th March

Eardley told me that when he was a boy at Winchester he stayed with a school friend, Andrew Shirley, at his home, Staunton Harold. The house even in those days, about 1917, was half closed, rooms under dust-sheets. The father Lord Ferrers had a black labrador of which he was extremely fond. Each morning on the portico he gave a peculiar order to the dog, which bounded away, over the fields and through a wood. It made for the main London–to–Leicester railway line which ran through the Staunton Harold estate a mile off. The guard on the train from London would at a certain spot throw a copy of *The Times* out of the window. The dog caught it and brought it back in its mouth to his master. This was a regular matutinal procedure.

Italy   *Saturday, 6th March*

Yesterday morning Eardley and I motored in his car through the East End of London, down the Seven Sisters Road, to Southend-on-Sea. What a beastly town, with nothing whatever to recommend it, save a mile-long pier stretching across the sands, with a train running up and down it. From here we flew in a ferry plane to Le Touquet. Drove hell-for-leather to Paris, catching a night train at the Gare du Nord. Car on the train. Woke up at Chamonix in the snow. Snow and fog all the way to Arezzo, down the motorway. We are staying for a fortnight at La Posticcia Nuova, Pieve a Presciano, a nice Tuscan farmhouse in the depth of the Tuscan country, half a mile from the village, down a narrow lane. On arrival were greeted by the owner, Jeffrey Smart,* an Australian painter of surrealist pictures. He is exchanging this house for E's London flat for the month of March. Nice friendly

---

* Painter and autobiographer (*Not Quite Straight*, 1987); b. 1921.

man who has treated us with much consideration, perhaps the first and most appreciated being his removal of himself at seven o'clock this morning. We said our goodbyes last night at midnight, having established our contact. Also staying with him a boy of twenty-six called Andrew Pfeiffer, a great admirer of *A. Voices*. So is Smart, it seems, for he kept quoting by heart passages which I had written and quite forgotten.

A native mason has been working daily on the studio. His face is extraordinarily like that of Federigo da Montefeltro, same swarthy skin, same hair of crisp dark thin curls, same extraordinary bulging eyes with sloe-like irises. He is the leading Communist in this region. Yet his manners are perfect and his attitude is to please. Jeffrey Smart told us that he took this man, called Velo, and his assistant to do a small job of work on his Rome flat in January, because his charges are so much less than a Roman builder's and he trusts the man. At midday Smart prepared a good meal of pasta and wine which he laid on a table on the balcony. To his surprise Velo would not touch it. On being asked why, he replied that one never ate out of doors in the winter months because the evil spirits entered your mouth while it was open. Smart with much presence of mind and without contradicting him said, 'You are of course quite right. But you have forgotten that this prohibition only applies to Tuscany. Now you are in Latium, where it does not operate.' Whereupon the leading Communist sat down out of doors and gobbled up everything set before him.

Sunday, 14th March

We have been to Arezzo and Borgo San Sepolcro to look at the Pieros. It is almost impossible to see those in the Augustinian church of Arezzo, because of the indifferent light and because of the height of all but the lowest range of paintings. In fact the best way of studying them is from the excellent photographs in K. Clark's splendid book, which I have read here. *The Resurrection* in Borgo is one of the world's greatest Christian messages. The risen Christ confronts the new world, with a face expressing some bewilderment, much anxiety, little expectancy, slight apprehension, yet steadfastness, determination and faith. The faces of the sleeping soldiers express the indifferent world over which the Christ is about to step. Of the Arezzo frescos the one which most moves me is that of Constantine sleeping in his tent, with the youthful lieutenant watching wearily at the bedside, leaning an

elbow on the bedclothes of his master. Can't unravel the angel in the
sky. Is it a pair of wings with one pointing arm?

Tuesday, 16th March

I am reading an interesting but unsympathetic book on the Fall of the
House of Savoy by an American, Robert Katz. He is a Leftist with a
bias against the Savoys. Today lunching with Harold Acton at La Pietra
in Florence I was talking about this book to Michael Rosse. M. told
me that Victor Emmanuel* had been reprehensibly weak with
Mussolini, from all he heard from his cousin Prince Filippo Doria, a
man of strictest probity. Prince Filippo was exiled from Italy because
he protested against Mussolini filching thirty per cent of the funds collected by Doria during the war for the Red Cross, of which he was
president. The King exiled him. When Prince Filippo asked to see the
King from time to time, a privilege he enjoyed because of his position as head of the 'white' Roman princes and a relation of the Savoys,
King Victor Emmanuel refused. When it came to a referendum,†
Doria voted against the monarchy.

Anne [Rosse] greeted me with the words, 'Did you get my letter?'
She had written to me since I came abroad to say she had received
from Queen Elizabeth a four-page letter about my book, which
Anne gave her. And has quoted chunks from it, she says. She was
looking marvellously pretty. Michael not looking at all well,
extremely pale, with sunk eyes and a squashy body. He fainted two
days ago and has been suffering from liver. I fear he is failing, and this
makes me sad.

We had but a short time in Florence, and visited Santa Croce in the
morning, which Eardley surprisingly did not know. Now, I don't
much like this church. The Giottos bore me and I know the Canovas
too well. Discovered a monument which I didn't know, to Bartolini,
in the cloisters. At luncheon at La Pietra, butler and footman wait in
white gloves and, what makes me uncomfortable, stand (while we eat)
behind a screen, their swivelling heads eyeing us. After luncheon
looked at the Pietà in the Duomo and Sir John Hawkins's fresco – E.
pointed out the beautiful carmine background – and the Ghiberti
door. That was all. Doors covered with dust. One might have thought

---

* Victor Emmanuel III (1869–1947); King of Italy 1900–46, when be abdicated.
† June 1946.

'they' could at least keep these world-famed and venerated works of art clean.

Pazzi Chapel was included. Can it be that the stained-glass windows are contemporary, by Baldovinezzi, as claimed? They looked to me nineteenth-century and ugly. As for the beautiful glazed Evangelists by Brunelleschi, they might be brand-new. This chapel is almost too clinically perfect. It is flawless architecture, and yet does not move me to any emotion but wonder.

Friday, 19th March

Overnight the weather changes in Tuscany. From bitter cold days and nights of hard frost, comes summer. These two past days I have been able to sit each morning in the sun on the first-floor balcony, and work, or try to work. I noticed yesterday walking with the dog that there were many butterflies, brimstones, tortoiseshells and little speck-led white ones; violets were on banks which they certainly did not adorn two days previously, scillas, grape hyacinths, and what look like mustard flowers in large patches. Round here all the hill houses are empty and falling into ruin, apart from those, like the we are in now, which have been renovated by the British. These little farmsteads are built to a pattern. On the ground floor are stables with a long row of mangers. An outdoor staircase to a small open lobby. Several small bedrooms clustered round one large, central *salotto*, with high ceiling and large open fireplace with projecting hood supported on colossal stone brackets. The breastsummer a monolith of stone. The inhabit-ants of these yeoman-type dwellings have all moved to bungalows in the neighbouring large village or town, in order to enjoy the com-forts of water, electricity, the tele. They motor daily to their land and back in large red Fiats.

Friday, 26th March

I am using Monica [Baldwin]'s typewriter which I gave her many years ago. It was originally bought by A. for Clarissa, who could not type, and bought by me from her and given to Monica, who cher-ished it, and wrote so many letters in its familiar script.* Her friend

---

* The machine had an italic typeface; J.L.-M. used it from time to time in typing up his diary notes.

Joan Arbuthnot gave it back to me. It is strange to be tapping away on keys which her fingers touched, as she wrote to me.

Wednesday, 31st March

The BBC are after me expressing a wish to do a television programme on Beckford and Bath.

Eardley writes that the city of Urbino is rejoicing over the stolen Piero's recovery. When the news was released the bells of the cathedral and the town hall were pealed. Now that is touching, if anything is. Imagine the British doing such a thing! It would never occur to them, for they would not care one way or the other.

I am reading *The Dukes*, by a young man, Brian Masters. It is fair, impartial and amusing. Full of funny stories. One amazing link with the past he gives. Princess Alice,* who is still alive, met someone who was present at the Duchess of Richmond's ball held on the eve of Waterloo, in Brussels.

On Thursday last I wrote a long letter to *The Times*, expressing horror at the number of objects taken from churches to be seen at the Feria Antiquaria, held at Arezzo on the first Sunday of this month. Eardley and I went to it. In a postscript I asked the Editor, before chucking the letter in the waste-paper basket, to show it to William Rees-Mogg,† who might think of giving the matter some other form of publicity. To my surprise my letter appeared in Saturday's *Times*. Monica [Dance] would have approved. So far it has provoked no replies in the paper, although one correspondent sent me a copy of a letter he had written, and several private letters have been addressed to me, including one from K. Clark expressing approval, and one letter of abuse from a certain Patrick Donnelly – Irish of course, bloody man – containing the idiotic argument that the Church was for the poor and not the rich, and asking was I not aware of the Gospel exhortation 'not to lay up treasures on earth'? My reply might well be: has he not read the story of Mary Magdalen pouring unguent on Jesus' feet? And which disciple rebuked her? Judas Iscariot!

---

* HRH The Princess Alice, Countess of Athlone (1883–1981), dau. of HRH The Prince Leopold, Duke of Albany, 4th son of Queen Victoria.
† Editor of *The Times*, 1967–81; cr. Life Peer 1988.

Wednesday, 7th April

Last night in London I re-experienced a sensation of my youth. I was alone. It was true I was staying with John Kenworthy-Browne and was to see him later in the evening. Therefore I had no genuine cause for loneliness. But I had tried in vain to get hold of a number of old friends, Patrick K[inross], Rosamond [Lehmann], and others, for dinner. Telephoned. No answers. Reconciled to dining by myself at Brooks's. Before dinner went for a walk round Westminster, looking at street buildings. Wandered into the Abbey cloisters just as the lights were turned on, in the twilight. Not a soul in the empty cloisters. Read the tombstones, to the Tufnells, surveyors to the Abbey in the early eighteenth century, to the composer Clementi who having died in Evesham was buried here. Looked again at the Cornewall memorial at the cloister entry. It is the most Rococo monument in England I know, rocks, shells and mussels, ropes and anchors. There I was smitten with the intense loneliness of my youth, when friendless and poor I used to walk the streets and think the passers-by so much happier than I, all so purposeful, so fulfilled, so content. I, last night, did not actually experience this unhappiness again, but I recaptured its flavour of sadness, nostalgia and utter hopelessness.

Sunday, 11th April

Watching the riders cavorting at the Three-Day Event at Badminton. What fascinated me most were the faces and expressions of the competitors as they rode past me – the intensity of their concentration, every fibre of their being, every thought concentrated, every muscle of their bodies directed to this one, single purpose, this test of endurance, this prize which hung by a thread, and meant so much to them. If I were an artist I would draw swift sketches of faces in deep, agonized concentration on fighting, winning, copulating, living, dying.

The whole Royal Family is staying at the House for the Three-Day Event. What shocks is that whenever they are here the church is filled to the brim for Sunday morning service. Since I go to the eight o'clock Eucharist and seldom to Matins, which doesn't fulfil me, I did not want to attend today, to be among the gapers. However, A. insisted; and we as villagers are given tickets. We sat in the middle of the nave close to the Royal Family, and so I *did* have a good stare. All the young princes, princesses and Mark Phillips* sat in one front pew, and a very pretty lot of children they were. Princess Margaret however looks miserable, trussed up like a broody hen, pigeon-breasted and discontented. I like the Royal Family to exist, but I don't want to know or be known by them. The P. of W. sporting a beastly beard, I hope temporary.

Thursday, 15th April

We dined with Pam to meet Debo who is staying. Just the four of us. Debo looking radiant again. She produced lots of samples of the lovely things she now sells in her shop at Chatsworth. I bought a shawl made from her Jacob's sheep and a pair of gloves for A. for Easter.

Much talk about Bobo. The sisters,[†] all the survivors but Decca, are as anti David Pryce-Jones's book[‡] as ever. They have ready a letter to send to *The Times* the moment the book is published – it is upon us shortly – dissociating themselves from it, and telling the world that they have all the papers to which he has not had access.

April 16th, Good Friday

Ann Fleming asked us to luncheon today, because Roy Jenkins and his wife[§] wished to meet us. We went. The Peter Quennells[¶] were staying, and Stuart Hampshire, Warden of Wadham, another guest. He a dour, distinguished man with white hair. I liked him. A. said, difficult to talk to. She sat next to Roy Jenkins, who was easy and entertaining. He was very polite to me, but I am embarrassed when strangers wish to discuss my books, and I endeavour to ward them off.

---

[*] Captain Mark Phillips, who m. HRH The Princess Anne (now The Princess Royal), 1973; m. diss. 1992.

[†] The six Mitford sisters, daughters of 2nd Baron Redesdale, were: Hon. Nancy (1904–72); Hon. Pamela (1907–94), m. Professor Derek Jackson; Hon. Diana (b. 1910), m. (2nd) Sir Oswald (Tom) Mosley, 6th Bt; Hon. Unity (Bobo) (1914–48); Hon. Jessica (Decca) (1917–96), m. (2nd) Robert Treuhaft; Hon. Deborah, m. 1941 Lord Andrew Cavendish, later 11th Duke of Devonshire.

[‡] Son of Alan Pryce-Jones; the book was *Unity Mitford*.

[§] Labour Home Secretary, 1974–76; first Social Democrat candidate to contest an election, July 1981; cr. Life Peer (Baron Jenkins of Hillhead) 1987; m. 1945 Jennifer Morris (Dame Jennifer Jenkins, 1985).

[¶] Sir Peter Quennell (1905–93); poet and man of letters.

This does not make me appear sympathetic, I am sure. He said he admired *A. Voices* as an important chronicle of the times. Could not put it down, etc. How often have I heard this said? Whereas Harold [Acton]'s *Nancy* bored him, and he could not finish it. Said she would be totally forgotten in ten years' time, whereas *Ancestral Voices* would be read in years to come. Flattering nonsense. A good talker, expletive, gossipy, indiscreet – overheard him tell Ann how he turned the new Lord Chancellor out of his room at the Ministry, '"Get out," I said. He is a worm.' Poor teeth, drinks a lot. Smokes a large cigar. Much addicted to the good life. No harm in this, were he not a Socialist. I was attracted by her much. Unfortunately did not sit next to her and had no opportunity of a talk before or after. I am too shy. She looked at me throughout the meal with a smiling, quizzical eye. Until we left I had no idea she was Chairman of the Historic Buildings Council and that she had wanted to talk to me about country houses, so Michael Astor told the Berkeleys. Why had Ann not told me? She supposed that I had known.

Jenkins is good company. I can understand why the socialites like him. Can he be sincere? And would I like to be governed by him in an emergency? No.

Wednesday, 21st April

I am still able to go for quite long walks, even after days, sometimes weeks of no walking. The other day in London I walked from Brooks's to John's house in Hollywood Road [about 2½ miles], after dinner and after walking round Westminster for an hour or more before dinner. How much longer shall I be able to do this?

Julian Fane brought his new wife, Gilly, who was at school with Clarissa, to luncheon on Sunday. Charming and very attractive, with hair like burnished copper. She said she had last met me in Thurloe Square with Clarissa; that our flat there was the first house to awaken her interest, rather to open her eyes to what was a beautiful interior. Until then she had never noticed houses either outside or inside. I accepted that as a compliment – to Alvilde.

Yesterday I was televised in Bristol at the HTV headquarters. Kept for two and a half hours. A sweet Welsh girl interviewed me, and only when the proceedings were over did she admit that it was her first interview; that I was her guinea-pig. The result was that we had one recital, then went through the piece from beginning to end; then that

was scrapped and we went through it again. By the third time neither
I nor she could remember whether we were referring to matters
which we had talked about earlier in the interview, or not, each being
slightly different. In fact the first was by far the best, I thought. I was
amazed when towards the end of the second she broke down, put her
head in her hands, and stopped the show. Then we had to go on again
ten minutes later from where we had broken off. All most difficult for
me. And I am not good at being interviewed as it is. Last week the
BBC interviewed me (both times about my Beckford book, out
tomorrow, and the exhibition) in the library in Lansdown Crescent. I
was made to walk into the room, holding the book, sit down at my
writing table and then be questioned. Felt foolish and was self-
conscious.

This girl asked me before we began our interview whether she
should address me as 'James'. As nicely as I could, I said my friends
seldom called me James; I thought Mr L.-M. might be more appropri-
ate in the circs. I was old enough to be her grandfather.

Why when one is tense and anxious does one's throat become tight
and dry? While waiting for the next session I was obliged to ask for
water.

Wednesday, 28th April

Sally Westminster said that Prince Andrew's charm was quite overwhelming. He is, she put it, overflowing with sex and mischief. I
could see that across the nave of Badminton church.

In *The Times* there is a letter from a correspondent who says he is
100 and that he was born when his father was 69. He asks if anyone
alive today can vouch that his father was born before 1807.

The Briggses* told us they were in Rome a fortnight ago for one
night. The boot of their car was filled with luggage and locked.
During luncheon a bag was stolen from the boot, the thief evidently
having a duplicate key. That was bad enough. They drove to where
they were dining, and considered whether they should empty the
boot, which they had re-locked. It would have entailed carrying
several suitcases up five floors, so they decided against. After dining,
they saw the boot of the car open. All the suitcases had been stolen.

---

* Michael Briggs, businessman, connoisseur and aesthete, of Midford Castle, Bath; his
wife Isabel Colegate, novelist.

Kenneth Clark opened the Beckford exhibition in Salisbury last Thursday. He made out that Beckford was a totally, irredeemably horrible man. Said that people loathed him, not because he was homosexual, but because he was odious. Now this just is not true. He was ostracized by society because of his homosexuality, and this treatment had a bad effect upon his character. Surprising that someone so intelligent as K. should adopt this attitude. He spoke very well, as he always does, and was funny. But he sacrificed sense to funniness, always a dangerous thing to do.

Today I was interviewed in Bristol by a man in Southampton. I spoke for nearly ten minutes, I guess, 'live', and acquitted myself fairly well.

Thursday, 29th April

Mrs Gulwell* says that so long as the blackthorn is in flower the cold east wind will continue. The wind has been exceedingly cold lately, and with the sun has made the ground as hard as a board. There has been no rain for weeks, and the water shortage is acute. This evening I walked down the Grittleton Ride, which runs straight as a die from the big house, not due south in continuation of the Long Ride from Worcester Lodge, but towards the south-east. It crosses two roads, the railway cutting and even the motorway. I walked as far as the motorway and could get no further, couldn't cross it. A lovely walk down this wide, straight avenue which spreads into hedged circles at intervals, and is bounded by dense coverts. Bluebells were out under the hedge facing west. I saw squirrels, rabbits and two foxes. One fox saw me. I stood stock still. It turned and watched me, and sloped quietly into the wood. I heard my first cuckoo this year. Glorious sound, stirring the spirit and evocative of eternal youth.

Hugh Grafton† has been made a KG. One is always amazed when people younger than oneself are awarded the highest honours and given the most responsible posts. There is Hugh, a dear man, no genius, made a Knight of the Garter for 'services to the amenities'. I introduced him to the amenity world not so long ago, it seems. I presented him to Oliver Esher‡ and intrigued that he should succeed

---

* Diana, Countess of Westmorland's maid.
† Hugh FitzRoy, 11th Duke of Grafton (b. 1919).
‡ Oliver Brett, 3rd Viscount Esher (1881–1963); prominent figure, as Chairman of the General Purposes Committee of the N.T., in J.L.-M's earlier diaries.

Oliver as chairman of the SPAB. It is most suitable that he should be given the Garter. But I would rather be given the Order of Merit any day, like K. Clark.

Saturday, 8th May

Henry, my great-nephew, told me that a contemporary of his was travelling in a London bus. A girl got in, so he politely offered her his seat. She slapped his face for his politeness, being Women's Lib. I asked Henry what he would have done in the circumstances. He said, 'Slapped back, to same tune'.

A. was complaining to old Mr Walker, our odd jobbing gardener, about the whiskers of the sweet peas, which have to be cut off if the plant is to flower. He said, 'Oh, I can't be bothered with them hurdy-gurdy things.'

On Tuesday a neighbour, Mrs Gough, and her husband, Bishop Gough, brought Lord and Lady Selkirk* to see the library. He is a Hamilton, younger brother of the last Duke, and a descendant of Beckford. Very nice man who knew little about his ancestor. He told me that the family always supposed Duchess Susan, Beckford's daughter, had been unhappy with her spouse. She was a good piano player. Selkirk's mother, who was not psychic, used to hear distinctly the sounds of a piano playing old-fashioned airs in the Beckford Gallery at Hamilton Place, where there was no piano. She was certain that it was Susan.

Yesterday I wanted to check a reference from Dante's *Inferno* and pulled from the shelf my copy of it, which was given to me by old Mr Allsebrook, the vicar of Wickhamford, in 1926. Evidently at the time I had not read it through from beginning to end, for I had to cut the last pages. It was a strange sensation, cutting pages of a book which had been given me exactly fifty years ago.

I have received the sweetest letter from Rupert Hart-Davis† commending *A. Voices*. He writes with such affection, reminding me of the Eton days when, as he says, I was the dreamy boy carrying a large

---

* George Douglas-Hamilton, 10th Earl of Selkirk (1906–94); 2nd son of 13th Duke of Hamilton and Brandon; succeeded to earldom of father under terms of special remainder, 1940; m. 1949 Audrey Drummond-Sale-Barker.
† Sir Rupert Hart-Davis (b. 1907; Kt 1967); publisher, editor, writer, and J.L.-M's oldest surviving schoolfriend.

volume of Shakespeare under an arm. He has become a recluse and never leaves the Yorkshire rectory where he has dug himself in.

In today's *Times* there is a letter from an old lady of 96 who has done better than the correspondent of 100 whose father was born in 1807. This lady's father was born in 1805, the year of Trafalgar, and her grandfather in 1759, in George II's reign, the year my Lees gt-gt-grandfather was born.

Monday, 24th May

[Jack] Rathbone and Norah Smallwood stayed last weekend. For some reason it was about the most enjoyable I remember. Norah an enchanting guest, very *à la page*, informative, and talkative. Indeed never stops talking. Yet is never boring. Is besides appreciative, attentive, sweet. Jack hit it off. We sat on the terrace or went for walks. More talk. Delicious food given us by A. I thought that satisfaction, happiness could not be eclipsed. Soon the tide must turn, disaster must follow.

Swallows' very late arrival. I have heard but one cuckoo, though A. says she has heard others. They must be disappearing from the English scene. This about the last indignity inflicted by man on nature, the greatest lyrical deprivation, hardly to be believed, only nothing today is unbelievable. On the other hand the hawthorn more in flower, more abundant than ever in anyone's memory. I would like at this moment to take a bus-load of highway authorities round this part of Glos. and show them that these blossoms come from the ordinary hedgerows which they are uprooting all over England.

Wednesday, 2nd June

Glyn Boyd Harte,* a friend of Colin McMordie, came down from London for the day to draw me. The result was rather startling, in garish coloured pencils; the eyes good and other features, except the mouth, which was not right. The most difficult feature always, and my mouth has no form and swims about like a jellyfish. The whole head a little too narrow. On the other hand, a goodish likeness. A work of art? He is to include it in his exhibition to be held in York

---

* Designer and illustrator (b. 1948).

(Festival) next week. A bubbling young man with whom it was a pleasure to be. We talked ceaselessly, yet with one in his twenties the gap
is a yawner. He belongs to the new although he is fascinated by our
oldie world. I liked him. Very plain.

Friday, 4th June

Having failed to telephone the Berkeleys last night I rang up this
evening at six to enquire after Patrick [Kinross] who had suddenly
gone to hospital two days ago. Babs* answered, and to my horror told
me Patrick had died at midday today. Lennox and Freda went to see
him in the morning. He recognized them, and smiled. At once they
realized he was in a very bad way indeed. They left for Aldeburgh.
The hospital tried to get in touch with them. Babs very upset, and
said Freda would be greatly distressed. I can hardly believe he has
gone. He was to have dined with me next Tuesday. He really was one
of my oldest and dearest friends. He has given more pleasure to more
people than most, on the minimum of money, for he has always been
poor. The irony is that at last the money he inherited from Violet
Trefusis had come to him; and his great book on the Ottoman Empire
had been accepted by an English (in addition to an American) publisher, and also accepted by the Turks for the Turkish *Times* in serial-
ization form for the largest sum they have ever paid a writer, Turkish
or foreign. All this anticipation must have given him pleasure. He was
a tiger for work, and would say he was only happy working. Luckily
he was pretty well able to work till the end, and I don't think he once
imagined that he would not continue to do so when he came out of
hospital.

   Only a few months ago I met him, one dismal, dank winter afternoon before Christmas, outside St Pancras Station. I said, 'What are
you doing, Patrick, here?' He said he had come from his doctor who
told him he had cancer of the intestine, but that it would be removed,
and there was nothing to fear. He was always optimistic. The dearest
old thing the world. He will be missed by hundreds of friends, for he
helped them all in one way or another.

---

* Bridget McKeever, nanny and valued friend of the Berkeleys.

Sunday, 6th June

While drawing me Glyn Boyd Harte said in the course of talk about art books, 'Now I am going to admit something which I fear will shock you.' 'I am sure nothing you have done could shock me,' I said politely. He proceeded to tell how he so coveted Mario Praz's book on conversation pieces that he stole one of two copies from, I think, his public library. He then went to the librarian weeks later and said he had unfortunately lost the copy which he had borrowed. The librarian said that did not much matter because there were two copies, but he must charge him for the loss, not the replacement. And fined him £1.50, which was about a tenth the value of the book. I *was* rather shocked. I gave a half-hearted laugh and said nothing. Now I, at twenty-one, stole a book from Lady Muir's house, but with the connivance of her daughter, Aunt Betty Moncrieffe.

Dining last night at the House I asked Mary Beaufort if I might bring Kenneth Rose,[*] who is writing a book about King George V and Queen Mary, to see her. She consented, then told me how well she always got on with George V, who terrified most people. He more or less adopted her when Princess Mary got married. He would bark at her and she barked back. He liked that. Dinners here are sticky, and the food is disgusting. The grey parrot in the Raglan room is a help after dinner, for he does say the most amusing things. Goodbye and good-morning, imitating the rather refined housekeeper Mrs Nettles's voice. He also imitates Master's[†] deep sighs on his return from hunting. The previous cockatoo they had used to fly to Didmarton and always returned, pursued by a host of furious wild birds. He alighted on the chimney-stack and roundly abused them so that they turned tail, and fled. Then he descended and walked into his cage. He used to follow the Bs to church and even peck at the church windows, so had to be locked in his cage during these absences. When Queen Mary was at Badminton and the bandmaster, with his stick, goose-stepped before his band, the cockatoo would perch on his toe. No movement would shake him off.

A. and I walked down Centre Walk looking for foxes after dinner. A still, mild evening. Saw one large dog fox slowly amble across the

---

[*] Biographer, and founder (1961) and writer of 'Albany' column in the *Sunday Telegraph* (b. 1924).
[†] The Duke of Beaufort.

ride. A cuckoo, thank the good God, was singing lustily in the distance. A posse of hunters out to grass gathered at the gate of a field on the Luckington Lane and allowed us to stroke and talk to them. Then an extraordinary scene took place. At first we thought two horses were fighting. They arched their necks so as to look like horses in a Géricault picture; they nibbled each other's necks. They stood on their hind legs facing one another like heraldic supporters. The mare pawed the ground violently. Then she deliberately turned her back on the other, all to no avail. Only then we realized it was a sex dance. Poor mare, she could evoke no response. A. had said we might ask Master what it meant. When we realized, we laughed. How embarrassed he would be. How ignorant he would think us to be.

Desmond [Shawe-Taylor] who stayed with us for three or four nights has the sweetest nature. He is one of the cleverest men I know, and one of the funniest. But he fusses to an extent which nearly drives his friends mad. He comes up to me and says he hopes he is not a nuisance, but could I find *The Times* newspaper of 21st May. 'Don't bother if it is not available, but if it is . . .' Then I can't find it, and he therefore goes into ecstasies of worry about the article he is writing and which cannot be completed because I have failed to produce the one newspaper he really needs desperately. He fusses about his travel, his packing, the hiring of a taxi, everything, everything. He is so restless that he makes me nervous to a degree unnatural in a man.

Monday, 7th June

I stayed the night with Eardley. He invited Eliot Hodgkin* and Mattei [Radev]. E. Hodgkin a sympathetic man, and a decent artist. Looks much younger than his 71 years. Is a mixture of Dadie Rylands† in his precise manner of speech and picking one up, and Bloggs Baldwin in his whimsical manner. His wife came in after dinner from attending a Christian Scientist meeting. She is French, or Swiss, and full of charm and common sense. Told us how she chased two burglars who had entered her house on the pretence of being electricity meter men. She ran after them, boarded a bus after them; no one helped; they got off, she followed, screaming 'Stop thief'. A man did stop them, she

---

* Artist and writer (1905–87); m. 1940 Maria Clara (Mimi) Henderson (née Franceschi).
† George Rylands, Shakespeare scholar and Fellow of King's College, Cambridge (b. 1902).

accosted them, found by lucky chance a policeman, they were arrested. She ought to have received a medal and been publicly commended, but wasn't. Retrieved some valuable watches they had stolen.

Tuesday, 8th June

Early for the dentist. Waited in St Peter's, Vere Street. Did not pray, but meditated. A venerable ancient man with grey beard was sitting on a bench by the door. Asked me for ten pence. I talked to him and said, 'Now you must tell me what this is all about. Why have you no pension?' Said he would not be 65 till next February. Was out of work. Could not afford the seventy pence necessary for one night's board in a hostel. Slept out. Came from Shropshire. Had been a countryman, farmworker. A sandwich-board man. I gave him fifty pence. He thanked me with dignity. I felt how lucky was I not to be in his position. But of course I ought to have asked why he did not receive the dole. Mr Plowman, dentist, to whom I related this tale, said, of course he had been in trouble or he would be receiving the dole.

Since Patrick was to have dined with me this evening, Feeble[*] and John Betj. had me to dine with them. J.B. very unhappy over P's death. Frank Tait[†] there too. Very sympathetic man. Slightly sardonic smile, yet compassionate, funny, very. He walks in an engagingly joyous manner as though at any moment he might levitate. J.B. recited in so far as he could remember it the ode on the Queen's Silver Jubilee which he has completed after much sweat and tears and submitted to the Sovereign. She is delighted with it, and so is the D. of Edinburgh, even over some complimentary and funny stanzas, not for publication, about HRH discreetly walking behind. The ode is very simple, and will most probably excite ridicule. J.B. aware of this. He is very pleased with a letter received from Ros Fisher about Patrick – the best friend of all our generation, she has written.

Patrick had beautiful, sensitive hands, with long elegant fingers. Why I so greatly lament his death is because he was one of those few to whom I could say *anything*. Vita was another. There are few such when one starts totting them up. Eardley, J.B. are others. Ros Lehmann too. Jamesey P.-H.[‡] was another.

---

[*] Lady Elizabeth Cavendish.
[†] Australian child psychologist (b. 1923).
[‡] James Pope-Hennessy (1916–74); writer; yr brother of Sir John Pope-Hennessy.

Friday, 11th June

Came back from London last night. Today went to Bath, and finished typing out another chapter of the novel. Heard my doorbell ring. Then saw a woman looking through the window. Threw up the window and asked her what she wanted. Thought she might be the new tenant of Jeremy Fry's flat. It was Jan Morris.* Went to the door. She asked if I would lunch today to meet Elspeth Hoare. Very kind indeed, but I explained I was just off to Patrick's funeral. Asked her to have a drink with me next Wednesday. Thought her face feminine, no signs of shaving, good feminine teeth, hair and bust. Did not inspect feet or hands. Next time. Nice of her, but I hate being dropped in on. The worst of my library is its being on the ground floor.

In the train wrote a review of the new Nat. Trust book on Treasures.† Train beautifully punctual. Walked to Paddington Green church. Well in time. Many society people assembling, some in tails and many in deep mourning. Spoke to a few, then sidled in; J.K.-B. there by chance and sat with me in the back of the church. Lovely church, splendidly restored by the late Erith.‡ A most moving, old-fashioned funeral, done with great style. Masses of country flowers. Large coffin in the sanctuary. I managed to avoid seeing it, only the candles on it. Had to turn away when it came out and by looking through the clear window beside, and biting my lip, managed to control myself. Deeply moved. Paddy§ read one lesson with his difficult voice. John Betjeman's address from the pulpit most beautiful. His excellent, calm, quiet, professional delivery. He likewise very moved. Said Patrick never got angry, yet could be caustic. Worked, worked. All tributes to him something to envy. I waited behind so as to avoid people but Natasha Spender came up to me, and was very sweet. Began by apologizing for being so cross with me. I apologized back. We held hands. And both said, Forgive, forgive. I was almost in tears by then. What could she have thought? Could not control my mouth which always gives me away. My weak feature, as Jamesey used to say. J.K.-B. most understanding. Accompanied me into the public park. We sat on a bench and I recovered myself. He

---

* FRSL; writer (until 1973 as James Morris) (b. 1926).
† *Treasures of the National Trust*, ed. Robin Fedden.
‡ Raymond Erith, RA, FRIBA (1904–73); architect in Classical Revival style.
§ Patrick Leigh Fermor (b. 1915); traveller and author.

then took me to Paddington, gave me tea in the hotel. Oh dear. Dreadful to watch J.B's painful ascent to and descent from the high pulpit. Osbert [Lancaster] there looking a million [years old]. Home for dinner.

Thursday, 17th June

Last weekend we stayed at Chatsworth. Andrew* only appeared for breakfast on Saturday, having returned the previous midnight. Then dashed off to deliver a speech at Burford, Oxon. We did not see him again. Other guests were Lady Cholmondeley† and the John Smiths.‡ I had always been bored stiff by the mention of Lady C's name. But she is delightful, and intelligent, and fascinating. *Très grande dame*, and sharp. Very friendly and pressed A. and me to stay at Houghton in August.

Praised *A. Voices*, and told me that Artur Rubinstein§ said I must publish a second volume. Have just heard from Norah Smallwood that Chatto's will publish vol. 2 in September next year. Quite right not to do so before then.

Debo says that the fate of Chatsworth hangs on a thread. Although their numbers are vastly increasing, the maintenance costs are £100,000 a year, exclusive of their other houses and personal expenses. They have three night watchmen, and three private telephonists, and I should imagine no staff in England is treated more generously.

Lady Cholmondeley's voice is so distinctive that I find myself talking like her for three days after leaving Chatsworth. Has that Edwardian preciseness and upper-class assurance. Delivery strangulated. No flush of sentimentality.

Billy Henderson¶ has been painting [a picture of] the library in number 19 [Lansdown Crescent] all this week, with me sitting on the sofa. From time to time he calls me from my typewriter and makes

---

* Duke of Devonshire.

† Sybil (1894–1989), dau. of Sir Edward Sassoon; m. 1913 George Cholmondeley, later 5th Marquess.

‡ Sir John Smith (b. 1923; Kt 1988); his wife, Christian Carnegy; he was founder of the Landmark Trust.

§ Pianist (1888–1982).

¶ Painter (1903–93); ADC to Lord Linlithgow when Viceroy of India and stayed on as Comptroller under Lord Wavell until 1946.

me read, cross-legged. Likeness already good, but my long legs won't come right. Room going to be v. good, in deep tones. B.H. a most sympathetic man whom I already know as well as anyone, so many friends in common. He told me while we walked up the hill after lunching that he was seduced by a master at his private school, when he was eight, during the Great War. Made him go to bed, sheets a morass, poor little boy bewildered and hating it. Had no father, and could not talk to his mother. A year went by before the affair came out. Whole experience so put him off sex that he had none till he was twenty-five.

Yesterday Jan Morris came for a drink. Billy there when she arrived. She is convincing as a female. Did I not know her story I would certainly take her for a woman. But she is tall, and fairly largely built. Pretty face, rather prominent chin. Convincing brown hair, streaked with grey. Good clear teeth. Good legs. Failed to notice hands. Has a giggly manner, rather coy. First thing I noticed when she stood talking to me in the small lobby of the flat was a slight feminine body smell. Billy left and I talked with her for half an hour. Feeling her way, not absolutely easy. Likeable, and very clever

Jan Morris said to Billy Henderson, who talked to her about successful and unsuccessful people in the world's eyes, 'I am all out for winners.' I asked if she was busy writing. She said she was finishing her trilogy on the British Empire.* After that she was compiling for the Oxford Press an 'Oxford Book of Quotations' on Oxford. Will be living in Oxford for this work, neglecting Bath. Wishes Bath wasn't so beautiful because she dislikes its provincial society.

I have finished typing out my novel and am giving it to A. to read.

Thursday, 24th June

When I went to a meeting of the Architectural Panel at Fenton House the other day, we inspected different methods of pointing old walls. Several specimens had been applied by an old mason to explain how the work should and should not be done. There was Mrs Dance. I always thought she disliked me, but she greeted me with such affection, calling me by my Christian name, that I

---

* *Pax Britannica* (1968); *Heaven's Command* (1973); *Farewell the Trumpets* (1978).

instantly responded with 'Monica', and when we parted embraced her warmly. We were both delighted with each other. Strange world!

On Sunday afternoon (20th) A. and I motored to stay the night with Mickey Renshaw* at Leeds Castle. The owner Lady Baillie† died two years ago and left it in trust to be kept exactly as it was – apart from some extremely valuable furniture, which had to be sold to augment the endowment, such as the duc de Choiseul's Carlton House writing-table. Castle is to be used for medical conferences, Anglo-American. Mickey is not one of the trustees but has been co-opted as the man of taste, he having been an intimate friend of Lady Baillie. The chairman Lord Geoffrey-Lloyd‡ was present and acted host. We were received by the family butler and were given tea, Mickey and G.-L. being out for a walk. House redolent of servants and gardeners. We stayed in a suite of magnificent rooms. Whole inside rather 1920 Hollywood style, vastly high bedrooms and tester beds, bathrooms marbled walls – not my taste, but some lovely contents, Meissen birds, a Tiepolo picture and one splendid room brought from Thorpe Hall. We were given an excellent dinner, waited on by the butler. The public see the Gloriette which is a detached part of the castle, furnished with rare medieval oak furniture and tapestries, stiff and rather boring. The 1820 wing kept for the occasional conference guests and, it seems, the trustees who go whenever they like, give orders and live in luxury and ease. A kind of All Souls élitist arrangement of which I entirely approve. Endowment apparently £2 million.

From Leeds, which outside is one of the most romantic and lovely castles I have ever seen, wide moat on which black swans drift, ragstone walls stretching straight from water, basin of hills, woods, gardens, bird sanctuary, romance – we went to Sissinghurst to stay with Nigel§ for two nights. Sissinghurst looking superb. A., who is critical, could find nothing to carp at. She thought the garden as good

---

* On staff of *The Times*; had a house in Cyprus.
† Wife of Sir Adrian Baillie, 6th Bt (1898–1947).
‡ Conservative politician (b. 1902; cr. Life Peer, 1974); Chairman, Leeds Castle Foundation.
§ Nigel Nicolson (b. 1917); yr son of Hon. (later Sir) Harold Nicolson and Hon. Vita Sackville-West; writer.

as when Vita left it. All due to the pair of ladies, gardeners, who still remain, having been taught all they know by Vita.*

Conditions very different from Leeds; almost spartan and very oaksy, but nice. Nigel's daughter Juliet staying. Aged 29, fine countenance, splendid large eyes, largish nose like Nigel's, good teeth, milky skin, whole impression very startling, slim figure like Vita's and the same dignified way of holding herself and walking, almost same articulate manner of speaking. Sweet to us, and very intelligent indeed. Great credit to Nigel.

Object of visit was for me to read papers and references to Harold for my *DNB* entry on him. Nigel v. kindly prepared a paper of notes for me, at the end of which, to my amazement, he wrote, 'Why, dear Jim, do you not write Harold's biography?' Amazement again; the very idea that I could possibly do such a thing! First reaction, No, no, no, unworthy, totally incapable, etc. Second was, well, perhaps I could. I am now in a state of indecision, perplexity and wonder. Must consult Raymond [Mortimer] and Norah S[mallwood]. But the thing truly is, could I possibly? I know nothing about diplomacy and politics. And do I find dear Harold whom I loved and revered quite my sort of subject? I like romantic figures, Beckford, Byron, and H. was never this. Vita was. Oh Lord!

Saturday, 26th June

I telephoned Raymond last night. He is going to dine with me on 13th. He is so affectionate that my heart warms to him. I am also seeing Norah. One of my doubts is this. A book on Harold would take me three years; The Squires another three years. Have I the time, the life, or rather the *mens compos* span in which to write both, even one? At my age this is a serious consideration. Besides, I have got novel-writing in my system. A. thinks my novel full of promise, the idea original, the composition better than anything I have written.

Pondering over Nigel's character. What an odd man he is. Likewise affectionate, fair, honourable, just, dutiful, extremely hard-working, a first-class writer, an exemplary parent, an aesthete, exceedingly clever, yet modest. At the same time, is he quite human? He speaks didactically, in a precise, academic manner. He is a cold man who wants to be

* Pamela Schwerdt and Sibille Kreutzberger, who went to Sissinghurst as head gardeners in 1959.

warm, and cannot be. He has humour, and understanding, being totally without prejudices. Discusses his parents' love lives as though they were strangers.

Wednesday, 30th June

Kenneth Rose having expressed a wish to meet Mary Beaufort to put to her questions about King George V and Queen Mary, on whom he is writing a book, came for the weekend. A grateful, appreciative and kind guest. We dined at the House, always an awkward proceeding. Master, wearing a blue pullover, greeted us with the words, 'I had no idea you were coming.' Present old Mrs Durant with whom I have a semi-historical flirtation, which is trying. Conversation sticky all round, though A. got on well with him [the Duke]. He said he wanted to pay us a visit. So A. said, What would you like? He replied, 'I would like to dine.' So she wrote a letter to M.B., quite properly, thinking she would refuse and he would accept, for next Thursday week; whereupon within minutes she telephoned to say she would come, but Master couldn't. We query whether in fact she ever told him. It is possible that he would like to come alone, but we cannot ask him to do so, for we don't know him or her well enough. Kenneth R. who is sensitive to situations remarked that he was short with her, and seemed irritated. We ate out of doors beside the cedar tree.

Brother Dick and Elaine stayed Mon. and Tues. nights. They were good and went out all day Tuesday. Dick as sweet as ever. She older. Dears though they are, we have nothing to talk about, except family matters. They had not seen this house before. Yet not one word of praise, or dispraise, not any notice taken of what we have done, no observations, no questions. I said to Elaine, 'You must see my bedroom.' She walked in, gave a quick look and walked out without a word. We suppose it is because they are frightened of saying the wrong thing that they say nothing. They do not know. That is the sad thing. Simon [Lees-Milne] came to dinner on their last evening. Same with him. Total non-registers. What communication can there be with such people? Total lack of interest makes for total dullness.

They left before me for Bath and must have halted for petrol on the way. For I who left for Bath five minutes later caught up with them, and passed them on the road. I saw a funny little old lady, so short her head was just visible above the passenger seat, beside Dick crouched forward, earnestly concentrating on the road in the way old people do. They looked so pathetic that as I passed them and waved – for they had not seen me – I could have cried.

Wednesday, 7th July

Stayed night of 5th with Eardley [Knollys]. Heat wave continuing. Never has there been a longer one. Whole country parched, and trees dying, beside elms which have been wiped out by this year's heat. Found E. naked but for a pair of long blue shorts, his white skin, his smarmed hair (for he had just had a bath), flabby muscles, pendulous breasts, looking like Picasso aged 90. I must have expressed my nausea by my looks. But how can aesthetic persons bear to be seen in this condition at the age of 74 even by their intimates? He advised me against the Harold book on the whole. Said I might not understand or be interested enough in the diplomacy periods, worse than the political ones, for I would have to discover what was the Persian government's attitude to the Soviet encroachments on the district of Izbah in May, 1924. Much in this. Had a long talk with Norah Smallwood, who was most interested and happens to be staying with Nigel next week and will discuss with him. She surprised me by saying she wondered if the present generation of readers had heard of Harold, and she is going to sound bookshops. This is the strangest reason for doubts. I still don't know, and await discussion with Raymond. Norah had been staying with Anthony Wagner* who applauded The Squires. Said I was just the person for it, but must decide what centuries to deal with; he would help me. As Garter King of Arms no one could be better. I fear the latter is to be my book.

Greatly distressed to read in this morning's *Times* death announced of Bloggs Baldwin. He was the sweetest of men I have known. I met him not very many times in all, but I felt from the first that I knew him intimately. We clicked, rather like William Plomer.† Enchanting dry sense of the ludicrous. Oh I mourn him!

Yesterday in London Freda [Berkeley] took me to Patrick [Kinross]'s house see if there was anything I would prefer to the little Etruscan vase under glass dome. I said No. That is what I remember each time I sat in the big armchair facing Patrick. It was on my left. House dread-

---

* Sir Anthony Wagner, KCVO 1961; KCB 1978 (1908–95); Garter Principal King of Arms since 1961.
† Writer, poet, and editor of the Kilvert Diaries (1903–73).

fully full of 'coffee cups'. His old writing-chair worn down by his weight, pens and writer's equipment, reference books, window wall covered with photographs pasted one next the other of his closest friends taken in their heyday, and looking their most beautiful.

Sitting in a bus which stopped in Piccadilly I watched from the top deck Peter Quennell descend. He was dressed in an immaculate dark blue suit, and a black Homburg hat, wide in the brim. I was on my way to luncheon in Brooks's. My bus kept stopping at lights: I watched for five minutes Peter walk towards me along the pavement. The heat was stifling. His face was drawn and he was encapsulated in that way one is in great heat. Yet I was much impressed by his handsome appearance, and his distinction, for he never wavered. How he could wear that hat I don't know. Upright, looking neither to left or right, he glided. At the corner of St James's Street he turned down, to White's of course, his funny, earnest, satanic, wicked face momentarily at rest and full of expectation.

Friday, 9th July

Have had Billy Henderson's painting of my library photographed, and sent it to Kenneth Rose, who is to use it as an introductory to his 'Albany' paragraph about my Beckford book. He telephoned to say he would publish the photograph slap across the two paragraphs of 'Albany'. That ought to be a help to the sale of the book. At Heywood's shop they say it is selling well.

Tony Mitchell motored me in the comparative cool of the evening to Coughton for my advice how to treat the wings on either side of the gatehouse. The dreary Roman cement* put on in the early nineteenth cent. has to be stripped; sample colours had been dabbed in patches for us. I thought the old brickwork underneath so nice that it should be retained, and no replacement of cement. Isabel [Throckmorton]† took me aside full of complaints and grumbles against the N.T. Two architects present. But she and Robert so jubilant over my decision, and the two architects conciliatory also, that I felt for once I had achieved something.

---

* Cement with added lime; supposed to be of a good colour, and particularly strong and weatherproof.
† Lady Isabel Manners, dau. of 9th Duke of Rutland, m. (2nd) 1953 Sir Robert Throckmorton, 11th Bt (1908–89), of Coughton Court, Alcester, Warwickshire.

Saturday, 10th July

Nick Robinson and his charming friend Nick Crawley lunched. They motored me to Dyrham, where I took them round. Think they were pleased. Both adorable, the other boy even easier than my Nick.

Monday, 12th July

Dear Raymond [Mortimer] dined with me at Brooks's. The heat appalling. He ate v. little, galantine cold and half a melon, I the same, plus one bottle of Pouilly Fuissé, and the bill just under £10. Upstairs in the subscription room we sat on a sofa under the *Dilettante* Reynolds. I cracked my head against the underframe and for a second or two believed I had broken my skull. R. said he had never heard such a noise as I made. I then consulted him about Harold. Like most old people, and as Eardley said, like Raymond always, he hardly listened to what I had to say, and instead talked, most interestingly, about Harold and Vita (her bad early novels, novelettish), and when I finally interposed, 'But dear R., what I want is an honest opinion whether you think I am capable of writing this biography?' the quick reply was, 'Yes', and on he went. The truth is that no person can give one advice. One must always make up one's own mind.

Tuesday, 13th July

At the Mutual Housing Association committee this morning the fatuity of my remaining on the committee decided me. I told Jack [Rathbone] at luncheon after that I was definitely going to resign. He did not oppose.

Then took train from Liverpool Steet to Bishop's Stortford, where met by nice Julian Gibbs,* who motored me to Mrs Crittall's house, New Farm, Great Easton. I went full of prejudices against this house built in 1934. But was fascinated, greatly to my surprise. Could not be objective because of the overwhelming charm of old Mrs Crittall, the widow. To my surprise Crittall, the man who invented those ghastly windows which have ruined the majority of old cottages the world over, must have been a craftsman of distinction. *All* the furniture in the house was designed by him, and the joiner was called Beckwith.

---

* N.T. regional representative.

Of good quality and design, traditional yet original. I would have been delighted to own nearly all of it. Walls covered with water-colours by him (delicate views), his friends Sir George Clausen, Steer, Sims, and others. What struck me was the walls themselves, hung with Chinese rice paper bought in China by Mr C. in the 1930s. Because I admired these Mrs C. took me into the studio and showed me rolls of them in mint condition. Some of silver background, the silver untarnished, patterns driving from the sixteenth century, the most beautiful imaginable, of birds and insects. I raved. The old lady, with whom I clicked, wanted to give me some, said she would let me have enough to paper a room. I demurred of course, especially in front of young Julian, who looked astonished at the sudden liaison taking place before his eyes. We parted bosom friends. Not sure how important architecturally the house is, but it would be a sin for all these objects to be dispersed.

Wednesday, 14th July

Norah telephoned from Chatto's. To my intense joy is enchanted with my novel, subject to one or two suggestions. Thinks last chapter needs amplifying. Was flattering about style, felicity of word use. I in seventh heaven. Also she talked to Nigel about Harold book. Emphasises that Nigel particularly wants diplomatic and parliamentary aspects dealt with fully. Sets much store by these aspects. I incline towards this venture now, the challenge. Will depend, must depend on talk with Nigel when he lunches with us next week.

Sunday, 18th July

Richard Shone* told a story illustrating Duncan Grant's *naïveté*. When traffic lights were first introduced they used to have on the red light the word 'Stop', and on the green, 'Go'. A friend who was a passenger in Duncan's car told Richard that when Duncan saw the green light and the word 'Go', he turned the car round and drove away.

Yesterday afternoon we were sitting in the garden after luncheon. The day was calm and balmy. True, there was a faint breeze. Suddenly shreds of straw fell on the roof, on the terrace, on the lawn. We looked up. There far away, a thousand feet above us against the blue sky, was

---

* Art historian; author of *Bloomsbury Portraits* (1976); now (1998) Editor of *Burlington Magazine*.

a drifting cloud of golden fragments. I have never experienced such a thing before. A whirlwind must have picked up the straw from some distant stack.

Today Sally W. brought Peter Coats* to luncheon. Peter, as ever, strictly polite and friendly towards me, but guardedly I sensed. Talked a lot about his forthcoming book of memoirs, and in telling us one silly story about Christabel Aberconway† in her cups, said, 'Of course I didn't mention that she was drunk. There are things which one must omit in autobiographies.' This was not lost on me. I cannot take Peter seriously. Society flibbertigibbet, forever quoting what the King of Italy said to him: 'Peter,' he said, 'what extravaganza are you doing?' etc. Yet however absurd, warm-hearted.

We dined with X. Ghastly evening. Other guests very off and pretentious. As we walked through his drawing-room door into the garden I saw and at once took against these people. It is the dog's instinctive hostility towards beings from an alien world. But one ought after 68 years to have learnt not to let these primitive emotions prevail.

Yesterday, in Bath, walking to the garage along the Bristol Road, I looked into the window of a junk shop. Saw and bought two small Lalique vases, rather suitable for tiny flowers. Having bought them looked at a miniature engraving. Recognized the face, that of Old Pretender. Looked at the back. Written by early nineteenth-century hand an explanation that the lock of hair was the Young Pretender's derived from Flora Macdonald. I bought it. Mistake about the engraving, however. Nevertheless I believe the lock of faded, grey hair to be Prince Charlie's. It couldn't be a fake, I think.

Why, when I receive and open a letter which I am exceptionally pleased to have, do I not read it there and then, but put it aside to read at leisure, at relish, and often leave aside for several days, when possibly it requires urgent attention? It is like the slice of cake with the icing sugar which I leave till last, and sometimes put aside on a plate, and forget to eat at all. How idiotic one's habits are. They must have some unconscious origin.

The few sad little strands of hair tied in a tiny bow must be part of

---

* Of the famous Paisley cotton family of J.P. Coats; son of 1st Baron Glentanar; an acquaintance of J.L.-M. since childhood; garden designer and horticultural writer (1910–90).
† Christabel, Lady Aberconway, widow of 2nd Baron (who d. 1953), of Bodnant, North Wales.

the tress which Flora cut off his head which he laid in her lap just before they parted in 1745. How romantic, how touching this is.

Tuesday, 20th July

Nigel and co-editor Jo Trautman lunched. N. rather engaging in telling us how he now regrets having asked Edna O'Brien to write Vita's life, since she does not intend to refer to Vita's writing. We said, 'We daresay you feel the same about J.L.-M.' N. laughed and said Ben[*] was delighted at the idea. V. sweet of Ben. Nigel again insistent that Harold's diplomacy and politics must be dealt with fully. I concur absolutely. Left it that I would have a go, and if at end of six months I found the task beyond me, would throw in my hand. In October I shall visit Sissinghurst and N. will let me take away loads of papers. The quantity is daunting, as is the whole project. I gave N. my draft of the *DNB* contribution on Harold for him to read and comment upon. Perhaps he will find it so bad that he will want to give me the sack at once.

Saturday, 24th July

Lunched with Constantia Arnold[†] at Swerford. Old rectory – just Cotswolds – of glowing orange stone, and good garden with hill in foreground sweeping upwards like a cup edge. Garden so dreadfully parched that the grass burnt white like Prince Charlie's hair. I have never, never seen the effects of drought so disastrous as now. The rain refuses to fall. Situation really alarming. As for the elms, they are all dead, and Warwickshire, formerly so luxuriantly wooded, is now a desert, with gaunt, leafless limbs. Every tree in this county seems to be an elm.

I often wonder how it is that certain figures in history are to me so vivid in personality when I know so little about their lives and deeds. For instance, I have in my mind a clear picture of what A.J. Balfour was like, the lethargic, easy-going, intellectual aristocrat, apparently weak though inwardly steely, but a man of honour, literary, quoting the Classics, a woman's lover platonically, and probably sexless. Yet I know nothing about his politics beyond his conservativeness, nothing

---

[*] Elder brother of Nigel Nicolson.
[†] Constantia Fenwick, wife of Ralph Arnold, publisher and biographer; she d. 1993.

of what measures he was responsible for in Parliament, no details of his life's action in fact. A picture forms nevertheless, willy-nilly. Perhaps totally erroneous.

Monday, 26th July

Last night after dinner we walked down Centre Walk in the twilight, looking for and seeing several foxes. How wary, canny they are. They are not the least disturbed or made anxious by horses and cows. But by humans, rightly, yes. They hear the footfall, but do not seem to notice one so long as one remains stock still. As we returned, inhaling the sweet smell of hay, I said to A., 'How did we ever consider living in London? The very idea strikes me as totally wrong, almost wicked.' She agreed. We both love this place. A. said, 'If I should die first, I really believe you would be happier living here than in Bath.' I said, 'Yes, Bath would depress me.' I hope that she will live on here after me, for I am sure to die first. The Somersets will look after her I feel sure. They are so sweet to us, and most Sunday mornings David walks in for a drink and chat. Beloved people.

Object of our luncheon with Constantia was to meet the Alfred Bakers,[*] after thirty years. She now an old lady, faded, but with the same beautiful eyes. V. sensitive, v. talkative, remembers everything I have forgotten about K. Kennet.[†] Disliked Lord K., was rather frightened of K. because she did not care for females. Said K. always surrounded by the most beautiful young men, like me. I laughed. I find it a problem picking up long-dropped threads.

Thursday, 29th July

Gerald, Peggy Bird's husband, working here last night, said that whenever you hear the train roaring through Badminton station, that's an infallible sign that it is going to rain.

On Tuesday Norah lunched with me at the Lagonda, Charing Cross Road. Quite an inexpensive luncheon, I think we had veal and broccoli, a cream ice each, one glass of white wine each, coffee. Bill

---

[*] Son of the architect Sir Herbert Baker (1862–1946); his wife Daphne; of Owletts, Cobham, Kent.
[†] Kathleen Bruce (1878–1947), widow of Captain Falcon Scott, m. Edward Young, 1st Baron Kennet of the Dene.

£5.50 without tip. Given away. Discussed the novel. Chatto's suggest
a few improvements and excisions. Are otherwise pleased. Ian Parsons
still working on the diaries. Norah only fairly likes my title,
Prophesying Peace. I said how difficult publishers are over titles. They
never like the author's choice. Discussed the Harold book. They are
mad keen. I have now heard from Nigel, approving of my *DNB* piece
about Harold, which I have sent off. It is double the length asked for.
Norah in a great state over a van driver whom the firm dismissed for
drunkenness and total inefficiency six months ago. Chatto's had to go
to court. Several directors obliged to present themselves as witnesses.
Infinite time wasted. Their costs, of counsel's opinion, solicitors' fees,
etc., £500. They won their case. The van driver pays no costs, and is
now living happily on the dole. Norah has a secretary who is incom-
petent and whom she would like to dismiss. Can't, unless she declares
the post redundant, which it isn't. Therefore she is obliged to keep an
inefficient secretary whom she dislikes, for ever. Such is the power of
the unions. Chatto's directors are not obliged to belong to a union.
Yet the unions send officials round to interview all the staff, bringing
every influence to bear upon the directors to join, threats included.

Went to Martha Graham's ballet. Impressed rather than pleased.
Acrobatics and drill beyond criticism. Effect boring on the whole.
J.K.-B. most wise about Harold. Says I must decide what aspect I want
to get across. Disagrees with me when I say H. not a romantic person.
Thinks he is romantic in that he abandoned his diplomatic career for
Vita, love, and entered politics out of idealism. Said too I must decide
which biography of recent years to model mine on. James [Pope-
Hennessy]'s *Monckton Milnes* for instance? Thinks something
lacking in my Beckford. Not dull, not clumsily written, flows, yet
lacks substance. Oh well!

A. has received a letter from Rosamond [Lehmann] who says
Isherwood* is delighted with *A. Voices* and is going to write and tell
me so. Disloyalty on his part to Spender, I say. But I am pleased.

Thursday, 5th August

On Sunday we motored to Aldworth to lunch with Anne and Osbert
Lancaster. I was rather shocked by how old O. has become; he is two
days older than I am. Anne told A. she is worn out, working at a book

---

* Christopher Isherwood (1904–86); novelist.

against time and having to look after Osbert who cannot do a thing for himself. Now he can't be relied on even to open a bottle of wine. Is forgetful – told me the same story twice of his grandfather commissioning Alfred Waterhouse to design the Prudential building in Holborn. Yet he is still full of fun and tells stories about his friends with the same relish and mischief. Took us across the road from their cottage to show us the medieval tombs of the de la Beche family in Aldworth church. Wonderful they must have been before being decapitated and disfigured by Cromwell's gangs. But too obliterated to excite me much. One later figure with folds in the dress almost Baroque. They took us to tea with the Iliffes at Basildon.[*] Wonderful how the Iliffes have saved this great house. I was struck anew by the superb quality of the plasterwork. House has been well decorated on the whole, though I question the propriety of so much gold in the dining room, done by the master, Fowler; the stair hall beautifully chaste in the Horace Walpole sense. This apparently Lady Iliffe's work. Lovely yellow stone of which the house built; presumably from the Cotswold quarries and brought down the Thames. Even the Iliffes are experiencing difficulty in living in this vast place. Hope against hope it may come to the Nat. Trust,[†] with whom I am cross for turning down Beckford's Tower. The Iliffes have made for their winter use a perfect little dwelling out of the east pavilion, a complete house of its own.

Friday, 6th August

A. gave me a gold cross for the gold chain round my neck. She had the date engraved. I received letters from Dick in Cyprus, and Audrey. No one else knows my birthday, thank God. A. and I motored to Euston near Thetford for the weekend. A terrible drive across parched country. Every elm dead, grass like parchment, and the bloody farmers in burning stubble have destroyed miles of hedgerows and even mature oak and ash trees. It is despairing.

The Brooks Richards[‡] staying. He now Ambassador in Athens.

---

[*] Edward Iliffe, 2nd Baron, and his wife Renée Merandon du Plessis; of Basildon Park, Reading, Berkshire.

[†] It has.

[‡] Sir (Francis) Brooks Richards, KCMG 1976; HM Ambassador to Greece, 1974–8; his wife Hazel Price Williams.

Nice people. I questioned him about Mount Athos, and he said many formalities had to be gone through which he as Ambassador was prepared to undertake for me. Might accompany me. Do I wish to travel intimately with someone I barely know and might not find sympathetic? Ditto the other way round? I wd like to go with Derek Hill.

Hugh has grown portly. Fortune* still more handsome than formerly. The eldest boy, James, stays in the Kent temple for weekends. A stick in manner, if not in physique exactly. He is immensely tall, bending over at the top like a question mark or a bishop's crozier. Could get no word out of him. Were taken to a house I have wished to see for many years, namely Giffords Hall, Wickhambrook. Over-restored half-timbering, moated, but great room upstairs with remarkable wooden ceiling such as seldom seen outside churches of East Anglia.

We went to Houghton on Sunday. Lady Cholmondeley sitting at the receipt of custom. On seeing us, left it and accompanied us round the state rooms, explaining. This is always very tiring. One has to attend to hosts, conjure up the expected reply, intelligent observation, and be generally polite, the most exacting of activities. She very attentive to me, and when we left took my arm and held my hand. This grand, once terrifying lady! I melted to her.

On our return home we lunched with Sachie and Georgia.† Both rather older, he a good colour, but a little bent. She not so good. I enjoyed being with them for two hours more than the rest of the expedition. I simply adore Sachie, one of the most lovable of men, like J.B., like Bloggs, like Wm Plomer. I fear though that Sachie is spent. He says defensively that he no longer can be bothered with publishers, and has his poems privately printed. Gave me a heap to take away.

Friday, 13th August

Poor A's birthday, and I elect to go to London for the day to see Dr Allison. My left testicle has become enlarged. The Vicar's son in this parish has had his left testicle removed. It is cancerous. I fancied that I too had the beginnings of slight pains in the groin. Fancied I had

---

* Duchess of Grafton; Mistress of the Robes to HM The Queen since 1967.
† Sir Sacheverell Sitwell, 6th Bt (1897–1988); m. 1925 Georgia Doble (d. 1980).

cancer. Was sure of it. Allison took a strong torch, put it below the
scrotum, made me look, ugh I said, and lo, no growth, thank the Lord,
but a duct filled with water. He says unless it gets larger still, it is best
to leave it alone. Nothing whatever to worry about.

I was motored up by Tom Parr[*] and Fulco[†] in their fast Mercedes.
Talked all the way. Too sophisticated for me, too rich, manservant,
Spanish chauffeur, yet very kind to me who has none of these things
and does not know the right set. I like splendour, but not luxury. This
is my cry.

Had nothing else to do in London apart from the London Library,
and so bussed back to Paddington. Missed train by an eye-whisker.
With time to spare, had a strange encounter in a bookshop, the sort
one should not enter. Door locked behind me. Smiling attendant, not
sinister, but personable with enormous charm. How can such a thing
be? How can someone engaged in this disgusting trade be so – highbrow and, dare I say it – conventional, a young academic? Talked
about Existentialism beyond my depth, then about the different types
– mostly pathetic – of his regular customers. I bought a frightfully
funny book. We parted with expressions of mutual esteem and hopes
of meeting again. I walked off to Warwick Avenue, feeling oddly
edified. Had a cup of tea with Freda [Berkeley] and returned to
Chippenham station where I was met by darling A. We dined with
the Barlows.[‡] Peter Coats there. Oh I can't take him seriously, I simply
can't.

Saturday, 14th August

David and Caroline [Somerset] dined here, alone. He was dressed in
a pair of white linen trousers, always narrow towards the ankles, a
snow-white shirt with wide collar open at the neck, bronze-browned
by the sun, a blue velvet jacket; always so immaculate, simple yet
splendidly dressed. Talk of funerals. When the last Badminton agent,
by name Rooke, died, he and Master attended the obsequies. The
small church was filled with a disagreeable stench. Master who is a
simple man whispered to David, 'I think there must be a dead rat

---

[*] Interior designer; partner in Colefax & Fowler (b. 1930).
[†] Fulco Santostefano della Cerda, Duke of Verdura (1898–1978); designer of fashionable
jewellery.
[‡] Basil and Gerda Barlow, of Stancombe Park, Gloucestershire.

somewhere.' David whispered back, 'No, I think it is a dead rook.' Master gave a guffaw, and suddenly remembering the occasion, pulled himself together and frowned back at David. David does not seem to know which of Master's titles will not come to him. He said, 'I know the Botetourt one [of 1305] won't.' I said, 'Horatia Durant told me the Herbert of Raglan one [of 1461] won't either.' 'Oh, bother!' said David. 'Anyway I think Glamorgan must. I like Glamorgan.' Caroline has a fine sense of what should not be done. It transpired in conversation the other day that the Beauforts have removed two figures of Prudence and Justice from the Grinling Gibbons monument to the 1st Duke, and propose to sell them at Sotheby's. I was appalled, at once consulted my David Green on Gibbons and found that these figures were specially designed to flank this tomb, by the sculptor. I had always thought this tomb rather gaunt and stiff, without realising that these Baroque appendages had been there in the first place. Begged the Somersets to stop the sale, which would be tragic and injurious to the Bs when known in the art world, which it undoubtedly would be. Caroline realizes that it would be an act of philistinism and must be stopped. She does not however relish having to tell Master so. The Bs of course are totally without aesthetic sense. I went with Horatia Durant into his room after luncheon on Wednesday. Huge portraits of nineteenth-century Beauforts on horseback with hounds, all chairs and sofas draped with scruffy blankets for the dogs, foxes' brushes mounted, and plastic models of foxes littered around.

In the London Library half-way up the stairs is a large photograph of Harold [Nicolson] which looks me straight in the eyes with a quizzical expression. I interpret it as reproachful and questioning, benevolent as always but expressing doubt as to whether I am capable of writing his Life.

I have now completed a chapter on the Powderham Castle scandal,* a long review of Philippe Jullian's book about Violet Trefusis, a chapter for the Future of Churches book, refurbished my novel, which I now think atrocious and adolescent, and have to cut down my diaries by 20,000 words, which appals me. Must complete these labours before we go abroad in September.

---

* This involved William Beckford.

Saturday, 28th August

The Vicar and his wife and son, Graeme, aged 23, who has developed incurable cancer, dined last night. A charming boy, with good manners and the right approach to life. Vicar told A. who met him shopping earlier in the day that he had seen the boy's specialist. His verdict was that he is riddled, in his chest, neck and all over his body; and there is no hope. His girl-friend, a sweet and pretty child, called after dinner. She is giving up her job in London to stay in the Vicarage in order to take Graeme to Bristol for his daily treatments and comfort him. What nobility and touching affection.

Mrs Gibson told me that Michael, the other son, has given up his interim job selling petrol on the motorway at nights (to supplement an exiguous income from designing book jackets). He was horrified by the fiddling that goes on between lorry drivers and the girls who take the money for petrol vouchers. Michael said the corruption is rife, and universal. In sending his notice to the firm concerned he pointed out what was going on. Reply he received was that the company was well aware of it, but powerless to take action. In other words, if they made a stand, all the workers would walk out on sympathy strike. This is the common depth which this country has plumbed.

In my whole life I have never experienced a drought such as the one we are enduring. Not a drop of rain for over two months, and that drop lasted half an hour. We have not had a proper day's rain since March. Grass burnt to palest straw, trees dying and stubble-burning reducing the hedgerows to cinders. Here we have fixed up a large plastic tub outside my bathroom into which all the water for washing ourselves, and the china, goes. Each evening we distribute this waste water in cans round the garden. There is no sign of the drought breaking. We wonder if it will ever rain again, if the drought is caused by man's interference with the earth's cycle, by atmospheric pollution, in short.

Sunday, 29th August

We lunched with Ian McCallum at Claverton to meet the American Ambassador, Mrs Armstrong, and her husband. A difficult position being Prince Consort. This one was a distinguished man. She very personable, attractive, well dressed, with that affability which is assumed but is no less acceptable thereby. Came in clutching a tussie-mussie presented to her by one of the guides, and gushing over it, and the beauty of everything she had seen. Quite right too. I asked my neighbour at luncheon, a nice, sharp American lady, what Mr Armstrong did all day in the Embassy. 'Counts his money,' came the retort.

This evening I rang up Moor Wood, and asked after Prue. Nick after some hesitation told me that she had been taken to Cirencester Hospital. Bad news. She was able to walk down the stairs, into the ambulance.

Tuesday, 31st August

Audrey's birthday, and we asked her to dine here, knowing how wretched she would be alone in her mill house. One of the grandsons to motor her over. They tossed up which of them it was to be. It was Nick. In order to leaven the family tension we invited Polly Garnett.* She came and chatted non-stop; very decent of her to come in the circumstances. We had warned her about the situation. At 9.10 Ted Robinson† telephoned from the hospital to say that Prue had died at five minutes to nine. Discussion what to do with Nick and Audrey and how to break the news. I called Nick to the telephone and let his father tell him. I took Audrey aside and told her. She was stunned, and as it were frozen. No tears, merely anger against fate. Nick drove off and Audrey stayed the night with us.

Thursday, 2nd September

Sitting at my writing table in Lansdown Crescent at 11.30 I heard an owl hooting. Thought it might be a child, but no, it hooted a second time.

Friday, 3rd September

We motored to Hay-on-Wye and delivered a copy of my *Beckford* which I signed for a young man working in Booth's bookshop, called Michael Cottrill. He is a great Beckford fan, like so many. I looked in

---

* Polly Devlin, journalist and author, wife of Andrew Garnett, entrepreneur.
† Prue Robinson's husband.

the shop for some of Harold's books. Managed to find three only – *Monarchy, Friday Mornings* and *Helen's Tower*, which is signed by Harold and dated 1938. It must have been his copy, but how did it get here in this case? Young Cottrill told me that Harold's books are difficult to come by since publication of *Portrait of a Marriage;*[*] Vita's quite impossible. They are in great demand, almost as much as Bloomsbury authors'. 'Cotters', aged 28, deprecated publication of *Portrait*. So even the younger generation think it a mistake.

We called with our picnic luncheon on Penelope [Betjeman][†] in her house on the hill above Cusop, without pre-warning. She was busily cooking in the kitchen. Received us as though we had been with her all the morning, went on cooking, talking, talking without cease, treating us with her extraordinary detached, candid manner. Is a round little tub with close-cropped grey hair, wearing a brown one-piece garment, trousers, the legs very tight, also the behind, which is enormous. From the behind a thick hair was dangling like a tail, of which she was totally unconscious. She is very worried about John. Thinks his health is impaired by what she calls his 'dichotomy', i.e., his divided allegiance to her and Feeble. She says F. is very possessive and John is afraid of her, which isn't true. Thinks John is killing himself with drink and drugs which his doctor plies him with. This is far more likely. It was distressing to see how old he has become, for in the film given on his seventieth birthday he walked like Charlie Chaplin, as though his legs did not belong to him. Very sad film, for he did not speak throughout. A background recitation in his voice taken from *Summoned by Bells*. At the very end he broke into that delicious smile, made a joke and came alive.

Saturday, 4th September

Poor Prue's funeral at one o'clock at the dear little church of Bagendon, at which I have attended Prue's children's baptisms and Dale's[‡] wedding, and at a which my old cousin Matty Leatham (née Constable)'s funeral also took place forty years or more before. Service

---

[*] Nigel Nicolson's revealing account of his parents' marriage.

[†] Lady Betjeman, wife of Sir John; author, as Penelope Chetwode, of *Two Middle-aged Ladies in Andalusia* (1963); dau. of Field Marshal Lord Chetwode, 1st Baron.

[‡] Dale Stevens, dau. of Audrey Lees-Milne by her 2nd marriage; m. James Sutton, yr son of Sir Robert Sutton, 8th Bt.

of family and close friends only. I bit my underlip and just managed to control myself until when all was over we left the grave-side, and Dale broke down and wept. It was moving to watch the three boys and Ted walk into the front pew next to ours. They were wonderfully controlled; also Ted, who organized things throughout, seemingly unconcerned. Afterwards we had to attend a buffet luncheon at Moor Wood. The Arthur family had come from Scotland, and I talked to Simon Glenarthur,* a charming young man resembling Matthew but better looking, and handsome Margaret G. who could not be more sympathetic. Her quiet dignity impresses.

Monday, 6th September

We called on Mr Crann in his tiny cottage, Shepherd's Lodge, and asked him to repair the escutcheon on the south side of our house. The mantling has disintegrated. This old craftsman showed us his workshop, and an infinity of tools with fine handles in maplewood. Told me the names of some of the implements, which I have forgotten. He is a splendid craftsman yet his own taste is execrable. Showed us gargoyles, garden figures, foxes, dwarfs he has carved: to be seen to be believed. In the evening Mr Gentry, the watch-mender in the village, called with the movement of my Louis XV clock. Came bustling in with it in his hand, almost in tears of vexation at what the previous mender (found for me by the late Mr Wallace of Wotton) had done to it. Put the pin of some important cog in an unorthodox place. Said he ought to be disgraced and struck off the register of horologists. Never seen a man more distraught. His life's training affronted. Then Mr Hayes the builder informed us he was an embalmer in his off time. Fascinating work. Told Peggy he would give her a lesson. It is not done as the Egyptians did it, he assured me (they spent three months to his three hours per client), but only to last a short time, before the corpse can be disposed of. I asked if he gutted the corpse. Oh dear no, only inject preservatives, he said, and something about removing offensive parts, 'but we are always obliged to restore them' – after treatment, I supposed, but could not ask for further details because the agent to the Beaufort estate came and interrupted.

---

* Simon Mark Arthur, 4th Baron Glenarthur (b. 1944); son of Audrey Lees-Milne's 1st husband Matthew Arthur (later 3rd Baron Glenarthur, d. 1976) by his 2nd marriage, to Margaret Howie.

Tuesday, 7th September

To London for the day. A Properties meeting in the morning at which Wimpole Hall discussed at great length. After lunching alone in the Carlton Club, which Brooks's members may use this month – a dim, dusty club, but fine building by Hopper – to Chatto's. Interview with Denis Enright* over my novel. Merely correcting and elucidating certain ambiguous passages. He v. friendly, but I don't feel at ease. Also I took back to Chatto's the diaries. Now have, I really believe, disposed of these two books until proof stages.

Spent twenty minutes at the L.S. Lowry exhibition at Burlington House. Must admit he had talent, showed great originality in delineating people, and found a new field in English Lancashire industrialism. A sort of Manchester Breughel. Photographs of him interspersed. Looks like John Betjeman.

Thursday, 9th September

A. and I had a splendid day. Left the house at 8.30, drove to Dartmoor – under two hours to reach Exeter. Reached Castle Drogo before it was open at eleven. Went round and over. Very satisfactory house of clean-cut granite. Inside exposed granite and plaster, rather Florentine Renaissance. Lovely little domed spaces in the corridors. Contents indifferent, bar some splendid tapestries. Wonderful setting. Robust, unambiguous, original, and the material most carefully worked and finished. A new family aspiring to, rather arriving at, landed gentryhood, and now the representative living upstairs in a tiny flat, all within my lifetime.

Picnicked on Dartmoor and at 1.45 arrived Yelverton. Went to interview Lord Carnock,† aged 93, in an old people's home. A midget's head: the back of it, what I could see, reminded me of Harold's. Small, dim, blue eyes, very *malin*; downward-drooping mouth. None of Harold's bonhomie. On the contrary. He greeted me with the words, 'Why on earth do you think Harold Nicolson's life worth recording?' I mentioned his having been a public figure. He said his political life was a complete failure. 'His writing,' I went on.

---

* Poet; Director, Chatto & Windus, 1974–82 (b. 1920).
† Erskine Nicolson, 3rd Baron Carnock of Carnock (1884–1982); elder brother of Sir Harold Nicolson.

'Everything he wrote was fictitious, and untrue,' he said sternly. I thought I was not going to get on with this old man. Nor did I elicit much from him but disparagement of H. Evidently resentful of H's success. But he told me some things about his childhood which I wanted to know – H's timidity, his sharpness, impishness, quickness, and wit as a child. Lord C. kept harping on the unreliability of H's historical books. Didn't do justice to their father, nor to King George V. Herbert Samuel* told him that Harold was a joke in the House. Said that in the thirties H. wanted to go back to the Diplomatic Service, but they wouldn't have him. Sorry as I was for this old, not undistinguished man languishing in a hideous little bedroom, with a few coloured photographs of horses and hounds framed and dotted on the walls, his pathetic little bottle, which a nurse ran in, while I was there, to empty, his three pipes, his fingering nervously with the wire of his deaf aid, I could not like him.

No man is a hero to his valet, or his family, it seems, yet he might have attributed some virtue to his distinguished, marvellous brother. Told me he only once saw Vita. Clearly had no love for her, either. Kept saying, 'But of course I am quite uneducated, and am stupid' – stupid he is not. I felt constrained to say, 'I think you are too diffident.' This provoked a spark of assertiveness. 'After all,' he said, and puffed himself, 'I did my duty in the first war, which is more than Harold did. He ought to have fought but didn't. I got the DSO, the Legion of Honour, St Anne with Swords.'†

After this strange encounter we motored to Powderham Castle. An open day. Wish I had gone while I was writing my *Beckford*. As it was, I went twenty years ago, and had forgotten much. The Rococo and neo-Classical additions extraordinarily interesting and good. Staircase a *tour de force* built by Kitty's‡ grandfather, elaborate plaster panels on ceiling and walls. But the present Earl of Devon a man of little taste. He has painted the walls of staircase a peacock blue and given the plaster relief a fawn hue, instead of white. The Music Room done for Kitty by Wyatt extremely beautiful, with niches filled with urns on

---

* 1st Viscount Samuel (1870–1963); Liberal statesman.
† He might also have included his Crown of Italy. The Order of St Anne was founded by Charles Frederick, Duke of Holstein-Gottorp, in 1735 in honour of his wife Anna Petrovna, dau. of Peter the Great, and adopted as a Russian Order of Chivalry in 1797 by their grandson, the Emperor Paul.
‡ William Courtenay, son of 2nd Viscount Courtenay, involved with Beckford, to whom he was known as 'Kitty', in the Powderham Castle scandal.

pedestals. I am sure this is how the niches at Claydon should be treated. A gorgeous full-length of Kitty in masquerade dress over the fireplace, which we could not get close enough to see properly. Also another likeness of him with father and mother, by I think Downman, likewise invisible.

Saturday, 2nd October

Just back from a fortnight and a day's 'holiday'. We flew to Marseilles, hired a car and drove to St-Rémy. Stayed at a delicious Hôtel de Roussan, two miles outside the town, an old *manoir*, of which the family lives discreetly and aloofly somewhere in the back premises. Furnished with delightful Empire pieces and rustic Louis Seize chairs and sofas with needlework, nestling beside ghastly trash. Fine old library. Wonderfully uncomfortable bedrooms, walls peeling, primitive wash-basins and sitz-baths behind curtains.

My zest for sight-seeing has diminished with my faith, I estimate. Wonderful landscape this round St-Rémy, the most Provençal area, hedges of cypresses marking boundaries and wind-breaks, mountains in near distance, water trilling through runnels in the garden. Apt church has two undercrofts, must be very ancient (Roman?) below. Over the presbytery arch an explosion of golden rays, like Spanish transparencies. L'Isle-sur-Sorgue church lined with seventeenth-century Baroquery, and fine picture frames of that century, as at Apt, containing dingy, poor religious canvases. Nave piers of the second painted in arabesques. Baroque rather than Rococo *boiseries*. Abbaye de Senanque strikingly pure Romanesque architecture, Benedictine rather. Empty church sad. The clean precision of architectural lines deeply impressive. Smell of mortality in the nave. Arles, St-Trophime – total lack of spirituality, which I notice in all Continental churches these days, especially in France. Here the Romanesque merges with the classical Louis XV in a way which makes me admire, namely the balustered galleries at the crossing, hollowed underneath smoothly. Aisles very narrow indeed, high and tight. Crystal chandeliers hang.

St-Rémy Roman mausoleum reliefs on four sides; those of the north-east more worn than the others. Panel of horse with head turned back to the viewer in high relief, exciting.

The Lukes have bought (through A.) a derelict farmhouse which calls for a fortune to make it habitable, near Uzès. Goodish situation, but not spectacular. I would rather die than live in it. The children play Box and Cox between this place, where they picnic in a hugger-mugger fashion, and a tiny house in a back street of St-Rémy, which Clarissa loves. All four spend their time with the town boys of St-Rémy. The three girls are boy-mad. Well, others have been boy-mad among my acquaintance, but these girls think of nothing else. Undergoing no education whatever, these children are in consequence uncommunicat-ive and -able. Conversation out of the question. However, they are a most united family, and nothing outside the family circle interests them in the least. All rather a pity in my opinion. Poor A. is worried, and sad, but can say and do nothing.

Stayed a few nights at Rory Cameron's* unfinished house, which is going to be *de luxe*, outside Ménerbes, called les Quatre Sources. Every stitch of clothing taken off is whipped away by Mahommed's wife and washed, even my pyjamas worn one night. Saw Hiram [Winterbottom],† lunched in the garden of his modern house. Plan fascinated me: only one spacious room to a floor, spiral-wise stairs, no communicating doors, no doors anywhere, vast windows down to the floor, no curtains, uncosy, and filthy dirty, squalor inconceivable. Hiram always invigorating in talk. Met Mrs Rintoul‡ with whom I had been communicating about characters in fiction. She told me that Victorian ladies never washed their hair. Merely brushed and brushed it glossy. Washed the hairbrushes only.

Flew from Marseilles in a tiny midget of a plane across the Alps to Milan. Changed for Venice. Stayed eight nights at the Calcina Pensione. Here we sight-saw like mad, walking every morning from church to church, and sleeping and reading in the afternoon. Some social activity. Met George and Diana Gage§ and ate with them several times on the Zattere. He is 80 and old in manner, puffs and pontificates. Did not approve of the Mosley boy's biography of his

---

* Roderick Cameron (1914–1985), American travel writer and resident, formerly of the French Riviera, now of the Lubéron.

† Hiram Winterbotham (1908–90), Gloucestershire native; one-time Executive Chairman of St Thomas's Hospital, Governor of Westonbirt Arboretum, Chairman of Rotork (engineering), etc., he had been instrumental in helping the BBC to set up the Third Programme; at 50 he retired to the Apt valley in Provence.

‡ Wendy Rintoul, indefatigable reader and researcher; author of *A Dictionary of Real People and Places in Fiction*.

§ Henry Rainald Gage (1895–1982), 6th Viscount, of Firle Place, Sussex; m. (2nd) Diana Cavendish, Hon. Mrs Campbell-Gray.

brother-in-law Julian Grenfell,* whom George never knew, and thought his picture of Lady Desborough totally wrong. Said Mosley considered himself such a great author that he could see below what did not in fact exist, and made wildly inaccurate interpretations. His not a case of getting his own back on the Grenfells because of his divorce. Just arrogance and silliness, says George G. Had tea with the old Clarys.† Prince Alfy now 90. Asked me to find out how the Cowper collection was formed. Told me again in brief the story of his and the princess's escape from Bohemia in 1945. Said it was better losing everything, even the clothes on one's back, which indeed happened to him, for a Russian soldier took his jacket, than having one's possessions whittled away by a corrosive government like ours in England. The worst thing was having to wear an armband, indicating that they were deprived of all human rights. No doctor was allowed to treat them. They were pariahs. Now he communicates with the curators of his castle, and is pleased to give them accurate information about its history. Has no bitterness in his soul. Is a deeply religious man. During the recent earthquake in Venice when their palace swayed and tottered and creaked, Alfy quietly prayed, so she said. He said to me, 'I didn't pray for us, because being so old we don't mind dying, but for the palace. I couldn't have borne it to collapse.' Angelic, sweet people. Lunched one day with Anna-Maria Cicogna,‡ who said that last week's meeting of UNESCO, à propos Venice in Peril, was fatuous. No agreements reached. Ashley Clarke§ told me the same. His work is ceaseless. The old priest of his 'parracho' told a friend that 'we have three saints in my parish, San Stefano, San Niccolò dei Mendicoli and Sant'Ashley Clarke.' Our last night we dined at the Palazzo Polignac with the [duc and duchesse] Decazes. Ate in the long

---

* Nicholas Mosley, 3rd Baron Ravensdale (b. 1923); son of Sir Oswald Mosley, 6th Bt, and Lady Cynthia Curzon, dau. of 1st Marquess Curzon of Kedleston; succeeded his aunt Mary Curzon, 2nd Baroness Ravensdale, eldest dau. of 1st Marquess Curzon (to whose Barony of Ravensdale she had succeeded in 1925). The book in question was *Julian Grenfell: His Life and the Times of His Death 1888–1915*; a soldier-poet of the First World War, Grenfell was the son of E.A.P. Fane (Etty), who m. 1887 1st and last Lord Desborough; she was one of 'The Souls', the self-named group of intellectually-minded aristocrats of whom A.J. Balfour (Prime Minister 1902–6) was the cynosure.

† Prince and Princess Clary, long resident in Venice after being forced to leave Czechoslovakia; he was the author of *European Past* (1978).

‡ Contessa Cicogna; friend of Nancy Mitford and long-time resident of Venice.

§ Sir Ashley Clarke, GCMG; retired diplomat.

sala under two huge and dimly lit lanterns casting shadows like a worn Aubusson carpet on the highly polished gesso floor. Table laid for fourteen, covered with silver. Two footmen in white gloves. Again sweet people, with the greatest respect for and admiration of his great-aunt Winnie de Polignac.* Enchanted with A's gift of Winnie's copy of the Carpaccio, which they have hung in a vast room, so skyed that it looks like a postage stamp; whereas in our dining room at Alderley we thought it vast. Sat next to the duchess who during the meat course, having cut with her knife, put it aside with the end upon the edge of the plate, and then used only her fork. The French always seem to disregard or minimize the part played by the knife when eating.

Sunday, 3rd October

Strange to be at Eucharist in Little Badminton at ten this morning, I among five old village women, whereas at this hour a week ago I was in the Gesuati, which was thronged with the most exotic persons.

Yesterday hounds met at the Kennels here at 7.30. Within three hours all was over. Miss Moore in striped bloomers passed me on her bicycle while I walked to the post office. With a radiant face, looking twenty years younger than the drawn, lined, sad countenance which seldom changes expression, she called out: 'We've had a super day; we killed five and a half brace of foxes.' A massacre. In the afternoon Master was out shooting pheasants.

Attended the annual Kilvert service held today at Kingston Michael church. Large congregation of old women and some old men brought in charabancs from Hereford mostly. I entered to a buzz of animated conversation, a thing which never used to happen in a church before a service. Dreadful service, dreadful hymns, but the sermon-address given by the Rector of Leominster was excellent. He said though Kilvert was not saintly, not perfect, he was almost the complete man; he gave all he had to God, moved in exalted and humble circles, going from one to the other within minutes; was the same charitable self to all.

---

* Princesse Edmond de Polignac, b. Winifred Singer, also known as Winaretta (d. 1943); friend and patron of artists, musicians and writers.

Thursday, 7th October

Last Saturday an urge, a prompting of conscience, a nostalgic kick
made me ring up Harry Ashwin,* who Audrey told me had been ill,
and I went to tea with him at Bretforton, having firstly called on Mrs
Haines† in Wickhamford. She looking thinner in the face but not frail.
In a great state of self-pity because she had only this morning learnt
of Prue's death in a letter from Elaine. 'Oh, it's one thing after another'
(she said) '– it's more than I can stand. What with my poor hands I
could barely get a wink of sleep last night.' I was constrained to point
out, feeling sure she would not hear, or care to hear, that she had not
known about Prue's death last night. We [J.L.M. and Harry Ashwin]
had a good heart-to-heart. Bretforton Manor seems frozen in time,
like a dead house whence all the family have fled, which is true, but
for Harry. When I was a child it was filled to the brim with brothers,
sisters, Mr and Mrs Ashwin, and cousins. Now only Harry, who lives
in the library. He is hardly recognizable, face twisted to one side, has
lost over two stone. Has had cancer of the jaw, palate removed, and
then what he called a stroke in his leg. But no self-pity, unlike Mrs
Haines (who said she wanted me to have the portrait by Barraclough
of my mother, after her death).

John Pope-Hennessy has lent me Harold's letters to Jamesey. In
reading them I have felt like an eavesdropper and ashamed of myself.
Also nervous of reading something disparaging about myself. But no.
Jim has a heart of gold, H. wrote before the war. Yet these letters to
Jamesey put me in my place, in that James meant so much more to
Harold on account of his lively little mind. Harold clearly loved James
until his dying day. He wrote to him when abroad that he missed him;
that when in the evenings the door opened and someone else entered
his room, he was disappointed. Almost an infatuation. Very touching.
But naughty Jamesey traded on this.

Monday, 11th October

One of the things which most appealed to me in Venice this visit was
the way the inhabitants string their washing from window to window.

---

* Of Bretforton Manor, Worcestershire, where the Ashwins were squires from the sixteenth to the twentieth century. Now gone.
† Mrs Norris Haines; her husband, who d. 1973, had been J.L.-M's parents' chauffeur for
sixty years.

Having no back gardens they have cunningly devised a system which presumably depends for its success upon the co-operation of neighbours. Often a line is slung across a narrow canal from one house to another. I watched women taking from a plastic pail handfuls of washing, and with great dexterity stringing vests, shirts, pants, trousers, etc. on the line with wooden pegs, and giving a deft pull so that the line moves across the water. Some of the back canals on washing mornings are festooned with Baroque swags and loops of multi-coloured garments.

Sunday, 17th October

Have just read and enjoyed Tony Powell's autobiography.* As I expected it is extremely well written, but his style lacks sparkle. Also he has a habit of economizing in words to an extent which induces ambiguity in his meanings. I have to re-read a sentence to find that grammatically he is absolutely correct, but that had he not omitted a conjunction the meaning would have been clearer at first reading. He discloses nothing about himself, but is revealing, albeit cautiously, of his contemporaries' foibles.

On Wednesday I motored (150 miles) to Sissinghurst for the night. Nigel had collected piles of files, boxes, wooden and tin, of letters, diaries and papers relating to Harold's life up to 1929, which is to be the first third of H's life. He also prepared a careful list of each item, descriptive of contents; also a pile of books relating to Balliol, Wellington, etc. He is the most thorough person imaginable. And so helpful that I am overcome by his kindness. He is alone, without the children and without any help in the house. So he took me to dine at Biddenden. On our return we talked about Harold and Vita till 1.45 a.m., v. late for me. Then I had to read one hour in bed before I could get to sleep. Up betimes in the morning, looked through the papers to see that I needed them all. In pouring rain we stacked the things in the back of my car. By eleven I knew that N. was longing to get to his work, so I said goodbye and wandered round the garden under my umbrella. Even in mid October, in drenching rain, garden looking splendid.

On the way to Sissinghurst I stopped at Petworth and went round the house, guide-book in hand, looking at the contents for the first

---

* First volume of memoirs *To Keep the Ball Rolling* (4 vols, 1976–82).

time without being bothered by caretakers or donors. Nobody there now knows me, mercifully. What a superb collection. There are about twenty Turners alone. While standing before the 'Sunset' Turner (taken from the house, of the lake and park) I recalled the dramatic occasion when I was once looking at it and the sun's disk on no provocation whatever dropped off the canvas on to the floor. Horrified, I stooped to pick it up. Drown's,* I believe, had to replace it. Stopped too at Upavon church, thinking it was where Sydney Smith was the incumbent for many lonely, isolated years of his life. Saw no signs of his memory, no mention on the list of incumbents. Drove on, and passed a signpost, pointing to Netheravon, and remembered it was that village. Then did not turn off, so failed to see S. Smith's church. Must do so the next time.

On leaving Sissinghurst I said to Nigel that it was a great responsibility having the loan of all his father's and mother's letters. He gaily said, 'It wouldn't much matter if they were lost. I have read through them all; and you will do the same. And I don't suppose anyone else will ever do so.'

Wednesday, 27th October

A. and I lunched with Harry Ashwin at Bretforton. He motored us to Bewdley for Bloggs Baldwin's memorial service. St Anne's Georgian church, so pretty outside, so grim inside. Absolutely bare, not even a cross on the altar; not a flower; hideous plastic light shades, and *hideous* coloured windows. Most genteel clergyman. No bishop. An old man conducted us to pews. Said he and I had not met for fifty years. He was Sir Thomas Lea† whose mother came from Arley Castle where Granny used to take us from Ribbesford. Harry talked so much before the service that A. who was sitting next to him made us change places. Harry's conversation is limited to discussing who people are. Never what they are. 'Yes, he is the third baronet. Her husband will be Duke of Sutherland if Lord So-and-So has no children.' Poor old Harry, he is a bore. Yet I am fond of him for ancient sake's sake.

---

* Picture restorers.
† 3rd Bt (1901–85); son of Sir Sydney Lea, 2nd Bt, and Mary Ophelia Woodward, of Arley Castle, Worcestershire.

Saturday, 30th October

Zita James whom we met (after many years) lunching with Eliza Wansbrough* told me that the young come from far and wide to sit at her feet and the feet of her sister, Teresa Jungman,† with whom she lives, just to hear them talk, and listen to their voices, and look at their hair-styles. Reason – that they belonged to the Twenties, and figure so prominently in Evelyn Waugh's diaries, and the diaries of other Twentyish persons. Yet to me Zita does not in any way represent a remnant of the Twenties. In place of the dashing, sophisticated, fashionable Eton-cropped friend of the Sitwells and Elizabeth Ponsonby‡ is a withered, soberly-dressed-in-tweeds, Cotswold lady of over seventy, without a trace of affectation or with-itry. Very sympathetic and sensible. Both are desperately hard up, the sisters. Zita told me that Teresa has masses of Evelyn's letters which she will not allow anyone to read, in spite of constant approaches from thesis writers, nor sell, although they must be quite valuable.

On Tuesday I went to Sudbury by train via Derby, for a meeting of the small management committee. Went round the house, which I can truthfully pronounce perfect. I can find no criticism at all of this uninhabited house, sparsely furnished. The walls, floors and ceilings are so self-sufficiently beautiful and so beautifully renovated by John Fowler that they convince me he has as certain a genius in leaving well alone as in decorating anew.

At our picnic luncheon I sat next to Councillor Miss Tunnicliffe. Had a long, intimate talk. She told me her history. One of seven daughters of a working-class man who, in her extreme youth, was at one time on the dole. The children were brought up extremely strictly and severely chastised for untruths or the slightest indication of dishonesty. She is a Socialist. Told me that undoubtedly the very young of today marry and have many children while living on the dole and enjoying benefits for each child. She advocates a means test, to use an ugly phrase in Labour circles. This woman has worked all her life and

---

* (Mrs) Elizabeth Wansborough, dau. of Sir George Lewis, Bt, well-known late Victorian solicitor.
† Teresa ('Baby') and Zita were the daughters of the hostess and talent-spotter Mrs Richard Guinness by her first husband, Nico Jungman; in the early Thirties Evelyn Waugh wanted to marry Teresa.
‡ Hon. Elizabeth Ponsonby (1900–40), dau. of 1st Baron Ponsonby of Schulbrede, was one of the first of the Bright Young People to wear her hair shingled.

is dedicated to social work. Marvellously dressed, elegant and *bien*, with piled-up grey hair and a peach complexion. Called me Love and has a broad northern accent – Luv. Says Derby has no immigrant problems because the number of such is limited.

Peggy De L'Isle called, bringing me a book of letters written during the first war to her husband, Wilfred Glanusk,* from the Prince of Wales, while in the Grenadiers. The P. of W. evidently hero-worshipped him. Began the letters 'Dear old Bill', and wrote many to Lady G., Toby's mother, to whom he must also have been devoted. Among this small group of young officers was Edward Marshall, A's half-brother, killed in 1915, to whom the P. referred in his letters to Toby. The P's letters those of a boy, mostly complaining that the King would not allow him to be with his friends in the front line. Rather touching. Not very educated. Peggy has now brought me an engraving in a maplewood frame of the second Sir Joseph Bailey, MP, who became the first Lord. He was my mother's first cousin and not, alas, my gt-grandfather Sir J., which is what I hoped for. I have no likeness of my gt-grandfather. Don't the least want this Victorian stuffed dummy.

Thursday, 4th November

Mrs Watkins in the Post Office at Badminton volunteered, while I was buying stamps, to tell me that I would not believe how many young – and she stressed *young* – men and girls claimed their weekly dole, when she knew that most of them either had jobs already – self-employed, or casual workers – or were too idle to take jobs they had been offered. She said it was a scandal that the young had absolutely no conscience or compunction in slacking and cheating. Christopher Chancellor, who came for tea yesterday, said that the young's ethics and our own just did not coincide. When I said that the young I knew struck me as more conscientious than my generation at their age, he laughed. Christopher said that we must change our social habits, must meet our friends between meals. He said he could no longer invite friends to meals. Sylvia, who is well over seventy and very delicate, spent the whole morning cooking for a luncheon party, and the whole afternoon washing up. It was no longer *on*. I said there was something slightly chilling in the prospect of going miles to the houses of friends

---

* Wilfred Bailey (Toby), 3rd Baron Glanusk (d. 1948).

and acquaintances and sitting round an empty table. Were drinks to
be allowed? Tea? Even biscuits? C. was sympathetic. Said piteously that
for him, an ex-executive, accustomed to power, to organizing huge
business concerns, retirement meant death. No fleets of motors, secretaries, telephones. 'For you, Jim, who have been nobody' (he didn't
put it quite like that) 'you have your books to fall back on. I have
nothing. The worst deprivation is no longer being in touch with
important members of the Government and the rulers.' His old
mother of 94 is dying. She has shrunk to a tiny horrid object. He confessed that the physical change so disgusted him that he could barely
bring himself to visit her. Understandable, but to be lamented.

   Rhodesia. To my expressions of total sympathy with Ian Smith* he
reported that he felt sympathy only for the third generation of the
original pioneering families. They amounted to at most ten per cent
of the white population. The rest were post-war immigrants from
Germany, England and Australia, people who had no disinterested
motives, but had for one generation enjoyed what they had exploited
from the country, were tax evaders from their original countries, and
deserved no pity. His father who had been Governor in the Twenties
told him in those days that black rule was inevitable and ought to be
faced up to.

Sunday, 14th November

We lunched with John Gwynne at Quenington in his lugubrious,
dark, dingy mill house. A good luncheon bought by him and hotted
up. Mrs (Tamara) Talbot Rice† the other guest. This highly intelligent
old woman is leaving her home on the Colne where she has lived for
over forty years for a small London house. Is miserable, yet philo-
sophic. While John was out of the room she told us that he had
decided to leave England for ever, to live in the East in some distant,
ascetic retreat, and cut himself off from his family and relations; that
it must be stopped. When he returned we taxed him with it. Yes, it
was true, this he intends to do. Can't face up to becoming a senile
embarrassment to his children, both of whom he dearly loves. The

---

* As Prime Minister of Rhodesia, Ian Smith had in 1965 issued a Unilateral Declaration
of Independence; Britain declared his regime illegal and introduced sanctions; in
September 1976 Smith at last accepted the principle of majority (black) rule in Rhodesia.
† Russian-born widow of David Talbot Rice, historian of Byzantine art; she d. 1995.

truth is that he is a follower of Sufi, and is hooked. Mrs Talbot Rice told me the whole creed was rot. We went to John's big room to look at two hideous surrealist pictures he had been given and that he much admired. There was a ring of chairs round an open space. 'This is where the Sufi faithful assemble,' she confided with a slight sneer. 'They are all John's friends. It is all the more ludicrous when they are upper class people,' she said. All the more pathetic.

Tuesday, 16th November

I am deep in Harold. Reading through all his letters, and Vita's to him. There are blanks in his life which I see no means of penetrating. One was the year in Madrid, 1911, of which I can find nothing. Precious little about the first war years beyond his somewhat scrappy letters to Vita. His letters to her are all love letters, not long, and less interesting than his letters to, say, Sligger Urquhart,* or even to his parents during his Oxford and German cramming days. Love letters are not on the whole rewarding. The great test of my endeavours will be searching through Foreign Office papers in the Public Record Office, I fancy. Burnet Pavitt† has put me in touch with someone in the Foreign Office library. That tiresome man Sir Alan Lascelles‡ refuses to see me. This is a great pity because he is about the only survivor of Harold's Oxford friends. I have always found Sir Alan disagreeable, grumpy and disapproving. Why does he dislike me? Is it *Another Self* or *Ancestral Voices* which has made him take against? Or merely that he considers me a poor fish? Or is it disapproval of Nigel's *Portrait of a Marriage*, and a distaste of being involved in further stuff of that sort?

Saturday, 20th November

Tamara Talbot Rice lunched today and disclosed that one of her godparents was Tolstoy. She told how she escaped from Russia in 1920 with her mother and brother and sister in a waggon, horse-drawn,

---

* Francis Fortescue Urquhart (1868–1934), Dean of Balliol College, Oxford 1916–33.

† Managing Director of Roche, 1948–73, and Trustee of the Royal Opera House, Covent Garden for 25 years.

‡ Rt Hon. Sir Alan Lascelles, PC (1887–1981); Private Secretary to HRH The Prince of Wales, 1920–9; Assistant Private Secretary to HM King George V, 1935, and HM King George VI, 1936–43; Private Secretary 1943–52; Keeper of The King's Archives 1945–52; of The Queen's Archives, 1952–3.

from their house outside St Petersburg, in the winter. The children were concealed under a sheet, but their breath froze and the sheet became stiff with frost. The children, furious at leaving Russia in these circumstances, started to sing. The peasant driver was so alarmed lest they be discovered that he refused to continue, and drove them home again. Whereupon the Danish Ambassador, who had helped the mother, smacked the children. Indignant but chastened the children consented to accompany the mother once again. This time, having obtained passes to Finland through the Finnish Ambassador, they boldly set out with cabin trunks by train. Many friends came to see them off bringing farewell gifts. On arrival at the river marking the frontier they got out. On foot they began climbing a steep, humped bridge, in the middle of which was the Finnish outpost. Half-way up they heard a telephone ringing in the Russian outpost and the mother guessed it was about them. But she would not allow the children to stop and they reached the Finnish outpost with rifle bullets from the Russian soldiers whizzing past their ears.

She said that their old home in Moscow is now the Afghan Embassy, and when she was last in Moscow conducting a party of American tourists her bus passed the door. When the Revolution broke out the family buried under a tree in the garden the mother's jewels. Before fleeing they tried to dig the jewels up but could not in their haste identify the exact spot and so went off without them. She knows that the tree has since been cut down, and wonders if the Afghans found the jewels or if they are still there.

Thursday, 25th November

To London on Tuesday staying one night with Eardley. Quite an enjoyable and profitable visit. London Library all Tuesday afternoon. Eardley took me to the circus on Clapham Common. Didn't like the animals, those proud lions made at the crack of a whip to stand on little pedestals and the noble elephants made to dance; but the acrobats took the breath away, swinging and turning somersaults and landing in nets. Ran into Bruce Chatwin* in St James's Square, overjoyed that he had handed in the MS of his book on Patagonia.

---

* Travel writer and novelist (1940–89).

Saturday, 27th November

Christopher Chancellor invited himself to tea with me in Bath yesterday, in order, it seems, to talk about his mother's funeral. She was cremated and her ashes buried in their family burial-ground near Edinburgh. Christopher much impressed by the distress of the old grave-digger, who was in tears. Then he read out to me the draft of an immensely long letter addressed to Raglan announcing his resignation as a trustee and going on to abuse Raglan for his past misdeeds and injuries to him, Xtopher. I said the letter was far too long and I doubted whether it would redound to his credit. Response from Xtopher: 'I don't think you are a fighter like me.' I said, 'I will fight to the last ditch when I am really angry over a cause I think worthwhile.' But I am bored stiff with this old issue which ought to be dead and buried.

Mary Beaufort came to dinner with us at her invitation. The Territorials were dining at Badminton and she had to get out, turned out of her own house as she put it, so that the men could tell each other 'coarse stories'. Her interests are confined to Badminton and the Royal Family exclusively. On no other subject does she have any views whatever. She asked what our Duncan Grant picture was. When I told her she had neither heard of him nor of Bloomsbury. Anyway she thought the picture perfectly hideous. Told us she went to the opening of Parliament this week in a dress worn by her grandmother the Duchess of Teck. During the Queen's speech Michael Foot,* dressed in a shabby blue serge suit and red tie, was looking around him and not attending respectfully, as he should. Master, standing beside the Queen with drawn sword, longed to cut him down to size. I wish he had. What a delicious scandal there would have been. Mary told us that the Emperor Franz Joseph she remembered was a benign old man with white whiskers, immensely distinguished in a white uniform with red tunic and gold epaulettes. She and her brothers used to drive from Schönbrunn to the Gloriette where they ate ices and rich cakes, and were sick in the wagonette on the return journey. Said even Princess Mary was terrified of King George V. When the King swore Queen Mary used to laugh if someone else was present, but when alone was not amused.

---

* Rt Hon. Michael Foot, PC; Labour politician; Lord President of the Council and Leader of the House of Commons, 1976–9; Leader of the Labour Party, 1980–3.

Tamara Talbot Rice suffers from palsy in the hand, very badly. She doesn't mind talking about it. Told me that by making a supreme effort of will she can control it for a few minutes, if, for example, she must endeavour not to spill something. But the effect is to make the shaking much worse when she lets out her breath, so to speak. For the same number of minutes the shaking is intensified. It is a ghastly affliction. She said that even at night her hand shakes, but not enough to keep her awake.

While I was driving after dark a beautiful cream barn owl flew across the road. It tried to avoid me too late and struck the bonnet with a thump and fell stone dead. I have been haunted by the death of this rare creature. How much wild life is destroyed by motor cars does not bear thinking about. And *I* try to be so careful, too.

Having read vol. 6 of the Byron letters, edited by Marchant, I think I have at last fallen out of love with Byron. This period, the Venice period of his life, shows him in a very unattractive light indeed – unscrupulous, inordinately vain, cruel and excessively vulgar. But then, one should overlook the shortcomings of genius.

Sunday, 5th December

When I went to A's room to say goodnight she said that Benjamin Britten[*] had died. Lennox [Berkeley] came on the television, asked impromptu for his first memories of Britten. So good he was, natural and unhesitant. Told how when they wrote some songs together – they were abroad, in Spain I think – Britten was listening to a man singing in a café. On the back of an envelope, he jotted down the melody of the folk song. It was to be the theme of their joint composition [*Mont Juic*]. I heard Tippett on Radio 3 before midnight. Good too. Identified Britten's music with his hatred of war and violence. Said that his music written for Peter Pears was inspired by his deep love of Peter. The news announcer referred to Peter as though he were the widow, 'his close companion'. That the Queen had sent him a telegram. Quite right, but I thought what an advance this was, that the Queen should tacitly but publicly recognize a homosexual relationship. They were a marvellous pair. I never heard one breath of scandal against either of them. Wonder when and how the romance started.

---

[*] Composer (1913–76); CH 1953; OM 1965; Life Peer, 1976.

I barely knew Ben Britten, but knew Pears a little better. Britten
didn't need people, I gather. Led an inner life, totally dedicated, and
good. My first memory of the two is in Ursula Nettleship's house,
next door to number 104 Cheyne Walk where I moved during the
war. I thought what a plain, abstracted, dim-looking man B. was. I
never made contact. He once came to Alderley and we walked round
the garden together, murmuring politenesses. Yet I felt an affinity
unexpressed. Lennox said with sincerity that long before Britten had
published a composition he recognized genius in him, so that when
his first piece (whatever it was – the Michelangelo sonnets?)* was performed he was not the least surprised by its reception. Britten was of
course suborned by the Soviets in Russia and foolishly claimed that
Russia was the paradise for artists – because he and P. Pears were
treated like VIPs in that hellish country.

Sunday, 12th December

Went to London on Tuesday. Attended the annual Nat. Trust representatives' dinner. Rather boring. Sat between two junior and affable
reps with whom I chatted, but by whom I was not edified. On the
way up to the dining-room walked with John Pope-Hennessy who
told me he was sure J.K.-B. would get the job at the Mellon Institute
for which he had applied. 'I shall be very cross if he doesn't,' said John,
who is on the committee. The Pope pronouncing. But J.K.-B. *hasn't*
got it, having set great store by the prospect. The Pope will be dis-
pleased.

Called on Diana Cooper† on Wednesday evening. Asked her questions about various early friends of Harold's whom she too knew. She
was very little help. Indeed, I don't believe people's recollections are
much use. It is the written word, or nothing. 'Yes,' she would say, 'I
remember Ozzy Dickenson well. The loony bin man we called him.
He looked after Charlie Chaplin's mother, who went mad.' 'Was he
governor of a lunatic asylum, or on the board, or a warder?' I asked.
She had no idea, of course. We sat very close on a tiny sofa, she
nursing her minute dog and kneading him like a piece of dough. She
was very kind, charming and helpful-intentioned. I liked the

---

* 'Seven Sonnets of Michelangelo' for tenor and piano (1940).
† Lady Diana Manners, dau. of 8th Duke of Rutland; m. 1919 A. Duff Cooper
(1890–1954), cr. Viscount Norwich 1953, diplomatist, ambassador, author; she d. 1986.

affectionate way she embraced me. She was in her drawing-room dressed in black with the felt hat (black) with broad brim, which she threw up over her lovely forehead and eyes. I liked the way she said how envious she was of Vita's superior brain to hers, when they came out together. Vita was, she said, not strictly beautiful, but very arresting. She had even in those days the suspicion, the shadow of a moustache.

Sunday, 19th December

Philip Magnus[*] lunched at Brooks's. When I said there was something I wanted to talk to him about, he said he knew already. Ben had told him. His strong advice was not to do two volumes of the book. One was quite enough, because, he said, and stressed, Harold was a 'lightweight'. I hate that expression. For who are the heavyweights? - Churchill, Lenin, Hitler, I suppose, men with no one perfected distinction to their credit, unlike Harold who was a writer of rare quality. How I hate politicians, great and small. Magnus did not much like Vita. Disapproved of her sloppy dress, trousers, chain-smoking throughout meals at embassies when they visited them during their cruises. Then, Magnus is a highly conventional man. He counselled me to tell all about H's sex life. Strange, from him. Then tea with Miss Niggeman[†] and maiden sister at Temple Fortune Court, North-something, miles beyond Golders Green. Took me more than an hour and a half to get there by series of buses. Dear sweet people in a 'how' sort of flat, not small, but decaying Twenties, parquet floors lifting and old-fashioned bath-tub with enamel off. Yet spotlessly clean; coloured photographs, framed, of flower pieces. Miss N. gave me some further papers relating to Harold, her book of lists of his friends who telephoned over the years, obituaries, etc., quite useful. I don't think Miss N. liked Vita much either. She disliked Sissinghurst, for its cockroaches, mice, moth and corruption, and said whenever she left the place she felt a weight off her soul.

Harry d'Avigdor-Goldsmid[‡] has now died, suddenly. A fine

---

[*] Sir Philip Magnus-Allcroft, 2nd Bt (1906–88); biographer; m. 1943 Jewell Allcroft, of Stokesay Court, Shropshire.
[†] Harold Nicolson's secretary, 1938–65.
[‡] Sir Harry d'Avigdor-Goldsmid, 2nd Bt (b. 1909); MP.

appreciation by Alan P.-J.* in *The Times*, comparing him to a Renaissance banker prince. He bore well the weight of great riches, great intelligence, contempt for fools. Was underneath a man of compassion and generosity. Art collector, and extraordinarily brave in war. I used to stay at Somerhill a lot in Oxford days. Then drifted away and never resumed the friendship. Harry, whom I respected but did not love, was not my sort: racing, banking, bullion, power politics and manoeuvre. But I mourn him none the less. A Jew worthy of much respect.

Charlotte Bonham Carter gave a a nice party of a choral concert in Paddington Green church, at which songs by Lennox and Michael Berkeley were sung to Michael's conducting. I predict that M's music may be greater than his father's. Is more tuneful, and also full of vigour which L's conspicuously lacks. Helen Dashwood in white fur tail dangling from a brown fur scone on her head. She deftly avoided me, poor Helen.

Thursday, 23rd December

John Betj. and Feeble stayed last Thursday night *en route* for Cornwall. He has aged alarmingly. Can hardly move. Passed the shuffling stage. Has to be guided along. With difficulty was able to enter our front door and collapse on an upright chair. There he sat till dinner, and ambled to the kitchen. Getting him upstairs and down the following morning a slow and laborious process. Talked after dinner about religion, and discussed how few practising Christians today really believed implicitly, whereas those of our grandparents' generation did believe without question, not all of course, but the majority. John said he *hoped*. Hope was greater than charity. All we could do was to hope. Last night A. and I watched the film about him, and telephoned Cornwall afterwards. Feeble said he was greatly touched for poets don't get this sort of recognition during their lifetime, and only when they are dead if lucky.

A. has had a cold this week, not a bad one, but has felt tired all the same, and is constantly sleeping. Living with a person is fraught with apprehensions. How I worry, how I fear for her health, how I dread, how I wonder how the survivor of us will suffer, will bear up. The

---

* Alan Pryce-Jones (b. 1908); man of letters and reviewer; Editor of *Times Literary Supplement*, 1948–59.

impermanency which hangs over couples is a glowering, lowering monster to spoil the sunlight of their love.

I have read the Nicolson letters down to 1920. Have got through the elopement bit, thank goodness. How am I to tackle it? Nigel has already done it so well. I am finding difficulty in discovering inf. about Harold's work, which after all is what matters. Norah has just telephoned that the galley proofs of *Prophesying Peace* have arrived.

Friday, 24th December

Off for Christmas to Englefield Green. Have not been there for two years; nor, I think, seen the Droghedas* since 1974 Christmas. Joan much smaller, frailer, Garrett with a stoop. Rhoda Birley† almost senile, forgetful and unable to converse at all.

25th December

Motor in two cars to St George's Chapel, Windsor, I with Derry who drives so slowly that Garrett ahead stops, gets down, and in a fury rebukes Derry for dawdling. Derry pays no attention. The Ds and Derry sit under the stalls, Garrett under his own yellow banner with red mullets and his moor's head and mantling crest. We three others on the knife board opposite them. Each time I notice something new. This time, the splendid closed gallery at the north-east corner of the chapel with portcullis emblem and rose emblem and fairy lattice coving. Was it constructed for Katherine of Aragon? The stall banner two away from Garrett's bore a pair of shoes, very modern in design and common, like Dolcis shoes. Are they Mr Wilson's, I ask myself? Had a splendid view of the entire Royal Family, headed by the Queen, passing by the opening on their way down the north aisle to the choir opening. Queen Mother's hat like an apricot cockerel, enormous and unbecoming. After the service to the new Dean's House where all the Royal Family assemble, they having walked through the Castle grounds from the west door. Found myself, having divested myself of G's borrowed overcoat, standing beside the drawing-room door. Couldn't back away. The Dean approached leading the Queen, fol-

---

* Garrett Moore, 11th Earl of Drogheda (1910–89); m. 1935 Joan Carr, pianist; their son Dermot (Derry), Viscount Moore (b. 1937).
† Rhoda Pike, widow of Sir Oswald Birley, portrait painter.

lowed by all the others, some of whom shook hands and said Happy
Christmas in a jolly way. I was perpetually bobbing my head. A. the
other side of me never stopped curtsying for five minutes.

Sunday, 26th December

Derry and I and Folly* walked in the morning across the Park to the
Copper Horse, to the Castle, about four miles. On the way Folly put
up a rabbit and dashing after it caught herself in a barbed-wire fence,
spun round and yelped with pain. Very worried about her, poor little
back torn. Arrived rather hot at the Charterises'† house, the
Winchester Tower, to find the P. of Wales, Princess Alexandra and A.
Ogilvy there. Was presented to the Prince and had a few words with
him. He began, 'Did you start the National Trust?' Told him it was
founded in 1895, even before my day. Thought the N.T. such splendid organization and asked me if I had read Roy Strong's excellent
book on the Destruction of the Country House.‡ Since I had contributed the opening chapter I had, but did not tell him this. He has the
best complexion of a young man I have ever seen, the picture of fresh-
ness and health. Examined his gold signet ring, which has a crown and
Royal coat-of-arms, somewhat worn. I longed to know to whom it
had previously belonged. He asked how we liked living at Badminton
and where our house was. It is the lodge, I told him, at the entrance
gate. He said, 'Master is my hero.' When we were beginning to have
a rather interesting and earnest talk about preservation our host interrupted by showing the P. a lump of carved marble, asking him what
he thought it was. Couldn't guess. Charteris said, 'I think it is two
people copulating.' P. of W. in his rather sweet, intense way, said, 'And
how do you make that out?' How indeed? He examined it with close
scrutiny, but could not satisfy himself. When he left he shouted to me,
'Give my regards to Master.'

---

* A new whippet; a companion, Honey, was acquired in 1977.
† Hon. Sir Martin Charteris (b. 1913); attached to the Household of HM The Queen
since 1950; m. 1944 Hon. Mary Margesson; cr. Baron Charteris of Amisfield (Life Peer)
1978.
‡ In fact John Harris and Marcus Binney were responsible for the book which accompanied their 1974 exhibition at the V. & A.; Roy Strong, who was appointed Director of
the V. & A. in 1974, wrote the Preface only, and there were many other contributors.

1977

At dinner last Sunday at the House A. sitting next to Master repeated what the P. of Wales said to me, namely that Master was his hero. He was touchingly diffident, surprised and delighted. Kept saying, 'But he can't have said that. It's not possible. You are pulling my leg.' A. said it was true and he must ask me if he wanted confirmation. How extraordinary these Beauforts are. Meals are dreadfully boring, and the food horrid, in spite of chefs and cooks. There is no waiting at table and he does all the handing round and collecting of dirty plates, and the stacking. Poor old Horatia Durant and Miss Betty Harford* staying. Conversation out of the question, and platitudes and *politesses* without end.

Watched a film about the habits of spiders which rather upset me. Nature is nothing but one animal or insect or winged thing preying upon another, ruthlessly. Nothing more calculated to persuade me there must be a God and the soul. Humans cannot subscribe to this ruthless, eternal, selfish, cruel process. As for spiders, the close-ups of these hideous beings, the appalling lascivious, grotesque postures of their sexual acts, enough to make one retch. I felt despair in my heart, if this is all life is about. Better it had never been.

I have had unfeigned tributes from the two partners in David Higham's agency to *Prophesying Peace*, David H. comparing me with Pepys. He thinks the first vol. a preparation for the masterly second vol. Whereas I know the second lacks the spontaneity and sparkle of the first, and this is what J., to whom I have sent a copy of proofs, thinks too. I have sent another to Rupert Hart-Davis, who has sent me a p.c. that he will give it his careful scrutiny and lynx-eyed analysis. I was v. bored with the penultimate entries. Last night in Bath I tore up the original manuscript of the last two years 1944 and '45.

A. and I were asked by George Weidenfeld† to his party given for Nigel Nicolson's sixtieth birthday. I didn't want to go, but on pressure

---

* A cousin of the Harfords of Ashcroft, Gloucestershire (Alderley neighbours).
† Baron Weidenfeld of Chelsea (Life Peer, cr. 1976); Chairman of Weidenfeld & Nicolson, publishers (b. 1919).

from A., agreed. Truth is she will go to any party; I will avoid any party if I possibly can. However, a drama over Folly, whom Peggy's husband will no longer have in their cottage because of her destructiveness, meant that A. came back from London the day before she meant. On her return Tuesday at tea-time she told me there was still time for me to catch the 6.30 train to London. So like a fool I went, and reached Weidenfeld's at 8.30. It was awful. Crowds and crowds of strangers. Hardly a soul I knew. Drank Dubonnet and waited, drank again and waited for the buffet to open. Seized a dry chicken leg and some carrots. No table to sit at. Mantelpiece too narrow to hold plate. Balancing wine glass in left hand, knife, fork and plate in the other. Finally Baba Metcalfe,[*] with the pertinacity of woman, forced her way to an armchair, sat in it, pushed me onto a stool beside her, and we ate from our laps and talked. She told me how she had to take away from Philip Magnus the papers on her father which she had lent him because it was apparent he would never start the book. He admitted to her that he could no longer concentrate. Instead she gave papers to Nigel [Nicolson], who suggested that since so many books on Curzon had been published, a book on his relations with the first Lady Curzon, Baba's mother, would be more suitable. Already Nigel has written half the book. B. says he works like a beaver, and never stops for anything else. Talked to Ben [Nicolson] who will lend me all the letters his father ever wrote to him. He has kept every one. Said never, never did two brothers have a more perfect, understanding, adoring father. Talked to Archie Aberdeen, and Anne Lancaster who says Osbert had another 'turn' in the Opera House five days ago and was rushed to hospital. They thought he had had a stroke, but she says it was merely overwork, and he is now quite all right again. He sent her to the party to accumulate gossip and regale him.

Wednesday, 26th January

Billy Henderson's portrait of A. sitting in the drawing-room here has come. It is charming as a picture. I should have been present when he began it for I would have insisted that she should be sewing with one hand outstretched and needle poised, or else sitting with her head up

---

[*] Lady Alexandra Curzon (1904–95), dau. of 1st Marquess Curzon of Kedleston; m. 1925 Major E.D. (Fruity) Metcalfe (who d. 1957).

in her characteristic, proud, alert way. As it is, she is reading quietly, calmly, which she rarely does. Moreover he has made the face that of a dear, demure little old lady, which A. by no means is. None the less I like it, and the detail of the room could not be bettered.

The *Sunday Times* came out with a list of books forthcoming this year, and apparently – for I didn't see it – included my book on Harold, which is of course absurd, for it won't be finished for years. Chatto's did not give them this information, so I don't know who did. Now Kenneth Rose, informed by Nigel at Sissinghurst, has telephoned to say he is writing a paragraph about it in 'Albany' next Sunday. Very friendly, anxious to help, says he Boswellized Harold and will lend me his notes; thinks that as the book will not be a best-seller, H. no longer being known by the younger folk, I might just as well go the whole hog and do two volumes, because there is such an immense amount of material.

Last week Nick Robinson brought Nick Crawley, his Cambridge friend, to lunch with me in Bath. Afterwards I showed them the Holburne of Menstrie Museum and Pump Room. We walked round the city. I broke through the barrier. It was a help having the other nice boy with him. Then on Saturday Richard* lunched with us alone, and we walked with his and our dog in the rain. He is delightful, and possibly the easiest of the three great-nephews. Told me he had a girl; met her at a New Year's ball, and is very excited about her. He is 19. Told me he had not imparted this information to the brethren, which flattered me. Also he talked freely about his father. This is a great worry, for the father, Ted, simply soaks, cannot attend to business and is a responsibility for the boys, who do not know what to do with him. He refuses to go to a nursing home. Richard said the one man who might influence his father was Bishop Bardsley.† So I have taken the bull by the horns, and am going to interview the Bishop and plead with him tomorrow.

Sitting in a bus in London last week, it being a raw day I took out of my pocket my white lip salve and applied it to my chapped lips. An elderly woman sitting opposite put on a strongly disapproving face, and said, 'Well!' in a long-drawn-out tone. I paid not the slightest notice.

On Sunday we were taken by Billy Henderson to lunch with

---

* Youngest of the three Robinson great-nephews.
† Rt Revd Cuthbert Bardsley (1907–91), Bishop of Coventry 1956–76.

Michael Pitt-Rivers* at Tollard Royal. His brother Julian and third wife were staying. This lady is French, a publisher, intelligent and very sympathetic. Julian P.-R. is extremely handsome and elegant, an exquisite not unlike Julian Fane and Claud Phillimore.† Michael must have been very handsome, now about sixty and a bit heavy. He has a friend, William Davies, who has lived with him for fifteen years and been dangerously ill with anorexia, owing to slimming. Incredible. Is v. affable, but frail and thin, with gold hair cascading over girlish face, but longish teeth which give away the age, wearing Mediterranean clothes, thin white, black-lined trousers and open shirt, adorned with gold rings, bangles and medals round the throat galore. Michael P.-R. also singularly dapper, wearing country tweed suit with blue velvet collar to the jacket. Immensely rich, large land-owner, breeder of Arab horses, planter of millions of trees. Interested in family connections, which are legion. Explained how his grandfather inherited name of Pitt-Rivers through his grandmother, Marcia, who was the third daughter of the first Lord Rivers, and married a Lane-Fox. M's real name therefore is Lane-Fox-Pitt-Rivers. What could be more territorial? House half-timbered, which is strange for Dorset, painted pink. No family portraits, and no outstanding treasures. A Japanese garden and pavilion just below the house, amusing but unsuitable in this context. Nice, civilized set-up. Enjoyed ourselves. A's friends, not mine.

Thursday, 27th January

Rupert [Hart-Davis] has returned my proofs. I opened the package with trepidation. But he has been very nice about it. Has spotted numerous mistakes in spelling, which he says is atrocious, and punctuation. Yet says it gives the best picture of London in the last war years, and of the decaying landed gentry in their decaying castles, that he has read. So I suppose I need not have any fears about its future reception by those whose opinion, like his, matters.

Snowdrops peeping up, not yet bursting, and still in bud. Stormy weather, but not yet the disturbing snuff of spring which I still dread.

---

* Owner of the Rushmore Estate at Tollard Royal; descendant of General Pitt-Rivers.
† Hon. Claud Phillimore (1911–94); architect of country houses; succeeded his nephew as 4th Baron Phillimore, 1990.

Wednesday, 9th February

Took the index of *Prophesying Peace* to Chatto's (what a mouthful that title is). It took me a whole week to do; there are so many names. Like the *Almanach de Gotha*. I feel rather ashamed. Even so I have merely put the names under their respective letter, not in alphabetical order. The office are going to do that, mercifully. Then Derek Hill's portrait of me is to appear as frontispiece – a melancholy likeness. Norah says it is not me; has no humour, or sharpness; is vague and dreamy. I stayed two nights, 8th and 9th, in London. To the 'Masked Ball'. Bought a little picture by George Barrett, jnr, *The Flight into Egypt*, with a sickle moon and distant blue mountains, because it was the nearest thing to an Elsheimer I am ever likely to possess; cost £150 and I can't afford that. It all happened by accident. I went to Agnew's marvellous exhibition of nineteenth-century water-colours. Made a note of this one. In Brooks's that evening Geoffrey Agnew pressed me to do a bicentenary article on the club for next year. And in euphoric mood I asked him if he would mark this picture for me tomorrow when he returned to his shop, if it was not already gone. It hadn't gone.

There is great excitement about the impending fate of Mentmore.[*] It was discussed at the Properties Committee on Wednesday after I had left, for it was not on the agenda. My strident and forceful letter in *The Times* caused a tiny stir, I fancy, for several people have congratulated me on it.

I believe I ought to record my reasons for having left the R.C. church and returned to the C. of E. The reasons are several, but two are paramount. First, this Pope [Paul VI]'s encyclical *Vitae Humanae*, condemning birth control out-of-hand. No argument can possibly justify in my mind a pronouncement which deliberately encourages more births. I regard overpopulation as the fundamental evil of our time. It is the cause of nearly all our ills, vandalism, guerrilla movements, the negation of beauty, physical, moral, spiritual, natural and architectural. Second, the effect of the Second Vatican Council upon the Liturgy; the scrapping of the Vulgate, and the vulgarity of the new rituals; in fact the abandoning of so many duties which when I became a Catholic were mandatory. Third, the hideous Irish situation. The

---

[*] Mentmore House, Buckinghamshire, owned by the Rosebery family; it was not considered a suitable house for the N.T. to hold, and the contents were sold by Sotheby's in 1977.

Irish Church is something so loathly that I cannot bear to belong to the larger body which contains it. The disinclination of the Catholic Church to condemn the IRA's activities. The very evident inclination, on the other hand, of the Catholic Church to support guerrilla movements throughout Africa, the East and South America, to boot. The Church's championship of Marxist policies. There are other reasons. But these two, now three, are my paramount ones. Furthermore, I no longer believe in dogmas which I used to take for granted, such as the Assumption, even Consubstantiation, which when I was fervent I never questioned. Now I regard Holy Communion as commemorative and a sort of pledge of betterment, a swearing-in of allegiance to God, an act of amendment, an act of supreme worship. It means more to me than anything in the world, but I no longer believe that Christ is in that wafer, and so by implication *not* in the air around the wafer, the trees, the fields, my neighbour, me. At the same time I am amazed that all sensitive, beauty-loving, goodness-searching people, of whom there are so many – I am amazed that they do not go to Communion, that they blissfully ignore it and give not a thought to the Church's supreme sacrament. Why don't they? Is it laziness? Is it indifference? It can't be hostility.

Monday, 21st February

Philippe Jullian stayed Saturday night with us. In motoring him back to Bath station on Sunday evening I pointed out the house in Marlborough Buildings where Jan Morris had her flat. I explained to him that she had changed her sex from male to female, and had four children. 'How remmer-kâble!' he exclaimed. Talking of Violet Trefusis's continual teasing of her friends by telling them she was going to leave them this and that, I mentioned how she assured me, the last time I saw her, that she would leave me a gold box with the Prince Regent's miniature surrounded by diamonds on the lid. And of course I never, never expected she would do so. Philippe said, 'But didn't you get it? I am sure she left it to you!' I was amazed. He is going to ask John Phillips, her heir.

We lunched with Joanie Altrincham* on Sunday. Oliver van

---

* Joan Dickson-Poynder, Lady Altrincham, widow of 1st Baron Altrincham; she lived at Tormarton, near Badminton.

Oss,* a highly civilized man, was staying. John Grigg† had been in his house at Eton. Oliver said to me after luncheon, 'Do you know a nicer man in England than John?' 'No,' I answered honestly. 'I am glad to hear you say so too,' he said.

Talked to John about my biography of Harold. People constantly ask me about it now Kenneth Rose has come out with the news in the *Sunday Telegraph*. I am shy of discussing the book. Feel it is bad luck, tempting providence. Don't want to appear too confident. Am hideously un-confident, as it happens. I said how strange it was that when Lloyd George was premier he could be living in sin with Miss Stevenson and nobody knew, or rather the public didn't know. John said, but everyone in high places knew well enough; on the contrary, in those days living in sin was no impediment to a politician's career, whereas today it is, and he instanced the sad case of Lord Jellicoe having had a tart.‡ We agreed the reason lay in the media today rootling out scandal and exhibiting it to the masses, whereas sixty years ago a public figure could be indiscreet discreetly. Today such behaviour is impossible. The unknowing public is far more censorious than a man's colleagues and friends.

Wednesday, 23rd February

To London for the day. Ostensibly to lunch with Nigel and Ben; or rather, to entertain them to luncheon at Brooks's. We discussed the book. Nigel not in favour of two volumes, which he thinks wd be too much of a good thing. People wd say, who *is* this man deserving of so much record? He suggests that I devote a third of the whole up to 1930, and two-thirds from that date onward. But of course the published diaries tell all of this latter period. I foresee that this latter part is going to cause me the greater trouble. Condensation is going to be torture. I asked them both many questions. Who was Aunt Frederica? Aunt Frederica? they repeated, and could throw no light. They are funny the way they talk about their parents as if they were persons of

---

* Eton College master to 1964; Headmaster of Charterhouse, 1965–73; Master of the London Charterhouse, 1973–84 (1909–92).
† Political journalist and writer (b. 1924); succeeded his father as 2nd Baron Altrincham in 1955, but disclaimed title 1963.
‡ A reference to the Lambton–Jellicoe scandal of 1973 involving a St John's Wood prostitute.

ancient history, nothing to do with them; quite dispassionately, too. 'I don't think Vita actually had an affair with her.' 'No, Niggs, she may well have slept with X.' 'My father was certainly much in love with so-and-so.' 'You know he wanted to go to bed with Patrick Buchan-Hepburn, who wouldn't let him.' Saw J.K.-B. in the London Library. He was smiling and seemed content and busy. What more can a man want? He is off to St Petersburg next Monday for a four-day tour, to prepare himself for conducting a party there in April.

Thursday, 24th February

At Lord Bath's request, I went to Longleat this afternoon, to express my opinion of a pair of fountains he has had built immediately in front of the south elevation of the house. They are pretty bad. In the first place I consider he has made the mistake of laying the pools too close together and not in line with the end bays; also projecting from instead of parallel to the front. They are of vertical shape, not horizontal as they should be. The fountains in themselves are ungainly; thin, too tall and attenuated. They have dolphins on brackets on all four sides. On top of a second attenuated, chimney-like plinth he has put basins with spindly feet, their brims encrusted with lesser dolphins, like sugar icing on a wedding cake. Of course the whole thing ought to be scrapped, but obviously can't be. So I advised strongly that the chimneys be reduced by two courses of stone (incidentally they are of pre-cast Bath stone, not the real thing), the dolphins and the whole of the basin and stem (of white fibre-glass that does not match the yellow imitation stone) be removed. In their place, put a cluster of balls, and let the water flow through and over them. Lord B. is rather disarming. He wanted to tip me when I left. I said in no circumstances whatsoever would I accept payment. Nice of him, all the same. Christopher Thynne was present in the Green Library when we had our discussion. Twice he called me 'Sir', which made me wonder if he were being deliberately derisive, or deferential, or what, considering he is Caroline's brother whom I frequently meet at the Somersets' house.

Tuesday, 1st March

Philippe Jullian in his bread-and-butter letter has written that he spent the following day after leaving us at Mentmore. He described the present condition of the interior and contents as '*très lugubre et poussièreuse*.' Lady Rosebery was kind to him and gave him luncheon. I had a letter from Hugh Grafton saying that the Government won't do anything about the place, and the Roseberys couldn't care less. A further letter in *Times* signed by the members of the committee of the National Art Collections Fund, urging instant action.

Went to see my new friend David Wiltshire* again this evening in the Lansdown Nursing Home. He told me the Prince of Wales was to give a dinner in the States during his next visit in aid of some charities he favours. One of them is the Palladian Trust's endeavour to acquire a long lease of Warwick House, St James's. I asked how many and which rich persons would be selected to dine with HRH for this purpose – i.e., extracting money from them. He said, 'The computer will decide, of course.' Apparently the computer gives the names of those persons most likely to stump up for specific purposes. Wiltshire says that within a few years the police will be able to ascertain which burglar robbed which house, and which murderer murdered which person by this extraordinary means.

A. had the Vicar call on her this evening. He did not complain exactly, but commented on the autocracy which governs this village and his church: that when the Queen stayed last year Master invited the Bishop of Gloucester to preach, without consulting him, the Vicar, whose sole right it is to approach bishops for such a purpose. Master just shrugged off his timid remonstrance. Then the Vicar said to A., 'Have you heard about the row over the Grinling Gibbons figures from the tomb in the church?' 'No,' she said. He then told that both David Verey† and the Archdeacon at separate times had got on to him, having heard a rumour that the Duke wanted to sell them. Both were very severe, so the Vicar, trembling, thought he must mention the matter to Master, who was furious, and said he would do what he wished with the figures. They were his property, because Queen Victoria had given the monument to his grandfather. The Vicar was instructed to retort that on the contrary any object, whether given or lent to a church, automatically became church property. So apparently the figures have been packed up again and put back in the stables.

---

* The Bath solicitor J.L.-M. had met for the first time in January 1975.
† Architectural historian (1913–84).

Wednesday, 9th March

Went up to London for the day, to give Raymond [Mortimer] luncheon at Brooks's. Just us. We had two courses each, and one glass of wine each, and coffee. Bill just over £10. Having read up to and beyond Harold's Persian epoch in which Raymond is introduced and features considerably, I asked him how much he would mind references to his love for H. Answer was that he would mind any direct reference to the love affair, because at his age he could not stand an onslaught from critics like Auberon Waugh (who, I feel sure, wounded him in a review of *Try Anything Once*). So I promised to be discreet. I could do no less. Raymond again deplored Nigel's publication of *Portrait of a Marriage*, considered it outrageous, and once again said it astonished him how deeply both boys disliked their mother. Anyway we had an enjoyable luncheon and talk for about two hours, at the end of which I got little. Philip Magnus is right – one gets little by word of mouth. Only the written word is of use. Yesterday I met Lady St Levan* at the Francis Hotel in Bath. She was very nice indeed, and has a twinkle like Harold. A sense of humour, and her eyes screw up like Harold's when she laughs. She told me Harold was the kindest of men but insensitive in one respect – that because he was always laughing at himself, so he imagined others would not mind his laughing at them. Many of them did mind. Raymond strikes me as unhappy. How can he be anything else? All his greatest friends are dead. His world has gone. The present world is worse than the old. He said he would read again H's *Paul Verlaine* and give me his opinion on its worth.

Thursday, 10th March

Claud Phillimore, passing through Bath, came to see my library and then lunched with me at the Lansdown Grove Hotel. A highly civilized, gentle man. He, like everyone else I meet now, talked about *the book*. Begged me not to analyse H's relations with men, and merely leave them to the imagination or interpretation of the reader. I said I intended to do this, yet was faced with the difficulty of withholding truth. After all, if the subject of one's biography loved women one

---

* H.N's sister, Hon. Clementina Gwendolen Nicolson, dau. of 1st Baron Carnock; m. 1916 Sir Francis St Aubyn, Bt, who succeeded his uncle as 3rd Baron St Levan (he d. 1978).

would be bound to say so. Why not, therefore, when men? Yes, he said, that's all right, but don't elaborate on whether they went to bed together. I said I would never do that in any case unless I had proof positive, and unless the action had a distinct influence upon the story, which was most unlikely.

Saturday, 12th March

The Rees-Moggs lunched, and Coote Lygon,[*] Caroline Somerset, and Jimmie Smith[†] who is staying the weekend with us. I believe William R.-M. is a friendly soul at bottom, but lacks the ability to unbend. He probably is very conscious of his stiffness and wishes he could loosen up. His wife[‡] is absolutely charming, and I daresay the very best complement to him. She is forthcoming, easy, yet clever, and bright.

Tuesday, 15th March

Had two letters this morning from people suggesting that we ought to be on Christian-name terms; one from the Ambassador to Athens, and the other from Lord Bath. I know that I am hesitant about using Xtian names, owing I suppose to my upbringing and a natural shyness, even with my contemporaries. It really does seem as though I shall be going to Mount Athos with Brooks Richards. He writes that he has got us an extension of permission from the Greek Orthodox authorities to one week. That will be enough. The other letter from my new friend Henry, inviting me to Longleat again to meet the friend of his who has designed a modified scheme for the two fountains. I shall go there the week after next. Caroline was appalled, when A. told her, that her father, when I left Longleat the last time, had asked me whether he ought to pay me a fee. But he did it so nicely. I only hope he does not think fit to offer me a present.

I have finished Raymond [Mortimer]'s *Try Anything Once*. Now, somehow his writing is not sparkling prose. There is a flatness, a lack

---

[*] Lady Dorothy Lygon (b. 1912), youngest dau. of 7th Earl of Beauchamp; known also as 'Pollen'; m. 1987 Robert Heber-Percy.

[†] Hon. James Smith (b. 1906); Governor of the Sadler's Wells Theatre and member of The Royal Opera House, Covent Garden Trust.

[‡] Gillian Morris, m. 1962.

of salt. I would go to him for correct style, but not flow. Can't make out why a man so intellectual, so entertaining, so experienced a writer, should have this dead effect.

Caroline was a little, just a little bit tight the other day, for she got extremely confidential with William Rees-Mogg, and embraced him on leaving. He was enchanted because she was so natural and sweet. And yet surprised.

That absurd, but decent I think, and certainly vulgar American Bernard Luce came to see me this afternoon for half an hour to talk about the appeal committee he is forming for Warwick House. He rattled off the names of all the dukes and marquesses in *Debrett*, then asked me if I would join too. I said I would, if my name could pos-sibly add substance to so august a collection of grand person-ages. But Hugh Grafton and Brinsley Ford[*] I do know. As he left I thought I would this time be un-stuffy, and suggested that we should be on Xtian-name terms. There is always their embarrass-ment whether they call me James or Jim. I wish I was never called Jim.

We had Jimmie Smith to stay last weekend. He snorted and coughed incessantly. In spite of these disadvantages, he is a sweet man, musical, intelligent, and fun to talk to.

Saturday, 19th March

Today A. and I attended a ceremony at Tewkesbury commemorating the hundredth birthday of the Foundation of the SPAB – the actual date of the first meeting was the 22nd, I believe. We lunched with a select few in the town. Hugh and Fortune [Grafton] were our hosts; I sat on Fortune's left, A. on Hugh's left. K. Clark on Fortune's right, Lady Pilcher[†] on Hugh's right. So we were greatly honoured, con-sidering that I have not been on the committee for twenty years or more. On my left was Liz Healing[‡] whom of course I did not recog-nize until she reminded me that in the 1930s she and Peter rented Hodys Place from my father. She said the house was cursed. Did I

---

[*] Sir Brinsley Ford, CBE, FSA (b. 1908; Kt 1984); member since 1927 of National Art-Collections Fund; Chairman, 1975–80.

[†] Delia Taylor, wife of Sir John Pilcher (1912–90), ambassador.

[‡] Hon. Mrs Peter Healing, of The Priory, Kemerton, near Tewkesbury – a much-admired garden.

know that when my father pulled down the row of cottages and built on the site the present house with its mock Tudor beams and ingle-nooks, an old resident put a curse on the new house? I said she was probably referring to Mrs Hartwell, the sexton, but I could not imagine her doing such a thing for she was always a friend of the family. Mrs Healing instanced the death of the Löhnises' baby in the house, the death of their nurse's young man whose aeroplane flew into the elm tree and crashed in the nearby field, countless disasters to the Healings, and the misfortune of both my parents in that beastly little dwelling. Then we went to the west door of the Abbey, which to my surprise was packed with SPAB members. We, the illustrious few, processed to the front of the nave. A. and I sat in the choir stalls. The bishop and other dignitaries in the presbytery. Good service, Hugh G. reading parts of Morris's original manifesto addressed to the Nation on learning of the threat to Tewkesbury Abbey in 1877, and K. Clark delivering a splendid talk about past and present threats to the heritage.

Monday, 21st March

A. and I had just got into the house from walking Folly in the park when the telephone rang. John Fowler in a husky voice announced that Robin Fedden died this morning in hospital, of cancer. He was apparently riddled with it. And we had not even known he was ill. It was sudden indeed. We both extremely sad in consequence. Dear Robin being the very essence of vitality, it is hard to believe his spark is extinguished. This morning Jack Boles* telephoned me in Bath. I knew immediately what he was going to ask – that I should write an appreciation for *The Times*. Spent the afternoon composing some words, which are totally inadequate, and read coldly. So difficult to do. It is an agony. However, fired it off before going to bed this evening. Robin was a brilliant man. I always felt he was wasted at the Nat. Trust, because he was not a mere expert. He was something better. He was a very good writer, in which capacity he never fulfilled himself. I had hoped he might on retirement write his masterpiece, but he was always diverted by pot-boiling. He did not lack industry, or facility in writing. If anything, his prose was too highly polished,

---

* Sir John Boles (Kt 1983), Director-General of the N.T. 1975–83.

but his style was impeccable. There was something a trifle too precious in his *Enchanted Mountains* and *Chantemesle* for my taste. But he
could, had he not needed quick money and had he not been so incor-
rigibly social, have done better. He was distracted, like Alan Pryce-
Jones, by the plaudits of rich and beautiful people – in his case,
women. A cold man, he yet was very affectionate, and very loyal.
Drink was his undoing, and I suppose it was drink that undermined
his extremely tough constitution. A pompous summary this! I mourn
him.

Peter Healing told A. that my father was a remarkable man, a great
craftsman, an enchanting companion, but of course a bad parent. He
was devoted to him. He said that physically I now resembled him to
an uncanny degree. 'Put a patch over one of Jim's eyes,' he said, 'and
you would believe he was George.' It is strange how when young I
exactly resembled my Uncle Robert, Mama's brother, and today I am
a Lees. I would prefer to look a Bailey, and not a Lees.

Tuesday, 22nd March

Today is the actual birthday of the SPAB founded exactly a hundred
years ago. A. and I lunched with Eliza Wansbrough and with Paul
Hyslop[*] who was staying with her at Broughton Poggs Rectory. We
went to Kelmscott church at 2.30. A short service in the little church,
in which presumably Morris did not worship, very informal, conducted by the charming old vicar of the parish. We followed him to
the grave-side, a beautiful coffin-shaped tombstone with pointed,
ridge-like top and splendid lettering on the sides thereof. A
flourishing bay bush at the head, and alongside two little square stones
marking the remains of Jane and May Morris, the daughters. I
remember May sitting next to the Duke of Kent at a dinner marking
the sixtieth birthday of the SPAB, just as I was present at the seventy-
fifth birthday ceremony in St James's Palace. Monica Dance, splendid
in a new turban hat, laid the vast bay wreath and delivered a few
solemn words. We then trooped into the village hall for a massive tea.
Apart from Donald Insall[†] and us, there was no one representing the
Society. Monica and I solemnly cut the birthday cake. Much merri-

---

[*] Geddes Hyslop (1900–88); architect in the Classical tradition; shared 5 Canonbury
Place with Raymond Mortimer.
[†] Architect and planning consultant; member of SPAB council.

ment caused by my desperately trying to slice a pink round piece of hardboard put on top of the cake, presumably for decoration since it was the same colour and indistinguishable from the icing, and practically breaking the knife-blade in the endeavour. I read out telegrams of congratulations from the N.T. and the Graftons and the Peter Heskeths.*

Friday, 25th March

In London I went to dear Robin [Fedden]'s Memorial Service in Victoria Road. The church, not a small one, was packed with his friends. Most of the N.T. agents and representatives had come to pay their respects. I slipped into a corner seat, and was joined by John Cornforth. Robin's daughter Frances read the lesson (couldn't hear), Mrs John Carleton† read extracts from *Chantemesle* (couldn't hear) and John Verney‡ delivered an address (could hear v. distinctly). This consisted largely of my article written for the National Trust *News Bulletin* four years ago, on his retirement, at some length – to my embarrassment, but pleasure. Slipped away after with Midi. Kissed poor Renée [Fedden] at the door. She looking drawn, and sad, but composed. Now, I was not moved to tears, as I was at Patrick [Kinross]'s funeral. Does this mean that I was not so fond of Robin as of Patrick (I think so), or that I was made of sterner stuff today? No, I think in the end it is a question of affection. Only when one's friends die and one accompanies them to the grave's edge does one realize precisely what they have meant to one. People seem to have liked my appreciation of R. in yesterday's *Times*. I wish now I had not put my initials, but merely put 'A friend writing', because it looks bad that two appreciations should be by me, when Robin had so many friends. There was that great concourse; there was the ripple throughout a host of people who loved and admired Robin; and within ten years he will be forgotten, and unknown.

Gladwyn [Jebb]§ lunched with me at Brooks's to talk about Harold

---

* Peter Fleetwood Fleetwood-Hesketh (1905–85); architect, writer and illustrator; member of West Midlands Regional Committee of the N.T.; m. 1940 Mary Cockayne Assheton.
† Janet Adam Smith (b. 1905); author and journalist.
‡ Sir John Verney, 2nd Bt (1913–93); painter, illustrator, author.
§ Hubert Gladwyn Jebb, 1st Baron Gladwyn (1900–97); diplomat.

with whom he was in Persia in 1925–7. He was friendly and helpful, without being particularly helpsome; he is a stiff and difficult man. Humourless, I daresay. Correct. Was curiously eager to read what Harold had written to Vita about him at the time. Begged me to send him extracts. An unexpected vanity. No, I don't find that these interviews with people who knew Harold in early days are any help to me at all. Gladwyn a clever, good, honourable public servant all the same, with a very keen mind.

Tuesday, 5th April

A. and I motored in the Mini all the way to North Wales, to stay Friday till Monday at Vaynol with Michael Duff.[*] A very long way, and a terribly big bite out of working days. The party consisted of Michael and three young men, all charming – Gervase Jackson-Stops,[†] nicknamed Jerks-and-Stops on account of his speech impediment, when he gesticulates and snaps his fingers while one tries not to look concerned by the extraordinary gymnastics, a very bright, gentle, sweet little puckish creature, his friend called Simon Blow,[‡] handsome but for a duckbilled platypus nose, also highly intelligent and sympathetic, albeit neurotic, and Tatton Sykes, son of that archaic stick Richard Sykes.[§] He too v. intelligent and gentle, wearing a moustache which makes him look just what he isn't – common. These three youths all aesthetes and good old Tories, with no nonsense. Michael much aged; stiff neck, neck corroded by radium treatment, but still straight as a poker and handsome, clearly not at all well. Very funny his stories of Queen Mary and her ladies-in-waiting are, though after three days one is surfeited. Besides, one cannot believe a single word he says. Very snobbish these upper-class people are. However, we quite enjoyed ourselves. Vaynol is a not nice house which has been poorly truncated by Michael lately so as to be lopsided. The fake plasterwork on staircase walls of poor quality. Went to Plâs-Newydd, not at all a worthy house for the N.T. to hold, apart from the Rex Whistler

---

[*] Sir Michael Duff, 3rd Bt (1907–80); m. 1949 Lady Caroline Paget, dau. of 6th Marquess of Anglesey.
[†] Architectural historian and adviser to N.T. (1947–95).
[‡] Journalist; author of profile of J.L.-M. which appeared in *The Spectator*, 1996.
[§] Sir Richard Sykes, 7th Bt (1905–78); his son, now Sir Tatton Sykes, 8th Bt (b. 1943), of Sledmere, East Yorkshire.

room which by any age would be considered an artistic *tour de force*. Situation of course splendid, although they have spoilt the lines of the tubular bridge, so much in the forefront of the landscape, since I was last there. Lord Anglesey* a hearty, bluff, casual man who reminded me of the late Charles Cobham without his endearing manner. Very polite he was to us. Michael doesn't like him, but then they are polarities, these brothers-in-law. Their estates march. Vaynol gives an impression of doom; already has that given-up look, for there is no heir, or rather a nephew-heir whom Michael does not care for and who presumably will not live here. Bangor, horrid town, is creeping up.

Tuesday, 12th April

Eardley [Knollys], with whom I stayed the night, asked Richard Shone to dine. The three of us contributed food which E. cooked, and we ate in his flat. Richard is v. bright. He knows Bloomsbury backwards. Knows what Clive [Bell] thought of [Lytton] Strachey's review in the *TLS* on E.M. Forster's book on, let us say, 12th April 1921. Will be helpful to me if I want to know what 'they' really thought of Harold and his writing. His book on Duncan [Grant] and Vanessa [Bell] has already sold over 3,000 copies. He is going to stay with Duncan and suggested my coming down while he is with him, for he can make Duncan talk, knows how to stimulate the old man. Alas, I cannot go until after Persia; and then Richard may not be with Duncan, and Duncan indeed may die. R. told me that Duncan did tuck up with Harold; hence Vanessa's caustic remarks about the Nicolsons, husband and wife, when they were together in Berlin in 1929, she, Vanessa, also being jealous of Vita's intimacy with Virginia [Woolf]. Gosh, those Bloomsbury incestualities!

Sunday, 17th April

Stayed this Friday to Sunday at Chatsworth. Motored there and back. We visited Haddon Hall as tourists, *en route*. Beautiful and romantic place. The Long Gallery and the Chapel two of the finest Jacobean and medieval apartments to be found anywhere in the land. Gallery panelling *sans pareil*; Chapel wall paintings equally remarkable. Effigy

---

* George Paget, 7th Marquess of Anglesey (b. 1922); military historian.

of Diana Cooper's elder brother, a little boy, is amateurish, yet exceedingly pretty and moving. We were with Diana the evening before, motoring her to dinner with the Droghedas, a funny dinner party. Persian Ambassador present, a young bachelor whom all the girls of London are after. Not strictly handsome, but has a seductive casual manner.

Andrew here this weekend, an unusual occurrence. Very charming he was with his superb manners, which can raise frontiers between him and those less sophisticated, but not between him and *hoi polloi*. He speaks fast in a rattle, and is inclined to laugh in anticipation of a subtle *dénouement* towards the close of his esoteric stories. Being deaf and dense I can't always catch the point of these stories, and so laugh in a wry, unconvincing manner. Much talk of Diana [Mosley]'s book,[*] which was out on Thursday. All papers full of it. I have now read. It is courageous for it makes no apologies for her pro-Nazi bias, although she does not condone all the horrors perpetrated. She is right however in stressing that the enormities of Hitler do not equate with the enormities of Stalin and other world Communist leaders, which are glossed over by our Left-sympathizing countrymen. Yet, as a reviewer has implied, one black is not rendered white by two blacks. Andrew good-naturedly preens from his wings the prevalent Mitfordism which might otherwise engulf him. Hasn't read Diana's book himself. Today too presents the first extract in *Sunday Times* of Decca's forthcoming autobiography,[†] which is going to be beastly. I spoke to Diana on the telephone. She asked if I had noticed the graceful tribute she paid me at the beginning of her book. I said, Yes thank you, thank you, but it was you all who taught me about the delights of Shelley and Keats when we were children, and not I you. Diana's prose style is better than Nancy's; it lacks N's débutantish touch, and is confident and adult.

Staying here are no adults but a host of Sophy [Cavendish]'s friends, all clever young things in their early twenties. *Very* agreeable and nice to us they are, and yet, and yet, I find it a strain coping with their earnestness. And again, I cannot hear what they say. They mumble so.

---

[*] *A Life of Contrasts.*
[†] *A Fine Old Conflict.*

Wednesday, 20th April

On Monday A. and I dined with the Hewers at Henbury. They have a charming Georgian village house and very good garden in what are Bristol outskirts, Henbury now being a mere appendage of the great city. From the garden can be seen a hefty square tower block of flats. The Hewers are most civilized. Tom Hewer is a botanist and explorer of note. Has travelled extensively in Persia and Afghanistan, bringing back plants for Kew, and, having seen buildings unknown to man, has taken photographs of them. His latest achievement is to have discovered the cause of virulent cancer among the Turcomans, a discovery which the World Health Organization failed to make. It is quite a simple one. Tom Hewer found that ninety per cent of the Turcomen tribes, owing to boredom, and being confined by the present Persian regime within a small area north of the Elburz mountains contiguous to the Caspian, smoke opium and, what's more, eat the tar which they scrape from the bowls of their pipes. The Persian government denies (because it is forbidden) that opium is smoked by these wretched people. But inevitably it is obtained on the black market. The Persian government is furious with Hewer for making the cancer discovery, and the WHO is highly embarrassed. They ought to award Hewer the highest medal of distinction. Anne Hewer is a remarkably handsome women with sharp-cut, classical features. In their dining-room is a family group painted by Henry Lamb just after the war. It is like a Reynolds group, which indeed is what, without my spectacles on and seeing it from a distance, I at first supposed it to be.

Sunday, 24th April

A. and I went to Holy Communion this morning at eight. In spite of the fact that Badminton is crowded up to the eaves with visitors, and the fields are jammed with caravans for the beastly Three-Day Event, there were only four of us in the congregation. When we passed through the garden there was no flag flying from the flagstaff. When we came out of the church at 8.30 the Royal Standard was up. Queen evidently sleeps with her window shut. Not to be wondered at, in that huge ice-box of a bedroom. Vicar looking distraught and rather older. Upset because Princess Margaret has signified her wish to attend Communion at Acton Turville at 9.15. I suppose it does add to his troubles. He also has to preach to the Royal Family at 11.15. I was

anxious to go to the early service; I want to be in a state of grace lest
I perish before returning from Persia – certainly won't return after I
perish. Reading that the victims of the last air collision shrieked until
the plane actually hit the ground, according to the recording of the
black box, makes me sick with apprehension.

I dreamt of Robin Fedden last night. Although he was not exactly
an intimate, I have been affected by his death. I dreamt that he was
looking haggard and bent, and his trousers were hanging in baggy fes-
toons over his crumpled knees. Usually I do not dream of people at
any particular age. This was an exceptional case. Usually, I repeat, they
are ageless.

We have Fortune Grafton and her daughter Rose FitzRoy staying
for the Event. The child is mad on horses. A strange child, with no
demonstrative feelings discernible. Seems surly, and is only thawed by
our two dogs whom she is interested in. Awkward manners which is
strange, too. She walks into the room, without the conventional
greeting, and starts picking up objects.

I did not go to Morning Service having attended H.C. But A.
accompanied Fortune. They were put in the pew in front of the
Queen. She gave a nod to Fortune which apparently meant, 'Come
in afterwards, whatever happens.' So after church she and A. went to
the House for drinks. Alvilde talked to the Q. who was totally relaxed.
A. began by saying she always got lost in the House in spite of the fact
that she showed visitors round on opening days occasionally. This led
the Q. to say that she was opening Sandringham to the public this
summer and had to go there tomorrow to arrange the house for that
purpose. 'Mummy is simply furious with me for opening it,' she said.
I agree with Mummy. I see no need, and it will be an awful imposi-
tion. A. advised her to cover with polythene any fabrics within reach
of fingers, for visitors touch everything.

Wednesday, 27th April

We went to Persia for a fortnight, returning Wednesday 11th May.
Vastly expensive but my ticket for the 'package' was paid by Chatto's
out of anticipated royalties for *Prophesying Peace*. Poor A. paying for
herself and Chloe* whom she took as an eighteenth birthday present.
We were not sure how much Chloe enjoyed it. She read no guide-

---

* Chloe Luke, A.L.-M's eldest granddaughter.

books, took no notes, and showed none of the enthusiasm which we felt on our first foreign jaunts at her age. I wonder if this child will be an artist. I believe girls are seldom dedicated by their own impulses. They are driven into ideals and careers by the men they hitch up with. Chloe is mad about boys, thinks of nothing else; and is v. boring on the subject. I am not good with young females. They get on my nerves and I criticize and do not make myself beloved. On this package tour of some thirty people there was no one disagreeable and only one person positively agreeable. She was a Contessa Tancredi, a woman of 75, Dutch by birth, married to a Calabrian nobleman, recently dead. She lives in Florence and is a friend of Harold [Acton]. We were enchanted by her; most distinguished, agile, interested, very well educated, amusing, with keen sense of the absurd. A sort of Orietta Borromeo,* tall, upright, regal bearing. We ate together and sat together in the long bus journeys.

Isfahan the only Persian town that I call entirely beautiful. The central rectangular square pre-planned. The Shah Abbas Mosque one of the most beautiful buildings I have seen; ditto Theological College, and the Ladies' Mosque; also the House of Forty Columns. Took notes throughout. The clear light, the changing colours of the bald mountains, the refreshing oases where are streams and plane trees, the pine-clad Demevend, the ever present blue hills on the near horizon, the carriage of the women still wearing *cholajs*. But filthy food, and the hotel servants not agreeable. Our last night of all, in beastly Teheran, we dined at the Embassy with the Chargé d'Affaires (Ambassador Parsons whom we much wished to meet being absent) George Chalmers, an off Glasgow fellow, clever, with friendly, dumpy wife. Met several charming and cultivated Persians, all on edge of events. Highly nervous.

Sunday, 15th May

Home again. Dined at the House to meet the Plesses.† Fearfully mournful, and the usual dry food, which could have been so delicious, fresh salmon and pheasant. Master said that the foxes of today differ from the foxes of yesterday in that they lack blood. When he has to

---

* Countess Borromeo, cousin of the Earl of Rosse's mother; often mentioned in J.L.-M's earlier diaries.

† Prince and Princess of Pless.

'blood' a child (this revolting habit still persists — I went through it and was proud as Punch) he has difficulty in getting enough of the liquid on to his fingers. The reason is that foxes lack sufficient carnivorous diet. There is little in the animal world left for them to eat. No rabbits. The rabbits have myxomatosis again. Whereas there were lots of rabbits in Centre Walk last autumn there are none this year.

That divine Contessa Tancredi's Sicilian husband came from a family just like the Lampedusas; brought up in a mad old *palazzo* in Palermo. He had a pious sister who was a nun. She became ill, and her death was expected. The moment the breath left her body, all the clocks in the palace chimed in unison. The conte's father rose quietly from his chair, left the room, presumably to visit his oratory, and murmured, 'This proves she was a saint.'

Friday, 3rd June

On Tuesday I motored to London, my little car filled with those files of Harold's papers which I have read through. Met John Cornforth in Brooks's, and spent an hour walking round the club, deciding which photographs should be taken for my article. As John said, articles on clubs are only a little less boring to write and read than articles on schools. He lunched and we went to the National Trust's Architectural Committee meeting. I am going to resign from this committee because it bores me looking at drawings of tea rooms and lavatories, and besides I am bad at forming and giving opinions on contemporary designs. Then motored to Sissinghurst via Sevenoaks. Ghastly drive out of London, no better than it used to be twenty-five years ago. Nigel took me to dine at a scampi inn at Benenden; food horrid, pretentious and expensive; and with tip, over £12 for the two of us. It was my turn to pay. I suggested we must not again go to a place like this; better eat a salad and boiled egg at home. The next morning filled the car with a second batch of Harold papers, up to the end of the last war. The next day motored to Charleston to lunch. There were staying Eardley, Richard Shone and Paul Roche,* and a boy of 23 who had returned from Canada in order to cook for Duncan. Air of decay about the house, of faded artistry. Duncan is a splendid patriarchal figure. Is wheeled in a chair; has a long benign Father Christmassy white beard, and wears a wide-brimmed straw hat with long pheas-

---

* Friend of Duncan Grant.

ant's feather swept back from the crown. Paul Roche ties his beard under a bib, when he eats. He is apt to clean his paint brushes on his beard. Is naturally distressed by the barn beside the house having been bulldozed last week to the ground by the Firle estate's orders, without a word of explanation, far less of regret to Duncan. After all Duncan has lived with this barn for over forty years, and it features in many of his paintings. It is a bit hard; cruel in fact at his age, 92.

Stayed the night at Wadhurst with Terence Davis,* not seen for many years. He has a charming young Belgian baron living with him. This B.b. has a bookshop in Tunbridge Wells. Is immensely tall; grandmother staying, a Mrs Vansittart, aged 86, who is not a widow, and has two husbands living. Terence Davis told me that having sold his London house to Ruby Holland-Martin he went to see Ruby one Christmas at Overbury. Took his parents, Birmingham business people. Terence was terrified lest his father would say 'cheers' when offered a drink. Was offered a drink; and said 'Cheers!' Immediately Terence tried to cover the deadly word up by saying, 'Chairs? Yes, I suppose they are by Chippendale.' 'No, Hepplewhite,' Ruby said. T. Davis a nice man, but queenly in spite of his strenuous efforts to be nothing of the kind. At the back of this quite small two-gabled cottage he has built one large square room, with gallery. In the gallery are books. Ceiling panelled with square caissons, filled with mirror glass.

This evening walked the two dogs down Worcester Avenue, in the warm sunshine. Dogs dashing after nothing in the long grass, their little heads occasionally visible, and eager ears. Heard one cuckoo plaintively receding as though the last cuckoo in the world. Maybe it is. Stuffy, sweet smell of Queen Anne's lace.

Wednesday, 15th June

Ben Nicolson and Norah Smallwood stayed for the weekend. A good combination, for they are both indoor persons, given to much chatter. The weather was atrocious. No sitting out, but cowering over a fire, while the rain poured down. Ben looks just like Harold's caricatures of him when he, Ben, was a boy. Stooping, rabbitty mouth open, long, drawn face, extremely thin, but now lame; owing, he told me, to having smoked too much, which has caused a blockage in his artery. I suppose inhaling. Now he smokes only three cigarettes a day. Very

---

* Architectural historian, specialist on John Nash (1924–83).

uncouth, unshaven and grubby. Nasty old clothes, and trousers too short, showing a length of sickly white legs. But sweet and benevolent, and intellectual. V. pleased with the issue of the *Burlington* entirely devoted to him last April in celebration of his thirtieth year as editor. Quite a record. Norah brought me the jacket of my book, pretty, I think, quite unlike that of *A. Voices*. This one an apricot ground with Reynolds [Stone]'s most Rococo squiggles round the letters. Also brought me a page of *Round the Clock*, which is in good large print. Reading the one page taken at random, I thought what drivel these few lines were.

On Saturday at one o'clock I went upstairs to my bedroom to listen to myself broadcasting on the Third Programme about country houses. I wasn't ashamed; my delivery was pretty good, no faltering, hesitations or 'ers'. But the first sentence was a slight shock because of the affected ripple in my voice. After a bit it seemed to wear off. Or was it that I accustomed myself to it? I wish the text had not been about country houses, this too-well-worn subject.

I am plunged this week into Harold in the 1930s. Surprising how few entries he made in the months of 1931 and 1932.

Poor old Charlie Harford* has died. Son Ben was sent for from Teheran. When father and son dined with us not so many weeks ago, we were pleased that Charlie for once seemed to have enjoyed himself. He was almost cheerful. But he never meant to us what dear little Joanie did. I wonder if Ben will cling on to Ashcroft, which he dearly loves.

I have resigned from the Architectural Committee of the Bath Preservation Trust. That has been accepted; also I wrote resigning from the Nat. Trust's Architectural Committee, but have had a telephone call from Bobby Gore and a letter from Terence Morrison-Scott, asking me not to go. Shall probably have to consent, and stay for a few years longer.

Had much talk with Norah and Ben N. about the book; advice as to length, not two volumes, not to fear repeating what is known already in H.N's *Diaries* and N.N's *Portrait*, yet to skate over the latter years – all rather contradictory, and unhelpful. I find no one can help me, which is doubtless as it should be.

---

* Of Ashcroft, Gloucestershire.

Sunday, 17th June

Midi has rung me up to tell me that her Brian [Gascoigne] is about to marry a charming Warner girl, daughter of popular Esmond Warner who runs the library at Brooks's and bores the pants off all and sundry. Otherwise unexceptionable. He is having as pages at his wedding – slap-up, in church (he agnostic of course) – his nephew and his illegitimate son, now aged seven and very handsome and delightful.

Friday, 22nd June

Last weekend we had to stay two boys A. has lately taken to – Sebastian Walker and Donald Richards, or the beast and beauty, for the first is v. plain with a turned-up nose and dreadful little toothbrush moustache, and bad complexion. Donald on the other hand is not what women wd call a fine figure of a man, for he is short, but he is extremely pretty, aged 27. They live together in a nice house in Islington in blatant sin, making no bones at all about their relations; in fact, a bit too much the other way. They say things like this: 'Unfortunately, being gay, we got no wedding presents two years ago.' This actually said at dinner to Alvilde. Really I like their frankness, but not the flamboyance. Sebastian is a cheeky monkey. He calls everyone by his or her Christian name, whether he knows them or not. Called Sally Westminster Sally when we took them to dinner with her Sunday night, they never having met her before, and referred to the Duchess of Beaufort as Mary. They both make a lot of money, Sebby as publicity agent for a publisher's, selling textbooks overseas. He taught himself French, German and Italian, and sticks at nothing. The other is a successful stockbroker. He is Australian. They say, 'We are so rich we don't know how to get rid of our money.' Sebastian used to work for Chatto's, and having made his pile is about to return to Chatto's as a director. He told me he intended to succeed Norah as chairman. They shocked us rather by disclosing that they used to shoplift, for fun. At first I thought they were teasing. When they told Caroline, she was aghast.

Yesterday I went to London for two funny little ceremonies. The first was the presentation of a red rose to the Lord Mayor in the Mansion House at 11.30 a.m. on behalf of Lady Knollys, in permanent rent, or rather contrition, for having built in 1381 a bridge across

Seething Lane connecting her house to a garden the other side, this
without first obtaining the Lord Mayor's permission. We (Eardley,
Knollys* and I) were lined up on either side of the Egyptian Hall. The
Lord Mayor walked in, wearing a badge (no chains) of office and a
tail-coat. Followed by a Master of the Watermen in long sable and
ermine gown. On either side stood a row of Doggett's Watermen,
wearing scarlet uniform and caps, holding an oar each. The Master
read aloud an explanation of the purpose of the ceremony. A clerk
presented to the Lord Mayor a freshly picked red rose on a golden
embroidered cushion. During the address the Lord Mayor stood, with
dignity and aplomb, only his eyes smiling. A nice man. Ceremony
over, we moved to the next room and were given sherry, and a red
rose each.

London Library, shopping and Sotheby's in afternoon. Consider
making a bid for a lock of Dickens's hair on 6th July. Then at 6.30 to
24 Chester Square to attend the unveiling of a plaque to Mary Shelley
who lived in this house towards the end of her life. A Mrs Hass organized the whole thing, and put up and paid for the plaque. She made
a speech just like Joyce Grenfell and called upon an earnest young lady
with scooped-back hair, *pince-nez* and a green cloak to read a poem
of Shelley's to Mary. This she did on the pavement in the most
affected, genteel and emotional manner, so that I could hardly contain
myself. Refrained from catching Sheila Birkenhead's eye for fear I
should explode. Traffic roaring past and passers-by on foot were
amazed at the spectacle. Called on John K.-B. for an hour; then
motored home, eating *en route* at the first motorway station – filth.
Arrived Bad. at 11 p.m.

Sunday, 3rd July

The Sitwells invited us for this weekend. We couldn't manage it
because of sundry engagements. So we motored to Weston for luncheon, on a summer Saturday too. Would only have done so for them,
having heard bad accounts of Georgia's health. A divine day, the first
this summer. Sachie very well, though bent about the knees, sinews
gone. He will be 80 this November. But poor Georgia not in good
shape. Had a heart attack and on recovery from that tripped in a torn

---

* David, 3rd Viscount Knollys of Caversham.

hole in Charlie Brocklehurst's* Aubusson carpet and fell on her face. Is very hollow about the chest and bent, and yellow in the face. Large, questioning brown eyes with a bewildered appeal in the pupils. But as full of chat and fun as ever. Only slightly *piano* (or is it *piana?*). Their recent burglary much upset them. They lost many small treasures – family miniatures, the canteen of Sachie's forebear which he used on service in the Peninsular War, and similar things. Sachie bubbling with stories – of the strange woman who fancied she was in love with Gerald Berners;† visited the church in Faringdon one Saturday. A charlady was cleaning the aisle floor with tea leaves. Strange woman got into conversation with cleaner. 'How wonderful is his lordship.' Cleaner, at first non-committal, said, 'Well, my daughter obliges his lordship from time to time.' 'Then,' said the strange lady, 'she should realize she is on velvet.' Made herself known to Gerald. Became disillusioned. But stayed in the Faringdon Inn. And said to Gerald, 'The fish there is not the sort that you and I are accustomed to.'

Talked to Sachie about Harold. No, it is true that they (the brethren) did not like Harold. Why, I asked? Sachie did not seem to know, but said Harold was too Foreign Officey for them. Had no specific reason. Agreed that Edith did not care for Vita. 'But then, women writers are always rivals.' I said that the Nicolsons were rather shocked by the Sitwell play taking off Sibyl Colefax.‡ 'Yes,' said Sachie, 'I see now that it was a cruel thing to have done. It only lasted one night. But that was so long ago I cannot judge. When young one did foolish and regrettable things.' We lay on garden *chaises-longues* in the shade at the back of the house. I *am* becoming deafer; it was a strain to hear both Sitwells. S. has just read Tom Driberg's book,§ and is horrified, and nauseated.

Wednesday, 13rd July

On grey days the wild geranium along the road verges is like a glimpse of heaven. I believe it to be the most beautiful of the English wild

---

* Charles Phillips Brocklehurst, of Hare Hill, Macclesfield, Cheshire.
† Gerald Tyrwhitt-Wilson, 14th Baron Berners (1883–1950); composer and noted eccentric.
‡ *First Class Passengers Only*, by Osbert and Sacheverell Sitwell, was performed for five nights and published in 1927 as *All at Sea*, with a long introduction; Sybil Colefax was characterized as Lady Flinteye.
§ Tom Driberg, MP (1905–76), cr. Life Peer (Baron Bradwell), 1975; journalist, lecturer and broadcaster; the book was *Ruling Passions*.

flowers. Plunged suddenly into midsummer the air is thick with the sweet, musty smell of elder, and mown grass. But already men are scything the road verges with mechanical cutters, and gone are the blue geraniums.

On Sunday we lunched with Coote Lygon and brought back from Faringdon Luisa Nicolson[*] for the night. She told us that the first time she met Harold and Vita was years before she met Ben. They were visiting I Tatti. Vita went for a stroll with Nicky Mariano[†] and said to her, 'Your Luisa is just the girl for Ben.' When her marriage with Ben was going badly, Vita went to her and said, 'You must divorce Ben.' Luisa took this badly, thinking it interference. I said she probably meant it helpfully, realising, more than did Luisa, how unsuited Ben was for matrimony. Luisa said that when she was carrying Vanessa just before giving birth, Vita sobbed in front of her, saying she was sure Harold would die before her, and asking Luisa what poison she could get, to take the moment H. died. Luisa said Ben's ingratitude was his worst failing. He took everything done for him for granted. Never thanked, or uttered one word of appreciation. Vanessa when she stayed with her father used to clean up the flat, wash and put away. No word of thanks ever from her father.

Juliet[‡] looked ravishing at her wedding at Sissinghurst. She wore a dress from Hardy Amies which cost £3,000. Ben told me this in a deeply shocked tone of voice. No wonder!

Friday, 15th July

This morning *The Times* has a longish obituary of poor old Joan Evans.[§] I had no inkling that she was on the point of death when I took Ben to see her a month ago. She told him before he left that he must go to the bookshelf in the passage and choose himself a volume. This is what she liked to do with visitors on the first time of their calling. Ben was very sweet to her, and obliged by taking a volume of the Touring Club Italiano provinces. She was full of sense and talk. I

---

[*] Luisa Vertova, of Florence; m. Ben Nicolson 1955; m. diss. 1962.
[†] Secretary and constant companion of Bernard Berenson (1865–1959), American art critic and authority on Italian Renaissance art; author of *Forty years with Berenson*.
[‡] Nigel Nicolson's dau. Juliet m. James Macmillan-Scott; m. diss. 1995.
[§] Dame Joan Evans, dau. of Sir Arthur Evans; academic, writer on art, and first woman President of Society of Antiquaries.

say 'poor old', yet I cannot pretend that I loved her. I grew to like her. She was so over-feminist, women's lib., the successful girl from St Hugh's, so pedantic, academic, censorious of others not so educated as herself, so – I fear the word is – conceited. Younger women are probably not like that today because they are brought up with the undergraduates, not isolated in glorious, superior virginity. Yet she was a scholar of some renown; she was a writer of good English; she was a very clever, well-informed woman. She was, too, generous indeed, and I enjoyed her company, although she did all the talking, never wished to know what I was doing, and as for what I was writing, she never once referred to the fact that I wrote at all.

We motored to stay at Long Crichel. On the way lunched with the David Cecils* at Cranborne. Sweet they both were. He told me that Dotty Wellesley† resembled a witch, with her great, pointed chin. She was not a clever woman. Joyce Cary‡ he was very fond of; he was a great friend, only David did not like his books. They were not for him. There was a hardness in his style which belied his good and splendid character.

Thursday, 21st July

If a single individual could report his experience of death, the conduct of every human inhabitant of the globe would be influenced by it; would be different.

On Tuesday went to Strauss's *Arabella* at Covent Garden. Enjoyed it immensely. Revelled in the romance of it. The New Zealand soprano§ in great good looks, and grand, sure voice. The sets very good indeed, especially the last act, of the hotel foyer, with wide stair-case and gallery. I was moved by this opera. I sat the first act with young Donald Richards in the stalls. Found my seat was next to Daphne Fielding's.¶ Introduced Donald who was thrilled with an unholy zest. Before I had fully explained that he knew her daughter

---

* Lord David Cecil (1902–86); Professor of English Literature, Oxford University; biographer and man of letters; m. 1932 Rachel, dau. of Sir Desmond MacCarthy.
† Dorothy Ashton, m. 1914 Gerald Wellesley, 3rd s. of 4th Duke of Wellington, who succeeded his nephew as 7th Duke, 1943; she d. 1956.
‡ (Arthur) Joyce (Lunel) Cary (1888–1957); novelist.
§ Kiri Te Kanawa (DBE, 1982).
¶ Hon. Daphne Vivian; writer; m. 1st Henry Thynne, 4th Marquess of Bath; 2nd Xan Fielding, war hero and author.

Caroline,* he called out to her, 'Daphne darling!' I was much startled. Daphne in her jolly manner showed no displeasure or surprise. Really, this does seem to me to be going too far. He had never met her before. Second and third acts I sat in the seat immediately behind the conductor, and feared that he was going to whisk off my spectacles with his baton. I have never witnessed such an expenditure of energy and vigour; yet the man never even sweated. After the opera Donald and Sebastian took A. and me, Jack [Rathbone] and Desmond [Shawe-Taylor] to a Chinese restaurant in Covent Garden. Very generous of them. But by this time, 10–11 p.m., I was so tired after a long day battling in London that I could not speak. Besides I find these two boys uninteresting, and pretentious. A brighter sprite than I am would be entertained by their antics.

Yesterday, Wednesday, was an enjoyable day. I went to Cambridge by 8.30 train from L'pool Street. Took a taxi to King's College, sought out the library, presented my letter from Quentin Bell, was handed the thirty letters of Harold to Clive Bell, and ten of Vita's, settled at a table, returned to fetch a notebook from my briefcase, when a youngish man introduced himself to me. He had seen my signature in the visitor's book. He was Robert Skidelsky.† For once I cottoned on, and said, 'You are the biographer of Tom Mosley.' He was full of praise of *Another Self*, which his great friend Michael Holroyd recommended so warmly. I asked if he was lunching, and we agreed to go to a quick bar at one o'c. Then said he was off to see George Rylands. 'Give him my love,' I said. At eleven Dadie appeared beside me. Very affectionate and begged to show me his rooms and have a talk, which I did at three. Skidelsky interesting about Mosley, whom he has grown to like and respect. Says Mosley has strong cosmic ideals in which he fervently believes. Diana is more politically passionate than he is. Says Mosley never hated the Jews; merely thought that international Jewry was a bad thing, and that East End Jews ought to be removed. Where to? I asked. Liked this man. He said I ought to write a book about the Mitfords *en bloc*. I couldn't, greatly tho' I love them. Dadie's rooms lead straight off the College library, to which he has a key and access at all hours. They are on the first floor. We sat in his bay window overlooking the broad sward, the Chapel, the river and the punt poles.

---

* Lady Caroline Somerset.
† Professor Robert Skidelsky; cr. Life Peer 1991.

All so tranquil and civilized. Dadie said he rather disliked it now. Knew none of the dons, felt out of things, was not interested in the young. But since he has his rooms for nothing for the rest of his life, couldn't possibly leave them. The room we sat in was the scene of Virginia Woolf's description in *A Room of One's Own*. Doors and fireplace surrounds painted by Carrington.* Curiously old-fashioned in that the shelves are jammed with china and the sideboards and occasional tables groaning with silver, brightly polished. 'My bed-maker does that,' he said. I thought the number of cups excessive. Showed me portrait of Lytton [Strachey] which he is leaving to the College. Dadie much older; little round pebble of a head, somewhat skull-like, too thin skin, stretched. Those piercing bluest of blue eyes. Somewhat concave about the middle and protuberant in the stomach to which he pressed my hand on greeting.

Got back in time for dinner at Eardley's. Richard Shone and J.K.-B. Richard out-Shone us all. Very clever, very well-informed, v. charming, absolutely unspoilt. How nice he is. John was subdued, looked as tho' he was not enjoying himself. I sensed a silent grievance. If only he would not deprecate himself, not be self-pitying.

Noticed Raymond Mortimer's slender hands; long, sensitive, closely assembled fingers.

In the train this morning a child banged the table next to me, ceaselessly, from when we left Paddington until we reached Swindon. The grown-ups in attendance never remonstrated, never showed signs of irritation. On the contrary their eyes met in doting adoration. I could have wrung its neck. And they too could have wrung its neck, if it had been an adult, or not their own. How idiotic people are about their own children.

At Long Crichel the dogs chased a hare round a field, the hare turning and facing me. As it ran desperately, it cried. I was miserable. Mercifully it got away in a field of tall barley.

Jack [Rathbone]'s neurosis. Complained to Desmond [Shawe-Taylor] of his increasing deafness. Desmond played a gramophone record to him to find out how deaf he really was. Jack's tortured comment was, 'Yes, I am definitely deafer now at the end of the record, than I was at the beginning.' 'Psychosomatic,' Desmond said to me.

---

* Dora Carrington (1893–32); member of the Bloomsbury Group.

Sunday, 24th July

Let me never cease to be grateful to Joan Evans for the life gift of her sumptuous Khorassan carpet, now in my Beckford library, and of the bronzey urn in the central niche of the east book-case.

Poor John Buxton,[*] walking oh so sadly alone down the wide nave of Malmesbury Abbey yesterday, and halting in the porch to shake hands with the congregation. How people have the courage to do this beats me. Since I was at the back of the church I was the first to skip off. But I shook him with both my hands and smiled. I said nothing, and walked swiftly away. He thanked me for my letter. 'In pastures green he leadeth me, the quiet waters by' in my ears.

I see Richard Shone doubled up with laughter as I read extracts from Harold's letters to Clive [Bell], with whom he was absolutely open and frank, as to no one else it seems, in spite of the fact that H. was semi-homo and Clive wholly hetero.

Monday, 25th July

Derry [Moore] motored Diana Cooper to us for the weekend on Saturday. To my amazement when A. warned Diana that she and I were to go to the Barlow–Llewellyn wedding that afternoon and would be away an hour or two, she volunteered to accompany us. Now, imagine another old woman of 85 wanting to do such a thing, a country wedding of people of whom she had never heard before! Such is her curiosity, love of the unexpected, the novel, and her enjoyment of – every event. If asked to describe Diana as she is today, how would I do it? Physically, she is tottery on those tiny feet (how tiny they are, almost like Chinese). Her face is still miraculously beautiful. That flawless profile, nose and chin. Less good full-face. Yet the cold blue eyes are absolutely clear and fresh, those eyes which I once thought insolent, and which frightened me. Again she told us how shy she is; she has to fortify herself with a stiff drink before she goes to any party. I must say this weekend she drank little, was never tipsy, and behaved admirably. When she doesn't behave admirably, she becomes slightly tiresome. For the same reason, shyness, she wears her wide-brimmed hat, to hide under, she said, while clawing the brim

---

[*] Of Cole Park, Wiltshire; author and don (New College, Oxford); his wife was Margery Lockley.

over her face. She never has been able to speak one word in public; when she was an MP's wife, and an ambassadress, it had its drawbacks. Yet she never could do it.

What puts her shoulder-high above her contemporaries is her interest in everything; her love of discussion; her voracious reading of new books; study of new theories; wanting to know the meaning of a word from the dictionary, a date from a dictionary of dates. She is ready to do anything, go anywhere. She is the perfect guest, being undemanding, taking the rough with the smooth. After lunching at the Barlows', and going to the church, where she put herself in the best seat while I parked the car (when asked by an usher whether she was the bride or bridegroom's friend, she said she knew neither), on return to Badminton she went straight to bed. Slept till dinner, which was with the Somersets. On return home sat up talking till midnight. Enjoys food, she says, though she eats nothing to speak of, like a bird. Doesn't mind what time she has breakfast, or what breakfast it is. She is exceedingly quick in the uptake, is naturally clever, and also well-educated. In spite of deafness, and use of deaf-aid, she hears everything. Her memory is phenomenal, and she can and does quote reams of poetry read fifty years ago, and what she was told by, say, Mr Balfour before 1914. She is a miracle of a woman. A phenomenon.

Oh, and the most distinctive, indefinable magic about her – her voice. It is one of those, now extremely rare, Edwardian patrician voices. Vita had it; Diana Westmorland has it. The words are thrown out from the back of the throat, so that each falls clear like a pebble onto water. The articulation is perfectly rounded and smooth. No syllable is slurred. It is a proud voice, having nothing to conceal, everything to declare about the personality of the owner. For it denotes lack of self-consciousness and self-importance; it denotes humility; yet it also denotes self-confidence and assurance without swank. It denotes that devil-may-care, dismissive manner of the well-bred, who knows he is as good as anyone, who takes nothing too seriously, himself least of all. What is the tone of this voice? Deep, a trifle raucous, commanding. Very intriguing, very splendid. Diana is constantly laughing, because everything, however serious in life, is a mild joke, yet she never laughs in a full-blooded way, like for example, Loelia and Midi. Her eyes glimmer; the corners of her lips lower with mild cynicism, and a short, silvery shout emerges when she is much amused, followed by a few trills. Never a guffaw like, say, Penelope [Betjeman]'s.

Monday, 1st August

Already a noticeable touch of autumn, which usually is not felt till my birthday. But this morning that golden-through-motes-of-mist, slanting light, and that crisp brush of the air, almost that sour taste of chrysanthemum. In the evening I took the dogs along the Verge, over the bridge behind the Somersets' garden, the humped bridge, towards the Bath Lodge. Deadly still; only a loud humming of flies, an occasional rustle of a pigeon's wing as though a sleepy bird had momentarily fallen off its branch, and a distant coo of wood pigeon. No other sounds, but the galloping little feet of Honey as she dashed past me through the fallen leaves. Too deathly; yet bright, too sad. I wished A. was accompanying me to Ireland tomorrow; I wished X was not abroad on the Mediterranean, staying with Y. I had a sweet letter from X this morning. But I don't see X as much as Y does, never for so long a time. In snatches only. It is awful, and absurd. What, I ask myself, are their relations? I can only guess. But they seem inconceivable, indecent, painful to think on. And I, being unpossessive – I protest – have no justification whatever for minding. And no right or claim, moreover.

The Droghedas stayed this weekend. Rather exhausting because if at the end of a story one says something which catches her interest, she wants one to repeat the whole story from the beginning, having missed the point of it. Each D. interrupts the other D. so that conversation is out of the question. I took Joan to see the Bath library. She told me that Isaiah Berlin,* David Cecil and I were her dearest friends. When she relaxes, which is seldomer and seldomer, she can become natural and talk of books that have moved her, for she is a true reader. Garrett is better alone too, but he is so restless he cannot be pinned down. Joan told me that he never reads a book from beginning to end. He merely leafs through half a dozen at a time. I said to A. that I only like having intellectuals to stay: the strain of social friends is too great, and too unrewarding. Yet I dearly love the Droghedas. Anyone reading these harsh words would scarcely believe me.

We do not improve with age. Our minds become muzzy. We are inclined to deafness. The sparkle diminishes to the hesitance of a car battery about to konk out.

---

* Sir Isaiah Berlin, OM (1909–97); President of the British Academy, 1974–8; Fellow of All Souls College, Oxford; philosopher.

Tuesday, 2nd August

I motor by myself to Heathrow, park the motor and take the shuttle service to Belfast. Am met there by a smiling colleen who works on the farm for Mairi Bury,* and am driven to Mount Stewart. Staying here for three nights. Mairi very kind. She has her sweet daughter Rose, Rose's husband Peter [Lauritzen] and their baby boy, recently born, and old Duncan Morrison from Stornoway. Duncan tells me that this is the fortieth consecutive year he has stayed at Mount Stewart, if you except one year during the war when he was unable to cross the waters. The return fare to Stornoway now is £90. Mairi is curiously unrelaxed, and is matriarchal, and much the proprietor. Meals are on the dot of nine for breakfast and eight for dinner. You are expected to be assembled promptly. On the stroke we proceed to the state dining-room. There we five persons sit in a straight row along one side of the huge table, facing the windows. All the other places are set with silver mats and plates and glasses for the benefit of the public who pass through this room. We are behind the ropes, an odd feeling. By dinner time the smell of BO is detectable, and no one has thought of letting some fresh air in. Very good food cooked by an excellent hired chef from London; rather rich but delicious. Courses hurried through, and only time for one glass of white wine. At every meal the same procedure; Mairi helps herself first, then me, then Duncan, then Peter. Hastily we stack and by 8.30 are off to the drawing-room.

Wednesday, 3rd August

No longer raining; sunny and storm clouds. Rose, Peter and I motor to lunch at Clandeboye. They return in the afternoon to attend to the baby. Lindy Dufferin goes off painting. I remain with Sheridan Dufferin† who devotes his afternoon to showing me round this ugly house, barely altered since Harold's youth. Maureen‡ put in some pretty wallpapers. Sheridan is unaccountably attractive, very in fact,

---

* Lady Mairi Vane-Tempest-Stewart (b. 1921), youngest dau. of 7th Marquess of Londonderry; m. 1940–58 to Derek Keppel, Viscount Bury; her mother was Hon. Edith Chaplin, who m. 1899 and d. 1959.
† Sheridan Hamilton-Temple-Blackwood, 5th Marquess of Dufferin and Ava (1938–88); m. 1964 Selina Belinda Rosemary Guinness (Lindy).
‡ Maureen Guinness, wife of 4th Marquess (killed in action, 1945).

thought strictly speaking not good-looking. Is silent, without being taciturn. Is humorous, informative, gentle and sad. Swarthy countenance, not sallow, odd nose, good brow, wears dark spectacles, good skin, a young-looking forty. To think that I was at prep. school with his father. I felt electric contacts with him. It was cold walking in the gardens and park. He lent me a duffle coat of his. In the Campo Santo where the Viceroy and his descendants are buried, there is a tomb to Ava (his father, and A's first cousin), although his body was never found in Burma. A melancholy circle once enclosed by Lawson cypresses, now mostly decayed. Sheridan told me he did not know what to do about Clandeboye's future. He and she go there to stay once in the summer and at Xmas; he pays occasional quick weekends for estate reasons. Doesn't really like being there; has no friends round about. What is the future of Clandeboye? They have no children. To me they seemed fond of each other.

Thursday, 4th August

Motor to Killyleagh Castle. Received by owner Colonel Rowan-Hamilton, a good-looking, straight man of 55, married with lots of children, whose presence marked by toys scattered helter-skelter in this untidy, inconvenient house, all floors and twisting staircases. The first floor rather interesting nineteenth-century wainscot by Lanyon; also main staircase in Jacobethan manner.

Went on to Castle Ward. Got caught by the curator, Colonel Kidd, who recognized me from eight years ago, and wd accompany me round every room, quoting from my books sentences which I had forgotten ever having written.

Mairi told me that her sister Helen has married a Swede who is thirty years younger than she, and has a boy-friend. Admits he is not in love with Helen, but is very devoted to her. Told me story of the disaster in late nineteenth century when a boatful of Mount Stewart servants were drowned in the Lough, the butler, two footmen, housekeeper and cook. Old Henry Chaplin when told the story by Robin Londonderry exclaimed, 'How on earth then did they manage for dinner that night?' Duncan Morrison says that Pakistanis are already installed in Lewis, having arrived ten years ago with nothing. They earned enough to buy first bicycles, then cars. Now they are lairds, and he knows one Pakistani girl who is teaching Gaelic in the school.

Thursday, 11th August

To my joy X rang me up in Bath on Tuesday afternoon just as I was departing for London, announcing her premature return. But I had previously arranged to dine with John and Feeble. F. has lost weight through a diet. She eats little and drinks nothing at all. John looking better, but very shuffly. Is suffering from Parkinson's, which he discusses merrily. Takes an infinity of pills. A lovely joyous evening. John quoting from a newly discovered queer vicar, the Revd —— Bradford, who wrote sentimental poems to boys in the 1920s. Very funny about his two new loves, one a girl secretary, two an announcer on TV, a young man whom Feeble and I both find repulsive. He is the sort of youth, John said, whom he would have fallen for at school and been turned down by. When the said announcer appeared on the screen John addressed him in heart-rending terms of endearment and howls of laughter.

John Betjeman says the two most inspiring pieces of architecture he has seen this year are the rooms newly decorated and opened at Somerset House (the view looking into the courtyard transcends anything of the kind seen in Italy - he hates abroad), and Scott's cathedral in Liverpool, far more exquisite than he had been led to believe.

Friday, 12th August

Spent all morning reading through back numbers of *The Times* in the London Library, for Harold's speeches. At one o'clock walked to Albany to lunch with K. Clark. Found his door open. He called from the basement where he was preparing luncheon himself. Unfortunately Lady Birk,* the object of this encounter, was ill and unable to attend. So just the two of us. He was charming. Said how much he had enjoyed my *Prophesying Peace*. I thought him much older. He totters, but does not shuffle. His eyes are watery, and somewhat dead. His mind as sharp as ever. He has not a grain of humour, and it is this which makes him seem so stiff. While we were eating downstairs in a tiny cubicle we heard a crash upstairs. I rushed up to see whether anyone had broken in because when I arrived the front door was open. In fact he had shut this behind me. I went into all the rooms, but could see nothing untoward. After luncheon we went to the

---

* Alma Birk (1917–96), cr. Life Peer (Baroness Birk of Regent's Park in Greater London) in 1967.

sitting room and K. smoked a cigar. Suddenly he said, 'Oh dear, my little Renoir drawing has gone.' There was a blank space on the wall facing him. I looked. The drawing had fallen off the hook without even receiving a scratch on the frame, and lay on the floor. I admired a small Constable coloured sketch of clouds. K. said he bought sixty such sketches just after the war for £100 each. They had come from the Constable family.

He said he had read all Roger Hinks's diaries, and thought them wonderful; his observations on works of art were those of an exceedingly clever and enlightened man. They were more important than anything Roger had published, yet they were unpublishable. How and why, I asked? He said they were so highbrow that no student of the arts would bother with them. Besides, they lacked human sensibility. He thought too Hinks's references to persons lacked interest because they were perfunctory, without warmth.

Talked of Sachie, introduced by me, I think, observing that altho' Sachie's books on artistic matters were unscholarly, they sold. 'They did sell once,' K. said. It was tragic how Sachie could no longer get any publisher to take his books now, and had privately printed an endless succession of poems, which were perfectly worthless. Said he did not at all like Georgia; she was totally mundane.

He has recovered nearly all his treasures stolen after Jane's death. They had been taken by an Irish substitute for the two nurses in attendance on Jane, whether with the nurses' connivance he did not know. But the woman they engaged for a weekend, while they went on leave, was a criminal. K. got the things back because he has photographs of every single thing he possesses, every medal, every ring.

Saturday, 13th August

In a London self-photographic box by the Passport Office I had two snaps taken. They were so gruesome, I looking like a sinister undertaker, only plus, that A. insisted I have others taken in Bath. She said she could not live with one of these every time she looked into my passport during the next ten years. I went to Woolworths in Bath today, and tried again. Result just as bad, although am rendered smirking like a sinister footpad, instead of snarling like a confidence trickster. My God, how absolutely hideous I have become. Sad really, when you think. As long as I keep clean. I suppose all I *can* do is to maintain that one standard.

Saturday, 27th August

Reading Harold's letters and diaries written during the last war I am struck by his intense patriotism, and Vita's too, the very polarity of Bloomsbury's contempt for such an attribute. It has set me thinking. Does anyone under fifty have these feelings today? How can they? For England just is not the same country, physically or ethnologically. Having been in London this past week I have seen that half the inhabitants are coloured. How can these people cherish the old affections and traditions which we were brought up to accept? They are aliens with alien beliefs, and no understanding of our ways and past greatness. England to them is merely a convenience, a habitation, rather hostile, where wages are high, and the dole is generous, and the State provides while making no claims from them in return. Then, physically – oh God! the decimation of trees is reducing the country to a barren waste. All the elms have gone; the beech trees are on the way out; so are the sycamores. And the ash trees. John Workman* whom we saw last weekend is in despair. Conurbation is what is happening to this wasteland. The traditional landscape will by the end of the century be extinct. And surely when a man feels patriotic, he is thinking of the hedgerows, the wild flowers, the woods, the green fields of the England of his youth.

Saturday, 3rd September

Joan Hewitt† staying here last weekend watched me winding up the grandfather clock in the kitchen. She told me how during the last war Aunt Dorothy had a visit from some evacuee youths from Glasgow. One of them said to Aunt Dorothy, 'I want to go to the toilet.' So she said, 'Go down the passage and you will find it the first door on the right.' Within a flash the youth was back, saying 'The door's too small. I couldn't get through it' – referring to the door of this clock. Mercifully he didn't pee through it.

On Audrey's birthday, 31st, the anniversary of the terrible dinner here when a telephone message came that poor Prue had died, we went to dine with Dale. Audrey and Richard and Nick there. On the

---

* Conservationist and tree expert (b. 1923); Forestry Adviser to N.T.
† Friend of J.L.-M's aunt, Dorothy Lees-Milne; lived with her for over thirty years of her widowhood.

way we were nearly involved in a nasty accident. Coming towards us
was a string of cars from Painswick. A blue van was overtaking another
car, and seeing us advancing, had to brake so violently that having just
passed us by a bee's knee it somersaulted and landed upright in a cloud
of smoke facing the direction in which we were going. I saw what was
happening through my mirror. We reversed, furious with the driver,
a young man in jeans, and tried to take his number. Fury is the
motorist's instant reaction, although we were not involved. I got out
and approached the young man. He was not drunk at all. He
explained that the car in front of him swung to the left down a lane,
so that he was obliged to pull up. He asked if we would give him a lift
to Painswick where he lived. We relented. There was a musical instru-
ment in a case in the back of his van. I asked if he had been going to
a concert. 'No,' he said very gently, 'as a matter of fact I was going to
church.' We gave him a lift to Painswick. He was charming. We felt
beasts for having approached him in a hostile way. He said, 'God bless!'
and walked away in a dazed, sad way. A. remarked to me, 'Did you
notice that he was clutching a bible?' He must have been about
twenty-five. So strange.

Dale's cottage is surrounded by and filled with animals. Outside a
white goat, two horses and flocks of white pigeons. Inside, two
macaws sitting on the door from kitchen to living-room, a hamster,
two guinea pigs, several dogs and cats and her python in a glass cage
in the fireplace. Two children. The girl child is likewise mad about
animals of all sorts and sizes.

Wednesday, 7th September

Lunched at the Étoile with Robert Harling who runs *House & Garden*
and works for the *Sunday Times*. He is a diary-fan of mine and is going
to write a profile about me in *House & Garden* for October. He is a
roughish diamond, in late fifties I would guess, for he was in the Navy
during the war. Said the war was the happiest period of his life. Told
me about his married life, present wife the second, seven years' interval, three children. We talked of Harold Nicolson. He is fascinated by
him and has made a study of him. Considers Harold the masochist of
all time; that his judgements were too bad for so clever a man and
must have been arrived at in order to flagellate himself; that he was a
deeply sad man. Now, I disagree with both these themes. We talked,
just gossiped. He didn't ask me any questions, and when it was time

to go, 'But I haven't told you anything you may want to know?' I asked anxiously. 'I have got what I want,' he said ominously. I liked him. He said, 'I know the Étoile is a favourite restaurant of yours.' I said, 'But I haven't eaten here for years. Can't afford it.' 'It used to be,' he said.

Thursday, 8th September

An awful day of interruptions. When I got to Lansdown Crescent the *Bath Chronicle* telephoned and sent a nice but ragged and smelly young man with a proof copy of *P.P.* in hand. I asked, what can I do for you? He said he hadn't yet read the book. Then, I said, we can't discuss it very profitably, can we? 'No,' he said, 'perhaps I had better go away and read it first.' I agreed that this was a good idea. Then his photographer called, and as is the way of bad press photographers he snapped several hasty poses, one after the other, in the hope presumably that one might be recognizable. He kept saying, 'Look at the camera, and smile.' Now, no good photographer would ask his subject to do such a thing. At 12.30 Derry [Moore] arrived from London, sent by *House & Garden* to take photographs of me. A. came over and gave us an excellent luncheon. Derry would not allow me to look at the camera: quite right. Then he insisted on taking one of me on the pavement, as though entering the house. Whereupon a young man who lives behind the Crescent came up, and asked to see me urgently about Beckford. Since my day had been so broken I asked him to return at four o'clock, which he duly did. He wanted to know what philosophers Beckford had studied. He believed that Beckford was an exceedingly good man whose life was spent working out a philosophy for the benefit and contentment of mankind. I doubted this. Then he told me he had had a dream that Beckford believed in the transmigration of souls. Rather cracky, he was. At 4.45 another young man, with spots, from the BBC came. I was so exhausted I had to drink tea before I could talk. He made me do a two-and-a-half-minute talk on a tape, not about *P.P.* although he mentioned that such a book was coming out on 22nd, but about my working in Beckford's library. What did it feel like writing in this particular room? Was Beckford a benign influence? etc., etc., all rather rot, and muddled. He kept breaking off without stopping the tape so that I despaired of his ever being able to cut out the irrelevancies, and tie up the beginnings and ends. But oh yes, he would do it all right, he assured me.

The present-day Beckford mania among odds and sods is most odd.
I am finding difficulty in typing with the fourth finger of my right
hand. There is little feeling in it, and it flexes slowly; has to be cajoled.
Since I type with all my fingers I shall never learn to do without this
one. If it does not regain its old stamina, I shall henceforth type haltingly. Hope it may be temporary – but it coincides with loss of feeling
in some of the toes of my left foot.

Tuesday, 13th September

A. and I flew to Venice, she taking me as a special treat to Cipriani's
for eight days. Sachie and Georgia Sitwell were staying. We spent
much of our time with them, and usually ate with them in the hotel.

Wednesday, 14th September

In San Marco I watch workmen raising the onion tester over the
pulpit which this time last year was missing: evidently for repair and
regilding. Then I notice the date 1845 scratched on it in stencil. Was
that the previous time it was repaired? From pulleys in the dome three
men hoist, three support ropes while a seventh from the gallery directs
and pushes the onion this way and that, a matter of inches. The said
onion is hollow within. The workmen have difficulty to avoid swinging it against a figure on a corner bracket. The new gilding has been
beautifully distressed so as to deceive admirers. In spite of all the
workmen in their brown overalls talking at once, giving and counter-
manding instructions, they are conspicuously confident. They are also
very enthusiastic over their task. There is no indifference as there
would be with English workmen.

In San Zaccaria the Giovanni Bellini, signed and dated 1505, has
recently been cleaned. Note, the deep, dazzling blue of the Virgin's
fallen cloak, like a sapphire sea. The angel at her feet with violin could
not be a musician by the way she holds her bow. She wears an apricot
cloak. St Jerome concentrating upon his Bible on the right is the very
apotheosis of solemnity.

Brickwork of the campanile is already perishing. The snow-white
Ischian stone chimney of the Library – an obelisk standing on its head
– has been given a little square lantern. Within, the exhibition of
Scythian gold from Russia was seen by us twelve years ago in the
Hermitage. The outstanding exhibit is a gold comb, every tooth pre-

served; delicately chased figures on the handpiece, of horses and horsemen (*Sciti* is Italian for Scythian).

While dining last night just after our arrival with Sachie and Georgia on the terrace of Cipriani there arose, without a hint of forewarning, a hurricane which blew the candles out, the flower vases and the tablecloths off the tables. We remained seated while eating our quails before moving indoors. Sheet lightning accompanied the untoward wind. We asked ourselves whether this was the precursor of an earthquake. It wasn't.

At luncheon, Sachie disclosed that all his shirts and collars were detached, and he still used studs on the starch bands. A. said, 'How incredible! You must note that down in your diary, Jim.'

San Giorgio Maggiore. On the right balustrade newel of the presbytery is a fine little Rococo figure of St George in a kilt slaying the dragon. He has too boy-like a face and expression for an action of such savagery.

Il Redentore: in the sacristy are to be seen through a glass door the wax, bearded heads of friars under glass cloches, like covered clocks on Victorian mantelpieces.

Thursday, 15th September

The church of the Angel Raffaele has a *baldacchino* coronal with fir cones or perhaps ears of corn which quiver under the sunlight from the dome.

A. and Sachie and I went church-crawling this morning. We took the *vaporetto* from Zitelle to the Zattere. Sachie in walking is rather bent about the shoulders and shaky in the knees. Took us, in addition to Angelo Raffaele, to Carmine, and San Nicolò dei Mendicoli. Has wonderful memory how to find his way up to gallery of the first. While waiting for the Cipriani motor-boat he told us that because he has no faith, he has much dread of death; that Denys Sutton's forthcoming biography* of him is very bad.

We dined with the Decazes at Palazzo Polignac. I had long talk with the duke about de Cossart's Life of Princess Winnie.† I told him there were no grounds for worry – only the references to her relations with

---

* *The World of Sacheverell Sitwell* (1981).
† *The Food of Love* (1978).

other women lacked refinement in the telling. The Abbot of ——,
known to his intimates as Fr Dolly, and another priest, were staying.
The Decazes are very devout. The Abbot very chic with gold chain
round the neck and an ancient abbatial ring of diamonds. Told me he
fought in the Irish Guards during First World War.

On returning to our hotel ran into Graham Sutherland standing
and talking with an unknown man like a painted monkey 'who has
written the life of Noël'. Were introduced. I thought the monkey said
Knole and replied, 'How interesting, for I love that house.' He so
flattered me about my books that I felt embarrassed. Graham is barely
recognizable, so aged and concave in the middle. I informed him how
pleased Eardley was with his visit to them at Trottiscliffe. Graham said,
'Yes, I am fond of Eardley, but I cannot discuss with him his painting,
if you know what I mean.' 'I do know what you mean,' I replied, but
did not add that I also knew that Eardley, to whom he and Cathie
owed so much, was no longer considered by them as important.
Cathie is so grand that she never leaves the special suite which they
are given by Cipriani, the VIP one. There still hovers around Graham
that unsureness, that tendency to spikiness, that fear of seeming too
gracious to the undeserving.

Friday, 16th September

'*Buon giorno, Maestro!*' I heard an Italian say, bowing stiffly from the
waist, as Graham emerged this morning from his enclosed suite. G.
gave a sharp look over his spectacles to make sure the man was not
himself another VIP, quickly decided he was not and returned him a
slight incline of the head. I tossed Graham a faint, wry smile.

Lovely sounds of syncopated, cracked church bells at midday from
S.M. Formosa and at two o'clock from St Mark's. Purposeful, masterful, relentless strokes, very nostalgic of pre-war Italy when these
sounds were far more plentiful than they are today.

Yesterday Sachie said the Gesuati (distinct from the Gesuiti) were a
religious order whose sole duty lay in distilling scents. The order was
dissolved by papal decree in the eighteenth century, one not noted for
intolerance of sinecures or un-onerous spiritual duties. Anyway, they
commissioned Tiepolo to paint the most beautiful ceiling in any
Venetian church.

A. and I went this morning to an exhibition in Museo Correr (fine
Napoleonic decoration, walls, mirrors and sconces) of German artists

who visited Italy in the neo-Classical era, *viz*: Friedrich Overbeck, *c.* 1820s and Pre-Raphaelites Franz Theobald Horny, Ernest Fries, Kart Blechen, and best of all – I have forgotten already. These exhibitions are extremely expensive, entry nearly £1 each.

Saturday, 17th September

Around two o'clock a.m. we both woke up, and within three minutes there was an earth tremor, as though someone was pulling the end of the bed in short, sharp tugs. A gale and pouring rain ensued the rest of the night and all today. It is impossible to go out of doors. We are frozen and our summer clothes are totally inadequate. Sat about in hotel all morning (have finished Virginia Woolf's diaries), half gossiping with Sachie. Woolf's diaries are a disappointment to me. Are too concentrated, too inward-looking, for all the light they shed on a great writer's mind-workings. Not easy reading. Yet noteworthy observations. When one writer compliments another upon his book, he withholds praise from a particular virtue which he senses the other prides himself upon.

Sunday, 18th September

The cold is Arctic. A bora wind from the Alps, or Siberia. Yet by evening the sky is clear, and the wind has dropped. Venice is serene.

Anna Maria Cicogna lunched with the Sitwells, and we joined them. I sat next to her, and she talked. 'She sees in you a fellow crusader,' Sachie said. She told me the Italian Communists were regarded by Moscow as irredeemable schismatics. To them French Communists were heretics – less unconforming.

The panel under the ridiculous equestrian figure of Victor Emmanuel on the Schiavone is worth noting. The King is greeted by an Edwardian lady with wasp waist and bustle, holding a parasol.

Monday, 19th September

Graham [Sutherland] may be a great artist – I am inclined to think he is – but he is not a great man. He addresses one with a studied affability, which means nothing. He models himself on K. Clark. But his graciousness is less insufferable than the affectation of Cathie which is so transparent, so assumed (her model being Jane Clark with a dash of Daisy Fellowes)* and so childish as to deserve her a good smacking.

Sachie this morning pointed out the mask on the façade of S.M. Formosa, a sort of leering John Sutro,† without the benignity, which a doctor friend of his once diagnosed as symptomatic of a rare disease.

Sightseeing with Sachie means dashing from church to church, barely casting an eye on a favourite object, and immediate flight to a neighbouring church. He told me while we were alone drinking coffee on the Campo of S.M. Formosa that he considered he had never received his due as a writer. 'I have written over ninety books,' he said, as though that had anything to do with his being a good writer. A fertile one, yes. There is some justification in his complaint, but not a great deal. I love Sachie dearly. He is a raconteur, and few of his books are sustained. That is his trouble. He dreads his eightieth birthday in November and again beefs about Denys's biography. It is poor, lacks humour and is heavy-fisted. Apparently another, consisting of essays of appreciation, is about to appear.‡ At all events he dreads any form of celebration, being a shy man. He loathes getting old, fearing death like all non-believers.

To return to Graham. God chooses his instruments for creating works of art mysteriously. Good artists can be men of little philosophy and small brain. Good writers must be men of brain. Composers and sculptors can be simple, even downright stupid.

Tuesday, 20th September

A message left at Cipriani's by Stuart Preston. So I met him after dinner. Sprucer than last time seen. Greeted me with effusiveness. 'To think that you should be here. What bliss!', holding me at arm's length. We stepped across the Piazza from Bel Sito, where he is staying, to Harry's Bar. Talk disconnected. He did mention *Ancestral Voices* which he has not read because Pope-Hennessy wrote advising him not, saying it was a disgraceful book. I told Stuart I had (have) a

---

* Marguerite, dau. of 4th duc Decazes (1890–1962); she m. 1st (1910–18) Prince Jean de Broglie; 2nd, 1919, Hon. Reginald Fellowes.
† Founder at Oxford of the Oxford Railway Club, which hired trains to drive about while the members on board ate food cooked by London restaurant chefs and drank fine wines (1904–85).
‡ *Sacheverell Sitwell – An Appreciation* (1977).

letter from John P.-H. warmly congratulating me. Stuart said he hoped he was left out of vol. 2. I said he was mentioned seldom. Really can't remember how much he comes in. He embraced me twice in the Piazza. Two kisses of peace, so to speak, rather dearly bought.

Wednesday, 21st September

Ran into Stuart in the street. Gave me a cappuccino and some useful advice what to discuss and with whom for H.N. data. The dear old creature.

A. returned to England. I flew to Salonika where I met Derek Hill, and together we set off the following day for Mount Athos. I entered our day-to-day movements, as a diary-letter to Alvilde, in a red note-book.

Thursday, 22nd September

It is now 6.15 and I have just left Rome for Athens, two and a half hours late, and I am already full of misgivings whether I shall reach Salonika tonight, or have to stay in Athens, and if so whether Derek will be in a great state, and what sort of state I shall be in myself, for I feel sure my luggage, last seen in Venice, will never keep up with me. In any case I feel quite lost without you, my darling . . .

It's now 11 p.m. in the air from Athens to Salonika. Oh, the hell I've been through, changing from one Athens airport to another, sharing a taxi with strangers, being motored miles out of the way and then robbed by the taxi-driver. Agony enhanced by not speaking one word of Greek. They are *hellish* people I think. I now don't know whether I have enough money to pay the next taxi in Salonika, at what will then be midnight - for we are one hour ahead of Italian time.

Friday, 23rd September

Well, I got to Salonika at midnight. The hotel was at the bus stop. Such luck. D. had booked me a room and left instructions that I should call him at no matter what time. Went to see him for two minutes and was cheered by his genial phiz.

Up this morning at 7.30. Spent hours at the Consulate, the police station, etcetera, getting papers. And visited one dreary old Byzantine church with invisible mosaics in the dome. After luncheon in Salonika (which is like a nasty Hove – but has pretty mauve hibiscus growing as trees along the streets) we took a bus to Ouranopolis – a three and a half hour journey in much discomfort. Greeks belching smoke over us. No room for legs, and v. cramped. Arrived here (which is the frontier) in pouring rain, the first drops for nine months. This strange medieval tower is inhabited by old Mrs Loch, Australian widow of the writer of the standard book on Mount Athos, several friends and a charming Polish prince of 80, a friend of Alfy Clary.

D. so far is the ideal travelling companion, capable, good-tempered, amused and amusing. Sees the funny side of everything.

The tower is well restored and reminds me of Lindisfarne Castle inside. We however are sleeping in a guest house run by Mrs Loch's maid. Conditions simple, but not absolutely primitive. We came back to guest house at ten p.m. to find a young American girl, almost completely nude, cooking her supper in the kitchenette-cum-lavatory-cum-washroom, we having dined in the tower on fried fish with their heads and tails on, and full of bones.

Saturday, 24th September

Woken at four by an appalling thunderstorm and teeming rain. Never heard such a din. Breakfasted off eggs and honey and toast and 'real' coffee before the final packing of haversacks. Mine is a beast to put on; so is Derek's old khaki canvas one, for that matter. In addition the little bag you gave me is bursting with tins we bought in Salonika.

At 9.30 caught the boat at Ouranopolis for Daphni. Beauty of the Athonic coast is indescribable; purple hills and the mountain sliding sheer into the water. Boat top-heavy, crammed with monks grasping umbrellas, and pilgrims like us bearing burdens. A very lop-sided boat, rolling and pitching. When boat rolling the monks on chairs are hurtled across the deck, and hurtled back again.

Bus from Daphni an hour and a half to the capital, Karyes. Again crammed. I stand all the way, head thrust into chest by roof. The road – the only road on the Athos peninsula – is like the bed of a *torrente* in the dry season. On arrival we have our passports examined by the police; then by the Church. This takes one hour. After which we eat in one of those pitch-dark caverns, off tepid bean soup and noodles seasoned with cinnamon. Not inedible. Then we call on the Governor – this is part of D's self-important activity – and are regaled with chat about the Mountain, and told that the number of monks is now on the increase.

I am taking my two Strepto-Triads a day and already have colly-wobbles.

We are this evening staying in our first monastery – Chilandari – Serbian – and I write this at a rickety table in my cell. Awful old iron bed with rug on mattress and a pile of grey sheets and one horse-rug on top. Washing place consists of a sink in the passage, cold tap, and round the corner a loo which I can locate by the stink. There is no electric light, only one oil lamp. On unpacking I take care to spread my clothes on my plastic mackintosh.

Dinner tonight in the kitchen with two nice Yugoslav pilgrims, uncle and nephew, both Greek Orthodox, and George, the Greek lay brother–servant, sitting in an overall at the head of the table, a sweet character, who sucks his teeth and wipes his moustache with the back of his hand. Derek talks to the Yugoslavs in fluent German. Dinner of cold potato, cold tomato and cucumber salad. Nothing else but the most horrible wine, like vinegar, which the others toss down as though it were nectar. D. and I empty ours into a flower pot. Bed at nine. Goodnight. I think of you tucked up with the two doggies. Curious that I am not the least bit hungry.

Sunday, 25th September

Rained in the night. Much colder this morning. Have I brought enough warm clothes? A wonderful view from my bedroom window of Limnos, exactly halfway between here and Turkey. Mount Athos wreathed in grey cotton wool. Breakfast consists of our own tea-bags (bless you for these!) and hunks of dry white bread. No jam or honey. We are off to Pantokrator on foot for the day, without, thank God, knapsacks. Derek this morning in a panic; he thinks the Council of Monks are ganging up against him and we won't get our extension of extra four days.

We walked this morning to Pantokrator monastery, downhill through chestnut woods, undergrowth smelling heavenly and autumnal in the sun after last night's rain. Quietness is the most notable thing about the peninsula. There are no machines of any kind, no mechanical saws – just as there is no electricity and no hot water. Walking is

not made easy by the cobbles and hefty stones of the paths. Haven't
set eyes on a mule yet, and hardly a donkey about. This monastery is
perched just above the sea. Lovely view of your island, Thasos, very
mountainous and apparently thick with trees. Our monastery has a
medieval pele tower, and a courtyard painted white and blue, with old
blue and white glazed china plates inset in the brick walls. We met an
archaeologist walking to the monastery and he showed us the icons
kept in a gallery not usually shown to visitors. The monks are reluctant to let us see their treasures. But the church, painted ox-blood
outside, contains some heavily chased chandeliers and silver icons.
The usual *disgusting* luncheon of beans swimming in grease which
gives me wind, and revolting wine. The meals are awful. We ate with
a young Greek and a young Polish pilgrim. Very earnest and devout
they were.

Walked uphill back to Karyes and the same hostel as last night. Very
bitter wind. We sent you a postcard this evening. I hope it arrives after
me.

This is the most beautiful Mediterranean country I have ever been
in because it is totally unspoilt. Mauve cyclamen and crocuses out, and
a little blue flower which D. says is a kind of grape hyacinth. But I
cannot support that notion at this season. Also that long spiky lilac
flower like the *Buddleia alternifolia*, only not weeping, but growing
upwards. The poke-weed very common, hollyhocks. On the whole
few flowers out. Orange trees in sheltered monastery courtyards and
camellias and magnolias, not blooming of course. The lushness and
greenery, sweet chestnuts, hazel nuts and cypress clothe the landscape.
There is no farming done; there are few vines. No wheat, no cattle,
goats or sheep. What the monks do beyond praying from two a.m. till
six p.m., poor things, I can't imagine.

D. tells me to say that other plants here are *Cineraria maritima*,
arbutus (whose pink berries we ate), samphire, *Erica arborea* (there,
how botanical I become).

Monday, 26th September

I write this in a small cell sharing with Derek in a monastery up in the
hills, called Konstamonitou. By my bed is an oil lamp on a chair. It is
8.45. The donkey bells below our window jangle in the cool, crisp
air, for it is oh! so cold now after dark – which, owing to the clocks
going forward on Sunday, comes at 6.30 sharp.

We have had such an odd day. Started off in the bus at Karyes after breakfast of BEA Nesc. coffee and a lump of bread without jam (no butter of course or anything resembling). Tremendous altercations between bus driver and passengers because there were too many of the latter. Eventually all the standers were made to get out. D. and I early in our seats refused to budge. Bus bumped down the dry bed of the '*torrente*' to Daphni. There, waiting for the boat, we had a fried egg each and yoghurt of the most delicious sort. This an unexpected treat, much relished. Boat came in. We piled ourselves into it; to be immediately ordered off and herded through Customs. Every cranny of our knapsacks examined and in the course of it I think my spectacle case dropped out, for now I have only the dark pair, through which I write this. For fifteen minutes we sailed northwards to Dochiariou Monastery which is on the sea and looks like Knole or Penshurst, a cluster of buildings round a pele tower. We looked at icons in the church, each one resembling its neighbour. Then in the monastic kitchen were offered on a silver salver tiny glasses of aniseed to drink, small cups of coffee and Turkish delight. Heavenly.

Soon set off along the coast, over shingle and a very rough path for three miles, turning inland and climbing, climbing to monastery of Konstamonitou, on a glorious site at the head of a valley overlooking the distant sea. A lovely sunny day which does not prevent us being boiled and frozen by turns. In carrying the bloody haversacks uphill in the sun we sweat like pigs. Five minutes later in the shady monastery we have to take haversacks off in order to unpack for a jersey.

We arrived at Konstamonitou at 4.30. Vespers were taking place in the chapel. We dumped our luggage on a bench. Went in, listened, prayed and on leaving the door were conducted by polite monks, without a word being spoken, to the refectory. Here given a Ritzy meal of fish, a sort of *bouillabaisse*, the inevitable tomato and sweet-acid wine. This over at five. With darkness at 6.30 there is nothing to do but go to bed. Straining the eyes over a book through dark specs is not on. Hence fumbling over this letter. It is now nine and Derek is fast asleep. He had an excruciating attack of cramp in the groin, and rolled in agony, screaming blue murder. I did not know what to do but give him whisky and tell him to relax. Luckily the attack soon passed, as these attacks usually do. This one I suggest was provoked by his use of muscles he is not accustomed to using. *En route* he looks so funny slung, like one of the knights in *Alice in Wonderland*, with cameras, canvas bags on long strings, and loose coats and pullovers dragging through the dusty paths.

The nights are the worst hours of this expedition – the rock-like palliasses, and tonight no sheets, only horse-rugs, not to be examined too closely. Good night, darling. Is this fearfully boring?

The beauty of the monastery by moonlight. Throughout the entire night the monks are celebrating the vigil of the Feast of the Holy Cross and chanting vigorously in the chapel.

Tuesday, 27th September

Elsewhere all lights were out by 9.30. D. and I both woke at 6.30. He a very good sleeping companion – no snores. The very worst moment of every day is the matutinal washing at a plug-less, dirty basin from a high-up, splashing tap of icy water, in an open cloister. On finishing my ablutions I found that D. had swigged the remains of his whisky tot and eaten half a tin of pâté spread on the smashed crumbs of Petits Beurres biscuit. There seemed small likelihood, the monks being still at prayer, of their giving us breakfast. Moreover the kitchen door was locked, so we couldn't boil ourselves water for the tea-bags (tea-bags nicer than coffee-bags). But on our descending the rickety stairs the monks came out of church, presumably tired, hungry and thirsty. Nevertheless they ushered us into the refectory. There was a spread of roasted chestnuts, beans (as usual) swimming, dry olives and chunks of dry bread like grey lead. D. insisted on my eating what was on my plate because it would seem ungracious to leave it: besides, you never knew when the next meal would be available.

The morning spent in a glorious walk downhill to the harbour of this monastery, called the Arsenal. At eleven the boat for Daphni arrived, crammed with black priests. The boat exactly resembled the one on the Raphael cartoon of the Miraculous Draught of Fishes. At Daphni we hoped to get fried eggs and yoghurt again, but no. Today being the Feast of the True Cross the monks do not allow fish, eggs or milk, of which yoghurt counts as milk (forbidden to be yielded on the Holy Mountain). The yoghurt is imported, and so in some way licit.

We changed into another boat southward bound for Karauillia, but the sea being too rough to land on the cape, the boat stopped at St Paul's, having passed three enormous monasteries, Simonpetra – literally growing out of the top of a cliff like a crow's nest, terrifying in its tiers of projecting wooden balconies – Gregoriou and Dionysiou. We landed at St Paul's and at 1.30 lunched on the shore off tinned spam like Kit-e-cat spread on Petits Beurres and your Kendal cakes, which aren't really Kendal cakes but squashed fly biscuits, rather delicious. Then we slogged up the hill, which with the luggage was agony. After an hour we reached St Paul's.

On the flagged path to the gatehouse an aged monk munching white grapes. He handed his bunch to D. and me. The guest master appeared and led us upstairs to the guests' saloon hung with portraits of the nineteenth-century Greek kings and photographs of the recent monarchs, including Constantine. He brought us a salver with aniseed, coffee and jam to eat with a spoon. This is the customary way of greeting strangers. He left us saying church service would be in a quarter of an hour. This we attended. Lovely chaunts, one with a jolly lilt in response to which a monk marched round the church swinging a censer with bells attached to it. The accompaniment to the chaunt like reindeer bells to a hunting tune. At 4.30 the fathers marched out, beckoning us to follow them to the refectory. The whole performance done with a reserved, unenthusiastic, or I might say unassumed, welcome and with much dignity.

Again, is this awfully boring? The refectory is enormous, and surprisingly pretty: whitewashed walls, lime green dado, and blue flowered frieze. The monks eat at their own tables. The pilgrims' table is separate. From a lectern a monk reads the Gospels throughout the meal. We eat and drink in silence. I love all this, and so does D. Having so short a time ago swallowed our spam we are not yet hungry, but this is the last meal of the day (at 4.30), and we must eat again somehow before the day is out, but how and where? Meanwhile we confront a huge tin plate of chips, raw cabbage and celery, washed down by the sweet-acid wine.

I have not been to the lav since I left Salonika on Friday. Too awful. All because of the Strepto-Triad, which I have now given up.

Wednesday, 28th September

Terrible gale whipped up in the night, and a grey, dismal morning in spite of the serenity of yesterday's sunset. Even I am up with the dawn, which is after six, and nine hours of bed. Bitterly cold it is padding down a dimly lit (one oil lamp) corridor the length of the village street at Badminton, to a stone trough for shaving and the lav of the sort that existed in medieval castles, a *garde-robe* flue with a hole through which you survey the ground three hundred feet below.

Breakfast once more of pâté and Petits Beurres which we find left over in the sack. Down to the beach for the boat to take us to Daphni at eight. But the boat does not come today because it is too rough to land. We wait in the wind till eleven o'clock. There are two Germans, two Greek-Americans and a Greek youth with us. We decide to walk, which means climbing a practically perpendicular path to the next monastery, Dionysiou, where we look at the painted refectory and cloister of sixteenth century. One picture depicts bombs being dropped from the sky on to a city and blowing it up. Then all are given aniseed drink, coffee and Turkish delight. D. who is fearfully greedy eats two lumps. We are about to walk to the next monastery when a large boat puts in to harbour. In turns we throw our luggage on board from the quay; and when the prow is wafted to shore by a tidal wave we hurl one leg over it, trusting to kind passengers to haul us up like a sack to the deck. An alarming and difficult operation. We learn that this boat has been hired by a rich Greek businessman bribing a skipper. In fact the sea is not really rough where we hug the shore. In the open it is obviously very nasty.

This is a sort of silly dream day. We reach Daphni at 2.30. The daily bus to Karyes has gone. There is no possible way of reaching it except by foot. D. resolutely refuses to climb the road with all his baggage. He discovers that a Greek bishop has landed with four chaplains, all in the same predicament. We persuade one of the chaplains to let us share their jeep when they shall have telephoned for it, and if there is room in it for two extra. The telephone on the whole peninsula closes down from midday till four o'clock. At four we find that today the post office is shut till five. I say to Derek that he and I must walk to the nearest monastery (which is two hours away) before it is dusk, when all monasteries shut their doors and will not in any circumstances admit pilgrims. Besides I do not trust the bishop's jeep, when and if it arrives, to have room for us. In any case the bishop is rather lukewarm, the evening is getting bitterly cold, and the sun is sinking. But Derek in a slightly querulous way insists on telephoning to some local VIP before he will reach a decision. Like Sibyl Colefax, he has to get in touch with every important person wherever he happens to find himself. When the post office opens we have a ghastly time inducing the cross and dirty post office boy to connect us. Then Derek speaks in German for half an hour to his important friend, repeating his request twenty times. I get restless and despairing. The important friend is no use at all. Derek sadly and I crossly make for our haversacks which we have left trustingly in the village street under a telegraph pole. A dog, the sole one on the Holy Mountain, has lifted his leg against mine. We are now obliged to walk to the monastery for the night, which we could have done three hours ago. Suddenly we hear a cry from the bishop. He and the four curates are snuggling together like sardines into a jeep which has appeared from nowhere. We are pushed head-first into the jeep by villagers and fall on to the laps of the fathers. Then the engine won't start. When it does we race up the hill, the road being as I have already described the bed of a dry river. As we go round corners we are hurled against each other in a helpless heap. The fathers' black hats fall off, their hair buns come undone. They cross themselves and then they giggle, which is endearing. We give them sweets, which they have never eaten before and at first mistake for marbles to be played with. They are incredibly naïve and unworldly.

Thursday, 29th September

How much I love you is borne in upon me when people who are fond of you, like Derek, talk about you. Then I purr inside and have longings for you. It was a week ago today that I left you like Cleopatra. The gondola she sat in like a burnish'd throne burn'd on the Grand Canal, you so upright, serene and goddess-like.

Although Mount Athos is one of the most wonderful experiences I have been through, I am longing to be home. There is certainly a spirit of holiness here, unique to me; and in talking to the young pilgrims I learn that spiritual ideals have not entirely departed from the world. I agree totally with Derek's fervent determination that the Holy Mountain must be kept as it is. There are immense pressures against the status quo, chiefly from tourism and the Greek government's resentment of Athonic independence, *and* of course from Communism, which does everything it can to discredit the way of life and broadcasts malevolent tales, such as abduction of children from across the border. All of these stories have proved untrue and yet the press rarely contradicts them. I have not once detected a suspicion of unbecoming behaviour (a phrase my grandmother used) in any monk. And Derek, who has been here four times, says the same.

Oh dear – to descend from sublimities to the frailties of flesh – I do wish I had never taken that wretched Strepto-Triad. It is precisely a week since I last 'went', which was in Venice. It must be a record of constipation. Lytton Strachey said constipation was the mother of invention, so perhaps mine augurs well for my next book. I write this nonsense at the kitchen table in Karyes while Derek talks (in German) to Father Mitrophan, the head of the community at Chilandar, about Athonic problems in which he, Derek, has deeply involved himself. He is like a man who has taken all the cares of the world upon his shoulders, and sees himself as Atlas staggering beneath the globe.

I think I may ask William Rees-Mogg, who himself is a holy man, if I may write an article for *The Times* about Mount Athos problems, no?

A remarkable trait in the Greek character is a total inability to compromise or to adjust to circumstances, which makes them insensitive. They seldom put themselves out to be pleasant by feigning politeness. Often they are downright off-hand. They are also devious, like the Irish, who on the contrary try to please, but in order to deceive. The evasiveness of the Greeks would drive me mad, and their inability to tell the truth when there can be no advantage to themselves not to impart it.

'Nature is place of God's calming Protect it' one reads in English on notice boards. And 'Nature is God's miracle Protect it'.

This evening we had to see Father Mitrophan (he is Serbian) off by bus because D. likes distilling little favours, and keeping the right side of those he knows and admires. Father Mitrophan, who has been our host in the monastery and in Karyes, absent or present, is a saint with sad eyes and a deprecatory manner. He travels all over the world, including Russia, proselytizing and attracting candidates for monkhood on the peninsula. But like all saints he lacks geniality and warmth. D. is devoted to him. Also going off on the bus was a man called Gerald Palmer (have you heard of him?), a dedicated Mount Athos man and member of the Reading biscuit family. Orthodox faith and even more revered here than D., who accepts this fact with graceful resignation. Anyway the encounter with Mr Palmer filled D. with delight as you may suppose – another link made less tenuous.

We had to visit the Governor's Residence to get the four-day extension to our *permis de séjour*. The secretary greatly pleased D. by telling him that the whole peninsula believed he was turning Orthodox and becoming a monk. 'Um, er, I very well might,' D. said.

We walked to a nearby monastery this morning called

Koutloumousia. There were signs of habitation, carpets spread over balconies and a dear little Carpaccio dog (the second dog we have met: cats abound in all the monasteries and are permitted to make messes wherever they like), but not a sign of a monk. They sleep at odd hours because they pray so much by night. It is said there are not more than five in this monastery. Very fascinating courtyards with tier above tier of arched galleries in brick. Between the openings Islamic plates and jugs have been inserted in 1767, mostly blue and white – some yellow. The church, painted ox-blood, as they nearly all are, has an ambulatory with seventeenth-century frescos, extremely lively for Byzantium, of saints dancing, fingers touching, more like Pompeian figures on a Roman mural than the stiff, stilted symbolism of the Byzantines.

We picked for you what looks like a wild datura, growing low on the ground, and sweet-smelling. Also saw a yellow crocus with rather attenuated petals. Also saponaria in flower. Shades of Meg Meade-Fetherstonhaugh.*

Gosh, this must be dull to read!

Having lunched off beans once more at our Serbian residence we are off with packs to Stavronikita monastery this afternoon. I am wearing all the clothes I have because the wind is bitter. We amble downhill for four miles, a gentle descent were it not for the boulders, with halts for picking up and eating walnuts as we go. This time we are going east, first to Iveron, a large, gloomy half- or rather nine-tenths-deserted monastery. A few decrepit old men usher us into the church which has a rich Cosmati floor, all circles and twirls. It lies in a steep glen by the sea, which is rough, with great breakers from the Aegean battering against the outer walls. We leave it for Stavronikita which we see in the distance, also plumb on the water. We follow a cliff path, up and down, and descend at times on to the beach, which is rather perilous because the tide is rising. After an hour we arrive. Stavronikita is an Athonic Knole, with gatehouse of stone, cobbled approach, rickety galleries and irregular courtyards. We put down our knapsacks on the bench within the porch and walk into the church. Vespers are already being sung. For an hour we listen, squatting in stalls, or rather perching on misericords, and rising to our feet when the others do. The monks are behind the iconostasis, apart from us. One or two laymen are in the choir. The incense-bearer, wearing

---

* Châtelaine of Uppark, West Sussex, who used saponaria to clean textiles there.

golden vestments, censes every icon, every pillar, every person one by one. When he has ceased we all bow. At the end of the service the priests troop out. One of them turns and asks if we wish to sleep with them. We indicate that we do. Without a smile, without a flicker of interest or disinterest, pleasure or displeasure, he asks for our papers, and examines them. D. asks to speak to the Abbot, to whom he has a letter of introduction. The Abbot is away. D. is vexed. He says it is too bad; he has no luck ever, anywhere. He seizes upon a priest who speaks a little English. The priest asks D's name. 'Ah!' he says, 'Dreek Hill who writes reviews of films in the English newspapers?' 'No,' says D., 'he is the wrong *Derek* (with emphasis) Hill. I am the right Derek Hill, who wrote an article on how to keep visitors away from the Holy Mountain.' 'Indeed,' says the monk, 'you are on the Holy Mountain.' 'I know that,' says the right Derek Hill. Then D. tells him all about his mission. Meanwhile another monk orders us rather peremptorily to go into the refectory. We obey. The other fathers and other pilgrims are standing, hungrily waiting. Grace is said and the Orthodox cross themselves with abandon over and over again. D. crosses himself rather a lot. I rather less.

This dinner (it is 4.45 p.m.) is about the best we have had. It is eaten in silence while a monk intones the Gospel. There is macaroni for a change, with lumps of cheese. The macaroni is delicious, but tepid. I am a slow eater and have learned from experience that the Gospels take less time to be read than I take to eat macaroni. So I leave half of my platter-ful (D. glances at it greedily). The platter is of pewter. So is the mug. So is the jug. 'Pass me the wine,' I mutter to D. He pours from it into my mug. It is water. 'How irregular,' says Derek, and I fear he may lodge a complaint. But his behaviour is gentlemanly. I turn to my pewter platter of yoghurt. 'Pass the sugar,' I say. D. passes me the salt. So I do without sugar. I just manage to finish the yoghurt and am beginning on the grapes, when Bang! goes the hammer of the sub-Abbot. I am too late. We all rise. Grace is repeated and we cross ourselves like mad. By now I have indigestion. Shortly, I also have my first evacuation since last Thursday in Venice. The relief is enormous.

We are taken up three floors to a nice, clean bedroom with bare white walls, bare floor, and clean white-painted iron bedsteads, white sheets and red horse-blankets. We settle in, light the one oil lamp and rejoice that no strangers are occupying the other three beds. I say to Derek, 'Which three persons would you most dislike to be ushered

into this bedroom now?' He says, 'Joan Haslip* and Charles Harding,'†
and I add, 'Douglas Cooper.'‡ We congratulate ourselves that we have
it to ourselves when the door opens and a silent, severe monk ushers
in an American with a moustache. The American announces that he
has a streaming cold. D. and I utter a shriek, rush for D's bottle of
TCP and tell the American to sleep in the furthermost bed under the
window which is made very draughty by the wind and waves howling
through the cracks. As I write this they are fast asleep. The American
is going to the Morning Service which begins at three and ends at six
o'clock. I suspect him to be a neophyte. I turn down the single oil
lamp and having swallowed my Dalmane sleeping pill am about to
undress – no, not totally undress: it is far too cold – and get back into
bed.

Today was such a beautiful day. The coast, the tree-blanketed
mountains and occasional broken-down towers pure Claude landscapes. Goodnight!

Friday, 30th September

We disgraced ourselves by sleeping till six o'clock and were woken by
a monk saying that breakfast was finished. D. said, 'Oh, I wanted to
go to church.' The monk said, 'That was over at 5.30.' Indeed, it lasted
two hours. Our American with the cold went at 3.30.

I forgot to tell you that in calling at Iveron yesterday afternoon we
were not allowed to see the Sponge, Mantle and Reed of Christ.
These and similar relics are kept well hidden away in the monastic
churches, quite properly, as is Our Lady's Girdle at Vatopedi, and the
left hand of Mary Magdalen at one of the other monasteries. They are
not on view. They may be revealed on special days in certain years.
But at Iveron we did see the icon of St Nicholas which crossed the
sea from Palestine on a holy beam. It took three hundred years to do
so, and grew an oyster on the saint's forehead, which is faintly discernible.

Disgrace or no disgrace I hastily shaved, dressed and tore down to

---

* Author (1912–94).
† Picture dealer.
‡ Art historian and critic, wealthy collector of Cubist paintings and author of *The Cubist
Epoch* (1911–84); famously, at a private view at the Tate Gallery he was punched by John
Rothenstein, the Tate's Director at the time.

the refectory, which was empty. I ladled some cold tea out of a witches' cauldron into a tooth tumbler and scraped some fig jam on bread as hard as rock. My week of total binding having ended last night, I allowed myself this indulgence.

The Abbot returned early this morning and before the wretched man had time to look through his letters D. insisted on an interview. I sat upstairs in the dormitory and resumed *Cousine Bette* – not the right choice of book for a journey such as this, and the print too small.

After an hour's talk D. rejoins me. I ask what the Abbot had to say and am told it doesn't concern me. We are shown the chapel by an English-speaking monk. All these monastic churches are pitch dark, so that it is next to impossible to examine the frescos and icons thoroughly. Besides I find it difficult to distinguish a good from a bad icon, as you know. I have learnt a bit on this excursion from Derek, who is knowledgeable. When you are able to distinguish, say, the wood carving of a choir stall, candlestick or some decorated feature, it looks or feels pretty coarse. But the general effect of gold under hundreds of little red lamps against the sepulchral gloom is conducive to devotion. Almost the most beautiful features of these churches are the great circles of brass chandeliers, suspended low and occupying the central space of nave under the dome. They are splashed with small icons and small crosses and heads of saints in brass and candle brackets.

We walk back to Karyes uphill – a slog. I don't think I can ever walk with a pack again. It is too fatiguing and irksome.

This afternoon we ambled into the woods looking at empty and abandoned *sketi*, or cells. Very lugubrious. Yes, on the whole I feel Mount Athos is doomed. I have seen enough for an initial jaunt and am ready to get away tomorrow. It is a lovely thought that I shall be with you the day after tomorrow at this time, 6.30, with luck. I am sick of the squalid side, the stinking lavatories, grubby stone lavabos, cold water, dismal food, and the ever-pervasive stink of stale sweat from unwashed clothes and limbs. Also it is dark by 6.15 and reading by oil lamp, especially when it is shared by others, is practically impossible. Besides, it is terribly cold in these barracks.

But I would not have missed the experience for worlds. And Derek has been a perfect guide and enchanting companion.

Last words! Not quite.

PS. To my unspeakable joy I have recovered my spectacles. I dropped them in the bus on Monday and the cross driver found and kept them on his dashboard. D. says miracles like this happen all the time on the Holy Mountain and one need never fuss. Something nice is bound to turn up.

The monks are thoroughly non-money-grubbing. On leaving each morning we insisted on paying for our keep. The only way to make them accept is by emphasizing that the oblation is for the church. Then they usually give way, but always with genuine reluctance. We believe that very few pilgrims offer contributions. Throughout the summer the monks have an average of ten guests a night, which must cost them quite a lot.

Saturday, 1st October

Hurray! shall be seeing you tomorrow. The irony is that the morning is divine, quite the first cloudless, windless one since we arrived. We are waiting on the terrace under the vine until it is time to descend to Karyes for the bus to Daphni. It is eight o'clock. The Holy Mountain is wholly visible for the first time. Not a sound is to be heard except the buzzing of a million bees which have come out of hiding. (No, I am wrong. Derek's nose having begun to bleed he is making the most terrible fuss, and I have had to unpack my knapsack to fish out the remains of the bumph roll from the very bottom.) We have visited eight out of the total twenty monasteries.

Sunday, 2nd October

Yesterday was a very tiring day. The awful bus drive to Daphni, the three-hour boat to Ouranopolis, the luncheon with Mrs Loch's old funnies in the Tower, the re-packing into the trunks we left there, then another three and a half hours' bus journey to Salonika with the radio (Forces Programme equivalent in Greek) blaring. Arrived Salonika hotel at eight. Derek instantly on the telephone to friends. Invited the Governor of Mount Athos to dine. I could scarcely keep awake or make sense. Yet the Governor interesting in telling us of the appalling threats to the Mountain from outside developers wanting to buy forests for felling, and even territory for prospective mining of uranium, not to mention the roads, tractors, lorries and other horrors which would follow. And the monks so innocent and naïve, and devoid of aesthetic sense.

Mount Athos is the most isolated, secluded, holy (nearest to divine) place I have ever visited. So far – and it may well not last another decade – the Holy Mountain is absolutely unchanged, certainly since in the middle ages, and barely changed since it was founded in the sixth century. The forests of chestnut and other trees, the plants and wild flowers (owing to absence of goats and of course cows), are preserved intact. Bar one road (of which the surface is as rough as a *torrente* when without water), from Daphni to Karyes, otherwise paths fit only for mules, donkeys and human feet. I have seldom been so imbued with devout spirit as amongst these Orthodox communities and the pilgrims we met on the Mountain – young and middle-aged, many from behind the Iron Curtain.

A. met me at Heathrow, and motored me home, like the angel she is.

Monday, 3rd October

Without opening most of my letters accumulated during absence, I motored with A. at 9.30 to Cheshire, to join the N.T. Arts Panel visit to Dunham Massey and Erddig. Dunham Massey is not a house of paramount importance. Its surroundings are suburban, but the 1500 acres and deer park are important because of the closeness of the place to Manchester. Yet the house is full of some very good things, a splendid collection of early eighteenth-century mahogany chests and tables. The small library is enchanting, each wall lined with old bindings, and two ancient orreries in the middle of the room. Over the fireplace is a space from which Grinling Gibbons' Crucifixion scene, which John Evelyn discovered him working at, formerly hung. The late Lord Stamford lent it to the V. & A. The Panel agreed that it must be put back where it belongs. Merlin Waterson's[*] work at Erddig is beyond praise. He has concentrated on the back premises, through which the public is ushered, with its carpenter's shop, forge, motor-house, coach house with vehicles, tack-room, and staff premises with ancient photographs and even eighteenth-century oils of family servants.

Friday, 7th October

John B. and Elizabeth come for the night. They arrive at 7.30 just when A. has to go to a concert at the House, arranged long before they invited themselves. They are *en route* for Cornwall. John looks

---

[*] N.T. area representative.

and is much better. Still shuffles but does not have to be helped in and out of chairs. We are all rather tired, but we gossip, and he recites from Laurence Binyon. Quotes the following couplet, composed by the Widow Lloyd* about Headley Hope-Nicholson,† that old painted (but nice) queen:

H is for Headley, the pride of Old Place,
What he earned from his bottom he spent on his face.

Tuesday, 11th October

To London for two nights. Went to see John Allison (doctor) in the morning about the swelling of my left testicle – he has given me an introduction to a specialist with advice to have the cyst removed. I think I may not take the advice, because of the expense and nuisance of going to hospital for twenty-four hours – and about the numbness and weakness of the fourth finger of my right hand. This he can't understand and says the blood is flowing through it satisfactorily and there 'ought' to be nothing wrong. All the same there *is* something wrong, because it hardly functions and makes my typing halt and cause mistakes. Then he talked about John B., in his indiscreet fashion, because we are both such friends. I respect his confidence accordingly. Says J's health is much affected by his happiness and unhappiness. The fact that Paul came over from USA and was nice to his father has helped to make him better. Allison says J.B. suffers terrible guilt over Paul. Why on earth? That now he suffers acutely from press persecution; references to 'our ageing laureate', and such-like wounding phrases, notably *The Times* in its boring Diary on the middle page. J.B. complained to me about this. If I saw such criticism I would at once write to Rees-Mogg in protest. I would always champion J.B. in any and every instance.

Sunday, 16th October

Walking down Broad Street, Bath the day before yesterday a short but sturdily built man stopped me by saying, 'Excuse me, sir, do you speak English?' – a foolish remark which set me on my guard. Then he

---

* John D.K. Lloyd (1900–78); conservationist and historian; known to friends as The Widow Lloyd from the peak of hair on his forehead.
† Brother of Felix Hope-Nicholson, collector, Chelsea.

began to ask me the way somewhere, and I knew what was coming. He was a sailor, going from Portsmouth to London, and could I help him? He was sorry to trouble me. So I gave him fifty pence, but with reluctance, making a wry face of deprecation.* He stared hard at me with would-be honest steel blue eyes. Thanked me, with a God bless you, sir. What is one to think? Should I have given him nothing and directed him to the town hall for advice how to get help? Was he genuine really? In any case I should have been more generous, and less grudging. But the truth is these days one is the victim of fraud, deceit, if not violence, and theft, which makes one wary, suspicious and reluctant to get into conversation with strangers.

Friday, 28th October

I am going to stay with Eardley today, and telephoned a week ago to John Fowler to ask if he would like me to call *en route*. His nice boy Graham answered and said John had just had another treatment of radium and was feeling too rotten to see anyone at the moment. Would I telephone again on Wednesday? I did. Graham said, Yes, do come, John is longing to see you. Thought I, thank goodness I am in time. Then last night on my return from Bath A. said they had telephoned again to say John was worse, and unconscious. Don't come. Thought about the poor old boy in the night, and this morning on waking up. At 9.30 George Oakes rang me to say John died last night at nine, peacefully, without suffering, without knowing. There was to be a memorial service soon, and John had expressly asked that I should give an address about him from the pulpit. Well, I suppose I can do this; I must, of course. But I must not be lachrymose. And at funerals I am quickly and regrettably moved. It was John who earlier this year rang me up in tears to tell me that Robin [Fedden] had died. I should have gone to see him immediately I returned from Athos. I dallied. Inexcusable. Anyway, he knew I was coming today, and died knowing that, which is one consolation.

Later

Motored to stay the night with Eardley at the Slade. Arrived just as it was getting dark. Delicious welcome, as always from dear E. Sat at the

---

* [1997: Only 50p? Good God! – even in 1977. J.L.-M.]

kitchen table drinking tea out of mugs. He tells me he will be 75 next month. Mattei [Radev] telephoned to announce he was arriving after dinner. We fetched him at Petersfield station. Talked to him about his meeting with a brother, who telephoned him from Salonika where he (the brother) was allowed to go for a week with his wife who has Greek relations. Their son aged 16 was held in Bulgaria as a sort of hostage. Mattei rushed to Salonika to stay with them. Hadn't seen his brother, who is over forty, since he was a child of 12. So never knew him well. Mattei slightly depressed by the encounter. I think suffering a little from guilt, because he knows his family have been in trouble on account of his flight thirty years ago. The brother and sister-in-law spoke openly about conditions in Bulgaria, which are awful. What's awful too is that the brother was too young to have known a pre-Communist Bulgaria. Says it is unimaginable living in a country of one-party system. You cannot vote for what you want. If you become a Party member, of whom there are few, you belong to a special class, favoured to the extent that you can take over the property of a non-member, who is treated as of lower caste. Non-members are limited to low-grade jobs, and can never earn decent money. Mattei still hopes to get his mother out. The father died last year, having suffered the previous thirty of his life from deprivations for which poor Mattei holds himself responsible, i.e., reprisals. Mattei, when speaking about Communism, becomes puce and shakes with rage.

Saturday, 29th October

Left at 8.30 for Knole. Found a good dual carriageway nearly the whole way to Sevenoaks. Was greeted by Lionel Sackville in the Green Court. We sat on a bench, talking. He never was a handsome man but with age and tribulation he has acquired a distinction which reminded me of his cousin Eddy and his Uncle Charlie. Did not go into details about his marriage, but merely said that his wife, whom he had left, refused to quit Knole. He had moved into rooms which Eddy once inhabited, over the Wicket, and eats with his brother and sister-in-law.* His condition is sad. Took me into the garden and then

---

* Lionel Sackville-West, 6th Baron Sackville (b. 1913), m. 2nd, 1974, Arlie, Lady de Guingand (m. diss. 1983); his cousin Edward Sackville-West, 5th Baron Sackville (1901–65), man of letters, reviewer and musicologist; his 'Uncle Charlie', 4th Baron (1870–1962), Major-General; his brother Hugh Sackville-West, MC, m. 1957 Bridget Cunliffe.

the chapel and, having asked one of his daughters if it were safe for him to enter his own apartments, tiptoed, finger on lips, through the colonnade room into the library. Then accompanied me round the state rooms, all looking very spruce and polished. I was rather shocked to see that some of the fabrics which we had mended twenty-five years ago were badly in need of attention again. Approved of the way they have regilded the furniture in the Venetian Ambassador's Room. I am sure that was right, i.e., total regilding. Lionel did not seem to know which were Vita's rooms. He is rather ignorant, for Nigel told me later that she never had rooms in the north wing, as Lionel suggested. So in a way my visit was wasted. However, we lunched with his brother Huffo and nice wife. I sat next to her and the eldest boy, aged 20, handsome but for spots. The future Lord Sackville, intelligent, alert and sympathetic; also sympathetic to my mission. They had kindly invited a couple called Martin who own Long Barn.* Funny little military man with grey moustache and Jewish-Greek wife. I took to her immensely. I followed them to Long Barn. They love it. It is *not* at all a covetable house, much bogus half-timbering, low doorways and sloping floors. Curious taste Harold and Vita had for ye olde, like my parents.

Alec Clifton-Taylor[†] turned up for luncheon at Knole, brought by a second couple. He has become an old buffer, rather too pleased with his broadcasting successes. I rather took against. Friendly to me as always, but absurd.

Stayed the night at Sissinghurst and fetched away quantities of further papers, including the full text of H's diaries in two heavy suitcases. Nigel's Juliet and her handsome husband James were staying. They cooked an absolutely marvellous dinner. Talked till midnight. A sweet couple, and so clever and bright. She works for publicity in Jamie Hamilton's[‡] office. Recently she met Diana Mosley and fell, flat, for her charm. Thought Diana the most beautiful woman she had ever seen.

---

* H.N. and V.S.-W's house before they found Sissinghurst.
† Architectural historian and broadcaster, specializing in cathedrals and churches (1907–85).
‡ Hamish Hamilton (1900–88); publisher.

Monday, 31st October

Went this evening to the specialist Patrick Smith at the Lansdown Home. He pronounced that my testicle swelling was quite harmless. It is a cyst, and he advises its removal. It will mean forty-eight hours in the Home, and a fortnight's convalescence. Bore about the fortnight.

Wednesday, 2nd November

A. telephoned early in the morning for me to meet her at Portmeirion Gallery where she had reserved a tiny picture by Fulco for me, having bought one for herself. I went, chose another of the Passing of the Host, for £150. Oh dear, the folly. But having just received a demand for nearly £4,000 tax for myself alone, I feel reckless. Luncheon to Peter Quennell at Brooks's. He asked me why the Somersets no longer invited them to stay. I thought it best to feign ignorance. Talked about Harold; but again, not much help. Peter said Harold made the mistake of sacrificing seriousness to flippancy. He could not resist introducing a funny anecdote regardless of whether it was *à propos*. This made scholars not take his biographies seriously. I wonder.

Tuesday, 8th November

My sermon about John Fowler is worrying me greatly. I have typed out three drafts already. Each seems more feeble than the last, and now the last is repetitious and inconsequential. Peter Hood whom I met in the Circus yesterday went to the actual cremation. Said there must have been a hundred people gathered. There were emotional scenes. John's devoted girls from the office and even Nancy Lancaster* in tears. He was greatly beloved. I have been thinking how the older one's friends get, the less beloved. One must remember them in the heyday. But the heyday vanishes slowly, so that one gets accustomed to the declension into querulousness, self-pity and lack of laughter.

---

* Nancy Perkins, of Virginia, USA; m. 1st Henry Field; 2nd, Ronald Tree, MP; 3rd, Colonel Claude Lancaster of Kelmarsh Hall, Northamptonshire; in 1945 became proprietor of the Colefax & Fowler decorating firm; horticulturist; she d. 1995.

When they die these last are the years and moods one remembers. One has forgotten the years of splendour, beauty and hilarity. Rosamond [Lehmann] who stayed on Sunday night has lost her mobility. Physically she has collapsed, into mountainous landslides of stomach, neck and cheeks. She is very slow, cannot get a move on, so one hovers with impatience, waiting. But mentally she is alert as ever. Up-to-date and wise. I love her still. May I continue to do so.

On Friday morning last week BBC 2 telephoned in the way they do, without warning. Will I consent to be interviewed by Robert Robinson in his books programme? They will send a girl (producer?) from London to see me on Wednesday. They will 'shoot' on Monday and Tuesday next. Before I have time to reflect I say Yes. Then the horrors of the whole affair dawn; the nuisance, too, the complications, the upset of my library, my dislike of my library being seen on television. The poor Loewensteins* have been badly burgled at Biddestone where they have resided only one month, not properly settled in yet. It happened while they were sleeping in the house; telephone wires cut; thieves stole the carving knife and a horrid sharp knife from the kitchen, not worth £1, but deadly, The police say they would have used these implements had they been disturbed.

Wednesday, 9th November

'A young lady', called Sue Anstruther, came down by the afternoon train to talk to me about the interview next Monday. Very nice she was, with a nervous laugh which reminded me of Betty Miller Jones.† Her job was to find out what sort of questions Robinson cd advantageously put to me. She stayed to tea and returned by the five o'clock train.

Thursday, 10th November

A. and I motored to Stroud to fetch the two darling dogs from the vet where they had spent the night after their operation – ovaries removed. Very piteous they were, still sleepy and unawake to things.

---

* Prince Rupert zu Loewenstein (b. 1930), financial adviser; his wife, Josephine Lowry-Corry.
† Hon. Betty Askwith (1909–95), dau. of Baron Askwith, m. 1950 Keith Miller Jones, author.

Strange too how within twenty-four hours their glossy coats and bright eyes had become scruffy, dull and tarnished. The shock, and the consequences, come quicker than with us. In a week they will be all right, God willing. We agreed last night that it is deplorable how deeply we already love them, and how agonizing it is to see them discomfited, not to mention distressed.

Wednesday, 16th November

Monday and Tuesday were devoted to filming for BBC 2. I was a little nervous, and not good. I lacked sparkle, and I lacked self-assurance. Robert Robinson, who interviewed me, was extremely kind and sensitive. He told me beforehand what sort of questions he would put to me, and when I objected to one he did not press, but let me off, which was decent. The team were charming. Consisted of young producer, David Speaght, Sue Anstruther, a sweet girl, secretary to Robinson and general (if I may so express it) dog's-body, four cameramen. Started off early Monday afternoon in Lansdown Crescent in the library, after I was made to do a preliminary walk along the railings of the crescent. Then was seated with my back to the drinks cupboard door, tied to my chair by wires attached to a tiny buttonhole like a dandelion flower when the fluff has been blown off. The process is extraordinary. When I had run through my piece Robinson was filmed putting to thin air, as it were, the questions he had already put to me. I asked if the original wording he had put to me or this new wording would be recorded. Answer was of course the latter. But I noticed that the second time he put a question it did not always correspond to the original one. At the end of every ten minutes the spool ran out. A pause ensued and we proceeded with the interrupted talk by me. This system does not make for continuity, and is putting-off. But the whole programme, I learn, is done in snippets, and will be pieced together in the studio. Not only will much of what I said be omitted altogether, but sentences will be joined up in a remorseless way, so that the sequence will be higgledy-piggledy. For example, on the second day we went to Lacock Abbey and Dyrham. I was filmed walking with Robinson outside these two houses. The cold was penetrating. I was so frozen that once I could not release the words from my mouth and had to get into the car with the engine running and the heater on in order to thaw before resuming. When we got to Dyrham Robinson said, 'Oh, you never told the story of the heiress

of Lacock jumping from the battlements to elope. Let's have it now.'
He told the cameraman to turn the machine upon me, so I added this
anecdote, very lamely – sadly, for it was a good one – there and then,
in between what I was saying about the architecture of Dyrham.
I enjoyed the experience, but did not excel. I might improve with
further tuition. I am sure I look glum. When all is over and it is too
late I think of a better answer than the one I haltingly gave. *L'esprit de
l'escalier.*

Sunday, 20th November

Stanley Falconer,* a great friend of John Fowler and his executor,
came to tea, bringing us each a present from John. A. had a little
French *jardinière* and I the marble profile relief of the Emperor
Claudius which used to hang in J's entrance hall; also the Palladio
volume of 1573 which I gave him when he lost his copy in the fire
which destroyed the Cardigan Chamber at Odiham.

Wednesday, 23rd November

A. and I motored to London. I had an important meeting of the
Corsham trustees in the morning. We decided to ask the Treasury to
take the house and contents immediately.
    A dinner party for Woman's† seventieth birthday in Elizabeth
Longman's‡ flat in Rutland Gate. Lots of old friends but oh so depressing! Difficult to hear owing to the low ceilings. But I sat next to Diana
[Mosley]. She retains for me the same ineffable magic. The same
Mitford jokes which require tuning in to. We talked about writing and
her experience in the publication of her book, and her interview on
television. Talking of Harold [Nicolson] she told me the story, which
was already familiar to me, of Sir O. refusing to see Harold who, on
an official delegation of MPs to Holloway Prison where the Mosleys
were incarcerated during the war, asked if he might visit him in his
cell. Diana's argument was that Harold had delivered such untruthful
propaganda stories about Germany over the wireless that Sir O. was

---

* Interior decorator; partner in Colefax & Fowler.
† Hon. Pamela Mitford (Mrs Derek Jackson).
‡ Lady Elizabeth Lambart, dau. of Field Marshal the (10th) Earl of Cavan; m. 1949 Mark
Longman, publisher (he d. 1972).

infuriated. But, I protested, Harold was not an out-and-out hater of Germany. On the contrary his views were very balanced and sober and fair. We kissed; we parted with unaffected protestations of deepest devotion. But it was no go really. I wonder if we shall meet again. Diana told me she was now a great-grandmother. I think of her, as it seems yesterday, that radiantly lovely Botticelli Venus aged 17, sitting on a Cotswold wall near Asthall, whom I, her elder by two years, worshipped.

Thursday, 24th November

Comes the morning of John Fowler's Memorial Service. Met A. who was already in the church (St George's, Hanover Square) by 11.40, sitting in the front left-hand pew, probably the one my grandparents occupied 73 years ago when my parents were married here. Church packed with friends. Beautifully arranged piles of flowers, lilies, on either side of the chancel steps. Very moving service, but I trying desperately not to be moved. 'Hark, hark, my soul', followed by Rachel Redgrave* reading faultlessly from the steps, 'Fear no more the heat o' the sun, nor the furious winter's rages, Thou thy worldly task hast done, Home art gone and ta'en thy wages; Thou art past the tyrant's stroke – Thou hast finished joy and moan', ending, 'Quiet consummation have, And renowned be thy grave.'

At the end of the Bach anthem, 'Jesu, joy of man's desiring', silence. I rose and walked to the lectern. Slowly arranged my pages, put on my spectacles, looked up, and read the first sentence: 'Sometimes, in the watches of the night, in order to induce sleep . . .' my voice clove the quiet air. It was all right. At least I think it was. A. told me afterwards that throughout there wasn't a stir in the congregation. Several people congratulated, which was nice, and I have received a few letters, which is reassuring.

Tom Parr offered to give us a lift in his chauffeur-driven car. He, Baba Metcalfe and we waited in Brook Street in the perishing cold. Car never turned up. So we were obliged to take a cab to Eaton Square, giving Baba a lift. I like her although she is, if not exigent, taxing, in that her presence is demanding of constant attention. She is *très grande dame*, but exceedingly friendly. Proffers in that truly

---

* Rachel Kempson (b. 1910), actress; m. 1935 Michael Redgrave (Kt 1959), actor, producer, writer.

womanly way a contribution towards the fare, diffidently and determinedly, yet knowing all the time that the proffer will be rejected.

Friday, 25th November

My broadcast tonight at 11.35. A. could not keep awake, I went to bed, and at 11.30 crept downstairs, wrapped in my brown sheep's plaid given me by Sally. I waited in trepidation, and with some reason. I am *furious*. Strong emphasis given to the social side; no mention at all of the National Trust's work and my part in it. All questions and answers of any seriousness cut out. Only the silly, frivolous questions and answers left in. Worst of all, a ghastly, vulgar man seen reading extracts from my diaries, but not even paragraphs. Merely random sentences of the most banal kind, strung together and read in a voice meant to be superior, disdainful, snobbish. A loathsome man. The whole performance geared to yesterday's anti-upper-class bashing. I am amazed at my own appearance. A drooling dotard, a mixture of Eddie Marsh* and Paul Hyslop, speaking in a quiet, subdued professorial voice. Embarrassing questions put to me about class. Damn, *damn* class! Oh how bloody the BBC can be! And what power they have to give a performance a strong slant by cutting, inserting, omitting, magnifying, and all by a sleight-of-hand which they cannot be arraigned for. Damn their eyes! I shall never do another, if invited.

Sunday, 27th November

Saw myself again on repeat performance. Really it is not I who am so bad, as the others. The ghastly man reciting, not even reading from the book, those shaming extracts, and Robinson with his casual, slightly off-hand manner. I am modest, in view of the questions put to me, rather distinguished and distinct. Nothing more.

Took the dogs to Westonbirt to walk in the gardens. Motoring down the long stretch with Ragged Castle in the distance at the end and Swangrove on the left, I thought never did an English scene in winter look more beautiful. The distant wood on the horizon was powder blue, the foreground tilled soil was deep chocolate brown. In

---

* Sir Edward Marsh (1972–1953); civil servant, scholar, and patron of the arts and of literature.

the west the beginning of an early sunset, which later turned to flames of orange streamers; and from the sky parachutists dropped from slow chugging planes. On my return I stopped and watched them jump out. One waited and fell several hundred feet before pulling his string. A cold, golden, quiet evening. The country at this season is all one's own.

Tuesday, 29th November

I am receiving lots of letters about my sermon and broadcast, most of which must out of politeness be answered. A letter this morning came from Ali Forbes beginning 'Dearest L.-Ms, I am so glad the hatchet is buried and that we are friends again.' He called on Sunday evening. I am sure that in spite of his mien of great self-confidence, his burbling conversation, his always-in-the-news air, he is like most of us a friendly, cosy old soul, anxious for affection. I wish him well.

Thursday, 1st December

I have received over a dozen letters approving of my sermon about John Fowler. So I believe it must have gone all right. Also a number of letters about the television show. On the whole approved likewise. Yet how does one know? For few people bother to write to say they have disliked one's efforts. They just don't write at all. So perhaps the majority didn't like it. This by statistics is the conclusion to be drawn.

Making the beds with Peggy this morning, she said in a worried voice, 'Have you heard that his Grace was taken to Tetbury Hospital yesterday? They sent for his bed this morning.' Then she said '*They* make too many demands on his Grace and her Grace. They ought to be left in peace at their age.'

A. left at dawn for London and is away for the night. I brought work back to Bad. for the day, remaining with the dogs. A dank, coldish, gun-metal day without a touch of colour. The sort of midwinter day on which I am quite happy. I worked hard at Harold, and in the afternoon walked the dogs across the Slaits into the Verge and beyond, and was surprised that I didn't come upon the main road, which must turn away westwards from Dunkirk before the point I reached.

I am sure that the only good diaries are those written by a writer who is constantly coming upon important people in the great world; and by a writer who stays at home, goes nowhere, sees few people, and sticks to the common round. Such a writer has time to ruminate and observe his surroundings. He alone can paint a picture of his complete life, little though it may be. Such a person is Francis Kilvert.

Sunday, 4th December

Nancy Lancaster told A. that she had been trying desperately to get a knighthood for John Fowler. The very day he died she had a letter from the Treasury agreeing. He, poor old thing, lived neither to receive or to know that he was about to receive it.

Saturday, 10th December

A. has been cross with me and hurt all day because when she told me after breakfast that we were going to a snack luncheon party at Petty France, for which she had bought two tickets, I said I wouldn't go. She has every reason to be upset, and I do not blame her. But what I cannot explain, and what she naturally cannot understand, is that I just could not. For the past few days I have been feeling *awful*, overcome with a loathing of my kind. Yesterday we had a luncheon party, and it was an agony for me to speak to my neighbours, silly Sally, and that idiotic woman, Clare Crossley. So today I could not face a repetition of this sort of thing.

I took the dogs for a walk up the Worcester Drive. They killed a squirrel. I did not see the actual kill but came upon the pair of them still tugging at its body from either end. It was quite dead, and the head had been torn off. Now there were these two little creatures, whom I had been watching a few hours earlier playing together on my hearthrug by putting their mouths inside each other's, those long, sharp fangs, but so gently, just as they playfully nibble our hands – now there they were, savages from the wild. I suppose it is the love of the chase inbred in them. But it is a disquieting sight to see.

In London last week I dined with the Skidelskys. Long, long, journey by tube an hour, from Knightsbridge to Stamford Brook, then walking down suburban streets in the dark. I was asked at 8 and arrived at 8.15, being full of apologies for lateness. We waited, the bell rang and a couple entered. Waited again, bell rang, and another couple. In the end we were a party of ten. All younger than I by a generation. Liked the Ravensdales.* He a sensitive, shy man with a

---

* Nicholas Mosley, 3rd Baron Ravensdale; m. 2nd, 1974, Verity Bailey.

slight stammer. Talked much of his father and Diana. Is fond of both, but has never sympathized with Tom Mosley's politics. I sat next to Mrs Skidelsky and Alexander Chancellor,* a plain man like that Edwardian Portuguese ambassador who was every lady's lover. Quick, clever, sharp. Mrs Skidelsky very pretty. How she manages to cope with a dinner party of this size with no servants, not even a daily she told me, and several young children? Said she read and re-read *Another Self*, a classic she called it. I have heard this before.

Wednesday, 14th December

K. Clark in his latest book, *The Other Half*, says that he cannot quote poetry when he delivers a lecture, because if it moves him, it reduces him to tears. Since I feel just the same, this little weakness appeals to me. I thought it was something shameful to admit. When I asked Peggy Ashcroft[†] if she ever was moved to tears by her own recitations, she said, with some acerbity, 'Of course not. Never.' But then, she is a trained professional. Today I received the sweetest letter from Rachel Redgrave – as I mention an actress – about her reading at John's memorial service. To return to K's book, it is full of endearing things which make him a more sensitive and vulnerable man than I supposed to be the case. Beautiful passages of course, but not a well composed book. To return in my senile way to Lady Redgrave, she told Alec Guinness[‡] with whom she is now acting, that she felt John [Fowler] to be present at the Service. Guinness, who is a Catholic, said, 'But he probably *was* there.'

Saturday, 17th December

I was complaining to our Peggy this morning that the local clock-mender had not yet come to attend to my gold Louis XV clock, which he has been tinkering with on and off for more than a year, and which has never gone properly since. He has a bad name, Peggy says, and her

---

* Son of Sir Christopher Chancellor; Editor, *The Spectator*, 1975–84.

† Dame Peggy Ashcroft (1907–89; DBE 1956), actress; m. 1st Rupert Hart-Davis (m. diss.); 2nd, Theodore Komisarjevsky (m. diss.); 3rd, Jeremy Hutchinson, QC (Lord Hutchinson of Lullingworth) (m. diss.).

‡ Sir Alec Guinness (b. 1914; Kt 1959), actor and diarist. The play was *The Old Country*, by Alan Bennett.

Gerald says he must never have another of their clocks to mend. Last time he took out the jewels. Now, how often have I not heard this remark about the 'jewels' in clocks? Are they really jewels, as we like to suppose, and do all clock-menders systematically 'take them out' and thereby enrich themselves to a vast extent? Or are 'jewels' an old wives' tale? Why should clocks need jewels rather than ordinary pins and screws?

A. went to London for the day yesterday; so I, much to my inconvenience, came back from Bath earlier than I wished, at 3.45, to take the dogs for a walk. Twice they bolted, and finally in the Slait field they bolted again. By now dusk was falling. It was bitterly cold. I whistled, and whistled. Nothing happened. I got crosser and crosser, and turned and walked home the way I had come. On reaching the house they were not there standing at the gate, as I hoped. So I got into the car and motored to the gate of the Slait field. There was Folly. I slapped her till she whimpered and drove her home. Still no sign of Honey. So back I drove to the Slait field. It was dark now; a sickle moon above the beech belt on the horizon. I hooted. Presently a guilty Honey sloped towards me. By now I was crosser. I lashed at her with the lead, she screaming as she always does whether one hits her or doesn't, squirming as I held her by the collar. I was angry, but I don't think I even touched her.

Nevertheless, I have been saddened ever since. Did I derive any satisfaction from thus belabouring them? Certainly not much, but possibly just a little. A satisfaction in letting off the steam of anger. I didn't want to hurt them, but I did want to make them understand they had misbehaved. How honest am I being? Am I a bully? For I love them so tenderly that I feel I have been a brute, taking advantage of my superior status in the hierarchy of living things over them. My remorse later in the evening took the form of almost passionate embraces and outpourings of love. Why do I love them better than any human being – save A. – in the world? I have only known them one year. It is absurd.

Sunday, Christmas Day

We are staying with Rory Cameron at les Quatre Sources, two miles north of Ménerbes. His house is only a little advanced since we stayed here in September of last year. At present it is not convenient. To get to the only sitting-room you walk down a circular staircase without handrail, through the kitchen to the dining-room. This is a temporary arrangement, for the west wing is not finished. We flew to Marseilles yesterday afternoon, and dined with Hiram Winterbotham. Rory has invited the Stephen Spenders to Christmas luncheon. When I told him that they disliked me he asked Hiram and his Ball to come too – a kind intention to make things better. As things turned out it was a mistake, for Hiram monopolized the conversation. The Spenders could not have behaved more kindly to us. She embraced me, and he brought us a present from his library, a book on Byron's sex life, with a *dédicace* from them both written on the flyleaf. I call this kind and forgiving.

There is little or nothing, beyond the large bright blue eyes, of the young Stephen I remember. As an Ephebe he had fine, strong features. Today his face and body have subsided. He is a collapsed pudding. Reminds me of Ralph Vaughan-Williams whom as an old man I met during the war. I was disconcerted by Stephen's camera. He is a compulsive photographer. He snapped away throughout luncheon. As I was sitting opposite him his camera was directed towards me. I didn't like it. I was embarrassed, remembering his remark to Ali Forbes that I resembled an undertaker, a sadistic undertaker. Wondered what sinister motives he had in these repeated snappings.

I have not enjoyed this visit much. Rory is duller than he used to be. His friend Gilbert is duller than anything imaginable. Ugly to boot, and a figure of fun, a market-gardener masquerading as a lounge lizard. Dressed in chi-chi clothes and highly scented. He has a good figure but an undistinguished, weak face. Horrid black moustache which conceals to some extent the weakness of his mouth. Has no back to his head. Has been in London learning English for months and can barely speak a word. His French conversation is limited to '*Plait-il?*' and '*Oui, les montagnes sont très jolies.*' Rory told us he still worshipped him. Our last night we dined with Ken Villiers, nice, bumbly and old. There were two women, one a decorator, Monro, chirrupy and spouting endearments, the other a widow of a prominent surgeon, dressed in a green evening 'gown' – and some six queers and their boy-friends. The horror of these sorts of people. Nothing to communicate; camp as can be.

I read this week, at Rory's, volume 3 of Virginia Woolf's letters, also Nigel's excellent *Mary Curzon* (a spoilt social climber), Dostoevsky's *The Gambler* and two other short stories, and dipped into Bruce Chatwin's *Patagonia*, which has had undeserved rave reviews.

No form to the book, a random selection of unpleasant incidents. What a ghastly country it must be. I think that the quality of a book depends very much upon the mood in which one reads it. I am in a bad mood; very depressed at present. Also physically tired, and stiff in the joints.

1978

Have received a number of letters from strangers about my television. One man simply demanded to see me and said he would get in touch after Christmas. Claimed he had met me thirty years ago. Yesterday morning he telephoned. Politely I said I was very busy and could not see him for several weeks. I took his telephone number (which I destroyed) and rang off. This morning the doorbell rang. I thought it might be Ernie come to mend the window catches. Went to the inter-com and a voice said, 'I am Mr Giles. I want to see Mr L.-M.' I pretended to be his secretary, and said Mr L.-M. was out. What message could I give him when he returned? The answer was None. So I said I was sorry. I returned to the library and since I did not hear the front door shutting I pulled down the blind by the window behind me. Ten minutes later I cautiously opened my door leading to the front hall, and saw through the glass door that a man was still standing by the inter-com bell. Shortly after I watched him leave the building and sit on the bench on the pavement in the cold. It is a bitterly cold day. I went to the kitchen, cooked myself something to eat, returned to the library and saw him still seated outside. Not till three o'clock did he leave. I have had manuscripts of books sent to me which I have returned unread (at the cost of seventy pence each parcel); I have been asked to write a foreword to a stranger's book; and so on. But today I received a letter from my old friend Archie Gordon* telling me he waited up till 11.30 to watch my broadcast, in apprehension, because Robert Robinson is a formidable interviewer. He thought I would be diffident and ill at ease. Archie says: 'Did you know how good you are on TV? I am a person who happens to know whether an appearance of this sort is effective, meaningful, or not. The whole occasion was a joy.' Now this is flattering because Archie was Director of Talks for years. Yet I know how nervous and un-positive I was. I was not as good as I could have been, or would be, if given another opportunity. Archie also says he did not like *Ancestral Voices*, but finds *P.P.* a masterpiece on its own. An amusing and amused letter from Diana Mosley

---

* Marquess of Aberdeen.

this morning about the 'rave' review, as she calls it, of *P.P.* by A.L. Rowse* who thinks all Mitfords ought to be shut up. Also another from Clementine Beit,† who thinks this sentiment is probably right, although she herself is a Mitford.

Thursday, 5th January

Nice, polite young man, called Luke Hughes, came to tea by appointment, to discuss his thesis on Beckford. My! how interested the young are in B. today. His idea was to take B's status as a landscape gardener. When I told him he would find difficulty in discovering more on that particular than had been revealed already in my book, he then thought he wd switch to Beckford as art patron. Could I help in this particular? Now, although I always like meeting young people who have interests in subjects which interest me, and helping them as far as I am able, I do find it a bore having to rough out for them the subjects of their theses. A letter this morning from David Carritt‡ asking if I can throw light on a small Fragonard sold at the Fonthill 1822 sale. It has turned up, and he wants to know how, from whom and on what authority Beckford considered it to be Fragonard's work.

Friday, 6th January

A., always ahead of me, finishes her breakfast first, and fidgets in her dear way to remove the breakfast things from the table while I am still munching toast; so she seizes instead the blunt scissors from the kitchen implement drawer, and snips off unruly bits of hair at the back of my head. I continue munching.

Sunday, 8th January

Lunched with the little Hoods in number 2 The Circus, Bath, the whole large house which they have bought. They are living on the two top floors at present. Gradually, they say, they will spread themselves as they become more prosperous. I was touched by them, and

---

* Fellow of All Souls College, Oxford: historian, poet and Cornishman (1903–97).
† Clementine Mitford, m. 1939 Sir Alfred Beit, 2nd Bt (1903–94), Conservative MP 1929–45, and art collector.
‡ Art historian, critic, and founder of The Artemis Gallery (1927–82).

their minute baby, the most beautiful doll of one year it is possible to imagine. It rolls on the floor and squeaks with laughter. Peter gave me a Fonthill Abbey Gothic bell-pull.

Wednesday, 11th January

Stayed the night with J.K.-B. There are builders in his basement and his sitting-room has a grand piano and two harpsichords in it. Went to Alec Guinness and Rachel Redgrave's play.

Thursday, 12th January

Paul Wallraf* lunched with me at Brooks's. I could hardly hear a word he said, for he speaks English badly, softly and seldom finishes a sentence. He was very sweet, and helped me with the correct spelling of a few German names. But he could give me no description of Harold's flat in Berlin. Talked about his horrid war experiences in the Isle of Man.† His release was deferred because he got into trouble. He used to work in a quarry for the sake of exercise and his health. Close by was a small cottage. He became friendly with the couple who lived in it. The wife was sorry for Paul and used to give him extra food and cigarettes. This was found out. I asked him what became of the couple. He said the wife was his secretary now, and she and her husband both lived in the Wallraf building, Grosvenor Place. He told me he was going to be 80 this year; Muriel is 81. He has two German boy-friends, neither of whom will consent to go to bed with any man under the age of seventy. The mind boggles beastlily.

I dined at Brooks's. At seven a meeting called by Tony Dulverton and Pat Gibson‡ of ex-Magdalen men who are members of Brooks's. A film shown, and several talks about the College's need – £3 million. Then we dined. After dinner, questions. I put two. I supported Ivor Thomas's§ concern that there should be a qualified architect employed.

---

* 'Prussian refugee from Hitler's Germany and dealer in rare works of art' (*Fourteen Friends*).
† Where he was interned in 1939; James Pope-Hennessy badgered the authorities tirelessly and ultimately successfully for his release.
‡ Patrick Gibson, cr. Life Peer 1975; Member of Council of the N.T. 1966–86; and of numerous other bodies concerned with art and architecture.
§ Ivor Bulmer-Thomas (1905–93); church conservationist and Director (1957–93) of Friends of Friendless Churches.

The Bursar told us they were employing a quantity surveyor only, and he brushed aside as nonsense a criticism by the *Architects' Journal* of the indifferent restoration of the College front on the High Street.

Tuesday, 17th January

Now that I have reached the years 1956 and '57 in my reading of H.N. and V.S.-W's correspondence I am getting depressed. Knowing as I do the actual dates of their deaths and the sad *dégringolade* in store for Harold so soon, so very soon, the ailments and minor illnesses I am reading about bring home to me the little of the life, which they both loved, to be left to them. And, it follows – how little is left to A. and me. I have read this morning of Harold's seventieth birthday celebrations and presents, which he pretended to enjoy and which he really hated. I shall of course not get the same recognition – indeed I pray that no one will know beyond my family – but I already feel what dear Harold felt. Another thing which upsets me is to read how much he disliked A. Vita took him to task once. He was irrational in his dislike. But it saddens me. This morning A. asked me to get her car out of the motor-house. Then we could not find the key. So she said, Oh never mind, I'll do it when I find the key; and I, without waiting or helping her to look for it, left. All day I have felt a penitent beast. I have grown to love her so deeply, for her goodness to me. As Vita wrote to H.N., A. fusses over Jim like an old hen. What is this but true, deep love? The darling.

Wednesday, 18th January

This morning I went to have the swelling next my left testicle drained by Mr Smith, the specialist at the Lansdown Grove Home, next door. I left number 19 at 11.30 and was back at midday at my typewriter. A prick, which was the local anaesthetic, and within one minute the syringe inserted. I looked away. Felt nothing. When it was over I asked to see what had been extracted. An abnormally large wine glass, as it were, full to the brim with straw-coloured liquid. I was amazed by the quantity, far more than it seemed the swelling could have contained, but I suppose the sac extended inwards. At once I felt lighter, more comfortable. It is likely the liquid will return, and then I shall have to have the cyst cut out.

Gave Peter Hood lunch at the Vendange. He told me he was decorating and rearranging Madame Tussaud's. Amongst the wax images there is a collection made by the original Madame Tussaud of some good busts of Marie Antoinette and contemporaries, saved from the recurrent fires at Madame Tussaud's. The original Madame escaped after the Revolution with her husband to England. Peter says the guillotine knife which beheaded the poor Queen is exhibited.

Thursday, 19th January

Peter Bradshaw, the odd boy who lives behind me in the Mews, came to tea. He is a Beckford loony. I asked him why. Although he is almost incoherent his worship is of the Martyred Beckford, who broke away from conventions of the Establishment, sex-wise. Told me that he, on the contrary, at the age of 17 had had a daughter by an Austrian girl whom he never married, but sees in Bath, where she lives, works and keeps the child. He is now 26. Yet he told me he disapproved of divorce, and of contraceptives. He believes in religion, but what religion I can't make out. His parents own the new house with large garden; his father a businessman with huge Mercedes; his mother likewise has a business. Yet this youth is living on the dole. He told me he hoped to receive £60,000 which he is claiming as damages for a motor accident. 'Why did Beckford spend his money?' he asked. Why? I said – presumably because he had it. 'What were his motives?' It tumbled out that he wanted advice how to spend his £60,000 if he got it. Should he dissipate it over, say, three years, on motor cars and girls? I told him he would be mad to do any such thing. It would render him miserable. He went away, thanking me for my advice. He is a nice youth, with an underlying wish to do the right thing, but without a clue. All he did tell me of interest was this: the black youths in this country, those who are not rebels against society, or vandals, are turning to religion; he believes there will be a religious revival which will derive, like all fashions today, from below.

Saturday, 21st January

We lunched with the Barlows. Peter Coats was staying. He has sold 125,000 copies of his garden book published by and on sale at Marks & Spencers. His book on the Buckingham Palace garden is about to come out and will sell as many copies – so he says. I have no doubt sales of both books will be immense. I said, 'How lovely for you to be so rich.' He said, 'Isn't it?' Then he asked me how I was going to deal with the, what he called 'pools', in Harold's life. Quite unsuspecting I said, I shall take everything of that nature for granted; neither explain nor comment. Then he said, 'You must take care not to implicate his friends who are alive.' Then I saw what he was driving at. He went on, 'I held it against you that you wrote such awful things about my dear old friend Chips.* All for the sake of three or four lines of scandal-mongering which could have been left out without lessening the effect of your book.' Peter went on, 'Harold was a friend of Chips.' I said, 'He didn't like him at all.' 'But he sponged on him all right.' I said testily, 'Harold never sponged on anybody. He was a poor man all his life, and the most generous person to his young friends who ever lived. You must know that.' These words were not spoken in anger or with raised voices. There was a pause. I looked at my feet. We moved into the dining-room. On leaving I waved distantly to Peter. I don't wish to appear unfriendly; on the contrary I wish to appear friendly, but at the same time to be utterly indifferent to his very existence. I think Peter is a fairly good man, a well-disposed man; but he is devious, shallow, and stupid.

Friday, 3rd February

On Sunday, a terrible day of bitter wind, horizontal sleet, and deep mud, I had elected to walk from Badminton to Ozleworth with Bruce Chatwin. Did not like to put it off when the morning arrived because a streak of wan sun appeared just as I was telephoning him. After my, not his, H.C. at eight and breakfast he was driven over by Elizabeth, his wife. Bruce had a dog and I took Folly. We strode across the park, via Worcester Lodge, Oldbury, across the main Stroud road, and halfway through Tresham where we decided to give up. We were very wet and the path from Tresham to Holywell was very bad, B. assured me; and I, knowing the path of old, well believed him. Elizabeth met us in the car. When we reached Holywell she plied us with hot lemon and whisky, and then a delicious lunch of pheasant stew and red wine. I gorged. Felt all the better. My acute depression lifted momentarily. I had an Up on the Chatwins, she for being so well organized and welcoming; he for being so clever and interesting. *En route* he told me

---

* Sir Henry Channon (1897–1958), MP and diarist.

what I was unaware of, that his Patagonia book and my *P.P.* were the choice of the year in the *Observer* of last month. I had not seen this. Maurice Richardson* the chooser. Bruce told me of hair-raising experiences he went through in South America. In one little country, I forget which, he was arrested for some misdemeanour, passport not visaed, and beaten up. He was hit about the face, stripped of all his clothing – what a pretty sight, to be sure – and humiliated in public. 'How awful!' I said. 'Well,' he replied, 'I must confess to having rather enjoyed it.' 'Then you are a masochist, I surmise.' 'Just a bit,' he answered.

Talking about hijackers, etc., Bruce assured me that they and the European guerrillas were motivated by religion; they were nearly all children of Lutheran or Low Church parents. They had devised some nebulous creed that whatever they did in defiance of the accepted principles of western civilization, must be right. There is no arguing with them. There is no solution to this particular problem, he is quite certain.

I am delighted. For once I have done something for someone. Denys Sutton telephoned to say he has engaged my gt-nephew Nick on staff of *Apollo* at £3,000 p.a. So there is a possible future for him, so long as that magazine can keep going.

Friday, 10th February

I spent two nights of 6th and 7th staying with Eardley in London. Two National Trust committees – occupying hours and hours; then London Library, tracking *Times* newspaper references to Harold. First night dined alone with Jack Rathbone. Extremely affectionate but to a degree to which I find it difficult to respond in mutual measure. 'We are the very greatest of friends, aren't we?' Well, I suppose we are. Second night Ros [Lehmann] dined with Eardley and me, I providing the grub, he the vino, in West Halkin Street. Talk with Ros always on so intelligent a level, candid and interesting. I went to see Mickey Renshaw for a quarter of an hour in his Cheyne Court flat. I fear he is dying. A terrible change, he is thin as a knife, moves painfully across the room, lies on the sofa and speaks with so weak a voice, with a boiling sound coming from his poor chest. Cannot eat, or even watch others eating; is undergoing radium treatment. So unlike Mickey, too,

---

* Journalist and writer (1907–78).

not to respond to any quip or gossip. I fear he is in a bad way. Talked of celebrating his seventieth birthday next August, which I doubt his reaching.

Last night returning to Badminton from Bath at dusk, the new moon was lying on her back with the old moon in her arms. I mean I could see the whole pearly orb distinctly outlined. I don't think this is visible all the year round. Perhaps it happens only during sharp frosts, which we are undergoing now. The Tormarton–Acton Turville stretch affords me after dark some wonderfully varied moonscapes.

Last night A. had invited to dinner the Vicar's youngest son, Graeme, and his little wife. Caroline Somerset very sweetly came to help and was a roaring success. This boy, having returned from visiting his grandfather in South Africa, has received very unfavourable reports of his [own] condition. The Vicar was told by the doctor that there is no hope. He is a terminal case. The little wife has been told. They do not know whether Graeme has guessed, or not. He is like a wraith, but cheerful. A general wastage, the whole body being gobbled up by this demon cancer. At the age of 25 it is extremely cruel. With cancer sufferers there is always conversation, albeit in an oblique way, about age. He was telling us that he supposed, since his recent birthday, that he was middle-aged. We all laughed in a wry sort of way.

Saturday, 11th February

In London I went to the Burlington House exhibition of Courbet paintings. Great crowds. Don't understand why certain artists draw the multitude; others, no less great, do not. Is it advertisement? I doubt it. Something topical captures the public's interest. I whizzed round within three-quarters of an hour. One cannot spend more time than this; and this was totally inadequate. I always wish there were ten paintings only; then I could study the ten in great detail, and remember them. As it is, a series of cinematograph flashes leaves the faintest impression on my mind. I wouldn't call Courbet great; stolid, matter-of-fact, competent; no hidden depths; no poetry; some conceit; much versatility. He reminds of Corot at times, at times of other contemporaries. Most of the frames, since the majority of the pictures come from French provincial museums, are the heavy mid-Victorian sort. How I wish I had not removed that of my little Corot. I kept it in the attic at Alderley, but when we left, must have thrown it away. French nineteenth-century paintings so often look like oleographs that I suppose a special varnish was used. They crack, too.

This black weather coincides with new aches and pains. At least A. comforts me by saying it is the cold which brings them out. I was fearing that the new pain in my right foot, moving to my right thigh, and never the two simultaneously, portended spinal trouble, a growth like that suffered by poor Nancy [Mitford] and Hester Chapman.*

Sunday, 12th February

Had another, shorter walk with Bruce Chatwin today. They lunched; so did Chiquita Astor.† But Bruce was not feeling very fit after a bad attack of influenza immediately following our last walk. We proceeded by the same route, stopping at the Jeffreys' farm where Elizabeth met us in the car. He is a stimulating companion, and when alone does not show off, but is diffident about his place in the world, as a writer; and is easy. I would happily go on an expedition with him. I have an Up on him. Today the ground frozen hard and stiff.

Wednesday, 15th February

Today I went to Magdalen, Oxford. Drove there, since the oil tanker drivers' strike seems about to end and no shortage of petrol threatened, after all. The anxieties we live through, on a perpetual knife-edge of some vital deprivation! I was given a special pass to park in the College precincts off the Longwell entrance. It was odd to ring the bell of the President's Lodgings boldly, and equally fearlessly to enter when a nice housekeeper lady, with whom I shook hands, opened it. I told the President that it was the first time I had set foot within these august portals since my interview with Sir Herbert Warren quite fifty years ago; for when I was resident in College I never once was invited inside by Sir Herbert's successor, I being an undergraduate of no distinction or promise. I lunched alone with the President, James Griffiths,‡ at the end of a long table in a large dining-room. Building dates from 1880s. Gothic but decent. Walls hung with

---

* Mrs R.L. Griffen (1899–1976); novelist, biographer, historian.
† Ana Inez Carcano, m. 1944–72 Major The Hon. John J. (Jakie) Astor (Kt 1978), 4th son of 2nd Viscount Astor.
‡ President of Magdalen College, Oxford 1968–79 (1908–81).

portraits of bewigged presidents. No one served at table. Sparsest fare of cold spam and mixed salad without dressing. Beer from a pewter tankard to drink. Followed by biscuits and mousetrap cheese. No coffee. Adequate but un-princely. I rather took to the President. A sensible, easy-going, un-pompous man. He described the problems confronting him concerning the reparations of the College buildings. And indeed, after being shown round for two and a half hours by the enthusiastic sub-bursar, Latham, I understood them. They are these: in the past and within recent times the buildings have been so poorly restored that hardly a stone of the original early Tudor time survives. I should say only the early eighteenth-century New Buildings are unchanged, and even so the middle of the south front was refaced just before my sojourn, in the late 1920s. There are moreover no photographic records of details of the gargoyles, heraldic emblems and carved work from which to judge whether the present sculptor's substitutes are faithful copies, or not, owing to the fact that in the Thirties they were replaced by synthetic stone copies. All the Thirties work both sculptured and façadal has deteriorated and must now be totally renovated. They are at least using a stone specially brought over from Lorraine, at great cost. It is very questionable whether the gargoyles should be copied from what they believe went before. And when one sees protruding from string courses the head of the present President, wearing collar and tie, one equally wonders whether this is correct treatment. I went away in a haze, uncertain how I am to report to Pat Gibson and what to recommend.

I liked the President, although not my sort of man. He is not a Classical scholar, but a professor of economics. But his love of Magdalen where he has spent the greater part of his life – fifty years, no less – is touching. He is a tall, ungainly, ill-dressed man with a smiling, pleasant face. There was a curious faint smell of scent about him.

Saturday, 18th February

Still fearfully cold, freezing all day. Peggy Münster[*] lunched, and the Somersets. Peggy is bent round like a hoop and resembles dear Eny[†]

---

[*] Margaret (b. 1905), dau. of Captain The Hon. Cyril Ward (d. 1930) and Baroness Irene de Brienen (Eny); m. 1929 Count Paul Münster.

[†] Baroness Irene de Brienen (d. 1974); m., 2nd, Vice-Admiral The Hon. Arthur Strutt.

already. Caroline was so noisy and so wild, hurling her arms around and shouting, that David, whose face had darkened, suddenly exploded at her: 'For heavens sake,' he said, 'don't shout!' I held her hand, and she giggled, but took heed. They disappeared for a walk, and Peggy remained. She read aloud for the second time her boring article on her garden at Bampton, to ask our approval. People should not read aloud their chapters to unwilling hosts. All I could say was, 'What a good description of your garden, which is the most beautiful I know.' Which is true. Then I walked with the two dogs on leads towards Alderley. Wearing two jerseys and my fur-lined coat and collar, I was frozen. A. picked me up near Dunkirk. We had tea with the Acloques.* Guy is just as noisy and hysterical as Caroline. Why, I ask myself, does one waste precious time vouchsafed one. Yet all the people I have seen today I am v. fond of. Therein lies irony.

Tuesday, 21st February

A. went to London today. Intending to catch the 8.30 from Chippenham she came to my room at 7.45 announcing her departure because the roads were still snowy. In ten minutes she was back, saying that she could not walk to the motor-house owing to the black ice. So I got up and we breakfasted together, and she thought she would try to take the next train. I said I would accompany her in my car as far as Acton Turville, where I knew the road to Chippenham was gritted. There I turned back and put away my car because I intended to stay at home with the dogs. Walking with great care on rubber-soled shoes back from the stable yard to the house I suddenly, without warning, fell flat on my behind. Several people witnessed this idiotic scene, but could do nothing. Mrs Munday was crawling along our wall to reach the milk van. The estate office kindly telephoned to ask if I was all right. I was, and am. Might easily have broken a wrist, if not a leg. Wasn't even bruised, though was shaken. The extraordinary consequence of my fall, which was a severe one, is that my sciatica, from which I have been suffering this past fortnight, went instantly. I suppose the fall put the dislocated spine back into position. Out of evil cometh forth good.

At 11.15 A. telephoned from Chelsea to remind me to put a potato into the oven to bake for my luncheon.

---

* They had bought the L.-Ms' house at Alderley, Gloucestershire.

Wednesday, 22nd February

I go to London for the night. I find myself dropping things when I am fumbling for money to pay the bus conductor. I can't manoeuvre parcels. In the bus this morning, I dropped my briefcase on the floor and when a kind girl stooped to pick it up for me, I dropped my umbrella. I stumble too, and knock myself against lamp posts.

Nick lunched. Adorable. I mustn't become soppy about my great-nephews. He was not looking at all well, having lost one stone since his wisdom teeth operation, followed by a nasty attack of red 'flu. There were no *longueurs*, no awkward moments. I really think I can be perfectly easy with him now. He pointed out that the curious head on the writing paper of Ezra Pound was a drawing of Pound by Gaudier-Brzeska. I had come from Christie's, where I read through seven letters which Pound wrote to Harold in 1935. Tirades of abuse and smut. He must have been raving. Nigel is selling them. I wouldn't give five pence for them. But Christie's estimate that they will fetch six to seven hundred pounds.

At four I had my interview with Harold Macmillan. I arrived punctually at Messrs Macmillans' office in Little Essex Street, a hideous building in this nice old area next to the Temple. Taken up in a lift, down a long passage, ushered into a dark and ugly and very hot board room. Mr Macmillan was sitting, back to the window, alone at one end of a long table. He is very old, was slumped in his chair, sucking at a pipe which was not alight. Voice rather hoarse. Said he had a cold and was evidently not feeling well. Kept running his hands through his long silken white hair, or patting his dark grey pullover on his rather protuberant belly. Gave impression of being lonely, sad and a little disillusioned. Said in the course of the talk, 'Nobody wants me now.'

In spite of this initial gloom, and the unattractive setting, he exercised his spell upon me. When he smiles he is very charming, and those leonine eyebrows are the most expressive features. He dearly loves and admires Debo.

Object of the interview was Harold N. He said he knew him very well, but not intimately. Liked him very much. He was a dear fellow; was a decent character; easy to get on with; was very kind to his colleagues, and particularly to Ramsay MacDonald when he was ill and gaga. But he lacked push and virility. Was too soft and sentimental for politics. Compared him with John Buchan* who was hopeless at

---

* Scottish author and statesman (1875–1940); cr. 1st Baron Tweedsmuir 1935, on his appointment as Governor-General of Canada.

organization. Admitted that at time of Munich H.N. showed distinct courage, but it was courage of the passive sort. I asked if the House listened attentively to his speeches. He said Yes, but the Chamber would not fill the moment it was known that he was to speak. I asked if he remembered H's maiden speech at time of Hoare–Laval crisis.* He did, but he said the speech Lloyd George made on that occasion was tremendous. Exhorted me to read it; it made Members sit up, and turn white. He could move mountains because he had the spirit of leadership. H.N. did not possess that quality. Thought that H.N. was on the upward grade since he first joined in 1935, making progressively better speeches, but once the Phoney War was over and the war in earnest began, there was no place for Harold – Macmillan spread wide his arms – he was no longer needed.

He, Macmillan, in those war days, saw Winston constantly. His little group of Pug [Ismay], Eden, Bracken, Cherwell, Macmillan himself could say what they liked to him. Winston relished argument and passionate disagreement, if need be. The inner group would say 'Winston, you are talking balls. The way you must act is like this.' W. would listen, complain that they were all against him, even cry, and then do what he thought best as a result of the discussion. Now, Harold was not on these terms. He would look at Winston with adoring eyes like a faithful spaniel. This is not what Winston liked, or admired. He did not care for deference, although he would not brook disagreement from those outside the favoured circle.

Duff Cooper was also hopeless at organizing. No good at all as a Minister. Yet, unlike Harold, he was pugnacious, passionate; a fighter. Macmillan said the person in politics today who most reminded him of Harold was President Carter.† The same shilly-shallying, the same sentimentality. I asked if his colleagues knew about his curious married life and his propensities. Macmillan said, almost aghast, 'No, in no sense whatever. In fact I don't think I knew then. I don't think anyone did. Besides, it was not a subject which we would discuss. You must remember that thirty-five years ago we were all – well, if not quite all, nearly all in the House were gentlemen.'

---

* This was 19 December 1935; the Hoare–Laval Pact, whereby the British Foreign Minister Sir Samuel Hoare and the French Prime Minister Pierre Laval proposed the cession to Mussolini's Italy of the most fertile part of Abyssinia (Ethiopia), prompted public outcry and was disowned by the British Prime Minister, Stanley Baldwin.
† James (Jimmy) Earl Carter (Dem.), elected US President, November 1976.

He said he hadn't been inside the House of Commons for fifteen years, and nothing would induce him to enter it again. Told me that for seventeen years he was a back-bencher and did not get office of the humblest sort during that time. 'That was unusual.' He repeated more than once that I must not think he considered Harold's political career a failure. There were plenty of men who went into Parliament with far less success than Harold, but they were not men of ambition. Harold *was* ambitious, and he himself considered his political career had been a failure. Of course he ought to have had a peerage. Pity Winston did not make him a peer. I asked if Attlee disliked him [H.N.]. All Macmillan said was, 'Attlee was a strange man, a cynical man. One did not know whom he liked or disliked.'

He thought Vita a great drawback. If H. had been an ordinary man he would have got rid of her. I dissented, and told him how devoted they were. Nevertheless he thought Harold enjoyed being a martyr, was slightly masochistic.

Finally, he said: rhetoric and writing are different arts. The greater of the two is writing. Harold was a great writer. Balfour's name came up and I suggested that he was as a person languid and soft. 'He was far from soft. He was lethargic, but he was ruthless. Unlike Harold, his spine was made of steel. He would sacrifice a friend of forty years without a murmur, without a moment's hesitation, if he decided it was necessary to get rid of him. That was the difference. Besides, Balfour did not care a damn what people said or thought about him. Harold did. He worried if he were criticized. He wanted to be liked. A fatal propensity.' He then made a curious comparison of Balfour to Lord Burghley. Surmised that Burghley, with his quiet, confident, astute manner, maintained Queen Elizabeth's confidence through not being flashy, passionate or volatile, but by remaining calm, apparently unambitious for glory. Balfour was this sort of man.

He thought Harold's father had been a strong man, tenacious and unyielding, in spite of his feeble physique. Sligger Urquhart, who had a great influence upon Harold at Balliol, was a saint, fortified during every incident of his life by his faith. Macmillan gave me a lift in his car as far as Charing Cross. On parting he repeated that he had been taking the part of devil's advocate, in order to help.

Saturday, 25th February

Having brought from London six copies of my novel I proceeded to read it, putting myself in the position of a stranger. I was so horrified by the jejuneness, the feeble dialogue, that I could not get beyond chapter 3. Now, how is this? When I finished writing this novel I was pleased with it. Until this moment I have been pretty confident that it was all right. Now I don't believe it is at all all right and am sure it will get a bad reception. I am plunged into a trough of anguish and dread the day of its launching on 16th March.

Friday, 3rd March

Having picked up *Round the Clock* again and read it through, I reverse my opinion just expressed. I think it is rather good, and well written; in spite of the passages between Adda and Jasper, and Adda with Mrs O'Connor, which are the feeblest in the book.

Nothing has brought home to me more strikingly the mortality of human beings than the discovery among the folded leaves of Harold's letters of cigarette ash dropped from his holder, and still powdery fresh today so long after his death. Even cigarette ash can be preserved longer than the flesh and blood of a genius. No, the ash I found was between the leaves of a pamphlet, *Swinburne and Baudelaire*, by Harold, given by him to Vita in 1930. So it is her cigarette ash, of 1930.

Thursday, 9th March

Philip 'the Coachman'* telephoned A. this morning in much distress to say that Mickey Renshaw died in his sleep during the night. Neither of us is the least surprised, but we are sad. Why do doctors have to torture terminal cases like Mickey's? It was so obvious to both of us who saw him recently that he ought to die.

Thought much about poor Mickey all day. We were very fond of him. He was a companionable man, and a wonderful traveller. We went to Turkey with him. He was always entertaining, tremendously giggly, and of course socially sophisticated. His friends were chiefly grand old women like Sybil Cholmondeley, Dow. Lady Salisbury and Maud Russell. He was thoroughly egocentric. Number one came first, and he could be ruthless and cruel; but was

---

* Philip Dimmick.

never so to us. He was a godson of Lord Kitchener, whom he resembled, with the same large, staring, fish-like eyes. Lord Kitchener was a great *ami* of his mother, Lady Winifred, but was not Mickey's father, so Mickey assured me once. The dates did not work out. Besides, starch and stiff Lady Winifred was not that sort of lady. We shall miss him.

Friday, 10th March

I heard on the 11.30 news last night that Roy Harrod* has died. Now with luck we shall see more of Billa who has devoted the last three years entirely to cherishing him.

Last weekend, staying with Loelia and Martin Lindsay, Loelia took us to the Watts Museum near Guildford. What a poor artist Watts was. There were some half-dozen pictures I would accept if offered: the rest I would spurn; wishy-washy, sentimental, devoid of solidity and substance. Wilfrid Blunt† the curator was out. A. wanted to discuss with him the provenance of her Watts portrait of Ellen Terry.

Tuesday, 14th March

John Sparrow‡ stayed the night. I met him in Bath and took him out to lunch. We talked in the library about Harold. Indeed we talked throughout the visit. He was charming, and more helpful than anyone else, apart from Nigel, so far. His considered opinion is that I should write two volumes – the first to be the shorter, and a life and assessment of Harold; the second much longer and a selection from his letters, articles, reviews, speeches, and diaries. I do not think this quite satisfactory, somehow. In the first place I wd find volume 1 difficult to condense and in the second material for vol. 2 would be difficult to select and to edit in a consecutive sense.

On Sunday we lunched with the [Anthony] Powells at Chantry.

---

* Sir Roy Harrod (b. 1900; Kt 1959); m. 1938 Wilhelmina Cresswell (b. 1911); Norfolk conservationist and founder of Norfolk Churches Trust; biographer of Maynard Keynes.

† Drawing Master at Eton College 1938–59 and author of several biographies (1901–87); brother of Anthony Blunt.

‡ Warden of All Souls College, Oxford 1952–77; man of letters and bibliophile (1906–92).

Duke and Duchess of Somerset* and their eldest son present. The
Duke like a Major in a dim line regiment; the Duchess a nice and
bright person. I liked her. Tony took John and me for a long walk
round the lake and grottoes.

John Sparrow told us the story of Leslie Hartley's† will. Apparently
the last novel he wrote was not accepted by Jamie Hamilton before
Leslie's death. The story very nearly anticipates what came to pass in
his case. Shortly after writing it he fell into a decline of drunkenness
and feeble-mindedness.

Fearing lest Leslie might leave all he possessed to a rascally manservant, of whom he had a succession, David Cecil (his greatest friend)
and Jimmie Smith prevailed on him to visit his solicitor and make a
final will. After some uncertainty and a good deal of prevarication
Leslie left everything he possessed to his maiden sister Norah, a very
decent woman who was already rich. She behaved generously and
made presents of money to Leslie's godchildren and gave lesser
mementoes to his friends. David Cecil had all the books he wanted
and I, who was never an intimate friend, was offered what books
I might select from those not taken by David. I took about thirty
in all.

Now John Sparrow has told A. and me that three years after Leslie's
death and the settling of his estate, the executor of a bogus clergyman
who had recently died found among his client's papers a later will by
Leslie, undoubtedly written in Leslie's hand and witnessed by the
defunct clergyman and another man, also since dead. This will left
everything to an elderly mother of a married daughter, whom she
claimed was Leslie's. When asked why she had never produced this
will before, the woman replied that she asked the clergyman witness
to keep it because she did not want to embarrass Miss Hartley in her
lifetime, but intended to produce it when Miss Hartley should die. It
seems that this woman has done the same thing with several other old
gents and amassed quite a fortune by this means. Stranger still, Leslie
made a second will in her favour when entertaining her to luncheon
in Claridges a few weeks before he died. Miss Hartley's solicitors are
being cunning. They cannot dispute that both wills are genuine. But
instead of disputing the motives of the woman, they are leaving it to

---

* Percy Seymour, 18th Duke of Somerset (1910–84); m. 1951 Jane Thomas; their son,
Lord Seymour, b. 1952.
† Leslie Poles Hartley (1895–1972); novelist – author of *The Go-Between*, etc.

her to prove that Leslie was of sound mind when he made the two
wills. This she will not be able to, it is thought.

Sunday, 19th March

On Wednesday I went to London by train. Lunched with Georgina
Stonor* who has become archivist to the Wellington papers. She had
written asking for information about Gerry's gift of Apsley House to
the nation. I told her all I knew – how badly and ungratefully he was
treated by the Government and the press. She then asked what I knew
of Gerry's marriage troubles. She says the present Duke won't ever talk
about either his father or mother. Too embarrassed by the whole
thing. Has a certain regard for his father's knowledge but clearly does
not revere his memory. On the other hand the son, Douro, whom
Gerry liked, is very interested in his grandparents and wants to collect
particulars for the archives room while his grandparents' friends
survive. I said I had never met Dotty, Gerry's wife.

Spent Wednesday afternoon and Thursday morning and afternoon
in the Script Library of the BBC in the old Langham Hotel, looking
through some of the three hundred broadcast scripts of Harold on
microfilm, a tiring process.

On Thursday lunched with Norah Smallwood and Ian Parsons. A.
came up for the occasion, to celebrate the publication of my novella,
Round the Clock. Two good reviews were produced, one in *Daily
Telegraph* which A. managed to buy in the country, there being no
copies on sale in London owing to strikes. Snarky reviews in *Listener*
and *TLS*. Complaints that the book is too upper-class!

To Royal Society of Literature lecture by a man called Gant† on
Masefield, John Betj. in the chair. Very dreary lecture and dreary
delivery. We dined afterwards with dear Sheila Birkenhead. Silly old
John had invited Gant and Mrs Gant to joint the party. I drove to
Wilton Street with Sheila who a little ruefully said how much more
fun we would have had without these people whom none of us knew.
In fact Gant turned from being dull to a very boring, pleased-with-
himself oaf. Elizabeth Cav. didn't like him one bit.

John told me that he wrote an appreciation of Billy Wicklow‡ and

---

* Sister of 7th Baron Camoys of Stonor Park, Henley-on-Thames.
† Roland Gant (1919–93); poet and (1978) Literary Editor at William Heinemann.
‡ 8th Earl of Wicklow, author (as Billy Clonmore) of *Shell Guide to Kent* (1935).

sent it to *The Times* who would not publish it. I told him that A. and I had just been to the Watts Museum. He said the picture called *The First Oyster* was meant as a deliberate joke, Watts having been piqued when told he had no sense of humour. Rather pawky humour his turns out to be. Humour through art never *is* humour, to my mind.

Wednesday, 22nd March

A young man came all the way from London to see me, having already been in touch with the National Trust of which he passionately wishes to join the staff. He promised not to stay more than half an hour and indeed only exceeded it by ten minutes. He is thirty-two, a bachelor as yet, and Australian. Has a job with the P. & O. Line at which he is earning £12,000. Yet he is prepared to throw all this aside in order to work for the Trust, no matter how menial the job he is offered, and even to work for one year for nothing if by so doing he could be taken on permanently. He has no special qualifications. I asked him why this quixotic idealism? He said he so disliked the attitude of money-making in the City and found his colleagues so uncongenial that he longed to get away. Money accumulation was no incentive to content of mind. Besides, when I asked if he had been able to put by from his earnings, he said Not really; so much went in tax, although he led a quiet and fairly abstemious life.

Tuesday, 28th March

My biennial tour with Alex Moulton* took place today. He called for me at ten o'clock precisely in his latest Rolls Royce, last year's model, for which he paid £22,000, no less. We drove to Staffordshire and looked at the dismal little bull-ring pavilion at Swarkeston where we picnicked. Purpose of this tour was to visit houses built by Smythson, who according to Mark Girouard was the builder of Alex's Hall at Bradford. Then proceeded to Wollaton, where I have not been these forty years or more. It was crammed with sightseers, but we walked round the interior which is exactly the same as I remembered, full of stuffed giraffes. Nothing inside to wonder at except the great hall, which is *tour de force* Elizabethan, with its very high clerestory

---

* Dr Alexander Moulton (b. 1920), of The Hall, Bradford-on-Avon, Wiltshire; innovating engineer and inventor of the Moulton bicycle and motor-car suspension.

windows and vulgarly carved roof figures. Also, what I had forgotten, the staircase walls and ceilings painted by Thornhill, which make a fine composition. Formerly attributed to Verrio; how the attribution could have been made I can't conceive, because the superior hand of Thornhill seems clearly apparent. Next looked at the outside of Wootton Lodge, Staffordshire, where I stayed with Diana Mosley in December 1936 and listened to Edward VIII make his abdication speech, while the tears poured down our cheeks. Then it was one of the most romantic old houses conceivable. Today, having been bought by a rich businessman, it is totally ruined. The window quarries [quarrels] have been replaced by plate glass, unsightly additions have been made to one side, a preposterous and hideous fence of high iron spikes, such as might have confined the inmates of a prison, erected, and behind it a belt of churchyard Lawsonias planted. From Wootton we drove to Baslow, on the edge of Chatsworth Park, and stayed at The Cavendish. Debo made and decorated this hotel which she took me round before it was opened. Extremely comfortable and *bien*, but fearfully expensive. Bill over £27 each.

I must say it is heavenly being driven in this beautiful motor. Indeed, I can imagine no nicer way of going to heaven than in a Rolls, listening to Mozart. It glides in a way that no other car in the world glides.

Wednesday, 29th March

This morning we walked in the park. Alex went right up to the house, but I turned back because I didn't want to be seen, as it were prying, by Debo, if she were about. Then we drove to Barlbrough which though a school is beautifully kept. Can't be faulted. No unsightly school extensions. Garden well looked after. Might be a private house. We rang the doorbell and the housekeeper said she was sure the headmaster would not mind us walking round the outside. He did not appear, and we did not see inside. I have often been here before. Roaring noise of the motorway about half a mile away. Then to Bolsover. The little castle still undergoing repairs and so not open. But what has been done to the riding-school and long open gallery very good indeed. Picnicked again and drove to Hardwick. Alex had not seen any of these houses and was amazed by Hardwick. Kept photographing frenziedly with evident enthusiasm. Now would I, if taken by him to a museum of bicycle wheels and gearboxes, have acted similarly? Probably not. My company ought to bore him, he being a v. distinguished scientist. On the contrary, he is tolerant of my whims. I asked to meet the new curator, a retired Air Commodore, nice man. He found us in the tea room. Said how much he enjoyed my books. Alex said brightly, 'I didn't see any of them on display in your shop,' to which the Air Commodore remarked, 'No, I'm afraid not.' Does this mean that the Trust considers my diaries unsuitable for their members? It gave me in its magazine a most grudging little notice of four lines on *Prophesying Peace*. On to Marston, near Grantham, to stay with Henry Thorold.*

This was a grim experience. Weather exceedingly cold. There is no central heating of any kind; bath water tepid and so no bath. We were shown to our bedrooms, which were large, and no electric fires even. I was so perished I could not even change my polo sweater for dinner, and put two extra jerseys over it. Special dinner party laid on for us – Myles and his Ambassador brother Toby Hildyard, the Barrington-Smiths (she was Penelope Packe, an absurd lady), and Henry's dear old senile aunt, aged 86. Party did not go with a swing, owing to the cold. We sat in the hall, an apartment with three or four open doorways, and one green log emitting a thin trickle of dun smoke. Henry is inexhaustible on his subjects, which are architecture and genealogy, particularly his ancestors. Good, clever, endearing man notwithstanding. O God, I am a cad!

Thursday, 30th March

Motored Henry and old aunt to Somersby Rectory, the birthplace of Tennyson. This was kind of Henry to arrange. Whereas the surrounding country is absolutely as Tennyson knew it, the house has been totally 'boiled', as Ted Lister used to say. Even the front door has been moved to another bay. All the rooms cut up. This was a sad disappointment. The owners of this house collect Staffordshire cows, and I thought I recognized one or two from Papa's collection. They told me they had bought several from Barney Kidd's collection, so it is probable that Papa's were represented likewise. Then luncheon next door with Holman Sutcliffe and his wife at a delightful plain Georgian

---

* Revd Henry Thorold (b. 1921), Squire of Marston Manor, Lincolnshire; Chaplain-General to the Forces and to King George VI; Chaplain of Lancing College, 1949–68; Lincolnshire county historian.

house called The Mansion House, Tetford, with a pretty Gothick library added recently by [Francis] Johnson. Holman Sutcliffe, whom I have not met since before the war, seemed pleased to see me, as I was to see him. Made me sign copies of my book. Last night Henry embarrassed me by reading to the company extracts from my diaries. (Will he ever read these aloud?)

We motored back to Badminton, having dropped Henry and aunt at Marston.

Sunday, 2nd April

Maddening that I have missed reviews of *Round the Clock* in last week's *Sunday Times*, which did not appear because of printers' strike, and in Thursday's *Times* which has been on strike all this past week. Norah told me that both papers had contained reviews. This is a blow because novels have small sales, and these papers might have helped. The *Sunday Telegraph* review of last week was very favourable. Also excellent review in *Financial Times* comparing me with Tony Powell and Evelyn Waugh – to make me laugh. But some captious reviews all the same, dwelling on the upper-class voice, as though this had anything to do with the merits of the book. I can honestly say that from my experience and from my own judgement of those few contemporary novels I do read, fiction reviewers are a poor lot. I dare to think that this little novel is the best book I have written.

Tuesday, 4th April

Motored this morning to Caversham outside Reading where is the Written Archives Centre of the BBC. Has a small cosy reference library with a few seats. I had to book mine a month ago. I spent all day from 10.30, when I arrived, looking through H.N's correspondence with the BBC, mostly about his own programmes, and only a few letters about BBC policy when he was a Governor, during the war. Rather a relief, this. I made some useful notes. All his letters were courteous and affable, and only a few caustic. Hardly any were cantankerous. He made friends with all those with whom he had dealings, and clearly they became fond of him. I enjoy researching in libraries. The other researchers are people after my own heart, nearly all young and earnest. During the short breaks for coffee and tea we talk about each other's work. There is a readiness to share and help which is *gemütlich*. One young man came upon a reference to the Germans during the last war making propaganda out of a talk given by H.N. on the wireless. The first day I ate sandwiches in the car, which A. had given me. The following day I went to the canteen in the big house, which once belonged to a relation, one of the Crawshays, in the last century. Much messed about, this house still preserves its south façade with extended colonnades, its giant order of Corinthian pilasters. In the grounds I noticed a charming Doric temple falling into ruin, one vast urn on a plinth, a group of a well-known rape, and a canal and terraces. A fine site now overlooking gasworks and the railway conglomeration of Reading.

The first day I motored on to London and visited Michael Rosse in the Nuffield Home. I had been worried about him from Anne's letters. But to my surprise he looked well in bed, as people usually do unless they are actually dying. He was very cheerful and optimistic. Says he will always have to keep his feet up and can never stand for long. Has had thrombosis. Talked of Princess Margaret and Tony, the latter having been to see Michael the evening before. Michael said the tragedy was that both of them only liked second-rate people. Their friends were awful.

Friday, 7th April

This afternoon sitting at work in my library in Lansdown Crescent the sun poured through the windows, half shrouded by holland blinds. For once there was no wind; and there was not a sound of motor cars. All was deadly quiet. Then I heard approaching the feet of horses, a cavalcade, clip-clopping past my door. The delicious sound of hooves grew louder and then receded into the distance. I put myself in the situation of Beckford as he sat in this room. I experienced exactly the sound that must have been so familiar to him.

Saturday, 8th April

Today the Hunt was pursued by a gang of antis. When finally they killed somewhere in the Vale near Hillesley the crowd of hooligans attacked the Duke, pulled him off his horse, kicked him, spat on him, and pulled a huntsman off his horse, gravely injuring him. He was only saved from death by Kershaw the MP* rushing to his assistance. The Duke who is 78 and has suffered two strokes was badly shaken, but more distressed by the hostility than by his physical hurt. I met Caroline walking to the House in the evening to enquire how he was. She dined with us and said that Master refused to discuss the matter, brushed all reference to it aside. The Hunt has to be very careful not to appear provocative or revengeful. But I am sure if I had been present I should have lashed out when I saw them assaulting. Yet I don't like witnessing a kill, and I think the Hunt would have been wise to go home sooner than kill.

Sunday, 16th April

We have Fortune Grafton and Rose FitzRoy staying for the Badminton Three-Day Event, for the second time running. It is a success. Rose has developed and improved since last year. She is less *farouche*. She adores our dogs, which endears her to us. Suddenly in the drawing room she leaves the sofa, throws aside her needlework and hurls herself into the dogs' cushion and embraces them. She clears the plates from the table, and without being asked, begins to wash up. She shuts up the house, shutters and curtains, again without being prompted or asked. Fortune says she loves doing this and shuts up at Euston. The Royal Family all in church this morning. Prince Andrew read the second lesson, well but too hurriedly.

Monday, 17th April

Tony Mitchell motored me to John Fowler's Hunting Lodge, where we had for some reason unknown a meeting of the Architectural Panel. We met in the Cardigan Chamber, now quite bare. I merely went through the house in order to visit the WC. Walls bare and no

---

* Anthony Kershaw (b. 1915); MP for J.L.-M's constituency, 1955–87; Kt 1981.

furniture. A blank oval space on the hall wall where my marble relief hung. All very sad indeed.

Staying with Eardley who returned from America yesterday. He had developed an appalling cold and was feeling rotten. I rather frightened of catching it by sleeping in the same room. He maintained that he enjoyed his visit. Kept on saying how exquisite, how wonderful the picture galleries are. This, I notice, is about all the English can find to say in favour of New York. Eardley admitted that the city was dirtier than London, filthy in fact. And that the risk of mugging was brought home by advice from everyone they met, not to walk the streets alone, never to loiter in front of shop windows; listening to ghastly tales of mugging from acquaintances.

Eardley said it was a remarkable thing how four Englishmen have come to the top of the art historical tree in America – namely, John Pope-Hennessy, Andrew Porter, John Richardson and John Russell.*

Ros [Lehmann] dined with me. Very enjoyable indeed. She told me she had received within the past few weeks three requests from obscure persons to write her biography, one from a woman who has crossed from the States and announced her imminent visitation from a London hotel. She asks to see all Rosamond's letters, and demands Xeroxes. What are Xeroxes? Ros asked me. I advised her to have nothing to do with any of these people and only to give material to a person of her choice, on condition that the book is not published in her lifetime. She is again upset by the impending publication by his son Sean of Cecil Day Lewis's biography.†
Ros asked if I had received a lot of letters about my novel. I thought some time, and said, 'None.' She says it is too good, or rather too deep, for people like Jack Rathbone or Eardley to appreciate. Incidentally, Eardley to whom I gave a copy has never said one word about it. Ros very upset by a recent review of her last novel by some young female, who begins, 'This is Miss Lehmann's first novel for 21 years. She need not have bothered to resume novel writing.' I tell her she must pay no heed whatsoever to tendentious criticism by ignorant juvenile and probably plebeian reviewers; that she will be read in a hundred years' time when

---

* Art critic of New York Times since 1974 (b. 1919).
† Cecil Day-Lewis: An English Literary Life (1980).

posterity will not judge the merits of her style by such yardsticks as datedness and class, etc. As if we assess Dickens, or Richardson, or Swift on similar counts!

Friday, 21st April

My poor father's birthday. He would be 98. I often wonder if he knows how sorry I am that I was horrid to him during his life and since his death, cruelly mocking him, making him a motley to the view. People eschew remorse as a self-indulgence which does no one, least of all the offended, good. But I believe that it does the offender, i.e., the sufferer of remorse, good in reminding him of the error of his past ways and encouraging him to be more charitable about others in the future.

I went this evening to Dr King about a new lotion for my eczema, and asked how the Vicar's son Graeme was. He said he has deteriorated badly within the last two days, which I took to be very ominous.

Saturday, 22nd April

At the post office this morning Mrs Watkins said, 'Graeme Gibson died during the night. Dr King was called at midnight', and Peggy when I told her said that Gerald her husband said he weighed five stone a few days ago. Why weigh somebody in that condition?

Dr King told me that eczema was as often caused by too much washing, which is deleterious to the natural oil of the skin, as by too little.

Audrey, who lunched with us today, and walked her dogs with ours along the Verge, told me she was reading my novel, and said, 'I suppose Alvilde finished off some of the chapters for you?' 'What on earth makes you think that?' 'Well,' she said, 'I fancied you got bored, and I thought I recognized her style.' An extraordinary thought, surely.

David Somerset brought John Wilton* to see us at tea time – but got no tea. We talked of voices, how the Victorian gentry spoke in

---

* John Egerton, 7th Earl of Wilton (b. 1921).

regional accents. 'Have you never been asked by the proletariat "to grow a chin"?' 'No,' I said, 'what on earth does that mean?' 'It means that the lower classes assume that everyone who speaks with a posh voice is chinless, a chinless wonder, like the late Billy Wallace.'* John W. said hardly a soul called him 'M'lord' these days. Only grand servants in grand houses. M'lord has quite died out.

A. and I went this evening to Malmesbury Abbey to hear Fauré's Requiem. I noticed that above the nave arches there is a running billet moulding, held in the centre by the teeth of a human mask; and each billet ends in animals' masks. Now, all these masks are foxes. On the south side, high up, under the clerestory, is a parvis with soffit painted with stars. Can it be that sermons were delivered from this height? Under the arcaded clerestory is a straight mould, Gothic of course, which nearly resembles the Greek key pattern. It must be a hangover or corruption of the Classical, I suppose.

Tuesday, 25th April

Went up by train to London for the Arts Panel, which met at 11.30, a mad time, for these meetings always go on longer than they are supposed to. I was to have lunched with Fulco, but he telephoned in the morning to put me off, because he was feeling ill. As it happened, the meeting went on till quarter to four. We were given sandwiches and white wine in the board room.

I dined with that funny old Philip Magnus, at Pratt's. He looks a million; is bent, and gaunt. One quarter of his left face is blotched, as with eczema. I enjoyed the evening. Pratt's is congenial and cosy. There is a cold billiard room on the ground floor, through which one passes to the staircase, and descends to the basement. Here is a kitchen room, with large open fireplace and glowing coal fire. A large dresser with blue and white kitchen plates on shelves. Red walls. Two stuffed fish in glass cases, caught by HRH the Duke of Edinburgh at Eastwell Park in 1880 and presented to the club. Coloured engraving of Captain Toosie Somebody (odd Christian name, or is it a nickname?) standing beside his horse at the Battle of

---

* Son of Euen Wallace and his wife Bambi Lutyens; associated with HRH The Princess Margaret before her marriage.

Inkerman. Drawings of D'Orsay gentlemen and prints and 'Spy' cartoons cover the walls. Next door the dining-room, pitch dark but for silver candlesticks alight. A large circular table. Everyone talks to his neighbour. There was Peter Rawlinson,[*] newly ennobled. I don't know if he remembered me. We talked. On one side I had Philip; on the other a nice man who was a member of the House of Lords but I did not hear his name. Kenneth Rose came in after dinner. Very sensitive he is, very knowing. Philip said to him, 'The first thing I read on Sunday mornings is your funny little paragraph in the *Telegraph*.' 'Funny little?' echoed Kenneth. He laughed it off. But Philip said later, 'I suppose I made a gaffe.' 'I suppose you did,' I answered. If I lived in London, and if I were a bachelor, I would like to be a member of Pratt's. Actually, Tom Mitford[†] proposed me during the war, but when he was killed I withdrew my candidature.

Wednesday, 26th April

After working in the London Library in the morning, went to Shaldon Mansions in Charing Cross Road where Robin Maugham[‡] has a sleazy flat overlooking the noisy bus-filled street – or rather his boy-friend, a tall American, has. Rang the bell and was greeted by tall boy-friend, and a smaller and younger boy, a sculptor, who immediately departed, giving Robin a smacking kiss as he went. I hadn't seen Robin for many years. He is rather handsomer than I remember; has lost that footman-y appearance, and has acquired some distinction. Must be about sixty. Looks delicate, moves delicately, and is I think very delicate. Has just had a minor exploratory operation and must undergo a major one, he tells me. He is not very articulate, and I being deaf found it hard to hear what he said. His voice trails off. He is economical with his words. He has very kindly lent me a large package of letters written to him by Harold, who was certainly very devoted to him. He said Harold was in love with him and his father knew it, and strongly disapproved. Told me also that his uncle Willy

---

[*] Barrister and writer; cr. Life Peer 1978.
[†] Hon. Thomas Mitford (1909–44); brother of the Mitford sisters and only son of 2nd Baron Redesdale.
[‡] Robert Maugham, 2nd Viscount (1916–81); novelist (as Robin Maugham) and nephew of W. Somerset Maugham.

was likewise in love with him, and this was the cause of Willy's ambivalent attitude towards him. Robin's book* has just come out, and he has given several broadcasts and I suppose it will sell like hot cakes. Stupidly I went and bought it from Heywood Hill's and read it quickly. It is very second-rate. He is a nice man, generous and friendly, and natural, but, as Harold remarked, a vulgar man with no literary style or sense. He lunched with me in Jermyn Street and we talked about Harold. I suppose I derive some useful thoughts about H.N. from these meetings with his friends, but I wonder how many. I am seldom told anything startling which I didn't know already. Robin said that he and Harold attended Richard Rumbold's† funeral together. Robin was astonished and amazed that Harold played noughts and crosses on the back of the service sheet, and kept passing it to Robin. The mourners in the church witnessed this apparent callous behaviour and seemed shocked. Robin was embarrassed. We agreed it signified H.N's dislike of church and clergy, for we know he was deeply upset by Richard's death.

Thursday, 27th April

David Somerset told me that Master, when engaging servants today, asks them what their religion and their politics are. If they are foolish enough to disclose that they vote Labour they are of course not engaged. If they admit to being Roman Catholics, this is worse. I said that I came across a letter written to my grandmother by some chatelaine presenting her compliments in the third person and giving a good character to Alice Spinks, but adding that she only left her service because she had become obliged to wear spectacles, which deprived her of the opportunity of getting a senior place in a respectable household. I said Master's attitude was on a par with this woman's of pre-1914.

Wednesday, 3rd May

A. and I motored to London in pouring rain – this the second day of rain without intermission – for Mickey Renshaw's Memorial Service at the Guards' Chapel; not a totally bad building but the material

---

* Conversations with Willie: Recollections of W. Somerset Maugham.
† Journalist and writer; committed suicide 1961.

horribly artificial and lifeless. That is the main difference between old buildings and the contemporary made of pre-fabricated stone and brick – that the old live whereas the new are born dead. The service was well chosen, beautiful psalms, hymns and Bach anthem. No address. Indeed, how could one eulogize poor Mickey. We took Philip Dimmick and Mrs Ratcliffe, M's old housekeeper, to lunch at Alfredo's restaurant. They both told us how impersonal Mickey was, and for this reason he would have approved this impersonal service – no warmth. There was little warmth in him. Philip, who was his lover presumably, said Mickey shunned all emotional expression. He never once asked Philip whether his parents were alive or where his home was. Mrs Ratcliffe, who had worked for him for thirty years, said the same. Mickey never once asked if she had any relations. He was strictly fair, and generous, but never cosy. Strange man.

I come home alone and watch a television film about the Parthenon. What horrifies me is that the Parthenon is not the only world-famous monument disintegrating from industrial pollution: apparently also the cathedrals of York, Lincoln, Chartres, Rheims, as well as Venice. Within the last thirty years more damage has been caused the Parthenon than between 400 BC and AD 1948. Also the millions of feet, literally one million pairs last year, are wearing the rock of which the Acropolis is made away to dust.

I forget to mention that Mickey left his flat and many of his pictures and priceless belongings, and some money, to Philip. Philip said that during the service he felt the inquisitive and hostile looks of Mickey's smart friends piercing the back of his head as he sat or knelt pious in his pew, discreetly isolated from but in front of the family mourners. None of the family mourned him as Philip did.

Friday, 5th May

I have at last finished reading Harold's unpublished diaries, and today I transcribed some of the letters from him to Robin Maugham which Robin lent me. I must now read again and take careful notes from Nigel's *Portrait of a Marriage* and Philippe [Jullian]'s book on Violet Trefusis; and visit the Foreign Office library, and Constable's [the publishers], when I should be through my researches. My next step, which I shall take next week, is to get my own voluminous notes in some order, and work out a detailed synopsis of the book. Then, who knows whether I can, after all, write it.

Monday, 8th May

Jack and Frankie Donaldson* come to stay for the weekend. Opposed as I am to Jack's political views, I find it impossible not to succumb to his – not charm, for I do not think that quality, which is there, predominates, but to his simplicity, sheer goodness and enjoyment of being what he is, Minister for the Arts in a Labour Government. He is modest about his qualifications, admitting that apart from music he knows little about art and literature. His life is full and his responsibilities are not overwhelming. He has few ambitions, and knows that at his age – seventy – there is no promotion in store. Therefore, he says, he is able to be outspoken. He is considered by his colleagues reliable, honest and wise. None of them is jealous of him. Nobody covets his job, which is a lowly one the hierarchy of ministries. He is a disarming man. One can speak quite candidly, disagree quite vehemently without causing offence. We went for a walk on Saturday afternoon, and he expanded in telling me of the joys of office, and the fun of being in the centre of things. Frankie on the other hand has aged. She is extremely verbose. Not boring, for she is so clever, but she is relentless, like a terrier with a bone. She gnaws, she plays with, she consumes her subject. Won't let go. Won't allow one to get a word in edgeways.

On Sunday morning I went to Corsham to attend the unveiling (by John Methuen) of two memorial tablets in the Methuen chapel of the church to Paul and his brother Lawrence. Nice, simple and good lettering. Merely their names and dates of birth and death, and below, in Paul's case, the one word Artist; in Lawrence's, Architect. The ceremony was over within half an hour. I was wrongly dressed, in my pale brown suit and a pink shirt and bow tie. Everyone else was clad in pinstripe suits, or black, with black ties. Yet this was not a memorial service, not an occasion for mourning. I did the wrong thing. That was clear. I got home well in time for our luncheon party – Coote Lygon, Ann Fleming and Ian Lowe,† a handsome but stiff, slightly precious youth. Before luncheon got into a friendly argument with Jack about the Government not putting up all the money required to save the Warwick Castle Canalettos. I said the Government ought not to

---

* John G. S. Donaldson (b. 1907); cr. Life Peer 1967; m. 1935 Frances Lonsdale (b. 1907), writer and biographer.

† Museum curator; successor to Ian McCallum at the American Museum, Claverton, Bath.

regard pictures and historic houses as bullion, commodities to be taxed; any more than they ought to regard land of natural beauty, the Peak District, say, as such, to be developed and spoilt in order to yield revenue for the Exchequer. Of course he could not agree, and claimed that he had done much for the arts in acquiring a larger grant from the Treasury. This is true, and I said I was grateful to him, but he had not answered my argument.

Tuesday, 9th May

Walking with the dogs down the Centre Walk I heard my first cuckoo this evening. A poor cuckoo. He gave two half-hearted notes, but enough to stir within me that nostalgia for sad and far-off things that distresses me deeply. I think it is the cuckoo which puts the lid on my spring misery. Nevertheless, thank God the cuckoos still return to this benighted country.

Forgot to say that Jack also totally rebutted my argument that the Italian terrorists should have been told that if they killed Moro, then all those terrorists now on trial in Milan, if found guilty of murder, would be shot at once.*

Thursday, 11th May

Having written to Eardley that I was in a depth of depression, he telephoned Wednesday evening suggesting that we go for a long walk next day, which is today. We agreed to meet at Hungerford at ten. To my surprise it took me less than one hour down the motorway. I took both dogs. They were the cause of angst. Whenever let off the lead they bolted. We walked down the canal (Kennet) to Pewsey, so inevitably there was barbed wire along the tow-path, and the dogs kept escaping into the fields and woods beyond. A lovely day, no bright sun as during the three previous days, but a hazy sun through mist. Cool wind, and perfect for walking. A. gave us a lovely picnic which E., who prefers for some extraordinary reason to carry a knapsack, chose to put inside it. Some long stretches of canal beautiful,

---

* In mid March Red Brigade terrorists had kidnapped the former Italian Prime Minister, Aldo Moro; he was found dead in Rome on 9 May after the government's refusal to make concessions to the terrorists; in 1983, thirty-two of them were jailed for his kidnap and murder.

with tall trees and steep banks. Banks covered with primroses, and a
few as yet unblown bluebells. Watched snipe dipping and darting over
the water. Some lengths of the canal recently restored, locks mended,
which is nice to see. Unfortunately the mud and stones and bricks
dredged from the bottom have been chucked on the banks, thus rendered ugly and untidy. At Great Bedwyn railway halt we looked at a
timetable which disclosed that from Pewsey station a 5.05 p.m. train
called at Hungerford, where we had left our cars. We hurried to get
there in time. Waited anxiously on the platform. At last a train
approached, but did not stop and roared past us. E. waved for it to stop
with his stick. The driver hooted madly as though infuriated by our
impertinence. Then we realized there was no stopping train after all.
We walked into the village. The only garage had no taxi. We were able
to catch a bus to Marlborough, which cost us 120 pence, the dogs
being charged the same as ourselves. At Marlborough changed buses
to Ramsbury. At Ramsbury changed for Hungerford. Had a drink of
cider in the Bear and separated. I arrived home at 7.45, tired but
happy.

On our walk we passed one long tunnel with entry of brick on the
curve. A large stone tablet, also on the curve, with beautiful lettering,
recorded that through the consent and with the enterprise of Lord
Ailesbury and his son Lord Bruce, Rennie made this waterway in
1810. E. very angry that the beautiful tablet, so carefully carved, so
carefully cut so as to be on the curve of the tunnel entrance, should
be allowed to disintegrate. He reminded me that some thirty years ago
he and I had admired it. In another thirty years' time, he said, we
would no longer be able to read the inscription at all. We sighed and
said no more. In thirty years he would be 105, I 100.

The blackthorn out in a haze of glory along the canal. But E.
remarked that the reflection was not pretty, for the stagnant water dis-
coloured the blossom, and the intervening spaces, which in reality are
black, were in the reflection muddy brown.

Wednesday, 17th May

Although during my walk with Eardley I heard several cuckoos, here
I haven't heard another. Perhaps it is too far north for them, Berkshire
being more south and less high up than Badminton.

My deep-seated depression remains – without any cause that I can
discern. Had a brief talk on the telephone with J.K.-B. who is just off

to Scotland for a fortnight with clever young John Martin Robinson*
who will be a great help over the book he is doing. They are to make
their headquarters at Susan Stirling's in Perthshire.

Thursday, 18th May

I have sent one lock of Dickens's hair to darling Ros who is a great
Dickens fan; and has been exhorting me to read Johnson's book,†
which I have bought and am enjoying. She even remembers Miss
Georgina Hogarth at her father's house.‡ It is fitting therefore that she
should have this lock with the card authenticating it in Georgina's
handwriting. Ros's great-uncle did the portrait of Dickens which is
illustrated in Johnson's biography.

I am going through my card index to square it up with the notebooks, i.e., checking that there are no references in it that I cannot
find in the notebooks, and vice versa. Then I have to go through the
chronological notes, deciding how to divide the book into parts and
chapters, and what to select from the notes, and what reject. That
must be my process.

Friday, 19th May

Is the cause of my depression disbelief in a future for this material
Earth, a disbelief unconceived by previous pre-nuclear generations,
for they had no reason – with the concomitant doubts of another
world after death?

A. and I went to a ghastly party, for which we paid £5 each, at the
House to hear Mr Heath speak. This he did very well for twenty
minutes at most, after we had spent one hour (and should have spent
two, had we arrived when invited) fighting for a glass of champagne
(which I dislike) and sandwiches. Heath told us succinctly why the
Labour Party had failed us, and why we must vote Tory. Simple
reason: that Callaghan§ cannot be trusted as a moderate man, since he

---

* Architectural historian; as an undergraduate he had called on J.L.-M. at Alderley in
1973; in 1978 he was working on the London Survey.
† Edgar Johnson, *Charles Dickens: His Tragedy and Triumph.*
‡ Charles Dickens's sister-in-law, who remained in his household after C.D. broke with
his wife Catherine, Georgina's sister.
§ Rt Hon. James Callaghan (b. 1912), Labour MP since 1945, was Prime Minister
1976–9; cr. Life Peer in 1987.

gives way on all critical occasions to the extreme Left. Mr Heath standing there on a small platform in the large green drawing-room seemed very out place. He looked like a figure cut from a turnip, as it were for All Hallows' E'en, quite square and pointed. His profile, nose and mouth, sharp gashes. Yet I admire the way he marshals his sentences, and he speaks with the authority of an elder statesman. Our local MP v. second-rate, with an ugly voice and a cataract of clichés.

Monday, 22nd May

I motored on Saturday to Oxford for Roy Harrod's Memorial Service in the Cathedral. Longish and a good service, well chosen hymns and psalms; anthem by Auden to music by Walton, very impressive I found. Lesson read by Henry Harrod, a splendid dark fellow. Cathedral full of dons in flapping gowns, like crows, and old friends, all in black. Billa, however, marched in wearing snow-white hat and pale fawn dress, not *en deuil* a bit, but brave and defiant. I thought the dons seemed as eccentric as they ever were in my day. Tousled hair, draped in hearing-aids, carrying sticks, mouths open, crocks for the most part, or if young, perky. I slipped away after the service, returning home in time to welcome John Betj. and Feeble. We had Richard Robinson and his friend, a funny little boy paralysed with shyness till he had something to drink, like a very young, fair Philippe Jullian, but clever as a monkey. Bettery [*recte* Bettley] by name.

They are going on a tour of Victorian country houses in July and wanted to pick our brains. John delighted by this, and by them of course, and very sweet to them. He is more crippled than ever; has difficulty in getting from the drawing-room to the kitchen, and has to be cajoled, and pulled by Elizabeth who is encouraging, and patient. He has to take dozens of different pills which he forgets. She reminds him; she in fact puts him to bed, and gets him up in the morning. He told me that without her he would die. Yet on Sunday morning he insisted on coming to church, not the early service, but Matins at 11.15 and Communion after. I feared great difficulties, but once out of the car he walked bravely from the gate. On his feet, and on the flat, and rested after a good night, he is better. Is stricken with Parkinson's, kept very under control by the drugs. As we approached the church door we were overtaken by a bevy of girl guides from their camp at Bath Lodge. 'Oh dear, they will be disturbing!' he said. 'It would of course be worse if they were boy scouts.' Says he very

much enjoyed *Round the Clock.* Hurrah! Said it was haunting, and
original.

Tuesday, 23rd May

This evening A. and I walked in Swangrove Wood. The bluebells at
their zenith. We had neither of us seen anything to equal or surpass
them. Through the slender trees the ground was deep blue like
Mediterranean seas. Against the fresh green the spectacle was extraordinary. Such vivid colours never to be seen on the Mediterranean.
Earlier in the month there were other wild flowers, garlic, primrose,
windflower, among the bluebells which make a delicious assortment.
But today these were over, and the bluebells reigned supreme. This
wood with its straight rides is peculiarly French. I don't believe I have
ever seen such beauty in any country of the world; the sun filtering
through the trees, speckling the astonishing blue groundswell.

Thank God I can still walk and can still see.

J.B. disclosed that ever since he can remember he has read poetry,
preferring it to prose, finding it easier to write than prose. 'It comes
easier to me,' he said.

Wednesday, 24th May

I went to London by an early train. Spent the afternoon in Constable
the publisher's office looking through some reviews of Harold's books
which I had not hitherto seen. It is not easy to read through quantities of reviews and get the pith out of them. Nearly all reviews are the
airing of the reviewer's knowledge of the subject, and little about the
writer. Besides, nearly all reviews of Harold's books are favourable, so
that I seldom come upon useful and pertinent criticism or objective
comments on his writing.

Went to tea in Ovington Street with Lady Ursula Horne, a cousin
of Harold's and first cousin of Ava.* She told me many fascinating
things about the Blackwood family. Aunt Lal disliked Harold as a small
boy, finding him spoilt; and having later discovered about his Berlin
life took against him in a big way. She said that Gwen† was a cruel

---

* Basil, 4th Marquess of Dufferin and Ava, killed on active service in Burma, 1945; an
exact contemporary of J.L.-M. at prep. school, Eton and Oxford.
† H.N's sister.

woman to her mother; had a hard streak. Ava was not liked by the family; was too arrogant and impatient with any but highbrows. He only loved his father who did not reciprocate his affection. Lady Ursula is a charmer. Aged eighty, she lives alone in a cosy early Victorian terrace house without servants, her couple of forty years' standing having died, or departed. As she said, gaily and without complaint, 'It is so odd being left servantless when one is aged and crippled with arthritis, after having had many servants and been brought up at Clandeboye, when hale and hearty.'

Stayed the night with Eardley. Richard Shone joined us and I took them both to dinner in Soho at an Italian bistro. A modest but good dinner with two carafes of wine cost me £21. Richard, in the course of telling me that he and John K.-B. both have articles in this month's *Burlington* mag., announced that Ben Nicolson died last Monday. While changing trains in Leicester Square tube station he fell down. By the time he was taken to the hospital he was dead. It took two whole days to identify who he was. The office had told the police he was missing. Luisa who returned from Italy by air on Tuesday expected to be met by Ben at Heathrow. The police had to break into his flat, thinking he might be there. I received a letter from Nigel on my return from London, telling me of his death. The brothers were devoted. Poor Ben. Such a good obituary in *The Times* by someone who knew and loved him well. Although I was never a close intimate of Ben, and disapproved of some sides of him, I have been upset by his death, and thought a lot about him. Probably because I have read so much about him in Harold and Vita's correspondence over the past year. They loved and cared and worried deeply about him. What I disliked in him was his near-Communist inclinations, his flouting of the ordinary social graces – for he was dirty, and ill- rather than bad-mannered. He despised all Vita stood for, and was never nice to her, was an inverted snob, anti-Establishment. But he was a true eccentric, honest as the day, a considerable scholar, and both innocent child and wily expert. I recall the delicious evening we spent some two years ago dining with the Jolliffes in the height of that hot summer, eating out of doors and drinking until eleven under the stars, talking of eternal things and Ben being at his sweetest, most gentle and entertaining. Then he stayed with us last year, talked a lot about his father, and could not walk to the post office, fifty yards away, for the pain in his legs. Poor Ben! I shall miss him at Brooks's – he will become just one more ghost – where he had been a member for over forty years, and where I would often see him slope into the coffee-room, later than others, perhaps at 1.45 or even two, clutching a book or a paper, bending forward with the weight of his own thoughts, dishevelled, his jacket collar sprinkled with scurf, his mouth half open, and not wanting to be talked to or disturbed.

Monday, 29th May

John Grigg tells me that Francis Haskell* wrote Ben's obituary. It was the action of a friend. I went to Joanie Altrincham's house in the evening, A. being obliged to attend at the House where a party for the Disabled was held. Joanie took me aside to the end of a sofa and proceeded to complain as usual; how much work fell upon her, how she had only one woman living under her roof, how she had no one in the garden (indeed, the trouble of everyone); how having nice John and Patsy [her son and daughter-in-law] to stay, not to mention the Reggie Winns† (sitting opposite), was too much for her. She insinuated by a toss of the head that Reggie Winn was gaga, a fact I already knew and was not going to acknowledge I knew. How boring she is, I thought, as I watched through the open French window the insects flying, like snowflakes there were so many, their little bodies and diaphanous wings caught in the setting sun. I was so delighted by the multitude of them that my heart rejoiced, and I could not listen to Joanie, who left me. Her place was taken by John, and we had an intelligent conversation about Lloyd George and Harold. He is a clever man. He argued against my support of Mrs Thatcher and my pleasure that she was strong right of centre. 'It won't do,' he said. 'But she will slide to the centre when she gets in, as they all do; and all will, so long as they are responsible leaders.'

Talking of gardeners, Diana Westmorland told me this morning (it is Bank Holiday) that the last years of her life have been ruined by the disagreeableness of her two gardeners, their beastliness to her, their laziness, their deceit, and their cheating.

---

* Professor of Art History, Oxford University, and Fellow of Trinity College, Oxford from 1967.
† Hon. Reginald Winn and his wife Alice Perkins, sister of Nancy Lancaster.

Tuesday, 30th May

I went to London to hear a symphony of Lennox Berkeley's. On return I dined with Alex Moulton. After dinner we sat on the steps before the porch on the garden terrace, just where we sat more than thirty-five years ago, discussing the future of this house.* He has quite decided to leave it by will to the National Trust, with the proviso that his great-nephew may live in it if he so wishes. Alex seems in no doubt that the Trust will accept it. When we first discussed the matter I had no doubts at all. Now I wonder. I told him to write to Bobby Gore at the Trust, and keep me out of all negotiations. I will support acceptance at the meetings when it comes up.

Driving home with the windows of the motor open there came in great wafts of delicious smells of mown hay, of may, which is in full bloom, and Queen Anne's lace which lines every verge. In my little garden in Bath the laburnum tree is dripping streamers of gold, the wisteria is out; and the solanum and the ceanothus ('Cascade'). Everything has blossomed at the same moment after the severe and gloomy winter.

Wednesday, 31st May

I motored straight to Kew to the modern Public Records Office. Brand new and worked by gadgets. Looking up Foreign Office papers is more complicated than words can express. The FO numerals, dashes and brackets have to be translated from the card index into the PRO code. Then you have to ask for the files by computer, which requires the mind of a higher mathematician if you are not to make mistakes. You are given a bleeper on arrival, and when your files are ready the bleeper squeaks and shows a little light, and you fetch the files from the counter. Absolutely boiling hot out of doors, but within cold as ice owing to the air-conditioning. I had to put on an extra jersey. By the end of the day I felt ill and by the time I reached John's house I was sneezing, streaming, with headache, nose irritation, throat infection and chest congestion.

---

* The Hall, Bradford-on-Avon.

Thursday, 1st June

Went to *Tristan und Isolde* at Covent Garden. I sadly miss the smell of fruit, which even pervaded the auditorium in the old days and gave a nostalgic ethos, if that is the right word, to this heavenly opera house. Jon Vickers an excellent Tristan, and Miss Knie as Isolde controlled, full but a bit brassy. Act 2 perfect, but long periods of tedium in Act 1 and Act 3. Listening to Wagner is like having a frustrated dream. A. and I motored home after, starting at 11.15 and reaching Bad. at 1 o'clock.

Sunday, 4th June

Strange clergyman visiting this morning, our Vicar being prostrated with sciatica in bed. For sermon he merely gave five reasons why we should go to church: 1, to worship God; 2, to give thanks for benefits received; 3, to learn something from the Gospel of the day; 4, to pray for others; and 5, to pray for our own improvement.

Leaving the church, Mrs Rich, the nice gardener's wife from the House, remarked on these five points. She was hurrying home to note them down. 'Excellent,' she said, and, 'You know, Mr Lees-Milne, I simply can't understand why the young don't come to church,' and she told me that her son, in spite of being in a racing stables where she said his companions were more pagan than in most other professions, never missed a Sunday. A nice young man, too, who sings in the choir here when he is at home, and attends Communion on occasion. I told her she must have been an exemplary mother. I can well believe she is, if not too good to be true.

Tuesday, 6th June

Hugh Montgomery-Massingberd comes for a midday snack at Lansdown Crescent today. A. provided the said snack. She enchanted with this young man's exquisite manners, which seem not to belong to this age. I let him look through my Red Books, with reluctance, because I shy at strangers seeing the idiocies, the embarrassing comments I have jotted down all these years about country houses. But if this new Committee on which I have agreed to sit to guide the compiler of the Country House Index wants my notes, I suppose I ought not to withhold them.

Monday, 12th June

Jack Rathbone lunched with me at Brooks's. I was awful in indulging my depression. I apologized and Jack sweetly said friends were there to be complained unto. But it occurs that I was selfish, in that he is the most neurotic man I know, who lives on pills to prevent break-downs, and I ought not to have appeared so gloomy. At 6.30 I called on Duncan Sandys* in his nice Georgian house in Vincent Square. We talked of old times with George Lloyd.† He told me how as a very young man he was looking for a leader and thought he found one in G.L. But it didn't come to anything, though he always admired and liked him. Recounted the story, which I vaguely remember hearing, of his flight in the early Thirties from Spezia, where he had been staying with the Lloyds, back to England in a Tiger Moth. Warned at Genoa not to fly across the Alps, he disregarded the warning and plunged into mountains and storms. Made for a patch of blue, which disappeared. After being tossed around he looked out and saw the patch of blue below him. Discovered that his instruments had broken, and he was flying upside-down. Eventually by flying low saw a patch of green, and crash-landed. It happened to be the only flat bit of Switzerland, and an airfield.

I watched this man who used to alarm me so, with his fiery red hair, his show of intense virility and heroism, his unscrupulous, mocking, rather diabolic manner. I could only see a broad smile, a twinkle in blue eyes, a kindliness, which were never there in old, or rather young, days. What hell the young can be to one another, to be sure. He was extremely friendly on this occasion and said we must meet more often. In fact received me as though I had been one of his oldest, closest friends, which I never was. But that comes with age, and the death of so many others who meant so much to us. Talking of politics, I told him that I was in favour of capital punishment but I wished the Tories would not refer to Hanging, a revolting way of putting to death, and one which upset the stoutest hearts. I said they ought to urge another means of killing, the prick in the arm. He agreed. He replied, 'I am in favour of capital punishment, but not of hanging.' Then talked about his efforts in the conservation line, his achieve-

---

* Conservative politician (1908–87); m. 1935–60 to Diana, dau. of Winston Churchill; cr. Life Peer (Baron Duncan-Sandys) 1974.
† 1st Baron Lloyd of Dolobran, statesman and proconsul; J.L.-M's first employer.

ments in founding the Civic Trust, probably the best achievement of
his life. He is now President of Europa Nostra, made to take it on by
Robin Fedden. Then talked about Harold Nicolson in the House of
Commons. He did not know H.N. at all well, but liked him as a man
very much. He told me that his maiden speech was an outstanding
success, so that when it was known that H.N. was to speak a second
time, the Chamber filled. The second speech was too like the first.
Thereafter Members did not trouble to listen to him again. He said
the way reputations are made, and held, in the House is quite fortu-
itous, almost inexplicable.

J.K.-B. dined. I told him I had met the previous Sunday Mrs
Molesworth,* Moley's widow, and that she was being tremendously
brave, and could talk of nothing but Moley, how clever, how modest,
how unambitious, how loving he was. John said he often saw them
together, at Langley in their beautiful Orangery – *orangerie*, she, an
affected lady, calls it – and they used to squabble something fearful. It
was quite embarrassing to witness. I suppose they had their ways with
one another, and his rudeness didn't mean to her what it meant to
others. Rather like the treatment of Elizabeth Chatwin by Bruce.

Wednesday, 14th June

Spent all yesterday afternoon and today at Colindale, looking through
Observer reviews by H.N. The studious quiet of the researchers is made
hideous by the occasional sounds of tearing. For they provide book
stands, and the huge folio volumes of the *Observer*, for instance, are
deposited on the stand. In the first place, from the low seat it is
awkward for me, with my bifocals, to focus the reading matter at the
top of each page. Secondly, the weight of the pages and the poor
quality of the wartime paper causes them to tear. I pointed this out
politely to the custodian at the desk; and suggested it might be wiser
to make researchers have the folios laid flat on the table top. 'We have
considered this point,' he said in a rather ungracious manner. I noticed
however that when the attendant brought me my next trolleyful of
folios he told me to sit at a flat table, without stand, and do what I had
suggested.

---

* Hender Delves Molesworth (1907–78); m. 1934 Evelyn Galloway; joined staff of V. &
A. 1931; Keeper of Sculpture, 1946; Keeper of Woodwork, 1954; retd 1966.

Went last night to see poor Keith Miller Jones.* He is bed-ridden, riddled with cancer, and yet cannot die. Betty ushered me into his bedroom, asking me not to stay with him for more than twenty minutes. His head seemed larger than I remembered it; his chest fallen in. Head falling on to the chest, and raised wearily to greet me, and each time he spoke. Meanwhile sipping at some lime juice from a glass. Mentally compos. Did not smile. No wonder. Said how much he liked the view from his bedroom window of Onslow Square garden and trees, yet he cannot see them from his bed. Cannot stand on his feet; never gets out of bed. Has a day and a night nurse, and Betty never leaves him. He told me how lucky he was in that he could still read, but I doubt how much he takes in. I asked if the wireless, Radio 3, was a pleasure to him. Said he did not listen to it. I notice that the very ill find no comfort in the wireless, music being I suppose a distraction rather than a delight. Yet Keith is very musical. Talked to Betty in the drawing-room afterwards. She reads all day in snatches. Said what hell old age was. Asked herself, were there any compensations? Answered herself that at least one no longer pined for love and affairs of the heart, or suffered from lack of reciprocation – a sad admission. She was not self-pitying. Embraced me warmly on both cheeks and thanked me. Keith called out as I left, 'Come again!' What does he say? I asked Betty. He says, 'Come again.' Walking down the pavement hastily to catch the tube for Covent Garden I felt a brute of selfishness, the first time I have bothered to see Keith, and there I was, able to walk fast and go to the Opera. Opera was *Falstaff.* I don't know why they say it is the greatest of operas. A. was much moved. I was not, merely irritated by the horseplay, and disgusted by the theme, the bullying and making a fool of a poor old man. I honestly prefer listening to this opera on the wireless, and not looking at the nonsense and pranks and jokes on stage.

Saturday, 17th June

Everything this year is out at the same time – now the elder flower in fat, cream saucers, and the eglantine, better than I remember it. Lovely, delicate pink and white dog rose, lovelier than any cultivated rose. The first fine careless rapture of spring went a fortnight ago. The grasses are long and dry and induce sneezing. The buttercups are

---

* Georgian Group member (b. 1899); husband of the writer Betty Askwith.

bedraggled. Our garden is however fresh and watered and full of colour, the achievement of A's tender fingers.

We lunched today with dear Billy [Henderson] and Frank [Tait] at Tisbury. Delicious food always. Only Cecil Beaton there. He greatly improved healthwise; and can talk consecutively now, and make jokes. Accused Harold of some beastly habit – a deliberate fabrication. I must have noticed it, were it so. I find people who were not Harold's friends do say very disobliging things about him. Cecil also said that physically he found H.N. repulsive. Well, every man his taste.

Frank Tait told a story about Nancy Mitford which typifies her peculiar sense of humour, or fitness. He was a very shy young man of 22, fresh from Australia, of middle-class upbringing, and learning to be a doctor, which he now is. He was sitting next to Nancy at a smart, cosmopolitan luncheon party in Venice. He took a large mouthful of lobster which he knew at once was bad. So, tucking the lobster into one cheek, he turned to Nancy and asked, 'What am I to do? I know what is in my mouth is bad.' Nancy's immediate reply was not 'Spit it out!' but 'Swallow it, if it kills you.'

Tuesday, 20th June

Eliot Hodgkin and his wife, who are staying in Bath for a week, came to tea with us at Lansdown Crescent. Charming couple. He has a wry manner of speaking, allied to great courtesy. Thus he contradicts one flatly without causing the least offence. Has no opinion of Paul Methuen's pictures. Has a humility about his own work. She is a Swissesse; intelligent. When they left I let fall that I had not met her before. She said Yes, we had, at Eardley's, not so long ago. Yet took no offence. This is with most women the unforgivable thing for a man to say.

Thursday, 22nd June

Began the actual writing of chapter 1 of Harold. I have divided Part 1 (will it be volume 1?) of the book into fourteen chapters. Already chapter 1 is going to be far too long.

Friday, 23rd June

We had a dreadful drive to Sissinghurst. Started at eight, and left the motorway at Slough. Thenceforward crawling at ten miles an hour to

Sevenoaks, in a queue of lorries and caravans. Lunched with Nigel. Juliet and Adam* there. First proper meeting with Adam, a sweet boy, very young, immature looking and intelligent. Nervous. Delivered the remainder of the files and boxes Nigel lent me. Is very distressed about Ben. Juliet told me that Ben had announced a year or so ago that his sudden death must be expected. Nigel thereupon left the room, and Juliet found him in his bedroom in tears. Of course Nigel has a soft side. Relations with his children about perfect.

We drove on to Firle for the weekend, arriving at six. The Beits staying. A happy weekend party. I got through to Rainald [Gage]. One has to persevere, and tease. He is nigh impossible to hear and half talks to himself, half to you. He took me to Charleston one evening because he wished me to see for myself the condition of the house. I had already seen it. Took no notice of my telling him I was there last year when Duncan was still alive. I was slightly embarrassed, for we drove up to the house and Angelica Garnett† arrived in her car behind us. Rainald merely asked if we might look inside. This shy, on-her-guard woman had to say yes. She brought us a delicious bottle of white wine, as though such a gesture was the *droit de seigneurie* expected of her. I must say that without Duncan and his court, and his pictures which lent colour to the background muddle, this house looks infinitely drear, dirty and dilapidated. Rooms adrift with old saucepans with unspeakable things sticking to their bottoms; empty toothpaste tubes on chairs, dust, dirt, peeling wallpapers, and the structure apparently needing £40,000 spending on it. Rainald to his credit does not wish to be accused of destroying a Bloomsbury shrine, yet has to do something by way of repairs. I suggested his selling the house outright to Angelica G. who says she wants to go on living there, where she was born in 1918. But R. says the house is in the middle of his estate, is the core of a farm, and understandably does not want to part with it to someone who might die or re-sell to a rich tycoon who would probably spoil it altogether. He left us to go and look at his cows; and we talked. I found her very sympathetic to talk to, and we got on. When we left she shook me with both hands, always a sign of cordiality, and asked me to call again at any time.

Then A. and I called on the Donaldsons at their house, newly built by them. Perfectly ghastly. A bungalow, like a public lavatory. In brick,

---

* Nigel Nicolson's son, b. 1957.
† Daughter of Duncan Grant and Vanessa Bell; m. David Garnett.

which is acceptable, but a sort of fascia board along the roof-line, of wood, already warping. Inside likewise terrible. One large room with wall of glass from ceiling to floor. No appeal whatever. No covetable furniture. Nothing. Already damp percolating from ceilings. The shoddiness of cement and new workmanship.

Sunday morning church. The Gages, Beits and L.-Ms sitting in a row in one pew. Few others in the church. Rainald reads both lessons, almost inaudibly. Parson likewise sermonizes inaudibly. Prayer books lovely red morocco, with prayers for Queen Charlotte and George, Prince of Wales. Charlotte crossed out of my book, and Adelaide substituted. We solemnly walk back to the house. Very feudal and old-fashioned.

Glyndebourne Sunday evening for *Magic Flute*, to Hockney production. Every one raving about Hockney but to be truthful it is poor stuff, coarse and child-like. Sort of Noah's Ark stuff, and shoddy. Very good performance, however. I met Lord Ferrers, whom I had once met twenty-five years or more ago. He thanked me warmly for being kind to his old father over the conveyance of Staunton Harold chapel.[*] Said his father always spoke nicely of me, and was grateful. A dear man, I remember, simple unlike the son, and very delicate. Son said that worry about the big house's future killed him.

Monday, 26th June

Beits drove me up to London Sunday night. I stayed in A's cosy little room at the Berkeleys' house; and this morning trained to Bath in order to meet Baba Metcalfe and the Ravensdales, accompany them to the Costume Museum and help choose two of Lady Curzon's dresses for an exhibition in Washington next year. My presence was quite unnecessary for Baba simply got her way by quietly bulldozing the terrified Mrs Mines who looks after the dresses. I was amused by Baba's deliberate action, her careful, loud diction, her proud, self-assured manner. Mrs Mines was defeated, and enchanted. Baba kisses me now, which is a sign of acceptance. I used to be terrified of her. I find her friendly. She is still handsome, and very energetic.

---

[*] 13th Earl Ferrers, PC, succeeded his 'old father', 12th Earl, in 1954. The church at Staunton Harold, near Ashby-de-la-Zouch, Leicestershire, is one of the very few built during Cromwell's Commonwealth.

Thursday, 29th June

Wonderful programmes on Radio 3. Last night I turned it on at random; there was an excellent reading of Shakespeare's *Venus and Adonis*, so well spoken by a man and a woman that I listened entranced, without attention wandering. Tonight a fascinating talk about volcanoes and the gases within the earth. Evidently it is not an old wives' tale that before an earthquake dogs and birds behave oddly, because in fact dogs smell the gases about to be released, and birds are affected by the preliminary tremors, neither of which are sensed by man.

Upset this afternoon by Denys Sutton telephoning to complain of my dear Nick. He *will* call him Robinson, which I find offensive. Apparently he comes in to the office late, at 10.30. Well, I said, you must tell him to come in at whatever time your office opens. But, I added, I thought he worked after hours and took proofs home to read over the weekends. Followed by a long dissertation by Denys about the young today from Nick's sort of background having no conception that the old life of hunting and shooting was as archaic as the dodo.

Friday, 30th June

Walk with the dogs this evening, up Centre Walk; the trouble is they will bolt, try as we may to stop them. Beating is quite useless. They always return, but I suffer agonies lest they get run over crossing a road after a hare, or get into trouble from Master and the keepers for chasing pheasant chicks, fox cubs, or sheep.

Noticed on the short return strip of road to the village that the hedgerows are full of flowers and blossoms. There was creamy meadowsweet, with its sugary smell; elder flower with its sour-sweet smell; a large mauve umbellifer with thick spiky mauve stalk; white and pink eglantine; flowering privet (sweet again), blackberry blossom, brilliant yellow stonecrop on top of the walls, and driblets or rather little frothy sacks of cuckoo spit. Thank God that we are spared even these wild flowers and plants.

Handed Alvilde my draft chapter 1 with some trepidation. She likes it but suggests my cutting out a good deal of description of Rowan Hamilton houses; some clarifications needed. Indeed I shall have to cut drastically. Chapter 1 has proved difficult in that I had little material from letters. And oh, Lord! the ensuing chapters will be more difficult owing to the mass of letters and diaries. How to select? Reading Anthony Hobson's[*] review of the Roxburgh Club publication of the Lindsay Library of Haigh Hall, I realize what a great man David Crawford was. For he knew about rare books as much as he knew about painting and the arts. He was such a patrician and so rich that he had no need to establish himself as an art historian in that rat-race of the museums and galleries.

Saturday, 8th July

An instance of memory failure: dining with the Somersets I overheard Alfred Beit telling Lady Salisbury my story of Lord Enniskillen and Lady Londonderry. He turned to me, chortling, and said 'Did you hear it?' I said I did overhear it while I was talking to someone else, and added, 'Yes, isn't it a good story? Do you remember my telling it you some years ago? You were so amused you rocked with laughter.' 'Oh,' he answered, 'but you didn't tell it to me. Lord Enniskillen told it to me. I remember him doing so at Florence Court.' 'No,' I said, 'he told it to me at Florence Court and I passed it on to you.' Since he seemed bewildered I didn't press the point. Besides it did not matter. But it is interesting that perfectly truthful, honourable people like Alf can make such mistakes. Their memories play them false. The story is this. Old Lady Londonderry was driving in her carriage through the Mount Stewart estate in Ireland, with little Enniskillen, then a boy called Cole, I think. They came upon a turf and thatch cottage on fire, with smoke pouring from the doorway and windows. Lady Londonderry sent the footman to enquire if they wanted help. There was probably no fire brigade in the vicinity. The footman returned, and jumped back on to the box, saying, 'It's all right, m'lady. There's nothing to worry about. They're merely smoking a whore for his lordship,' his lordship being the Marquess, her husband.

---

[*] Bibliophile and book collector (b. 1921).

Sunday, 9th July

Lady Abel Smith (Henriette)* asked us only yesterday to luncheon today. She had her sister-in-law Lady Wallinger, who is a daughter of Zilliacus,† staying; also Bill Bentinck (Lord William Cavendish-Bentinck to me).‡ Both of them knew Harold and wanted to talk to me about him. So A. and I went. As we arrived at Quenington too early, we stopped to let the dogs out. Immediately they put up a hare and bolted. We whistled and shouted to no avail. So A. told me to go ahead and warn the Abel Smiths what had happened. They were charming, and said it was always happening with their dogs. She accompanied me back to A. who by that time had recovered both dogs.

Lord William was interesting; had something to tell about H.N. He said that in the Foreign Office he was regarded as too partial to Greece and Venizelos at the time of the Peace Conference. Also rather soppy about Romania. He said that he (C.-B.) was Tyrrell's secretary and had a great regard for him. Denied that he got drunk in public, as Harold alleged. He had a serious breakdown after his second son was killed in action and his daughter was gravely ill. He, Bentinck, and another FO man persuaded the doctors to have Tyrrell sent home from Lausanne. Curzon had to be squared. He agreed. Told a story about the late Schwarzenbergs, Prince Johannes and his wife, brought to Sissinghurst by him. Harold was an old friend from Foreign Office days but Vita had not met him. She took Bentinck aside in the garden and said, 'You can understand why I loathe the Foreign Office, when I hear Harold obsequiously saying "Yes, Your Highness, No, Your Highness", like a little boy talking to his schoolmaster.' 'But', Bentinck retorted, 'he isn't saying anything of the kind. He is calling Prince Schwarzenberg by his Christian name.'

---

* DCVO; Lady-in-Waiting to HM The Queen (and as HRH The Princess Elizabeth) 1949–87; Extra Lady-in-Waiting from 1987; m., 2nd, 1953, Sir Alexander Abel Smith (he d. 1980).
† Konni Zilliacus (1894–1967); born of Finnish-Swedish and Scottish-American parents; served First World War in RFC; Labour MP; author, lecturer and journalist; Stella Irena Zilliacus m. 1958, as his 3rd wife, Sir Geoffrey Wallinger, diplomat.
‡ Succeeded his brother 1980 as 9th and last Duke of Portland (1897–1990).

Monday, 10th July

Went to see Lord Boothby* at 5.30 in his flat in Eaton Square. He was in pyjamas and dressing-gown. Looks much changed. The sofa and armchairs all covered with towels, I suppose because Bob Boothby is incontinent, but it was not attractive. Lady Boothby came in almost immediately after me and stayed throughout the conversation. Then his publisher came and talked about his forthcoming book of memoirs. Boothby showed me several letters he had received from Harold, very sympathetic, generous, helpful ones they were, written at a time when Boothby was in some trouble. They disclosed that H.N. was homosexual, Lord Boothby remarked to me. I thought they disclosed that Boothby was too, or H.N. would not have written to him recommending a harbour in Greece where pretty sailors were to be seen drinking and smoking.

Dined with Eardley and Richard Shone. Delicious gossip and much laughter as always. Richard is a heavenly young man. His laughter enchanting.

Spent a ghastly day at Kew in the new Public Record Office for the second time. Simply could not find anything I wanted. The computer drives me mad and I am so stupid working the bloody thing that I am humiliated every time I approach it. I do think an attendant ought to sit at it and translate into computer language what one wants to get out. As it was, those files I tried to get were away at the Foreign Office.

Sitting in the tube reading the advertisements I was amused by somebody's careful deletion of letters on the corner notice in front of me announcing that the seat is pre-reserved for old people. The abbreviated version read: 'Please eat elderly and reserved persons.'

Poor Boothby is a warning example of how the old become painfully vain. He kept reading extracts from the books of famous contemporaries in which they praised him. He praised himself, spoke of his power of rhetoric. Said he would speak on any occasion about any subject, knowing that he was swaying his audience. It is love of power, I suggested. Yes, he said, smiling. An engaging fellow. Not a great man, as Eardley observed.

---

* Robert (Bob) Boothby (1900–86); cr. Life Peer (Baron Boothby of Buchan and Rattray Head) 1958; Conservative politician; m., 2nd, 1967, Wanda Sanna.

Friday, 14th July

Tonight Julian Berkeley* and his friend Tony Scotland came to dinner with us. Two such handsome young men, Julian a real pin-up like his mother, and improved beyond all words. Now adult and intelligent. A very earnest, serious youth, a deep thinker I should say. So is the other, whom I liked immensely. In the middle of dinner we listened to a broadcast on Edmund Gosse which I was determined to hear. Gosse was recorded speaking about Hardy after Hardy's death in 1928 and a few months only before Gosse's own death. Most interesting listening to the voice and pronunciation, absolutely different from anything heard today. Choice of words and phrases archaic, precision of diction, 'litera-cher', 'pick-cher', which surprised the commentator and the two boys, but not us who were accustomed to this form of pronunciation. But we would think someone talking like Gosse today too unbelievably pedantic for words. I wonder if Gosse was typical of the professorial class of his day rather than the landed gentry. I think so.

The spotted flycatcher nested a month ago in the coronet of the coat-of-arms under A's bedroom window, as it habitually does. We have watched the appearance of eggs and hatching of three chicks with interest. When I looked at them a fortnight ago I wondered how the little birds could remain in so shallow a nest, built with no rim. Then two disappeared, either fledged or fallen out of the nest and devoured by cats. Yesterday we found the third out of the nest on the ground, its parents assiduously flying to feed it with flies, and insects. By the evening it had somehow reached the cedar trees, but still quite unable to fly properly. So we got a ladder and A. having caught it handed it to me and I put it into a disused blackbird's nest in the fork of one of the cedar trees. We waited and within half an hour the parents had discovered it and were feeding it again. Will it survive?

Saturday, 15th July

In the obituary columns of *The Times* this morning two announcements next to each other, one of poor old Keith Miller Jones, the other Oliver Messel.† On Tuesday Anne and Michael Rosse lunched

---

* Son of Sir Lennox and Lady Berkeley (b. 1950).
† Theatrical producer, decorator and artist (b. 1904); brother of Countess of Rosse.

with us in Jermyn Street. No mention was made of Oliver's illness, so I presume he went quickly. Anne will be devastated. She adored him. Two such old friends gone. I wrote to Betty and told her that Keith was the kindest and wisest man I had known; he bore no one malice, and he never expressed disapproval of his friends' peccadilloes although he may often have inwardly disapproved. I told Anne that Oliver had the innocence of childhood, of the creative artist which he was (though not of the highest calibre). But *The Times* this morning says he was one of the four greatest stage designers of this century, Gordon Craig, Charles Ricketts and Lovat Fraser being the other three.

Went to three exhibitions in London this week, Matisse, Bonnard and twentieth-century portraits at the Nat. Portrait extension in Carlton Terrace. Matisse is not a great artist; slovenly stuff I call it, thrown casually off and choice of colour combinations often displeasing, reds and oranges. Bonnards not as good as ours! The portraits enjoyable. Graham Sutherland self-portrait of last year very good. The portrait of Daisy Fellowes the first time seen by me. Would not have recognized it as Daisy but then she must have changed, she did change towards the end of her life. Here fat in the face, Cortisone I daresay. None of the extreme elegance I remember; little of the wickedness and chic.

Sunday, 16th July

Boothby again. Another sign of my senility is that I remember days later incidents and words spoken. I try and train myself while listening to someone who is telling me what I want to record, by making a mental note, or mental numbers, saying to myself, 1, 2, 3 points I must record when I get outside; but no, when I get outside, I have forgotten; but they often return. Well now, Lord Boothby told me that he is still remembered by strangers for his old broadcasting days. Taxi drivers will not take a fare from him; others recognize him and drive him home to number 1 Eaton Square without waiting to be given the address. Yes, he said, it was a dreadful bore being a celebrity at the time, you couldn't step outside the house without being molested and asked to write your autograph. He was pleased as Punch telling me this. He is a jolly, bluff, rather lovable, very likeable man.

A. has read chapters 2 and 3. They get shorter and shorter, but

Chapter 4 will be long. Damn this article for *Country Life* on Brooks's which I must write. I resent any interruption.

J.K.-B. has suggested our going to Rome in October now. Eastern Germany is off, dreadfully expensive and beastly; besides he has been there twice lately. I just might join him in Rome where he has to go for his cataloguing of huge collection of Nollekens drawings. I would like to be with him for a week at a stretch, because he takes time to unfold his extraordinary arcane knowledge of the Classical world.

Tuesday, 18th July

Met Sachie [Sitwell] by chance in Sotheby's. He was walking with a stick, rather bent and very much older than last year in Venice. Had that hollowness behind the ears which is a sad sign. He said Georgia's walking was worse than ever, and he could not think what the trouble was. The doctors did not seem to know. I suspect that they know only too well. Poor Georgia, poor Sachie! I was told he was very upset by the book which is coming out this autumn about the three Sitwells, and the disclosures of Osbert's queerness.* David Horner has given the author letters from Osbert to him written from Balmoral, compromising love letters. 'What will the Queen Mother think?' Sachie said. I then went to Maggs and asked them to bid for a lock of Browning's hair and failing that his spectacles in a tortoiseshell case.

Tuesday, 25th July

Miss Rose of Maggs telephoned that I did not get the lock of Browning's hair, which was bought by an Eton schoolmaster who is a passionate Browning fan,† but I did get the spectacles. Would rather have had the lock. I see that Byron's lock went for only £100. I should have bought this also, only I already have two.

Wednesday, 2nd August

Last night, reading in bed Rupert [Hart-Davis]'s delicious letters to George Lyttelton, a moth flew in through the open window and settled on my left hand. It fluttered prettily, and waltzed up and down,

---

* *Façades: Edith, Osbert and Sacheverell Sitwell*, by John Pearson.
† Michael Meredith.

tickling. So I blew it away. It returned and nestled happily beside my sleeve, and was so good that after half an hour I grew attached to it. Honey was sleeping peacefully in her basket beside me. Suddenly my moth decided to move and flew away towards the bedside table. An hour later I took a sleeping pill and then a gulp of water from my silver mug – the one Great-aunt Jane gave to my Uncle Robert. That was all right. Before turning out the light I wanted another sip. There, floating, with wings outspread, quite still and dead, was my pretty moth, drowned. The surface of the water was covered with grey flecks from the poor thing's wings.

Friday, 4th August

I firmly believe that the most beautiful lines of English prose come in the Benedictus – 'And thou, Child, shalt be called the Prophet of the Highest, for thou shalt go before the face of the Lord to prepare his ways . . . Through the tender mercy of our God, whereby the dayspring from on high hath visited us, To give light to them that sit in darkness, . . . and to guide our feet into the way of Peace.' What does it matter if these truly divine words mean little? In fact they mean a lot to me, but if they didn't, they are magical, numinous and enough to turn the sensitive atheist into a member of the Church of England. And then the ancient chaunts that accompany these words, the canticles, do not detract from the poetry but somehow strengthen it and add to it. Usually I disapprove of fine poetry being put to music, for the one destroys the other, the music destroys the poetry because the scansion of each conflicts with the other. But not so with the Psalms. Yet our vandal bishops can scrap these divine god-like poems and substitute words of ineffable banality. They make me sick.

Last night too I listened to Glück's *Orfeo*. Likewise sublime, perhaps my favourite opera because it too is numinous, magical and tragic. How wonderful are works of art from true genius, how uplifting, how transporting, how only worth while. Everything else one does, and reads, and thinks is dross beside these immortal moments. Pretty banal observation this. Not unworthy of Q. Victoria.

Saturday, 5th August

In the Verge, walking with the dogs this evening, I encountered one of the keepers who was very rude to me. He said, 'I will not have these whippets in this wood. I have told the woman before that I won't allow it. She pays no attention to me. I am seeing his Grace tomorrow morning and I will tell him.' I was furious but for once contained my temper, because I knew I was, if not in the wrong exactly, on the Duke's land and he has the right to make what restrictions he wishes with his own property. So I merely said, 'You are referring presumably to my wife, whom you must know, for we live at Essex House. I too will speak to his Grace, or Mr Somerset.' And I put the dogs on the lead and walked off, and out of the Verge. But it was disagreeable. I hate these restrictions, these holy coverts for foxes which are preserved in order to be killed by hunting people. I hate the whole Beaufort lot, and their archaic out-of-date values. I rather hate this place because there is nowhere one can walk, because of the holy deer, the holy hares, the holy foxes, sheep, horses. Such tommy-rot, as my father would have said, though he would not have said it about foxes, which he too thought holy.

Sunday, 6th August

My seventieth birthday. My dear God, how could you do this to me? The obscenity of it, the ugliness, the squalor of old age. Well, I feel well, thought doubtless I look mangy, mouldy and a million. We had our party today. I was dreading it. I need not have, for I enjoyed it very much indeed. Everyone has been so kind. The whole thing was organized and run by Alvilde, who is a genius in this sort of thing. We had Clarissa over from France staying, and Billa. Billa is the best value, just the same in spite of her recent widowhood and so sensible about Roy's death, seeing it as a sort of triumph, or transfiguration. She and I began the day going to Holy Communion at eight.

We had about fifty to luncheon. We hired a tent from Cheltenham, thank goodness, because the weather was, is still, lousy, cold and grey and rainy, off and on. The tent just outside the kitchen door held twenty-five; the rest of us in the two little front rooms. The Droghedas chucked, the Rosses couldn't come, and Debo couldn't come. She and John Betj. sweetly telephoned. But Diana Cooper motored down with Jack Rathbone and Philip Dimmick from London. Eardley came; the Somersets; Osbert Lancasters, he looking very frail and shaking. I gave him a copy of my novel. He left his present for me behind in London. I rather hope it may be one of his drawings. The Lancasters stayed with the Somersets, so did Derry

[Moore], and Archie Aberdeen. I was given masses of presents, all of which were things I wanted. They were mostly books. How lucky I am. How kind people are to septuagenarians. My dear beautiful gt-nephew Henry came and helped wait and hand drinks and was generally useful and adorable.

Monday, 7th August

Stayed at Badminton all day, writing some thirty letters of thanks, and taking back jugs, china, cutlery (beastly word) lent by friends, also garden seats and trestle tables for the tent. Looking at my presents. My gratitude to A. knows no bounds. How sweet she is to me. She wants me to get some recognition, and thinks I do not receive enough. Bless her heart. I received a letter today which drew tears from my eyes.

Saturday, 12th August

Nick rang me up from London and is much distressed and hurt that Denys Sutton has sacked him from *Apollo*; the only reasons given that Nick's heart was not in his work. This is what Sutton told me, too. Of course Sutton is a beast and no one can work under him for long, but Nick is so calm and industrious that I hoped he would stick it out for a year or two, and gain much valuable experience under this very clever, informed taskmaster. Nick is coming to lunch today to talk about it. Norah Smallwood lunched with me in London on Thursday. I told her about Nick. She remembered meeting him here and liked him, and said she could give him a job, of a publicity sort, in Chatto's. I don't know if it is the sort of work he wants, but at least it is something.

A. has been overwhelmed with letters thanking her for the party last Sunday. It really does seem to have been enjoyed. Among my presents Rupert's letters already read. What a clever, what an industrious publisher he was; must have known every author that ever was, and became his friend and adviser for life.

Norah told me that Dirk Bogarde whom she is mad about is editing some letters between him and an un-met old lady (rather like Monica Baldwin and me); said to her he didn't know that he could make a good job of it. 'That tiresome fellow L.-M. with his diaries has made it impossible for anyone following him to do as well.'* Flattering from him; but nonsense of course, for there is no artistry in my diaries. They were just a day-to-day jumble of thoughts and recorded events. Now I am reading Fanny Partridge's† diaries of her war years; and they *are* art. Her observations of nature, the trees, the animals are poetic. Also she writes about an enclosed circle, by nature of her and Ralph's solitary life in the country limited by intellectual friends with exclusive pacifist views. This makes for better writing, whereas my diaries bring in too many people. It is my theory that novels are better in which the dramatis personae are few.

On Wednesday, before leaving Bath at five o'clock to catch the London train, I wrote about 5,000 words of my biography; and in the train wrote 1,000 words on Ivy Compton-Burnett for *Twentieth-Century Literature*. I told Norah that I would be sending her the first six chapters, up to the end of the First War, for Chatto's to look through. That if they thought them no good and requiring to be entirely re-written, then I would chuck 'it'. If they merely approved but made suggestions for improvement, then I would persevere. I am rather surprised by the speed with which I seem to write. Because I type straight on to the page, perhaps.

Monday, 21st August

Today is the birthday of my revered Uncle Robert who was killed in 1917. *There* was a saintly, beloved man, clever, with a useful and honourable career as Clerk in the House of Commons, who would have risen in his profession and become an ornament to his country, now remembered only by me who just knew him and recall his appearance and gentle manner, and his goodness to me as a child. Apart from my sister Audrey there is probably no one else alive who even knows of his existence, let alone his birthday. How quickly mortality engulfs us.

---

* Derek Niven Van Den Bogaerde (b. 1921); actor and writer; the book in question, *A Particular Friendship*, was eventually published in 1989; Kt. 1992.
† Frances Marshall (b. 1900); diarist and literary reviewer; m. 1933 Ralph Partridge (who d. 1963); these diaries were *A Pacifist's War*.

Saturday, 26th August

The depression from which I suffered so grievously during the spring
and early summer has quite gone, and I am content again. On
analysing this return to 'normality' – if it is normality – I can find no
explanations for it. Because I am not in better health; if anything, in
weaker health: I get more tired and I suffer from eczema and tingling
on my face, and palpitations. Nor have I particular reason to be more
self-confident than I was in the spring. I still do not know whether
my biography is going to be any good. When I was depressed, I had
not even begun it. Now that I have begun it I have reason to suppose
it is not a success. And the verdict of Chatto's, to whom I am sending
the first few chapters while A. and I are to be in Cyprus, is a cloud
before my eyes. No, it is altogether strange. I believe that I suffer from
depression when my mind is clear of fog and I can and do look into
life with penetrating eyes, and see life for what it really is, a hollow
sham. Now that I am out of depression I am living in a happy sort of
daydream, avoiding the truth and realities and delusions of existence.
I know this is not the customary way of looking at this matter. When
one is depressed one is supposed to be ill, mentally if not physically. I
find the very opposite to be the case. When one is happy and contented one is living in illusion, a fool's paradise in glorious fact.

A. and I stayed last week two nights at Euston and one with Billa
at Holt. We found Hugh Grafton rather less self-confident than hitherto. He worries inordinately about things. For instance, he begged
A. for her advice about the garden at Felbrigg, which when she gave
it, upset him. She said, 'Scrap all these hideous beds in the walled
garden and keep one narrow border along the north wall for flowering
shrubs that require little attention; keep the rest in grass and plant fruit
trees. Thus you will save two gardeners and the place will look
simpler.' Hugh, having engaged two more gardeners, which the place
can't afford, and agreed with the silly Garden Adviser's advice to make
the place a mass of bedding-out, was dreadfully upset in consequence.
He went on and on, arguing his case, until A. told him he should not
have asked for her advice since he had no intention of taking it. Then
he took me to the Kent temple in his park which has had dry rot and
is costing him £40,000 to repair. He asked for my candid opinion,
whether I approved the plaster ribs he had had put inside the dome.
Well, he has copied the thin, narrow ribs from the church. But the
church dates from Wren's time, and the temple from Kent's. I thought

what he had done was a mistake, and gently told him so. Result, more distress. The trouble is that he rushes into things. Poor Hugh, his determination to do right is getting him down. Then he took A. aside to tell her how worried he was about my forthcoming biography. Feared I was going into Harold's sexual deviations. Why mention such things when writing about a man of letters?, etc. It was bad for Jim's image. But Jim hasn't got an image, she said, and he does not care what happens to something he hasn't got. Hugh is incredibly honourable, but incredibly old-fashioned.

Saturday, 2nd September

Golden autumn days, the very air washed like brightly polished guinea pieces of my youth; the cubbing mornings crisp with sharp tingles and the hedgerows that remain – most are burnt to cinders by the bloody stubble burners – netted with silver spiders' webs. The beauty of England at this time! and we are going abroad in a week. Now is the moment to stay in England. It is the only reliable time of the year, weatherwise, and seldom lets one down. All other seasons do, the summer worst of all. No summer this summer, so to speak, at all, at all.

I have written six chapters and A. is taking them to Chatto's on Monday for them to give an opinion, but I make a mistake probably. I should have waited till I had finished part 1 or vol. 1, and then sent the whole thing, for if they start criticizing or complaining of excessive length of these admittedly too-long preliminary chapters I shall be thrown into confusion and depression, like Hugh indeed.

A. and I were talking last night about sense of humour, when she said, 'Do you think I have a sense of humour?' and I replied, 'No, not really.' 'Oh!' – and I knew at once she was hurt. 'But I always laugh at what is funny, and don't laugh at what is not.' So I, endeavouring to mitigate the cruelty, added, 'But I certainly have no sense of humour either. Because people laugh a lot, that doesn't mean they have a sense of humour.' And I instanced those people we both know who rock their sides off, like GA and CF, and have none at all. It arose, I recall, because Diana Westmorland surprised A. by remarking at tea that Caroline S. had no s. of h. Now she does have a whimsical turn, and is frightfully jolly, candid and disarming, yet I have never felt absolutely as one with her as to laughing, any more than I am with Osbert [Lancaster], who is renowned for s. of h. I said to A., 'You must remember that it takes two people to make one sense of humour, just as it takes two people to make one bore.' I don't think that helped. People take it as the deadliest insult to be told they lack s. of h.: is worse than being told their breath stinks. I shouldn't have said what I said. I regret it, just as I regret having told her a year ago that H.N. didn't like her. Needless, heartless cruelty. Poor darling, I am sorry. And to think of the numbers of scintillating people who leave me unmoved like a stone, and the numbers of society stars who look upon me as a death's-head. The truth is, one cannot be candid, or honest, with one's dearest. One cannot be honest or truthful. Truth is not Beauty. It is something to be hidden in the deepest depths of one's inmost being. One must act all the time. All the world's a stage, indeed.

Friday, 8th September

A. and I and Philip Dimmick flew to Cyprus to stay with Dick and Elaine. We changed at Constantinople. While we were in the trolley-bus on the tarmac on the way to our plane I saw our luggage on a truck being driven in the opposite direction. I said to A., 'There goes our luggage. I recognize my blue suitcase on the top of the load.' Sure enough, on arrival at midnight our luggage was not unloaded. It had been sent to Ankara. We had to wait twenty-four hours before it arrived, and then poor Dick had to drive to the airport to collect it.

Weather very warm, beautiful in fact, each day cloudless. I felt very languid and devitalized. Hardly had strength to stack the dishes. But I enjoyed the bathing in a nice cove, practically deserted. Walking along the shore we could see nothing but the range of Kyrenia Mountains, and no horrors. The horrors exist, however, in a beastly development, round Kyrenia; houses unfinished, with clusters of wire sticking up from the truncated storeys of cement. This seems to be customary in the eastern Mediterranean. Dick and Elaine most kind and hospitable, but I fear found us boring guests because we did not want to go to cocktail parties or meet their just as boring friends. In fact, the day after we left they gave an enormous party, according to Philip, who remained behind, to celebrate their freedom it seems. To us their lives are dreary in the extreme. They have no interests, they do not even garden. And they drink far too much, whereas Elaine eats the minimum. I would say her life's prospect is a poor one.

The 18th to 23rd A. and I spent in Constantinople. First two days very fine; warm and beautiful; the two remaining days weather horrid, overcast and raining. Went up Bosphorus the first day. Shores over-built, old wooden houses mostly gone, the rest going. Hideous substitutes. The waters swarming with jellyfish. Never seen so many, a revolting spectacle, like drifts of spermatozoa, dirty milk. The Golden Horn even more disillusioning, a stinking sewer. Dead, black water. We held our noses until the ferry boat got back. Factory effluent and drains. And hideous. Town pullulating with people. Population has trebled within one generation. Conditions of people bad. Trouble brewing, and I should guess there will be a Marxist revolution within five years. Santa Sophia does not disappoint. Even more wonderful than when last seen, the scale and proportions reducing men to insects. Stone ramp upstairs for the horses which carried the Empress of Byzantium and her suite to the galleries. Blue Mosque disappointing. Being repaired and redecorated, not well. St Saviour in Chora a true gem of a church, with double narthex, and the finest frescos of the time of Giotto to be seen anywhere. But oh! the walking difficulties, up hills, narrow pavements, holes in the pavements so that each step has to be watched. I visited the old British Embassy, built by [Sir Charles] Barry. Rather like Bridgewater House or the Reform Club. A very good building, one of the few secular buildings left of any merit. Fine grand staircase with double flight, marble walls, portraits of King Edward VII and Queen Alexandra. Ballroom huge with high coved ceiling through two floors. Very splendid, and a good walled garden. How much longer will the Government keep this building before finding its maintenance too expensive? What a power in Turkey Great Britain was in the nineteenth century! Harold and Vita's house has gone. I saw the street in which it was, but no trace of house, or garden, where Vita began her horticultural career on steep terraces overlooking the Bosphorous and Santa Sophia.

I lost my precious pocket comb in Cyprus. It slipped from the pocket of my bathing pants while I was in the sea. In Kyrenia tried to buy another. In the first shop I entered, the man serving whom I asked for a comb said, 'Since you have no hair, why do you want one?' There was no answer to this sharp Turk. Then the most extraordinary miracle happened. Philip Dimmick a few days later, while swimming with goggles on to watch fish, saw my comb at the bottom of the ocean, dived and retrieved it.

I can't forget the filth in the Bosphorus; the boys bathing in it; the young men fishing in these stinking waters, the obscene jellyfish which presumably batten on the polluted waters; the stone fortresses; the tumble-down remains of wooden houses, some with Baroque frills and furbelows; the vast, out-of-scale hotel dwarfing the little village of Therapia where the smart palaces for *villeggiatura* were; remains of gardens with umbrella pines, cypresses and planes. There are still remnants of the forest called Bulgaria behind Therapia and Buyukdere; the croaky voices of the ferry boats when the pilot blows his whistle. The large palaces along the water like the Casino and opera house at Monte Carlo, wondrously ornate and fascinating – Dolmabahce and Kucuksu by the architect Kikogos Balyan. I would like to know more about him. And who was Abdul Mecit for whom the second, smaller palace on the Asian side was built? The railings and gates are of incredible opulence and delicious bad taste.

Wednesday, 4th October

We dined with Sally Westminster to meet Sir Bernard Lovell and his wife* who are staying the night at Wickwar. This eminent man does not look outstandingly distinguished, but he has the face of a sage. He is short, bald and has a stomach. An odd mouth, regular yet twisted, and thin lips. A nice modesty, a good manner. I sat next to his wife, a charming woman, intelligent, bright and fun. After dinner I had a long talk with him. Of the swallows this autumn which, deprived of insects during the cold spell, when they decided to emigrate dashed themselves to pieces against window panes and walls. Was it suicide in desperation, or merely looking for insects in unaccustomed places? Swallows are unusually temperamental birds. He deplored pesticides as much as I do. I asked if their use in such quantities since the war had increased the crops of corn, and he doubted it. I asked if the oxygen belt on which all living things depended was being impaired by the rapid diminution of the rain forests of the world; he confirmed that this was so. He said the temperature of the earth had already increased by one degree within the last thirty years owing to the increasing generation of electricity in the West. That if the Third World was to be supplied with the same amenities, electricity and machines of all sorts, then the threat to the earth would be very serious

---

* Sir Bernard Lovell (b. 1913; Kt 1961); Director of Jodrell Bank Experimental Station, Cheshire 1951–81; Professor (later Emeritus) of Radio Astronomy, University of Manchester 1951–80; m. 1937 Mary Joyce Chesterman.

indeed. That the left-wing politicians never gave a moment's consideration to the appalling consequences of population increases in their desire to spread what he called the amenities more equably. There was a lesson to be learnt from the planet Venus. Why? I asked. Because the sending of rockets there and taking of photographs have shown that Venus was once about the same temperature as the earth, with very similar conditions as to oxygen, and probably vegetation, although that planet is appreciably nearer the sun than we are. But something happened to cause its temperature to rocket, so that today nothing can survive on its surface, and lead would melt. He said politicians had no understanding of the grave energy problem, nor interest in it. Said he was very pessimistic about the future. Within fifty years some terrible catastrophe may happen to the earth. It is no consolation that we shall be dead by then. He said no scientist today can be anything but a pessimist.

Like other great men I have met, Bernard Lovell has many interests. He is a keen gardener, is mad keen on birds and nature, and music. Said that he came from a large family near Bristol, all musical. With a family orchestra, what fun they had. Such a thing is unknown today among the young. He complained that too much of his time was wasted in doing executive work in his office, leaving too little of it for his researches in outer space. This seems dreadful. Surely, I suggested, he could have a vice-chairman or someone whose job it was to relieve him of questions of personnel, pay and morale.

Thursday, 5th October

Had a successful day. Left by the 8.53 from Chippenham, reaching Paddington, actually early, at 9.50. Was met by Philip Dimmick who motored me to Chelsea Court, Mickey Renshaw's flat, where I chose one thin dinner jacket suit with smart satin collar, a blue velvet smoking jacket with frogs, and a summer jacket of Mickey's. Saw the red leather Victorian dining-room chairs which I have already bought from him. I am putting these in the downstairs flat in Bath and giving Simon* six of the Hepplewhite chairs from Crompton Hall. Jane, his first wife, already has five of this suite. I think it right that Simon should have these Crompton Hall chairs and Guy should grow up with them and perhaps learn to love and cherish them. Philip motored

---

* Lees-Milne (J.L.-M's nephew); his son Guy.

me to Heywood Hill's shop. There I collected some books and, most extravagantly, bought for £200 two volumes of John Scott's visit to Paris in 1815, which had belonged to Beckford and Lord Rosebery. Then to Brooks's where I gave the Secretary the pulls of my article on Brooks's for *Country Life*. Everyone there seemed pleased with the article. Then London Library. Then walked carrying my briefcase and sackful of heavy books to the Savile Club. Lunched with Julian Berry and the committee of the Country House Dictionary, and sat round table after luncheon, discussing until five o'clock. Just had time to catch a bus to Paddington, and the train back – also one hour's journey. Was unable to meet Eardley, so have arranged to stay with him next Wednesday after Sheila Birkenhead's dinner for the launching of Freddy's book on Kipling, and to walk with him next day on the Downs near Swindon.

Tuesday, 10th October

John Betj. and Feeble stayed Sunday night on their way to Cornwall. I would say he is rather more decrepit than before. Mind active as ever, and quoting reams of poetry which always puts me at a disadvantage. Has re-read *The Deserted Village*, which was the first poem he knew, for his father read it aloud to him. He now realizes that all his own poetry stemmed from it. After we had been sitting in the drawing-room A. said come and look at the sunset. John said he would like to be driven round the park. So I drove him, and we came out at Little Badminton and I took him to look at the outside of the church. The lights were shining through the windows and we heard singing. This determined him to join Evensong. It turned out to be Little Badminton's Harvest Festival. The tiny church was packed. We sat at the back beside the font. I was not properly dressed, wearing a pullover. All the rich farmers and their wives dressed to kill; and Master and Mary in the front pew. A moving little ceremony, church decked with vegetables, every candle in the chandeliers, if the round rings with cups can be so described, burning while the light outside waned. Congregation sang the Nunc Dimittis without looking at their prayer books. Vicar gave a good sermon, exhorting them not to concentrate upon material things – which of course they do – and to remember that someone outside themselves controlled their lives and the produce which enriched them.

Sunday, 15th October

On Wednesday I motored to London in the evening, reaching Eardley's flat at 6.45. Fanny Partridge talking to him. Congratulated her on her diaries. She says she has enjoyed receiving letters from all sorts of people more than writing or preparing the book. People always talk as though they receive hundreds of letters from strangers. I am sure Graham Greene does, and Iris Murdoch, but I wonder if the little-known authors really do. I receive about two a week, but seldom more. I changed and drove to Warwick Avenue. Picked up A. and we went to George Weidenfeld's buffet dinner given in honour of Freddy Birkenhead's Kipling book. Sure enough, neither of us enjoyed it much. It was an extremely hot evening. Crowds of people we did not know, and indifferent food difficult to eat, balancing plate and glass on a knee. Clarissa Avon* talking to A. who said, 'You know Jim?' as I approached. She said, 'I have known him since I was ten, and he made me write a sonnet.' She was agreeable enough, but as I never once saw her all the years she was married to Anthony Eden, I don't feel very warmly towards her. Found myself, with a plate of ham, sitting on a sofa next to Lady Hartwell.† Never met her before. We have both known of the other for years: Nancy her friend. She puts me in mind of the gypsy lady in *The Masked Ball* whom the King consults for his fortune. She has a strong, masterful face and manner. Has strong dislikes; thinks Ali Forbes should be boiled in oil, and said she would leave the room if he entered. Is worried about *Daily Telegraph*, on strike for a week. I asked if it was sheer bloody-mindedness on the part of the strikers, intending to destroy the reputable daily papers, and through them a vehicle of democracy, the correspondence columns being the one way left in which the ordinary man, if he was lucky, could give voice to his opinions? She said yes. But her son, to whom I also spoke on the same subject, who tells me he works on the *D. T.*, said No, they did not want to destroy, they merely wanted, like every working man in England, more money for less work. Lady Hartwell said when Harold Acton asked for the loan of Nancy's letters to her,

---

* Clarissa Spencer Churchill, niece of Winston Churchill; m. 1952 as his 2nd wife Anthony Eden (1897–1977), Conservative politician, prime minister and statesman, cr. 1961 Viscount Eden and Earl of Avon.
† Lady Pamela Smith, dau. of 1st Earl of Birkenhead; m. 1936 Michael Berry, 2nd son of 1st Viscount Camrose, newspaper editor; cr. Life Peer (Baron Hartwell) 1968; Chairman and Editor-in-Chief of the *Daily Telegraph* and *Sunday Telegraph* (she d. 1982).

she looked through them and, finding them all about trivialities, did not send them. She supposed Nancy adapted her letters to the correspondent, and that she thought she, Pamela, was only interested in gossip and un-serious matters. I said, No, I thought Nancy was not a deeply serious person, and gossip was her usual fare. Tried to sit with Sheila Birkenhead and talk to her, but the noise too great, and I could not hear. We left at eleven o'clock. Not a successful evening.

The next morning, Thursday, at 9.15, E. and I motored to the Berkshire Downs near Ashdown House, which we never found, left the car in a lane, and walked for five hours straight as a die across them [the Downs]. Not a house or human in sight for infinity. A glorious walk, wonderful sunny day, only too hot to be exhilarating. I felt tired out, and so did E. But he is 75. Got back to the car at 2.30 having covered, we estimate, ten or eleven miles. Drove to Marlborough and, the pubs being shut, went to Polly's Pantry and had a heavenly blowout, iced coffee with cream, and scones and apricot jam and cream. Deliciously bad for us and undid all the good of the walk. Put E. on the train at Chippenham. Loved this walk.

Thursday, 19th October

Dear, good, kind Philip Dimmick motored from London for the day just to deliver the things of Mickey's which we have bought, including the six red leather dining-room chairs for me. When we were going through Mickey's clothes the other day we found some pornographic photographs in the pocket of one coat.

Lunching last Sunday with the Chancellors, the Lees Mayalls were there. They left before us. Seated in their car, Lees had his foot on the pedal when Christopher went to the window and began talking again. Sylvia shot at him, 'Don't, whatever you do, stop people leaving when they want to go.' Both the Mayalls rather drinky, he very nice and intelligent. Has taken on the chairmanship of the Bath Trust, a good thing. Her voice wonderfully affected in the Thirties manner. Exaggerated emphasis up and down the scale.

Monday, 23rd October

A. and I motored to Newburgh [Priory, Yorkshire] on Friday for two nights to stay with Malcolm Wombwell, her first cousin, who is recently widowed and aged 85. *En route* we lunched with Myles

Hildyard at Flintham. His companion, David, is a marvellous cook and a jolly, very friendly creature.

Malcolm lives in what he calls the flat, on the first floor of the new wing, comprising the drawing-room with three inner domes and plasterwork on ceilings and walls. The visitors' book, still in use, is the earliest I know. It begins in 1858. Victorian signatures are splendidly Baroque, with flourishes. Ours today like housemaids'; unreadable and inelegant.

What has given me immense pleasure is a visit to my dear old friend Rupert Hart-Davis who lives in a rambling rectory at Marske near Richmond, in Swaledale, the river rushing below, the moors behind. A. was not feeling well so I went alone, and lunched. I had misgivings about seeing him after so many years, but A. insisted. It was a great success. He was so affectionate. His wife is sweet and lovely, clever I should say, retiring and adoring. I liked her immensely. We talked non-stop for hours. Since my return I have had a letter from Rupert offering to read through my Harold book. His house is more crammed with books than any I have ever seen. From floor to ceiling there are books in every room, and all so neatly shelved. He can lay a hand on any one he needs. He lent me several letters to him from Harold. He fetched them from Harold's books. Took a book from the shelves and out tumbled letters. What an orderly man. He has an orderly mind. I do love him. I think he is a great man in his way, which is scholarly without being pedantic. He is a practical man, yet poetic. He looks like a retired major, with his long, thin face, a little heavy about the jowl, and the absurd little grey moustache. A little of *embonpoint*. He said I was sadly bald. What an honour to be asked to let him read my manuscript. He is the successor to Eddie Marsh as England's proofreader-in-chief.

Saturday, 28th October

On Thursday I took the six p.m. train to London, arriving Paddington just after seven. Went to the Berkeleys'. Joined A. and we drove to dine with the Blakistons in Markham Square. At eleven we motored home, arriving at 1.15. I would not do this for many people, but they are such old friends. Giana [Blakiston] has the old woman's skin, thin, filmy and mother-o'-pearly about the temples. Snow-white hair, but more distinguished than ever. Noel has lost his beauty and is a venerable but no longer striking man. Made me sign some five of my books on our arrival. This embarrassed me because Honour and Fleming were present, and quizzically watching. Haven't seen them for ages. Very nice, Hugh much calmer. They have been commissioned by a kind of Rainbird individual in America to write the History of World Art. Gigantic undertaking for which they are paid a vast sum they could not resist. They hope on completion never to have to potboil again.* Hugh said the absurd complications with Americans amount to this sort of misunderstanding: referring to a Classical statue of Venus with one hand before her pudenda, he had captioned it the Pudic Venus. American printer altered this to Pubic. American editor crossed word out and put in margin, 'Not very nice'. He says they speak and write another language. He had referred them to the word *pudic* in *Webster's Dictionary*, to no avail. John Fleming has been made Harold Acton's literary executor, and is pleased.

Walking the dogs in the playing fields this morning at nine o'clock the ground covered with a film of gauze, no more than a coverlet, three inches from the ground. It was cobwebs, sparkling with rime. Now I don't believe that there are cobwebs here every morning when there is no rime, for I have looked carefully to see. So why do the army of spiders do their work only when there is a ground frost, at this time of year too?

Sunday, 5th November

Chloe is staying. Has come over from France to stay in her father's flat for the winter. Thinks she is going to paint. A. took her to Chatto's where Norah received her kindly and ordered a painting from her. So did Maclehose, her partner, so they must think she has talent. But this child will never thrive in my opinion because she is wholly undisciplined, and not dedicated. Is a hard little nut, a proper little madam, and not very easy to communicate with. She might well join the Baader-Meinhof group if she fell in love with a member of that gang.

Sally W. brought to dinner on Saturday one of her royal Siamese boys whom she befriends in the holidays from Malvern School. Not an attractive boy, a bit of a podge with large round horn-rimmed spectacles, *décolleté* to the navel, wearing bejewelled bracelets and chains

---

* Hugh Honour (b. 1927) and John Fleming (b. 1919); writers, separately and together, on art and architecture: *A World History of Art* was published in 1982 and won the Mitchell Prize.

with charms around the neck. Now, this makes him sound more exotic than he is. Said he dislikes his housemaster at Malvern and does what he can to disoblige him. Proudly told us that the whole house went on strike, or rather put themselves into Coventry the other day, and refused to speak at meals. Who on this earth would be a school-master unless driven to it by extremes of penury? A. said to him at dinner, 'Won't you have some salad?' He replied, 'Oi don't loike greens.'

Today, Sunday, we lunched with Hardy Amies* at Langford near Lechlade. He has converted a Victorian school into a house. Whimsical. All his furniture is oak, Jacobean gate-leg tables and buffets and chests of drawers; old prints; one or two oil paintings of the Stuart family. Nothing Georgian. What a refreshing change! How the wheels of taste go into reverse. We are back to the Broadway of my youth, and the hang-over of the William Morris tradition. Hardy is a friend of the Hornyold-Strickland family of Sizergh. He was staying with friends in the Lake District where the late Princess Royal was a guest. His friends just before luncheon told the Princess whom they had invited, to include Mr and Mrs Hornyold-Strickland. The Princess said, 'The Who?' They repeated the name. Whereupon the Princess went into one of her *foux rires*. 'Horny old,' she gasped and went off into further peals. She could not stop. Finally she was able to say, 'Send for Emily at once.' This was her maid. 'Emily,' she spluttered, 'you know what to do.' 'Yes, Your Royal Highness,' Emily said, and rushed off to fetch a bible. Came back, and standing up read a verse or two at random. This brought Princess Mary back to her senses. She was perfectly composed, and when the H.-Stricklands were pre-sented, she kept a straight face and was most genial. I can believe this story, for British Royalty are like this.

Walked with the dogs in the twilight. The falling field to the left of Park Piece was spread with mist from the wood along the fence, bounded by the road; in fact the entire field was evenly swathed as though it were a lake, a kind of Swan lake. Above it, and the dark trees, a sickle of moon.

---

* KCVO 1989; Dressmaker by Appointment to HM The Queen, and gardener (b. 1909).

Thursday, 9th November

To London for the day, specially to attend Oliver Messel's Memorial at St Martin-in-the-Fields. Went first to London Library; looked up names of Foreign Embassy officials mentioned by Harold in 1924. Called at Chatto's to leave a letter from A. Asked to see Nick, who appeared looking more handsome than words can express, but pale. His long dark, glossy hair, like a Bronzino portrait. Don't think he is very happy but assures me he will stick it out. Church full of old people, Peter Coats with snow-white hair, but hair; Diana Cooper in trousers which upset Michael [Rosse]. Princess Margaret. Went on by tube to 18 Stafford Terrace for buffet luncheon. Anne very upset indeed because she must leave the house she loves above all others. I understood it was to be turned into a museum. Met Tony Snowdon by front door. We grasped each other's hands. He said he had not been invited to luncheon and was leaving. We swore eternal friendship, in that way friends do who meet once in ten years for ten seconds after obsequies. I congratulated him on the way he read the second lesson. He said he was terrified, and when I told Anne after, she said crossly it was high time he snapped out of this rot, and made a speech somewhere. With him was Linley Messel's boy, Thomas, who read the first lesson. He said, Are you the author of *Heretics in Love*? For a time I could not think whether I was. Harold Acton there. Had a long talk with him and together we walked to the bus stop, but found a taxi instead. He said the new book on the Sitwells is shameful: readable, very, but journalese and containing the love letters which Osbert wrote to David Horner. Harold said he never would speak to David again, for Osbert was an extremely circumspect man and made no reference to his queerness. Sachie is dreadfully upset thereby. At Heywood Hill's I bought the Kipling book, Mina Curtiss's book,* Alfy Clary's memoirs and Virginia Woolf's second vol. of letters. John S. Smith said that Denys Sutton's book on Sachie was so bad that no publisher would take it. He had read it and told Denys he must improve it.

---

* *Other People's Letters.*

Monday, 20th November

Got back from Rome last night. Although the journey was easy
enough I am tired – very. Flight at 10.45 but woke up at 7.30 and by
eight left the British School in much anxiety lest on a Sunday morning
there would be no taxis about and no buses running. J.K.-B. accompanied me to the station terminus, where we had a cup of coffee and
a filthy bun – no nice *pannetone* nowadays – and he bade me farewell
on the step of the bus, and went off. A lump momentarily. We had
stayed eight days or rather nights together at the British School, which
is beyond the Villa Papa Giulia just outside the Porta del Popolo and
approached on foot through the Borghese Gardens. We were wonderfully fortunate in the weather. Every single day fine, with full unin-
terrupted sun, colder than England, but crisp, fresh, and perfect for
walking. For most luncheons we met, often sitting in the sun in the
Piazza Navona, twice at my favourite restaurant (once again func-
tioning after closing for several years), Mestre Stefano. But now they
are robbers. We consoled ourselves in the fact that we were eating in
the November sunshine.

In spite of the daunting reports I have received over the last few
years Rome seems to be no more dangerous than before. No signs did
we encounter of mugging, or bag-snatching. For the first two days I
hugged to my bosom the little bag on a strap containing my guide-
books, notebooks and pens. Then after dark I often walked home
across the Borghese Gardens when there was hardly a soul about. No
molestation. On the contrary Rome seemed improved. The centre is
unchanged architecturally, and traffic-wise it is emptier, many streets
now closed to traffic, round about the Piazza di Spagna to Corso area,
and Piazza Navona. Told that all the pine trees in Rome were dying.
Not so, they looked flourishing, also cypresses. The Forum lush and
green with vegetation, which for November is surely remarkable.
Walking along the Embankment under the plane trees through leaves
falling and fallen, otherwise flourishing. How the branches dip over
the river. In the Palazzo Braschi museum are many water-colours of
Rome scenes dated 1888. No embankment even in that year. And the
buildings looked in decay. Rome is always in decay I daresay; but what
is deplorable is the graffiti daubed on the walls of every palace and
building.

San Pietro in Montorio: first chapel on south side after entry – by
Bernini. The monument on the left wall to member of Raimondi

family has slanting face of sarcophagus carved, the Last Trump. Skeletons rise from their tombs; all have smiles on their faces, most cheerful expressions of resurrection, such an odd vision.

Walking home at dusk past the Villa Medici I heard a very loud growl as of a waterfall. Could not think where it came from. Looked. On turning the corner on Pincio and passing the iron grille of the garden the sound was deafening. Starlings roosting on the large pine tree.

Most noticeable things to be deplored are, after the daubing with political slogans in indelible paint, first, the number of Japanese visitors: hideous little beasts crawling like insects everywhere. While I was in the church of the Cosmedin there was an inrush, chattering like starlings, giggling like schoolgirls. I said *Hush* very loudly and shook a finger. I would not behave like this in a Japanese temple, damn them. Second: no one prays in churches. Twenty years ago in every church, especially at dusk after work time, the pavements of churches would be strewn with figures on their knees. Now no one. I walked through S.M. Maggiore at six with John and the pavement of this vast temple was almost empty.

Staying in British School was an experience. I said to the Provincial, a nice man, Whitehouse, but a man of little personality, that I supposed they had never had so old a student as I was. 'Yes,' he said, 'age does not count. Come again.' Residents are divided into artists and art historians, and they don't mix much. All young, scruffy but very nice boys and girls, tolerant of me, but I found it difficult to communicate. John too complained of their unrelieved earnestness.

Since I really went to Rome in order to be with John who was working on his Nollekens drawings – explanation needed: Heim Gallery, having acquired for sale a large collection of Nollekens drawings of statues done while the sculptor was in Rome during the 1760s, are employing John to identify as many as he can – I had to have a job. I made one. It was to revisit in turn each of the eight monuments I described in *Roman Mornings*, and book in hand make corrections and a few additions for future paperback issue. But on re-reading this little book I at once realized it could never be republished for it is terribly amateur, and out of date. The truth is that I must be studying, researching for a specific new book in hand, otherwise my wanderings became aimless, purposeless.

Rome is a curiously sexy city. I watched at nightfall men and women wandering aimlessly and furtively in an enclosed garden at the top of steep steps in front of the Museum of Modern Art. I went inside to have a look round. Against one stone wall of the south boundary was a long hedge of evergreens. In the hedge at intervals were openings. Between the openings and the wall were couples, some with their trousers down and skirts up, blatantly having sex. No one seemed to be the least disturbed or perturbed by my intrusion. They went on with the job unabashed. And when satisfied strolled away, without a word being spoken. I did not see any money passing. And the total silence sinister.

One day J. took me to lunch with Malcolm Munthe, son of Axel,* in his castle in the Campagna, called Lucretia, or rather a corruption of this word, for Lucrece was raped by Tarquin here, so it is said. A large medieval castle with early Renaissance windows and doorways, but cold and dusty and dank. Would not stay the night here at any price, yet Munthe seems not to mind. He is a charming man with a boyish manner, but inclined to the boring; he never ceases talking for one second, and although what he has to say is interesting, it is tiresome not to have the opportunity of interjecting a word. He adored his mother, who loved the castle, and he has laid out a terrace walk with box hedges spelling her name, Hilda. From the windows one sees pylons, tenement blocks and wires.

Munthe told us that the tendency in Italy among Italians is not to use their titles any more. Only among the nobility are titles recognized. For instance, he had to telephone Prince Colonna, and asked the servant who answered if Doctor Colonna was available. Also the rich are terrified of wearing their jewels. When he dined at the British Embassy for a party his wife met Princess Doria in the cloakroom taking her jewels out of a little bag to put on, in the safety of the Embassy precincts.

Tuesday, 21st November

Watched on 'Panorama' the dispute in *The Times* office. It is terrible that this paper may cease altogether at the end of the month if the Unions don't accept the management's offer. We saw management

---

* Axel Munthe (1857–1949); Swedish physician and writer; practised in France and Italy, was Swedish Court Physician, then retired to Capri where he wrote his autobiography, *The Story of San Michele* (1929).

and men, and heard the arguments of each. To me it was apparent that the men were behaving atrociously.

<hr>

Sunday, 26th November

Leaving church this morning Mary Beaufort asked us to dine tonight; old Horatia Durant was staying. We were told to arrive at 7.45 because they wanted to look at the film about Lily Langtry. After a rushed drink of sherry we were bustled into the dining-room. I sat next to Horatia with no one the other side of the huge table. Mary was opposite me behind a pot plant. Dinner eaten with great rapidity. No waiting. We choked over soup, fish, fruit salad; hardly time to toss down a glass of white wine. Master stacked the plates. Hustled back to the panelled room. Master turned on the telly and for quarter of an hour we watched a film about naval privateers in Regency times in which a whore was being tossed from hammock to hammock. 'Unlike Lily,' Master growled. Then I ventured to suggest that it was not the Lily film, but another, as it proved to be – viz., *Mutiny on the Bounty*. Hurriedly we switched on to the right film. Therein Lily made to go to bed with a young man for a diamond necklace. Raped another called Sir George Arthur. Mary did not see for she was asleep. Neither Master nor Horatia made a comment. At nine the News came on. When it was over, we rose, and left. Mary already yawning. A purposeless occasion, surely.

Such a funny thing told to A. by Caroline [Somerset], to whom A. said she wondered why Peggy De L'Isle having taken us up hot and strong, dropped us like hot bricks. 'Oh,' said Caroline, 'if you really want to know it is because Jim made out to her that his great-grandfather Bailey when an impecunious youth walked barefoot from Yorkshire to South Wales – no doubt with his cat – and she did not like that. She maintains that the Glanusks belong to the high aristocracy.' How can she be so silly? After all, Sir Joseph was *my* gt-grandfather and not hers. She merely married my distant cousin, likewise descendant of the implied Dick Whittington.

Tuesday, 28th November

Alan Pryce-Jones whom I had invited to lunch with me at Brooks's today at his suggestion did not turn up. Nothing surprising in that, tho' sorry not to see him. I lunched alone. At the next table William

Rees-Mogg was eating with a friend. Friend left the room for a moment so I went across and said how deeply sorry I was about *The Times*'s troubles, and wished there was something however humble that I could do. He naturally said there was nothing. He seemed quite cheerful, and said they would resume after an interval; which is encouraging. I asked, 'On a different basis?' No, he said, but in improved conditions. A. and I dined with John Betj. and Elizabeth in her house, which is more topsy-turvy than usual, the builders in process of installing a heating system.

Indeed the heat was asphyxiating. John says he never can be too warm. Talk of the Thorpe* case. John said that in no circumstances was he ever shocked by sex cases. A. said, not even when children are seduced? Never, John answered. I said I am often shocked by things, violence for instance, and the Trades Unions' concerted malice against the established order of things.

Stayed the night chez J.K.–B. and read his Preface and Introduction to his book on country houses.† Both excellent, the first a tribute to Robin Fedden, the second an original article about houses, not pedantic, not architectural; and is interesting.

Wednesday, 29th November

Suffering from acute pain in the back. Struggled on foot to the Hayward Gallery in the belief that defiance of a complaint often cures it. Looked at a terrible exhibition of German paintings of the Weimar Republic decade. Prostitutes, poverty and big business. They made me feel sick. Walked to Marlborough Galleries and looked at Derek Hill's exhibition. Derek came in and talked, and was pleased. Some very good indeed, notably two Cardinals, better than Sutherland's. But he is erratic. Others not so successful, viz., the late Lord Salisbury and Garrett's‡ portrait. Some of the little landscapes – sleight-of-hand, rapidly thrown on the canvas – best of all. Good sketches of Berenson in bed in old age, Nicky Mariano reading to him.

---

* In August the former Liberal Party Leader Jeremy Thorpe had been charged, along with three others, with conspiracy to murder Norman Scott, and Jeremy Thorpe with incitement to murder; the committal hearings in November resulted in lurid press coverage; at the ensuing trial in May–June 1979 all four men were acquitted, but Thorpe abandoned his political career.

† *The Country House Guide* (1979).

‡ Earl of Drogheda.

At six to St James's Palace, Georgian Group party, attended by the Queen Mother. We were lined up in the Throne Room to be presented. Next to the Fleetwood-Heskeths; Mo shrunk to half size. Queen Mother reached us. Peter Chance who was piloting her murmured about me being an art historian and A. a garden expert. Queen Mother thereupon said to me, 'Is it very dry with you?' That is all that passed. But the poor, sweet woman spent an hour and a half on her feet talking, non-stop, no respite, with some 150 people. I suppose she could do it in her sleep, just exuding sweetness and charm, and talking inanities. After a quick and filthy dinner at Brooks's – every meal this visit has been disgusting – we motored home.

Sunday, 3rd December

Have thought of a new book to be called *An Old Man Walks*. I go for a long tramp, describing the scenery through which I pass and every single object my eye lights upon, whether tree, bird, blade of grass, church, barn, pylon, beautiful or revolting, and each object makes me go off at a tangent upon some theme that perplexes or worries or saddens or enrages me. Also the memories that they induce, the hopes they engender, the philosophy they arouse – life and death, God and the Devil, belief, disbelief.

Thursday, 21st December

A. has just read my chapter 10 and found it dull. Too many dates and no interest in the Balkans. She is right, but there must be some Balkan stuff. She is the sure plain man's guide; always right until she comes to grammar. But her taste is impeccable. She knows as it were by instinct what is good style and what bad.

It is extraordinary how these days I never get a letter, but never. Merely bills and demands for money, subscriptions, etc., in buff envelopes. The cause may be the high postage. True, I get no fan letters any more. Not a soul has written about *Round the Clock*.

The promise of the Lees family and the only male of his generation in existence has no neck, is spoilt, ignorant and commonplace. Poor child, I daresay he may improve, but I much doubt it. He has his grandmother's looks, and probably will have her shape. God help us.

Stayed Monday night with Eardley. William Cavendish-Bentinck lunched with me at Brooks's. He is 81. Came from a board meeting and had to return to it, so we did not have much time. Luckily I had a list of questions which I fired at him during luncheon. Unfortunately, room very noisy and I could not hear him well. He said he was the last survivor of those attending the Lausanne Conference, so I had better make the most of him. Nice old boy. He is leaving tomorrow for Paris, staying at the Jockey [Club], then returns next day. Liked Harold very much. Is sensitive about his old boss, Tyrrell, and said allowances must be made for him for losing his two sons, both killed in 1915. Ever after he could not stand up to crises, and took to the bottle.

Went to Plowman my dentist. He told me that his elder son, now 28, is so brilliant he is the leading researcher of chest cancer. Lives for his work, is totally dedicated, and has little time for recreation. Plowman wishes he would marry a woman who might humanize him a little. He said, What can you expect of a man who sees children dying daily of cancer? He is always on call because the cancer cells which he puts in bottles develop at odd times of day and night, and suddenly it is essential for him to be present at the right moment of florescence. So he usually sleeps in the research place. Then to call on Emily and Dolly. Poor old dears. Conversation is invariably the same. 'And how is Mrs Stevens? How is Miss Clarissa?' And when I descend their steep and seemingly endless flight of stone stairs I look back, and there they are, waving from their bathroom window. I wave back. As I turn the corner of the colonnade into the street I turn again and wave. They are still there. Ah well, each time may be the last, I think to myself, and then I shall be spared another duty. Yet I love them. Or is love too strong a word?

Eardley and Richard Shone dined with me at Alpino's restaurant: £16 on top of £10 luncheon today. Eardley said his mother had a printed Evangelical Questionnaire, Victorian. It consisted of questions and answers. One went as follows: 'Q. Is it not true that Roman Catholics bow the knee to the Lord's Table? A. Yes, it is true. Q. If God knew, would he not be angry? A. God does know. He is very angry.' Then E. told me he has got to know Mrs McCorquodale, a novelist of best sellers, an absurd woman, dressed to kill, covered in jewellery, with dozens of secretaries and living in a palace outside London. He was so fascinated by a coloured photograph of her that he did a painting, a version of it, and wrote and told her. She asked him to visit her and bring it. I asked him if she bought it. No, he said. She thought it too impressionistic. Naturally. This shows some ignorance or insensitivity on E's part. Mrs McC. clearly hoped Eardley would be a young man, and the portrait as nearly resemble a coloured photograph as the original. She was disappointed. But E. was surprised that she was.

Saturday, 30th December

Christmas Day fell on a Monday, for the first time, the Vicar told me, since he had been ordained. We had Burnet Pavitt and Betty Miller Jones to stay.

Betty clearly sad, with that strained look of the recently widowed. I think however she enjoyed herself. Ian McCallum and Betty Hanley lunched on Christmas Day. He left for America the following morning, so I gave him a letter to John Pope-Hennessy which he said he would post in New York for me. He should have got it within two days. On Boxing Day we lunched with the Hyltons* at Ammerdown. They live in this large house which contains a number of good family portraits and some good French furniture and porcelain. I had thought they sold most of the best things when they inherited, but no. They exude piety, and have some five children, and intend to have more, in that Catholic way. I suppose they never have coitus unless they mean to propagate, so enjoy less sex than pagans. Very sweet they were. He is stiff but smiling, and not easy. She is rather intense, with literary aspirations. She asked me earnest questions about my books which embarrassed me.

Harold is nearing the end of volume 1. I have two more chapters to do. Then will come the hard work, pruning drastically, trying to improve the structure, for at present it lacks shape, and introducing some assessments of H.N's achievements up to date. A. goes through each chapter religiously, and is a great help.

---

* Raymond Jolliffe, 5th Baron Hylton (b. 1932); m. 1966 Joanna de Bertodano; involved in many charitable activities.

Address

A Memorial Service to celebrate the life of James Lees-Milne was held on 12 March 1998 at the Grosvenor Chapel, South Audley Street, London. Nigel Nicolson gave the following address:

We all know the purpose of a memorial service. It is to bring together in collective affection the people closest to a friend who has died, and to record in the best way we know, by our attendance here, our gratitude for all he gave us.

There would be many others here had Jim not outlived them, for he was 89 when he died, and few people had a greater gift for friendship. He preferred his friends to be like himself – energetic, cultured, well-mannered, and with a touch of eccentricity. He once said that he preferred houses to people, but that was only because houses last longer, and what really delighted him was the company of people whom he loved in delectable surroundings, as when he had Alvilde to himself at Alderley, Bath or Badminton; or take this scene from his diary of 1973:

> Yesterday I spent at Uppark with the National Trust Arts Panel. Sitting round the dining-room table, on which incongruously Emma Hart once danced, there were some of the most understanding, cultivated, earnest men of good sense and taste it was possible to find: Robin Fedden, Brinsley Ford, Johnny Walker of the Metropolitan Museum, Roddy Thesiger, Lord Plunket, Bobby Gore, young Martin Drury, Gervais Jackson-Stops and Merlin Waterson. Could there be a better lot? No, there couldn't.

Some of those he named have died. Some are here with us today. I believe that they would all have felt about him what he wrote about them – mutual affection, mutual regard, mutual trust, and a shared commitment to save for future generations irreplaceable treasures from the past.

James Lees-Milne was not an aristocrat by birth, but he was by nature. I think he was aware of this, but he never traded on it. I once asked him where he had spent the past weekend, and he replied, 'With friends in Derbyshire', when he had been staying at Chatsworth. Once he wrote, 'I am acutely conscious of, and amused by, class distinctions, and hope they endure for ever', but his critics, if he had any, in quoting this with relish, would always omit the next sentence: 'Class *barriers* are a different matter, which no sensible person would advocate.' He admired people for their gifts and dedication, whatever class they came from. There was an affinity between him and the thousands of craftsmen who, centuries ago, built the houses and filled them with works of art for the few who could afford them, and the thousands more who care for them today.

Jim's delight in the past sometimes made him contemptuous of the present. He had a breathtaking disdain for fashionable ideas, but nobody was less supercilious, nobody less arrogant, nobody more candid. He must be the only Englishman to have expressed publicly his regret that he never fought for Franco in the Civil War. He was given to self-reproach, but never to self-pity or self-praise. Few people were capable of rising to such heights of exhilaration or sinking to such depths of despair. For someone who was apt to say that the country was going to the dogs, he extracted a great deal of pleasure from it, both in his private life and in his work. I remember a passage in his diary when Alvilde fell and slightly grazed her knee, and Jim wrote in the privacy of his room, 'It makes me realise how precious she is to me, more and more as the years roll by, and I dread ever losing her.'

That was one side of his nature. Another was his love of literature, and his own contribution to it. He was an art historian of great imaginative and scholastic gifts, a biographer who included among his subjects the parents or forebears of some of us here today. He was an autobiographer of superlative merit, even if he sometimes cast himself as a character in an Evelyn Waugh novel. But perhaps he will be best remembered for his diaries, which he never intended for publication, and as the most successful house-hunter that the National Trust has ever had.

'I was not born in the heroic mould', he wrote, but his achievement as a young man was truly heroic. As the executor of Lord Lothian's and Lord Esher's concepts, he toured the country before, during and after the war in an unparalleled pilgrimage of grace. He was not always successful. Having failed to add Longleat to his day's bag, he heard Lord Bath courteously suggest that it might be time for Jim to ring for his chauffeur and have his car brought round to the front door. Jim had to confess that he had no chauffeur; indeed, he had no car. So a footman was despatched to the stables, and returned, smirking slightly, with Jim's battered bicycle, on which he rode away, casting over his shoulder a last, lingering, regretful look at that incomparable façade.

On another, less melancholy, occasion when he and Eardley Knollys went fishing for Dyrham Park, their host grew bored with their exclamations of delight at his wonderful possessions, and turned to his wife to say in his dreadful French, 'My dear, *pensez-vous qu'il faut les inviter* to dinner?'

But what a catch resulted from these trawling expeditions! Jim's houses – let me be excused for calling them that – read like battle honours: Dyrham itself, Charlecote, Blickling, Montacute, Stourhead, Knole, Polesden Lacey, Cliveden, Lacock, West Wycombe, Gunby, Cotehele, Petworth, Osterley, Nostell Priory, and many others. When you consider that the Trust had almost no money of its own, and a minute membership, it remains a miracle how it was done. Indeed, Jim often wondered himself. 'If the N.T. knew what I was up to, what promises I am making in their name,' he confided to his diary, 'they would be shocked by the extreme zeal of their servant.'

They are shocked no longer. He preserved an essential part of our history and inheritance. He was the most civilised of Englishmen, and we have come here to celebrate the excellence of his life, character and achievements, and to express our gratitude for what he has bequeathed to us.

Index

Index